Key Issues in Contract

Key Issues in Contract

John N Adams   LLB
of the Inner Temple, Barrister;
Professor of Intellectual Property,
University of Sheffield; Director of
the Intellectual Property Institute

Roger Brownsword   LLB
Professor of Law, University
of Sheffield

Butterworths
London, Dublin, Edinburgh
1995

United Kingdom	Butterworths, a Division of Reed Elsevier (UK) Ltd, Halsbury House, 35 Chancery Lane, LONDON WC2A 1EL and 4 Hill Street, EDINBURGH EH2 3JZ
Australia	Butterworths, SYDNEY, MELBOURNE, BRISBANE, ADELAIDE, PERTH, CANBERRA and HOBART
Canada	Butterworths Canada Ltd, TORONTO and VANCOUVER
Ireland	Butterworth (Ireland) Ltd, DUBLIN
Malaysia	Malayan Law Journal Sdn Bhd, KUALA LUMPUR
New Zealand	Butterworths of New Zealand Ltd, WELLINGTON and AUCKLAND
Puerto Rico	Butterworth of Puerto Rico, Inc, SAN JUAN
Singapore	Reed Elsevier (Singapore) Pte Ltd, SINGAPORE
South Africa	Butterworths Publishers (Pty) Ltd, DURBAN
USA	Butterworth Legal Publishers, CARLSBAD, California and SALEM, New Hampshire

A CIP Catalogue record for this book is available from the British Library.

ISBN 0 406 50936 0

Typeset in Bookman by Grahame & Grahame Editorial, Brighton
Printed by Clays Ltd, Bungay, Suffolk

Foreword

English lawyers already have available good expositions of the law of contract as it is in standard textbooks. But it is the function of academic lawyers also to keep under constant review the rationality of our law. It is essential therefore that writers should critically examine and re-examine the doctrines and principles of our contract law. Here English lawyers have until now been less well served. It is true that Simpson's *A History of the Common Law of Contract* (1975) and Atiyah's *The Rise and Fall of Freedom of Contract* (1979) gave us an excellent historical perspective of the problems. Treitel's *Remedies for Breach of Contract* (1988) placed the problems in a much needed comparative context. And it is right to pay tribute to many excellent critical examinations in learned journals of the orthodox doctrines and principles of our contract law. The publication of Atiyah's *Essays on Contract* in 1986, bringing together in revised form his articles on the subject, was a notable step forward. But until now there has been a need for a comprehensive and up-to-date book which systematically and critically examines the doctrines and principles of our contract law. There was a gap. In my view this book admirably fills that gap.

The authors explore many fundamental and topical questions, such as whether the privity of contract rule is a rational restriction on freedom of contract and whether there is scope for a wider recognition of duties of good faith in English law. The authors subject those questions, and many other doctrinal questions, to rigorous analysis. This book is a valuable contribution to our legal literature.

The authors state in the preface that they have attempted to address a number of key issues in the law of contract in such a way that student readers would be provoked and stimulated into considering the rationality of a variety of doctrinal matters. In that aim the authors have succeeded: the book will quickly become essential reading for students. But practitioners and judges will also find in it a fund of insights on important questions of contract law. And the more fundamental the question, and the higher in the judicial hierarchy it arises, the more useful will it be to practitioners and judges alike.

The book will prove to be an important aid to the examination of fundamental questions of contract law.

Johan Steyn   June 1995
House of Lords

Preface

In this book, we have attempted to address a number of key issues in the law of contract in such a way that student readers are provoked (and we hope stimulated) into considering the rationality of a variety of doctrinal matters. To do this, we have restricted our exposition of basic contract doctrine to just one chapter (Chapter Two) and we have reserved the rest of the book for a critical evaluation of the law. Although we are mindful that a little knowledge of the law can be a dangerous thing, we are also mindful that the dead-weight of doctrinal overload can inhibit the spirit of inquiry – and it is this latter consideration that has prompted us to strike the balance between exposition and evaluation in the way that we have done in this book.

We cannot claim that our critical reflections on the law have all been newly minted for this book. Indeed, this would scarcely be possible, given that we have been working in this field for some twenty years. During this time, we have individually and jointly published a number of papers in which many of the reflections that we now bring together have been aired – sometimes in embryonic form only, at other times in a more developed form. This is the first time, however, that these fragmented thoughts have been gathered together and developed into a sustained and, we hope, progressive critique of the law of contract.

The roots of Chapter Three, in which we discuss both standard form and relational contracting, can be traced to three of John Adams's papers ('The Standardisation of Commercial Contracts or the Contractualisation of Standard Forms' (1978) 7 Anglo-American Law Review 136; 'The Battle of the Forms' (1983) Journal of Business Law 297; and 'Consideration for Requirements Contracts' (1978) 94

Law Quarterly Review 73). In Chapter Four, where we evaluate the classical exchange model of contract, we draw on John Adams's discussion of promissory estoppel and waiver ((1972) 36 The Conveyancer 245) as well as on our more recent comments on *Williams v Roffey* ((1990) 53 MLR 536) and the *Blackpool and Fylde Aero Club* case ((1991) 54 MLR 281). Chapter Five, in which we deal with the vexed question of privity of contract, draws to some extent on our paper 'Privity and the Concept of a Network Contract' (1990) 10 Legal Studies 12 and our comments on the *London Drugs* case ((1993) 56 MLR 722). However, our assessment of the Law Commission's proposed dual intention test relies heavily on our (hitherto unpublished) submissions to the Commission (during the consultation period), which submissions were co-authored with our colleague at Sheffield, Deryck Beyleveld. We gratefully acknowledge the important part that Deryck played in formulating our three-handed response to the Commission's proposal. Chapters Six and Seven, which consider respectively the right to withdraw for breach of contract and the possible incorporation into English contract law of an explicit requirement of good faith, are based very closely on two of Roger Brownsword's more recent papers ('Retrieving Reasons, Retrieving Rationality? A New Look at the Right to Withdraw for Breach of Contract' (1992) 5 Journal of Contract Law 83, and 'Two Concepts of Good Faith' (1994) 7 Journal of Contract Law 197). Chapter Eight, which focuses on modern intervention against unfair terms in contracts, has some diverse roots: particularly our general paper on the Unfair Contract Terms Act ('The Unfair Contract Terms Act: A Decade of Discretion' (1988) 104 Law Quarterly Review 94), our two papers on indemnity clauses and UCTA ('Contractual Indemnity Clauses' (1982) Journal of Business Law 200, and 'Double Indemnity – Contractual Indemnity Clauses Revisited' (1988) Journal of Business Law 146), and a recent comment by John Adams on the exclusion of set-off rights in franchise contracts ((1994) 57 MLR 960). Finally, in Chapters Nine and Ten, where we first analyse a co-operative model of contract and then set out a general framework for assessing the rationality of contract doctrine, our discussion is based on two papers by Roger Brownsword ('From Co-operative Contracting to a Contract of Co-operation', which was prepared for publication in David Campbell and Peter Vincent-Jones (eds) *Contract and Economic Organization* (Aldershot, Dartmouth, 1996) and

'Towards a Rational Law of Contract', which was first published in Thomas Wilhelmsson (ed) *Perspectives of Critical
Contract Law* (Aldershot, Dartmouth, 1993)). We are grate-
ful for permission to draw on and, to a limited extent, to
reproduce these works.

Finally, it remains only to record our appreciation of the
publisher's patience with this project. The contract for this
book was signed many years ago; the delivery date has long
since passed. Had the publishers insisted on their contractual pound of flesh, this book would not have been
written. In a book that has a good deal to say about trust
and confidence in contract, it is perhaps fitting that the book
itself should have been produced in such a conspicuously
co-operative spirit.

John N Adams   March 1995
Roger Brownsword

Contents

Table of statutes

References in this Table to *Statutes* are to Halsbury's Statutes of England (Fourth Edition) showing the volume and page at which the annotated text of the Act will be found.

List of cases

Chapter 1

Introduction

Adopting Jeremy Bentham's famous distinction, we might say that the jurisprudence of the common law has two aspects, the 'expository' and the 'censorial'. Whereas expository jurisprudence is concerned with expounding legal doctrine (with stating 'the law as it is'), censorial jurisprudence is concerned with critical evaluation of legal doctrine (with articulating 'the law as it ought to be'). For the most part, textbooks on the law of contract place their emphasis on exposition rather than evaluation, seeking to present the law as it is in an orderly fashion. Without doubt, such books have an important place in any student's library. However, their very existence – and, indeed, their existence in such numbers – makes it both possible and desirable to offer a book that strikes the balance between exposition and evaluation rather differently. Accordingly, this book reverses the standard priorities, being fairly short with regard to exposition of the law of contract but rather longer with regard to its critical evaluation.[1]

The book is divided into three parts. In Part I, the main contours of contract law (particularly the principal doctrines and the leading cases associated with the so-called classical law of contract) are sketched. In Part II of the book, a number of key doctrinal issues are addressed. Some of these issues arise from the lack of fit between the classical model of contract law and modern transactional practices and expectations. Other issues concern the scope and application of such distinctively modern contract notions as

---

[1] Cf Roger Brownsword 'Teaching Contract: A Liberal Agenda' in Peter Birks (ed) *Examining the Law Syllabus: The Core* (Oxford, Oxford University Press, 1992) 42.

1

economic duress and unfair contract terms. The vexed question of the availability of the right to withdraw for breach of contract is also discussed, this being something of a crossroads where classical and modern thinking threaten to collide. In relation to each of these issues, our intention is not so much to expound the law, but to encourage the process of critical evaluation and reflection on current legal doctrine. Finally, in Part III, we gather up our reflections in two ways. First, we explore the idea that the classical model of contract should be abandoned in favour of a model that takes co-operation between contractors as its cornerstone. Secondly, we develop a view of rationality in the law which enables us to locate our reflections within a framework that facilitates systematic evaluation of contract doctrine (and, indeed, of legal doctrine generally). We will say a little more about the idea of rationality presently; but, before we do so, it is important to understand how critical evaluation relates to the study of the law of contract.

1. CRITICAL EVALUATION AND THE STUDY OF CONTRACT LAW

Generally, students are asked to do more than 'parrot' the law of contract. They are asked to manipulate the law in various ways, particularly by applying legal doctrine to problems (problem-solving) and by writing reflective essays about the subject. It is fairly obvious how critical evaluation relates to essay-writing because students are not invited to recite all they know about a particular topic – characteristically, students are instructed that they should 'critically evaluate' some doctrine or some statement about doctrine. Where, however, does critical evaluation touch base with problem-solving?

The problems which students are asked to solve rarely involve routine applications of the law. On the contrary, they typically hinge on one or more 'nice points of law', that is, questions of law where the authorities (mainly the precedents in the case-law) are divided, or are unclear in either their articulation or their application, or are silent on the particular issue, or the like. Where the authorities are divided, students who cite only those precedents favouring one side of the argument will be marked down for failing to take account of the rival precedents. A good answer to a problem looks a bit like a tree-diagram with a number of forks in the branches and with arguments extended along the branches as appropriate. However, once the competing streams of authority have been identified, and the various branches of the problem explored, how is one to arbitrate and produce the 'right answer' to the problem? Textbook writers sometimes oblige by offering their version of the 'better view' on some thorny issue – but there is no basis for adopting that view unless one is satisfied as to its credentials. What we need is some defensible criterion relative to which we determine the 'right answer' and the 'better view'; and, it will be appreciated, this is where the process of critical evaluation intersects with problem-solving. For the essence of critical evaluation is that legal doctrine is assessed as 'good' or 'bad' relative to some given criteria, and it is these same criteria that form the basis for preferring one reading of the authorities to another – for asserting that such and such really is the better view. It follows that the more students understand evaluative criteria, the more explicit and reasoned they can be in breaking the deadlock in problem-solving as well as in handling the critical aspects of essay-writing.

Whilst, in the light of these comments, some students might see the strategic sense in taking critical evaluation seriously (because it promises to improve their grades), they might nevertheless think that evaluation is marginal to the study of law. Such a perception, of course, is encouraged by the dominant expository approach and, concomitantly, by its supporting 'black-letter' educational philosophy. This philosophy assumes, first, that there is a body of materials which represents 'the law' ('the law as it is') and, secondly, that the task of legal education is essentially to offer instruction in finding, stating, and applying these materials. It is also assumed that these materials are divisible into discrete doctrinal packages marked 'contract', 'tort', 'criminal law', and so on. Accordingly, the primary function of a textbook on the law of contract is to expound that part of the law which is regarded as comprising 'the law of contract'. From time to time, academics rail against these assumptions. Some think that the accepted divisions of legal doctrine are artificial or unreal (so that, for example, parcels of law comprising contract and tort, or contract, tort, and restitution, are preferred). However, so long as the emphasis remains on exposition of legal doctrine, the black-letter philosophy continues to hold sway. More radically, some contend that the study of contract must address not only the law-in-the-books (the formal legal materials) but also the law-in-action (the relevance and use of the formal materials in practice, and the existence of informal rules governing the practice of contracting). Since investigation of the law-in-action may reveal that the law-in-the-books has only a limited effect on actual transactional practice, the point of expounding formal legal doctrine to the exclusion of other lines of inquiry is thrown into question. Where, then, does our own emphasis on critical evaluation stand in relation to the ruling black-letter view?

Our starting point is that the study of law must be viewed as a broad-ranging inquiry seeking to get to grips with all facets of the practice of law – quite simply, to study law is to seek an understanding of the regulatory and dispute-resolving phenomena that we associate with the practice of 'law'.[2] Mastering the formal legal materials is part of that inquiry, but it is not the whole. In particular, our understanding of law is deficient if we cannot explain its dynamic (if we cannot account for its operation) and if we have no developed view of its legitimacy. If we treat the law of contract as that branch of the law that regulates transactions, then we have not tried to understand contract law unless we have asked how it works in the field of transactions and whether its doctrines are legitimate. It follows that critical evaluation of the law of contract is not a marginal exercise – on the contrary, it is a central line of inquiry for any serious student who aspires to understand the law.

2. CRITICAL PERSPECTIVES

Critical evaluation, as we have said, must operate with some criteria on the basis of which positive or negative assessments can be made in relation to particular legal principles. Two criteria which are regularly relied on are certainty (or

---

[2] For an extended statement of this manifesto for legal education, see John N. Adams and Roger Brownsword *Understanding Law* (London, Fontana, 1992). For similar statements with specific reference to contract law, see Roger Brownsword *Teaching Contract*; and John N. Adams and Roger Brownsword *Understanding Contract Law*, 2nd edn (London, Fontana, 1994) especially ch 1.

predictability, or calculability) and justice (or fairness). However, these criteria do not necessarily pull in the same direction: certain rules might prove unjust, and legal doctrines aimed at procuring justice might prove uncertain in their application. We can give as examples three well-known instances of such a tension, each relating to doctrinal matters which we discuss in some detail in Part II of the book.

First, there is the doctrine of privity of contract,[3] according to which a third party, C, is not permitted to enforce a contract made between A and B even though it was the express intention of A and B that their contract should confer a benefit on C – even though, in the classic case of *Tweddle v Atkinson*,[4] A and B not only mutually agreed to pay a sum of money to C, but also agreed that C should have the right to enforce their mutual promises. Asked to evaluate the privity doctrine, we might say in its favour that it is certain: at least A, B, and C know where they stand. Against this, however, we might argue that the doctrine is unfair. For example, if B fails to perform and, for some reason, A is unable to enforce the contract so that C gets the intended benefit, not only does B get away with breaching the agreement with A, C loses out too. In 1991, the Law Commission provisionally recommended that the privity rule should be amended so that a third party, such as C, would have the right to enforce the contract between A and B provided that A and B intended (i) that their contract should benefit C and (ii) that their contract should create an enforceable obligation in favour of C.[5] Whilst this proposal might promote fairness between the parties (A, B, and C), it is arguable that the Commission's recommendation jeopardises certainty. For, in place of a clear rule denying rights to third parties, the Commission proposes a test that hinges on the (uncertain and contestable) intentions of the contracting parties.

A second example of the potential tension between certainty and fairness concerns the right of an innocent party to withdraw from a contract for breach of 'condition'. For example, section 13 of the Sale of Goods Act 1979 (following the scheme laid down by the Sale of Goods Act 1893) provides that it is an implied condition in contracts of sale

---

[3] See ch 5.
[4] (1861) 1 B & S 393.
[5] See Privity of Contract: Contracts for the Benefit of Third Parties (Law Commission Consultation Paper, No 121, 1991).

that the goods shall correspond with their description. The significance of treating this requirement as a 'condition' is that the buyer has the right to reject the goods should they fail to correspond with their description.[6] Where the extent of non-correspondence is such as seriously to affect the acceptability of the goods, a right of rejection seems perfectly reasonable. However, the courts sometimes interpreted section 13 somewhat literally, such that the right to reject applied even where the failure was trivial, in the sense that it did not interfere with the intended use of the goods. Such an interpretation encouraged opportunistic behaviour, buyers rejecting on the ground of trivial breach as a pretext to escape from the contract in order to take advantage of more attractive prices elsewhere. To counter such opportunism, a number of strategies might be employed. For example, one might follow the lead given by the Court of Appeal in 1962 (albeit in the context of a charter-party rather than a sale) when it introduced the so-called *Hong Kong Fir Shipping* test[7] which, on its most robust interpretation, excludes the right to reject (or withdraw for breach) unless the actual consequences of the breach have deprived the innocent party of substantially the whole benefit of the bargain. Somewhat similarly, section 4 of the Sale and Supply of Goods Act 1994 provides that non-consumer buyers will not have the right to withdraw for breach inter alia of section 13 if 'the breach is so slight that it would be unreasonable for [the buyer] to reject'. Whilst such tests can claim to promote fairer results, there is more than a little vagueness in the concept of a party being deprived of 'substantially the whole benefit of the bargain', or of a breach being 'so slight' as to render it 'unreasonable' for the buyer to reject the goods. Thus, if certainty is our preferred criterion, we may want to stick with a literal application of section 13 (occasionally unjust results notwithstanding); whereas, if we prefer just outcomes, we may go along with the *Hong Kong Fir Shipping* test and its cognates (an element of uncertainty notwithstanding).[8]

---

[6]   See further ch 6.

[7]   *Hong Kong Fir Shipping Co Ltd v Kawasaki Kisen Kaisha Ltd* [1962] 2 QB 26.

[8]   Another way of dealing with the problem of opportunism is to require that contractors act in 'good faith': see further chs 6 and 7.

A third example arises in the context of standard form contracts where one party purports to exclude or restrict its liability for breach.[9] In the case of *L'Estrange v Graucob*,[10] the plaintiff purchased an automatic vending machine from the defendants. The terms of the contract were contained in a written sales agreement that the plaintiff buyer had signed. One of the small print conditions in the sales agreement purported to exclude any liability on the part of the defendant sellers. When the machine proved faulty and the plaintiff sued for breach of contract, the sellers relied for their defence on the small print exclusion clause. The Court of Appeal held that, in the absence of fraud or coercion, or some other vitiating factor of that kind, the plaintiff was bound by the terms of the agreement that she had signed. Clearly, the position taken by the court was designed to promote certainty (and, to some extent, caution on the part of buyers). The rule was simple: if a contractor signed an agreement, the terms were binding. However, by mid-century, the courts, particularly the Court of Appeal, had adopted a much more protective approach, holding that the small print could not exclude liability for a so-called 'fundamental breach', or for a breach of a 'fundamental term'.[11] The precise meaning of these protective concepts was never made clear. The basic idea of a fundamental term was 'something which underlies the whole contract so that, if it is not complied with, the performance becomes something totally different from that which the contract contemplates'.[12] As for a fundamental breach, that, Viscount Dilhorne said in the famous *Suisse Atlantique*[13] case, was rather different:

> 'In relation to a fundamental breach, one has to have regard to the character of the breach and determine whether in consequence of it the performance of the contract becomes something totally different from that which the contract contemplated.'

Whilst this smacked somewhat of a distinction without a

---

[9] See further chs 3 and 8.
[10] [1934] 2 KB 394.
[11] See eg *Karsales (Harrow) Ltd v Wallis* [1956] 2 All ER 866; and see further ch 3.
[12] *Smeaton Hanscomb v Sassoon I. Setty, Son & Co* [1953] 1 WLR 1468, 1470 (per Devlin J).
[13] *Suisse Atlantique Société d'Armement SA v NV Rotterdamsche Kolen Centrale* [1967] 1 AC 361, 393.

difference, and whilst the distinction between (excludable) conditions and (non-excludable) fundamental terms remained obscure, so long as an element of doctrinal looseness enabled the courts to shield contractors in hard cases, the position was accepted as tolerable – not least by Lord Denning who, having previously acted as counsel for the defendants in *L'Estrange v Graucob*, was destined to play a leading role in the mid-century shift of priorities from considerations of certainty to considerations of fairness.

Although critical evaluation often hinges on judgments of certainty and fairness, these are not the sole criteria. For example, legal doctrine is often criticised on the ground of some 'anomaly', or because it fails to protect legitimate expectations or reasonable reliance, or because it is 'inconvenient'. Dealing with this last-mentioned criterion, removal of inconvenience is frequently linked to the question of whether a proposed rule or a ruling would threaten to 'open the floodgates'. The floodgates argument can mean several things. Sometimes, the argument is that the courts could not cope with large numbers of claimants – in other words, there would be inconvenience to the administration of justice. Thus, in *Balfour v Balfour*,[14] the leading case on the requirement for contractual formation of an intention to create legal relations, Atkin LJ said that, if domestic and social agreements were to be ordinarily enforceable as binding contracts, then 'the small Courts of this country would have to be multiplied one hundredfold'.[15] On other occasions, the floodgates argument is not so much about the number of claimants as about the extent of potential liability. The idea is that defendants, and their insurers, can absorb only so much liability before passing the costs back to the community (by raising prices) or ceasing to trade in a particular sector. So, for example, whilst there might be some attraction in awarding damages for disappointment, or in releasing parties from onerous contracts, this might precipitate a liability crisis or restrict the range of useful (and desired) contractual options available in the marketplace.[16]

---

[14]   *Balfour v Balfour* [1919] 2 KB 571.
[15]   At p 579.
[16]   See eg Michael J. Trebilcock 'The Doctrine of Inequality of Bargaining Power: Post-Benthamite Economics in the House of Lords' (1976) 26 University of Toronto Law Journal 359.

In our consideration of various key issues in Part II of the book, questions of certainty, justice, convenience, and the like, regularly impinge on our discussion. Our discussion, however, takes place against a background that assumes that there is a systematic tension between the values associated with the classical law of contract and those associated with the modern law. At the risk of some oversimplification, we can say that, whereas the classical law gives priority to certainty, calculability, and convenience, the modern approach is more concerned that the law should be capable of responding flexibly, with a view to producing just and reasonable outcomes and to accommodating the legitimate expectations of contractors. Thus, whereas the classical view emphasises that contractors must be held to their bargains (enshrined in the ideas of 'freedom of contract' and 'sanctity of contract'), the modern view favours intervening in order to protect weaker parties (particularly consumer contractors); and, whereas the classical law takes a fairly inflexible view of the prerequisites for forming a contract, the modern law favours a more relaxed approach where this fits with commercial practice and expectation.

To a certain extent, the tensions between the classical and the modern approaches can be relieved if the classical view is applied to commercial contracts (ie contracts made between businesses), leaving the modern view to be applied to consumer contracts (ie contracts made between a business on the one side and a non-business contractor on the other side). The common-sense rationalisation for this compromise is that commercial contractors can be fairly held to their bargains because, unlike most consumer contractors, they can be assumed to have some control over the deals they make. However, although there is now a fairly clear bifurcation in the law, with commercial contracts and consumer contracts being subjected to different regulatory regimes, one might question whether such a convenient solution is 'rational'.[17]

Given that it is a recurring theme of our discussion that the law should aspire to be 'rational' (with this idea systematically elaborated in Part III of the book), it is necessary to introduce the essentials of a rationality-based critique in these opening remarks.

---

[17] See further our discussion in ch 10.

3. CRITICAL EVALUATION AND RATIONALITY

Our proposed framework of rationality treats critical evaluation as having three dimensions: formal rationality, instrumental rationality, and substantive rationality. Our thesis is that law is fully rational only where it meets the criteria regulating each of these three dimensions.

The first dimension of rationality, formal rationality, represents a fairly straightforward concern (as in the black-letter tradition) that legal doctrine should not be contradictory. At one level, this requires no more than that contract law should establish clear ground rules for the making of transactions – settling whether, for example, a letter accepting an offer is legally binding at the moment of posting or at the time of arrival. Different legal systems may (and do) adopt their own (different) rules in relation to such questions; and this is unproblematic. What formal rationality demands is that *within a particular legal system* there should not be competing ground rules. Avoidance of contradiction, however, is not always so simple. In our next chapter, for example, we discuss a notorious trio of cases concerning mistakes of identity.[18] In each of these cases, the courts were called upon to adjudicate between two innocent parties who had been deceived by a rogue. One innocent party, A, had been tricked by a rogue, B (who used a false identity in dealing with A), into transferring possession of goods to B on credit; the other innocent party, C, had in good faith bought the goods from B. In two of the three cases, it was held that A could not rely on a mistake of identity to nullify the 'agreement' made with B and, thus, open the way to recovering the goods from C; but, in one of the cases, the court ruled that A could so rely on the mistake of identity. Since the material facts of these cases are indistinguishable, the cases seem to involve a contradiction and prima facie the demands of formal rationality are not satisfied.

Secondly, there is instrumental rationality, which has two aspects – generic and specific instrumental rationality. The generic aspect seizes on the idea that the law of contract, no less than any other branch of the law, should be capable of guiding action. For contractors, particularly commercial

---

[18]   *Phillips v Brooks* [1919] 2 KB 243; *Ingram v Little* [1961] 1 QB 31; and *Lewis v Averay* [1972] QB 198.

contractors, it is axiomatic that the law should be calculable (the requirement of certainty). In line with this axiom, the classical model of contract strives to lay down general rules with predictable applications. However, as we have said, in modern times judges have become concerned not only that the classical law licenses dealers to take unfair advantage of ordinary consumer contractors, but also that it fails to keep in touch with the expectations of commercial contractors. These concerns have led to contract doctrine being manipulated to produce the right outcomes. On occasion, judges have been pretty open about these manipulations. More often than not, however, doctrine has been covertly massaged. This has bred a form of irrationality which we will encounter with some frequency: namely, there is a lack of fit (or congruence) between contract doctrine as expounded and the underlying imperatives of judicial decision-making. In other words, there is a gap between the law-in-the-books and the law-as-applied-in-the-courts.

Turning to the specific aspect of instrumental rationality, the question is whether particular legal interventions have their intended effect.[19] Whilst some interventions may seek simply to facilitate commerce, much of the modern law of contract aims to protect contractors (particularly consumer contractors) against sharp practice. For example, s 3 of the Unfair Contract Terms Act 1977, and art 3 of the EC Directive on Unfair Terms in Consumer Contracts (93/13/EEC), seek to regulate the inclusion, or the effect, of a wide range of terms in what, for these introductory purposes, we may loosely refer to as consumer contracts. However, if such interventions have little or no impact in practice (for example, because consumers are unaware of their legal rights, or because small claims procedures are not sufficiently user-friendly, or the like), we might condemn the law as irrational in failing to be effective relative to its desired end. Conversely, if the law proves very effective in regulating terms in consumer contracts, but as a result there is an unintended negative effect (escalating prices, goods or services for which there is a significant need no longer being offered, or the like), then the law again

---

[19]   See eg Richard Lewis 'Contracts Between Businessmen: Reform of the Law of Firm Offers' (1982) 9 Journal of Law and Society 153.

fails when judged by the criterion of specific instrumental rationality.

Finally, there is the dimension of substantive rationality. Here, the question is whether the law is legitimate, whether it conforms with some given justifying principle or end. In response to such a question, a number of criteria of substantive rationality might be suggested. For example, if one approaches the matter with an eye to modern moral positions, the principal choice lies, we suggest, between those theories that follow Bentham by employing the maximisation of utility as their criterion, and those theories that work in the Kantian tradition by equating legitimacy with respect for individual rights and with performance by each party according to his or her duties. To express the difference somewhat bluntly, for utilitarians, convenience and the general good override considerations of fairness; for Kantians, fairness overrides considerations of convenience. Alternatively, instead of looking for one's criterion of substantive rationality in moral theory, one might look for it in economic theory. To the extent that economic theory restricts itself to explaining and predicting the incentive and disincentive effects (from an economic point of view) of various regimes of legal doctrine, it is relevant to matters of instrumental rather than substantial rationality. However, where such accounts of the incentive and disincentive effects of doctrine are deployed in a cost/benefit calculation, economic theory may offer a basis for evaluating the legitimacy of legal doctrine. On analysis, though, economics-as-applied-to-law does not offer a fresh criterion for substantive rationality; for the cornerstone of justificatory economic theory, the maximisation of welfare, is simply another rendering of utilitarianism.[20]

To sum up, in reflecting upon some of the key issues in contract, we will encounter many doctrinal features which give rise to concern about the rationality of the law. We will find tensions and contradictions which suggest some

---

[20]   It may be argued that the maximisation of *wealth*, not the maximisation of *welfare*, should be treated as the cornerstone of normative economic theory: see Richard Posner 'Utilitarianism, Economics, and Legal Theory' (1979) 8 Journal of Legal Studies 103. For the claim that wealth maximisation, once divorced from utility, loses its normative plausibility (both categorically and instrumentally), see Ronald Dworkin *A Matter of Principle* (Oxford, Clarendon Press, 1986) ch 12.

element of formal irrationality; covert manipulation of doctrine which violates the requirement of congruence;
questions about the effectiveness of the law; and, throughout our exploration of the key issues, we will meet concerns
about the legitimacy of the law. Critical evaluation, therefore, sets a taxing agenda for students of the law – and,
indeed, for lawmakers. However, without approaching the
matter in this way, one cannot be satisfied that the law is
fully rational – and, if the law is not fully rational, it is not
fully defensible.

Part I

Key doctrines and key cases

Chapter 2

Contract law: the basic doctrines

Introduction

As we suggested in our introductory chapter, the study of law has tended to be dominated by the 'black-letter' approach, which focuses on a narrow study of the legal rules which make up the subject. In the case of the law of contract, these legal rules are expounded in a number of well-established student textbooks. Although there are differences between these books, in many ways their similarities are more significant than those differences.[1] An important feature they share is a canon of cases. In the areas of law developed by the courts, which contract pre-eminently is, the rules are laid down in what are usually termed 'leading cases'. This constitutes the canon we refer to. One purpose of this chapter is to guide the reader through that part of the canon which lays down the basic rules of the common law of contract. However, before we embark on this task, we might pause to consider the concept of a 'leading case'.

1. THE CONCEPT OF A 'LEADING CASE'

Cases qualify in more than one way to be described as 'leading' and therefore to be included in the canon. Some cases come ready labelled, as it were. A superior court may seize on a particular case in order to try to lay down guidelines in a particular area. For example, in 1932, the majority Law

---

[1]   See Adams and Brownsword *Understanding Contract Law*, 2nd edn (London, Fontana, 1994).

Lords, led by Lord Atkin, not only laid down the modern framework for the law of negligence in the great case of *Donoghue v Stevenson*,[2] they also set out in *Bell v Lever Brothers Ltd*.[3] the principles applicable to cases involving mistakes as to the subject-matter of a contract. What the majority were concerned to emphasise in *Bell v Lever Brothers* was that a 'mistake' would not serve to release a commercial contractor from a contract simply because a bad bargain had been made. Just over twenty years later, in *Davis Contractors Ltd v Fareham UDC*[4] (the leading modern case on 'frustration' of contracts), the House of Lords set out similar restrictive principles regulating a contractor's right to be released from a contract, this time on the ground of supervening difficulties – again, as with mistake, frustration was not to be used as a convenient escape from a bad bargain. In another landmark case, *The Heron II*,[5] which is a leading case on remoteness of damage,[6] the House of Lords was concerned to offer guidance on where the law of contract draws the line in allowing an innocent party to recover compensation for the consequential losses flowing from a breach. On other occasions, a judge may deliberately take the opportunity provided by a case to float an idea. If the idea is accepted, the case in which it was floated comes to be regarded as 'leading'. Denning J's dicta in the *High Trees* case,[7] the seminal case on promissory estoppel, is a good example of this. These are examples of cases which may be regarded as having been born great. Other cases, however, have greatness thrust upon them. A commentator may have chosen a particular case as a subject for an exegesis of a body of law. Some such cases are quite ancient. An example of this still to be found in modern textbooks is Coke's notes on *Southcote*'s case[8] which lay down a number of important principles on the law of bailments, including the special acceptance rule which was to be of central importance in the development of the use of standard forms in contracts for the carriage of goods.

---

²   [1932] AC 562.
³   [1932] AC 161. See pp 38–39 below.
⁴   [1956] AC 696.
⁵   [1969] 1 AC 350.
⁶   See pp 50–51 below.
⁷   *Central London Property Trust v High Trees House* [1947] 1 KB 130.
⁸   (1601) 4 Co Rep 83b.

Serjeant Williams's notes on *Pordage v Cole*[9] in the same way became the standard guide to the complexities of the law of dependent and independent covenants which was of importance in the development of the law relating to discharge by breach.

Without question, it was the nineteenth century that was the great age of the leading case. In 1837 John William Smith published the first edition of *Smith's Leading Cases*, a work which was to remain in print until its thirteenth edition in 1929. In his Preface to the first edition, Smith claimed to address two needs. First of all, he addressed the needs of students who are advised to read for themselves the original cases, rather than rely on commentaries and abridgments, but find themselves perplexed simply by the quantity of reported cases. Which are the ones to read? The answer according to Smith was the '*leading cases*': 'embodied in which [the student] might discover those great principles of Law of which it is necessary [he] should render himself thorough master'.[10] The other group of readers addressed by Smith were the practitioners requiring a portable collection of leading cases. Smith hoped his collection would prove useful to both classes of reader:

> 'The cases it contains may all, it is believed, be properly denominated "*leading cases*". Each involves, and is usually cited to establish, some point or principle of real practical importance.'[11]

Like Coke, and Serjeant Williams and others of their kind, Smith appended a commentary to the cases, setting out other cases in the process of expounding a body of doctrine.

Another category of leading case is a product of the fact that the modern law of contract is to a very large extent the invention of certain nineteenth-century textbook writers, notably Sir William Anson, and Sir Frederick Pollock. Indeed the style of contract textbook which they wrote was comparatively novel at the time. The tradition seems to start with John Joseph Powell's *Essay on the Law of Contract* (1790). What distinguished it from what had gone before was that instead of being a patchwork commentary built on particular decisions, it expounded an organised and rational

---

9   (1669) 1 Wms Saund 548.
10   Preface to the first edition, p i.
11   Ibid.

framework of contract into which the cases were fitted.[12] Obviously the framework was in part at least derived from leading cases, but where a case did not fit the framework, but had nevertheless enjoyed more or less the status of a leading case, it was simply given the Procrustean treatment and slotted in, either by the judges, or by the textbook writers, who enjoyed a symbiotic relationship. *Lampleigh v Brathwait*[13] is a good example of this. It appears to have been decided under the old rule that a promise made where a moral obligation was owed, was made on good consideration (and was thus enforceable).[14] This did not square with the modern theory, explained below, that consideration was a part of a bargained-for exchange. Consequently the case was reinterpreted as having involved an implied promise at the outset that the plaintiff's services in seeking a pardon for the defendant would be paid for.[15] Occasionally a contemporary case was seized upon because its fact situation provided a convenient peg upon which to hang a thesis. *Raffles v Wichelhaus*,[16] which was supposed to be an illustration of the proposition that where the parties are at cross-purposes the contract is void, never in fact involved a decision by the judge, Pollock CB, that the contract was void for mistake. Indeed, mistake is only discussed in an exchange between counsel and the judge. Nevertheless, *faute de mieux*, the fact situation was too good to pass over, and the case went down in legal history as a leading case on something it never decided. The symbiotic activities of the textbook writers and of the judges produced the rule-book which constitutes the law of contract as it is usually studied by students. It is the object of the remainder of this chapter to sketch out the contents of the rule-book, for it is the classical canon that sets the framework (and the foil) for our reflections on the key issues of contract law.

---

[12]   See Simpson 'Innovation in Nineteenth Century Contract Law' (1975) 91 LQR 247.
[13]   (1615) Hob 105.
[14]   See Simpson *A History of the Common Law of Contract* (Oxford, Oxford University Press, 1975) pp 322–3.
[15]   *Kennedy v Broun* (1863) 13 CBNS 677.
[16]   (1864) 2 H & C 906.

2. THE LAW OF OBLIGATIONS

The law of contract belongs to the body of legal rules known as the law of obligations. Obligations come into existence in two ways: (i) by act of the parties themselves in agreeing to be bound to each other; (ii) through the law imposing them independently of agreement. The latter category includes first of all the emerging law of restitution (which, in general terms, deals with cases of unjust enrichment, as eg where the law imposes an obligation on a party to repay a sum of money paid under a mistake of fact), and secondly the law of torts, which imposes civil duties which if broken render the wrongdoer liable to the injured party. The common feature of each of these categories is the legal tie which connects the parties.[17] The rights conferred by the law of obligations are personal, as opposed to the rights in rem enjoyed under the law of property. It is the first category of obligations, those created by agreement of the parties, which concerns us in this chapter.

3. ELEMENTS OF A SIMPLE CONTRACT

Contracts are of two sorts: formal contracts made by deed,[18] and 'simple contracts', ie all other contracts. It is simple contracts which are the principal focus of this book.

A contract is an agreement giving rise to a legally enforceable obligation between parties. Usually, the law of contract is expounded as a narrative starting with a magical moment known as 'formation', and ending when the contract is discharged by breach giving rise to an action for damages, or in some other way. Like a Greek tragedy, all subsequent events are controlled by those fateful first events, ie the circumstances existing at the time of formation. They control, for example, the interpretation of the contract and the award of damages.

---

[17] *Vinculum juris* in the Roman law terminology from which this categorisation is taken. Roman law is the basis of continental civil law systems. The influence of civil law writers on the development of the modern common law of contract was, as we shall see, considerable.

[18] The formal requirements of a deed are set out in the Law of Property (Miscellaneous Provision) Act 1989.

Every contract entails a free agreement,[19] but not every agreement results in a contract. A contract to be binding must have four elements. There must be: (1) intention to create legal relations; (2) offer and acceptance; (3) consideration; and (4) certainty of terms.

(i) Intention to create legal relations

The courts set a threshold for an agreement to surmount before they will take cognizance of it. This threshold is expressed as a requirement that an intention to create legal relations must exist before an agreement will be regarded as a contract. Now, in general, only in formal contracting will the parties consider the legal consequences of their agreement at all. In other cases, usually the first time they consider the matter is when something goes wrong. The requirement of intention to create legal relations is therefore a way of signalling that there are categories of agreement over which the courts do not wish to have jurisdiction. For instance, if a friend invites you out to dinner, and then cancels, you may be very disappointed, but you will have no legal redress. On the other hand, if you book a table at a restaurant and fail to turn up, the restaurant may sue you for breach of contract – and, indeed, there have been cases of this kind in the County Court. In the leading case of *Balfour v Balfour*[20] a man who was returning to his job abroad promised to pay his wife in England a monthly allowance. It was held that this promise did not give rise to

---

[19]   So that if a contract is the result of duress or undue influence it will be void or voidable. For duress, see section 5 of this chapter. For undue influence (which may be actual or presumed), see *Allcard v Skinner* [1887] 36 Ch D 145. Recently, undue influence has become a much litigated issue where male mortgagors have applied undue influence to female partners with an interest in the mortgaged property; the question then arises whether the normal right of the mortgagee bank to have possession of the mortgaged property against a defaulting mortgagor is in any way restricted. The leading cases are *Barclays Bank plc v O'Brien* [1993] 4 All ER 417 and *CIBC Mortgages plc v Pitt* [1993] 4 All ER 433; and for some of the many cases applying *Barclays Bank plc v O'Brien* to the question of whether, on the particular facts, the mortgagee banks have constructive notice of the undue influence, see eg *Massey v Midland Bank plc* [1995] 1 All ER 929; *Banco Exterior Internacional v Mann* [1995] 1 All ER 936; and *TSB Bank plc v Camfield* [1995] 1 All ER 951.

[20]   [1919] 2 KB 571.

a legal obligation, because the parties had not intended to enter into legal relations. On its facts, the case is close to the borderline. Had the parties been about to separate, it is probable that the promise would have been enforceable, but the principle is clear that in general the courts do not wish to have jurisdiction over domestic agreements. Non-domestic agreements (ie commercial and consumer contracts), by contrast, are generally held to involve an intention to create legal relations, but not necessarily so. In *Esso Petroleum Ltd v Comrs of Customs and Excise*[21] a revenue case which turned on whether Esso had sold the World Cup coins they offered with every four gallons of petrol purchased, the Court of Appeal, and two of the five Law Lords thought that the coins were a gift, ie there was no intention to create legal relations, but the view which prevailed was that they were transferred under a contract.

(ii) Offer and acceptance

Every contract is supposed to involve an offer and an acceptance. Sometimes, the offer is preceded by a so-called invitation to treat (or tender) – for example, goods displayed in shops are generally regarded as invitations of this kind (rather than as offers).[22] Thus when you go into a shop and ask for the goods you have seen in the window, you are making an offer (in response to the shop's invitation to treat) which the shop assistant can choose to accept by selling you the goods, or not. The assistant might choose not to sell you the goods if, for example, they are an alcoholic beverage and you appear to be under-age. If the assistant agrees to sell you the goods, a contract for the sale of the goods is formed from the moment acceptance of your offer is indicated.[23]

The requirement of offer and acceptance had its origins in the doctrine that a contract must involve a meeting of minds. The reason given for this requirement of a meeting of minds was that every legal obligation involves a limitation

---

[21] [1976] 1 WLR 1: for analysis, see Roger Brownsword 'Of Cups and Coins and Contracts' (1976) 27 Northern Ireland Legal Quarterly 414.

[22] See eg *Fisher v Bell* [1961] 1 QB 394. For discussion of tenders, see ch 4, section 4.

[23] See eg *Pharmaceutical Society of Great Britain v Boots Cash Chemists (Southern) Ltd* [1953] 1 QB 401.

on individual freedom. The only justification for this limitation was that each party was *ad idem* as to the freedom they were respectively surrendering, ie that there was a meeting of minds. Now if minds had to meet, there had necessarily to be some point of time at which this occurred – namely, the moment at which the offeree indicated acceptance to the offeror. This doctrine is to be found fully worked out in the writings of the French eighteenth-century jurist Pothier, whose *Treatise on Obligations*, and *Treatise on Sales*, were highly influential in the development of the common law of contracts in the nineteenth century.

Clearly the doctrine created a problem if contracts were made by post, for there could be no point in time at which both parties could know each had assented to the other's terms. Pothier solved this by presuming a continuing will on the part of the offeror to contract in the terms of his offer, such will enduring until the offeree indicated acceptance. In effect, the offeror by indicating either expressly or by implication that posting an acceptance of the exact terms offered would suffice, had dispensed with communication of the acceptance.[24] This doctrine disposed of a problem which had existed in the common law of contracts before the nineteenth century. Under that old law, a promise could be consideration for a promise, only if it were itself actionable. This entailed that promises be made at the same instant, otherwise the first promise made would be without consideration, and the one subsequently made would be made on a past consideration. Consequently no contract could come into existence.[25] This problem confronted the court in the well-known case of *Adams v Lindsell*.[26] The plaintiffs were woollen manufacturers in Bromsgrove, Worcestershire. The defendants were wool dealers in St Ives, Huntingdon. The defendants wrote to the plaintiffs on 2 September offering them a quantity of wool on certain terms. They misdirected the letter, and it did not reach the plaintiffs until 5 September. The plaintiffs immediately posted off their acceptance. On 8 September, not having heard from the plaintiffs, the defendants sold the wool to third parties. On

---

[24] And consequently by implication would still be bound if the letter of acceptance went astray in the post – *Household Fire and Carriage Accident Insurance v Grant* (1879) 4 Ex D 216.

[25] *Cooke v Oxley* (1790) 3 TR 653.

[26] (1818) 1 B & Ald 681.

9 September the plaintiffs' letter of acceptance arrived. The court appears to have adopted the Pothier analysis, for it held that there was a contract brought into existence by the plaintiffs posting off the letter of acceptance on 5 September; consequently the defendants were in breach. This case, by which the so-called 'postal acceptance' rule was introduced into the law, left open the question of what would have happened if the defendants had changed their minds and decided to revoke their offer before the plaintiffs posted off their acceptance on 5 September. The meeting of minds theory logically would hold there to be no contract. Certainly, this view was current as late as the case of *Dickinson v Dodds*.[27] However, *Byrne v Van Tienhoven*[28] settled that a revocation of an offer (even a revocation made by post) must be communicated to the offeree.

An acceptance must match the terms of an offer, otherwise there can be no meeting of minds. If A offers to sell goods for £1,000, and B replies offering to buy for £950, clearly there is no contract. What is less self-evidently correct is the view taken in the famous case of *Hyde v Wrench*,[29] where the court drew the conclusion that the 'counter-offer' (in that case, a counter-offer to buy a farm for £950) was a rejection of the original offer. Although the courts may be prepared to hold in such a case that such a reply is a mere inquiry and not a counter-offer,[30] in general, a reply in different terms from the offer will be treated as a counter-offer, and a rejection of the offer.

This is of importance in the resolution of the so-called 'battle of the forms'. A makes an offer on his standard printed form; B replies purporting to accept using his standard form which differs materially from A's. Even if either A or B's form states that its terms shall prevail over any differing terms in the other party's form, it is not clear whether the law should give effect to such a provision (and, if so, how). One solution to the battle of the forms is to regard the last act capable of constituting an acceptance as being an acceptance. Thus, if following B's reply, A dispatches the goods, A's act is arguably an acceptance of B's counter-offer.

---

[27]   [1876] 2 Ch D 463. *Cooke v Oxley*, n 25 above, was anachronistically explained as an example of the same proposition.
[28]   (1880) 5 CPD 344.
[29]   (1840) 3 Beav 334.
[30]   *Stevenson v McLean* [1880] 5 QBD 346.

But, as Lord Denning MR pointed out in *Butler Machine Tool Co Ltd v Ex-Cell-O Corporation (England) Ltd*:[31]

> 'In many of these cases our traditional analysis of offer, counter-offer, rejection, acceptance and so forth is out of date.'

In short there is no mechanical production-line solution to the problems raised by these production-line contracts.[32] In fact, in the *Butler Machine Tool* case, Lord Denning was prepared to apply traditional theory because the original offeror had signed and returned to the (original) offeree, the offeree's tear-off acknowledgment slip, which stated: 'We accept your order on the terms and conditions stated thereon' – a fairly positive act showing acceptance of the (original) offeree's terms.

(iii) Consideration

The third requirement for an enforceable contract is consideration. As noted above, in the seventeenth-century case of *Lampleigh v Brathwait* a promise of a sum of money made where a moral obligation was owed (because the plaintiff had obtained a pardon for the defendant from the king), was held to be made on a good consideration. By the nineteenth century, however, in *Eastwood v Kenyon*,[33] it was held that a moral obligation was not a good consideration. The plaintiff had acted as guardian for a girl and had spent money on her education and for the benefit of her estate. She promised to reimburse him when she came of age. She then married the defendant who also promised to pay. Lord Denman held that the moral obligations of the promisors notwithstanding, the promises were unenforceable. The doctrine of consideration in this and other nineteenth-century cases was remodelled into an essential part of a bilateral contract. The older doctrine, by contrast, was simply concerned with the enforcement of promises by asking whether a promise had been made on a good consideration, ie in circumstances which indicated it was meant seriously;[34] it was not concerned specifically with bilateral transactions.

---

[31]   [1979] 1 All ER 965, 968.
[32]   On the question of the battle of the forms, see Adams (1979) 95 LQR 481, and (1983) Journal of Business Law 297.
[33]   (1840) 11 Ad & El 438.
[34]   See Simpson *History of Common Law of Contract*, p 321 et seq.

The classic (nineteenth-century) definition of consideration is that of Sir Frederick Pollock:

'An act or forbearance of one party, or the promise thereof, is
the price for which the promise of the other is bought, and the
promise thus given for value is enforceable.'[35]

It is possible that this classical view of consideration has
been significantly altered by the Court of Appeal in the late
twentieth-century case of *Williams v Roffey Bros & Nicholls
(Contractors) Ltd*.[36] One consequence of the classical view
was that a promise by A to perform for a party, B, that which
the other party, A, was already bound to perform, was unenforceable. Thus in the famous case of *Stilk v Myrick*[37] a
seaman who had contracted to complete a voyage for a certain sum of money sued for the bonus promised by the
captain for completing the voyage after two sailors had
deserted. The claim was rejected for want of consideration.[38]
However, in many modern commercial situations, it makes
perfectly good sense to promise a party more for doing
what that party is already contractually obliged to do. For
example, if a sub-contractor has under-estimated, it may be
that the choice is paying more for the job, or letting the sub-
contractor go bankrupt. In the latter case there will be the
delay and expense of getting a new sub-contractor to the
site. A cheaper solution may be to promise the original sub-
contractor more for completing the job. In *Williams v Roffey
Bros & Nicholls* it was held in just such a fact situation that
the sub-contractor was entitled to recover the extra amount
promised. This seems to come close to returning to the older
doctrine of consideration, which simply held that a promise
made on a good consideration (using that word in a more

---

[35] Pollock on *Contracts* (13th edn) p 33. This definition was adopted in
     Dunlop v Selfridge [1915] AC 847, 855.
[36] [1990] 1 All ER 512. See further ch 4.
[37] (1809) 2 Camp 317.
[38] Although Lord Ellenborough based his decision on the ground of want
     of consideration, he may have used the term 'consideration' in the older
     sense of reason for making the promise – remember that in the
     appalling conditions on sailing ships at the time, desertions were very
     frequent – rather than in the sense given to it in Sir Frederick Pollock's
     definition. In the earlier case of *Harris v Watson* (1791) Peake 102, Lord
     Kenyon had rejected a similar claim because it might promote black-
     mail of a master by the crew to allow it. As to the older doctrine of
     consideration see Simpson *History of the Common Law of Contract*
     pp 322–3.

normal sense than the modern technical legal sense) was
enforceable.[39]

(iv) Certainty of terms

If no certain meaning can be extracted from the terms used
by the parties there cannot be a contract. Thus in *Scammell
v Ouston*[40] the plaintiff wished to purchase a new van from
the defendant. He gave the defendant a written order which
included the words 'This order is given on the understanding that the balance of the purchase price can be had on
hire-purchase terms over two years.' The defendant refused
to deliver the van, and the plaintiff sued for damages for
non-delivery. Evidence was given that there was a wide
variety of hire-purchase terms, and there was nothing in the
agreement to indicate which of them the parties had
intended. The House of Lords held that there was no contract. As Lord Wright said:

> 'In truth, in my opinion, their agreement was inchoate and never
> got beyond negotiations. They did, indeed, accept the position
> that there should be some form of hire-purchase agreement, but
> they never went on to complete their agreement by settling
> between them what the terms of the hire-purchase agreement
> were to be.'[41]

An important corollary of the certainty requirement is
that, on the classical view, 'a contract to negotiate, like a contract to enter into a contract, is not a contract known to the
law'.[42] Recent case-law, however, suggests that a contract to
negotiate may be enforceable where it takes the form of a
'lock-out' agreement under which, for a fixed period of time,
it is agreed between A and B that A will not negotiate with C
(thereby giving B a clear run at completing the deal with A).[43]
In the leading case of *Walford v Miles*,[44] though, the House
of Lords put down an important marker. There, the House
ruled that a lock-out agreement of *uncertain* duration (in

---

[39] See Adams and Brownsword 'Contract, Consideration and the Critical
       Path' (1990) 53 MLR 536.
[40] [1941] AC 251.
[41] Ibid at p 269. Compare *Hillas & Co Ltd v Arcos Ltd*, p 43 below.
[42] *Courtney and Fairbairn Ltd v Tolaini Bros (Hotels) Ltd* [1975] 1 All ER
       716, 720 (per Lord Denning MR).
[43] See *Pitt v PHH Asset Management Ltd* [1993] 4 All ER 961.
[44] [1992] 1 All ER 453. See further ch 7.

that case, an agreement between the Mileses who were selling a business and the Walfords who were prospective buyers) could not be salvaged merely by substituting a 'lock-in' agreement whereby the parties undertook to negotiate in good faith. In short, certain lock-out agreements are 'in' (contractually speaking), but lock-in agreements are 'out'.

(v) The inter-relationship between the formation requirements

The famous case of *Carlill v Carbolic Smoke Ball Co*[45] will serve as a vehicle for illustrating the inter-relationship of the four above-mentioned requirements for the formation of a simple contract. The defendants advertised that they would pay a £100 'reward' to any person who caught influenza after having used their smoke ball three times daily for two weeks as directed by the instructions supplied with the product. They indicated that they had deposited £1,000 with their bankers to show their sincerity in the matter. Despite using the smoke ball as directed, the plaintiff caught influenza. The Court of Appeal held that she was entitled to the reward. The Court took the view that the (alleged) deposit of £1,000 indicated that the defendants intended their promise to be taken seriously, ie the Court held that the advertisement constituted an offer (rather than mere sales talk) and, concomitantly, that the defendants intended to enter into legal relations. The act of acceptance was using the smoke ball as directed, and whilst the usual rule is that the acceptance must be communicated to the offeror, it is open to the offeror to indicate expressly or by implication that some other act will suffice as acceptance (with the need for communication being waived). The consideration for the defendants' promise was either buying the smoke ball (thus enhancing the defendants' sales), or using the smoke ball as directed (which the Court deemed to be a sufficiently inconvenient and unpleasant process).[46] In coming to this

---

[45] [1893] 1 QB 256.
[46] The curious idea that sniffing carbolic acid powder could guard against influenza is put into the context of medical knowledge of the time in a fascinating article by Professor Simpson 'Quackery and Contract Law: the Case of the Carbolic Smoke Ball' (1985) 14 Journal of Legal Studies 345. Some of the remedies prescribed by orthodox medicine at the time were scarcely less outlandish.

conclusion the Court also rejected the defendants' argument that the agreement failed for lack of certainty. While the advertisement was vague in some respects (especially with regard to the period during which the offer of a reward applied), the Court's basic approach was that the defendants could not expect to escape their obligations by appealing to their own copy-writing inadequacies.

Some readers may have begun to ask why we need both a doctrine of intention to create legal relations *and* the modern doctrine of consideration. The answer is that it is partly an historical accident that both doctrines exist in the law, for as Holmes pointed out in his great book *The Common Law*[47] the same act may or may not be consideration as it is dealt with by the parties (that is to say, depending upon the intentions of the parties). For example, if I say 'You can take my car to York' I may mean *either* 'You want to go to York, and you can use my car to do so', *or* 'In consideration of your delivering it to York, you may take my car'. Only the surrounding circumstances will indicate which I meant, and only in the latter case is there intention to create legal relations, and therefore consideration. In other words, the doctrine of intention to create legal relations, which is in fact quite close to the pre-nineteenth-century doctrine of consideration, ought in principle to be sufficient by itself. As we will see, however, the requirements imposed by the classical doctrine of consideration have had a number of implications, the most significant of which is the doctrine of privity of contract.

4.   THE DOCTRINE OF PRIVITY OF CONTRACT

According to the classical theory of consideration, if A promises to pay B £100, A's promise is unenforceable by B unless B has given some consideration for A's promise – meaning, unless there is some detriment on B's part for which A has bargained. In the absence of such an exchange, the agreement between A and B is unenforceable. It follows that, if A promises B that he (A) will pay C £100, then in the absence of any consideration, neither B nor C can enforce A's promise. So far, the logic of this seems impeccable – the

---

[47]   Little Brown & Co (1881) pp 293–4.

gratuitous third party C surely cannot be in a better position than the gratuitous promisee B. The privity doctrine, however, takes the apparent logic of consideration one step further. What the doctrine of privity of contract holds is that C (being a stranger to the consideration)[48] cannot enforce A's promise even if B has given A consideration for the promise, even if in other words there is an enforceable contract between A and B. Of course, if there is an enforceable contract between A and B, B will be able to enforce A's promise.[49] However, the privity doctrine disallows any contractual claim by C. As we explained in our introductory chapter, where we discussed the classic case of *Tweddle v Atkinson*,[50] this doctrine is capable of working serious injustice in relation to the intended third party beneficiary.

The problems created by the privity doctrine are not restricted to simple situations such as that in *Tweddle v Atkinson*. They run deep into commercial contracting where contractors are commonly linked in networks of main contracts and sub-contracts, networks of distribution contracts, and the like. By holding that only the parties to a contract can sue and be sued on it, have burdens imposed by it, or derive benefits from it, the privity doctrine artificially treats each contract as a private bilateral arrangement between the parties to which all other parties are strangers. This important topic is discussed at length in Chapter 5, and we will not therefore deal further with it here.

5. COERCION AND ECONOMIC DURESS

According to the classical view, contracts are the products of *free* agreement. Although, as both philosophers and

---

[48] In ch 5 we argue that it is a fallacy to reason from C being a stranger to the consideration to C being unable to enforce the contract between A and B.

[49] Note, though, the difficulties that B may face in recovering substantial damages on behalf of C. See eg *Beswick v Beswick* [1968] AC 58; *Jackson v Horizon Holidays Ltd* [1975] 3 All ER 92 (family claim on consumer contract); the consolidated appeals in *Linden Gardens Trust Ltd v Lenesta Sludge Disposals Ltd* and *St Martins Property Corpn Ltd v Sir Robert McAlpine and Sons Ltd* [1993] 3 All ER 417; and the direct challenge to privity in *Darlington Borough Council v Wiltshier Northern Ltd* (1995) 11 Const LJ 36.

[50] (1861) B & S 393.

psychologists will testify, there is no simple line to be drawn between free and unfree action, there are some fairly clear cases where a transaction is procured by coercion – for example, where a transaction is concluded at gunpoint, or where there is a threat to one's family or property, or the like. Not surprisingly, the law treats contracts as voidable where agreement has been obtained only because of a clear coercive threat.[51] The modern law, however, is prepared to take a fairly broad view of what constitutes coercion, so much so that English law now recognises a doctrine of economic duress.

The root of the modern thinking on economic duress is *North Ocean Shipping Co Hyundai Construction: The Atlantic Baron*.[52] In this case, a shipyard applied pressure on a client to pay more than the agreed contractual price for the construction of a tanker. Reluctantly, the client acceded to the shipbuilders' demands. Although, on the facts, it was held that the client acted too slowly in trying to avoid the agreement to pay additional sums for the tanker, it was accepted that, in principle, the client had the right to escape the additional obligations on the ground of economic duress. Since the decision in *The Atlantic Baron*, the jurisprudence of economic duress has been developed by the courts to the point where one can say that the paradigm of this form of coercion involves the following three elements: (1) one party, A, applies illegitimate pressure (that is, pressure going beyond legitimate commercial pressure) to B in relation to some demand (eg that B should pay more, or that A should pay less); (2) as a result of which B has no reasonable alternative but to accede to A's demand; and (3) the net effect of the transaction is manifestly to B's disadvantage. Such a paradigmatic case arose in *Atlas Express Ltd v Kafco (Importers and Distributors) Ltd*,[53] where the plaintiff carriers, having (through their own carelessness) under-priced a contract to transport the defendants' basketware goods to various retail outlets, threatened not to perform the contract unless the price was adjusted upwards. Because the carriers' threat was made at a time of year when it was not possible for the defendants to find an alternative carrier, and because they could not afford to let down their retail

---

[51]   See *Barton v Armstrong* [1976] AC 104.
[52]   [1979] QB 705.
[53]   [1989] 1 All ER 641.

customers, they had little choice but to go along with the demand for an increased price. Whilst, no doubt, there will be many cases where it is moot whether the situation displays all the ingredients of economic duress, the dealings in *Atlas Express v Kafco* were thought to be plainly coercive.

The modern development of a doctrine of economic duress has an important bearing on the willingness of the courts to relax the consideration requirement. Thus, in *Williams v Roffey*,[54] the Court of Appeal ruled that the main contractor's promise to pay additional sums to the financially troubled sub-contractor was binding provided (i) the promisor main contractor derived some practical benefit (or obviated some disbenefit) from the arrangement, and (ii) the promise was *freely* given. In fact, in *Williams v Roffey* itself, it was not argued that the sub-contractor had applied economic duress to the main contractor. However, the modern thinking seems to be that contractors, who are vulnerable at a particular time during a contract, should be protected against unfair demands not by the doctrine of consideration but by the emerging doctrine of economic duress. These are matters to which we will return in Chapters 4 and 7.

6. ILLEGALITY

A contract may satisfy all the requirements set out above, but yet be one the courts will refuse to enforce because it is made in furtherance of an objective rendered illegal by statute (such as price fixing contracts between manufacturers),[55] or against public policy (such as contracts in restraint of trade). Classically, the position is summarised by the maxim '*ex turpi causa non oritur actio*' (the gist of which is that the courts will not assist those who found an action on an immoral or an illegal act). In the twentieth century, this has crystallised as the so-called *Bowmaker* rule,[56] according to which the material question is whether a party is seeking to rely on, or to found its claim on, the illegal contract. If a party is not so relying, the action may not fail on the ground of illegality. For example, in *Tinsley*

---

[54] See above.
[55] These are contrary, inter alia, to Art 85 of the Treaty of Rome, and may amount to an abuse of a dominant position contrary to Art 86.
[56] See *Bowmakers Ltd v Barnet Instruments* [1945] 1 KB 65.

v Milligan,[57] T and M were parties to an illegal agreement: namely, that they should jointly contribute to the purchase of a house, but that they should register it in the sole name of T, thereby enabling M to make fraudulent claims for welfare benefits which T and M would use to meet their joint expenses. When the relationship between T and M broke down, T claimed ownership of the house and M sought a declaration that T held the house on a resulting trust for them in equal shares. By a majority of 3 to 2, the House of Lords ruled in favour of M, the illegal arrangement notwithstanding – with reference to the *Bowmaker* rule, M did not need to rely on the illegal agreement to establish her interest in the property.

We shall have a little more to say about illegality later.[58] However, it may be observed in passing that the courts have tended to be reluctant to police contracts in the name of public policy.

7. MISTAKE

A natural corollary of the meeting of minds theory was that if one or both of the parties did not consent in the same terms, the contract was void. One of the ways in which consent could be negatived was mistake. The classical common law doctrine of mistake (which operates to render a contract void *ab initio*) applies only to a restricted range of situations as follows:

1.   where one party makes a mistake as to the identity of the person contracted with;
2.   where the parties are at cross-purposes;
3.   where the parties make a mistake as to the existence of the subject-matter of the contract;
4.   where one party makes a mistake as to the terms of the contract and the other party is aware of this mistake.

We may add to this list, as a sort of appendix, a fifth circumstance in which a contract will be void for mistake, though it originates from a different source than the above

---

[57]   [1993] 3 All ER 65.
[58]   Ch 10.

doctrines:[59] this is where a party is mistaken as to the nature of the document he or she is signing, eg a party is tricked into signing a guarantee thinking that he or she is witnessing a document.[60] However, in the absence of trickery a party is estopped by signing a document from denying assent to the contents. For instance, in *L'Estrange v Graucob*[61] (which we mentioned in our introductory chapter) the plaintiff, who owned a café, agreed to buy a cigarette machine from the defendants. The agreement which the plaintiff signed included a clause exempting the defendant from liability for breaches of conditions and warranties. The machine proved to be defective. It was held that the plaintiff was bound by the exemption clause though she had never read it. By signing she had estopped herself from denying her assent to it.

(i) Mistake as to the identity of a party

If A makes an offer to B, only B can accept it, and not C. Similarly, B to whom the offer is made must address the acceptance to A the offeror, and not to C. All this sounds eminently reasonable until we examine the working out of its consequences in the cases. The leading case here is *Cundy v Lindsay*.[62] A rogue, Blenkarn, hired a room at 37 Wood Street, London, near to the premises of a respectable firm Blenkiron & Sons who carried on business at 123 Wood Street. Blenkarn then proceeded to order a large quantity of handkerchiefs from the firm of Lindsay, signing the order 'A Blenkarn & Co'. Lindsay, thinking that the order had come from Blenkiron & Sons, dispatched the goods on credit. Blenkarn received them and sold them on to a bona fide third party, Cundy, who paid Blenkarn. Needless to say, Lindsay were never paid, and sought to recover their loss by suing Cundy in tort for conversion of the handkerchiefs. If the contract between Lindsay and Blenkarn were void for mistake, then Cundy would have no title to the handkerchiefs and would have committed the tort of conversion. The House of Lords held that Lindsay had indeed intended to deal with Blenkiron, and not with Blenkarn, and that consequently

---

[59]   See eg *Thoroughgood's* case (1582) 2 Co Eliz 9a.
[60]   *Foster v Mackinnon* (1869) LR 4 CP 704; *Saunders (Executrix of Will of Gallie) v Anglia Building Society* [1971] AC 1004.
[61]   [1934] 2 KB 394.
[62]   (1878) 3 App Cas 459.

the contract between Blenkarn and Lindsay was void for mistake, and Cundy had committed a conversion.[63] Now, however logical this result, two obvious criticisms can be made of it. One is that between two innocent parties, Cundy and Lindsay, the loss should in fairness be placed on the party best able to prevent it, ie Lindsay.[64] On the facts, Lindsay were careless: 37 Wood Street is clearly different from 123 Wood Street, and should, if Lindsay had noticed the discrepancy, have put them on notice not to dispatch the goods on credit. A second objection is that the question of the identity of the rogue was raised only because the plaintiff had not been paid: if Lindsay had been paid, they would almost certainly not have cared in the slightest whether they had sold to Blenkarn or Blenkiron (although, in theory, the contract would nevertheless be void so that Cundy would not get title to the goods, and indeed, the money paid to Lindsay would be recoverable by Blenkarn).

Cases subsequent to *Cundy v Lindsay*, possibly for these reasons, exhibit degrees of hair-splitting which would do no disservice to a mediaeval schoolman. In *King's Norton Metal Co Ltd v Edridge Merrett & Co Ltd*[65] it was held that where the name used by the rogue was that of a fictitious firm, so that there was no other party in existence with whom the dispatcher of the goods could be supposed to have intended to deal, the contract between the rogue and the dispatcher was not void. Similarly, when the parties are face to face, it is said to be more difficult for the courts to conclude that the plaintiff intended to deal with someone other than the person before them. This conclusion was drawn in the well-known cases of *Phillips v Brooks*,[66] and *Lewis v Averay*,[67] but a different result was reached in the virtually indistinguishable case of *Ingram v Little*.[68] In *Phillips v Brooks* a rogue called North entered the plaintiff's shop and selected a necklace costing £2,550 and a ring worth £450. He then

---

[63] Ie had dealt with the goods in a manner inconsistent with Lindsay's ownership. Because the contract between Lindsay and Blenkarn was void, Lindsay retained the property in the goods. See now on conversion, the Torts (Interference with Goods) Act 1977.

[64] This, for example, is a principle upon which the law of negotiable instruments operates.

[65] (1897) 14 TLR 98.

[66] [1919] 2 KB 243.

[67] [1972] 1 QB 198.

[68] [1961] 1 QB 31.

wrote out a cheque for £3,000 saying as he did so, 'You see who I am, I am Sir George Bullough'. The plaintiff had heard of Sir George Bullough, and upon consulting a directory found that he lived at the address given by North. The plaintiff then asked North whether he would like to take the articles with him, but North replied that the plaintiff had better have his cheque cleared first. As an apparent afterthought, however, the rogue said that he would perhaps like to take the ring as it was his wife's birthday the next day. North then took the ring and pledged it for £350 to the defendant who took it in good faith. It was held that the plaintiff had intended to sell to the person present in the shop, ie North; in consequence there was a valid contract of sale, so that the pledgee was entitled to keep the ring. On the other hand, in *Ingram v Little* a rogue falsely calling himself P G M Hutchinson (again the name of a real person) called on the plaintiffs and negotiated the purchase of their car for £717. He proffered a cheque for this amount. Initially, the plaintiffs were reluctant to accept a cheque, but after confirming the name and address given by the rogue in the telephone directory, they allowed him to drive away. He sold the car to the defendant, who acted in good faith. It was held that the plaintiffs intended to sell to P G M Hutchinson, and that the contract was void for mistake, so that the plaintiffs might recover from the defendant in conversion. The facts of *Lewis v Averay* were virtually identical, a trusting seller of a car again taking a cheque from a rogue who was allowed to drive away with the vehicle which he then sold to an innocent third-party purchaser. Yet, in *Lewis v Averay*, the Court of Appeal reached the opposite result to that arrived at by the Court in *Ingram v Little*.

In cases of mistaken identity (where the mistake has been induced by fraud) similar to those discussed above, the plaintiff has another avenue of recourse. The fraud on the part of the rogue renders the contract with the plaintiff seller voidable in equity. However, the seller's right to avoid is lost if it is not exercised before the goods have been sold to a bona fide purchaser. In consequence, as soon as the third party buys in good faith, the plaintiff's right to avoid the contract for fraud will be lost. The effect of this allocation of risk is to place the loss on the party best able to prevent it (ie the seller who surrenders possession of the goods on credit). This line of thinking goes some way towards explaining the hard-nosed approach to mistake taken by the courts in *Phillips v Brooks* and *Lewis v Averay*.

(ii) The parties are at cross-purposes

Virtually the only known example of this kind of mistake in the books is the mis-cited case of *Raffles v Wichelhaus*,[69] mentioned above. The defendant agreed to buy cotton to arrive 'ex Peerless from Bombay'. There were two ships called 'Peerless' sailing from Bombay one of which would arrive later than the other. The judge appears to have thought that if the plaintiff meant one ship and the defendant the other, the contract would be void, but this was never actually decided.

(iii) Mistake as to the existence of the subject-matter

Mistake as to the existence of the subject-matter would occur, for example, where parties insure something which unknown to them has ceased to exist.[70] Where the subject-matter ceases to exist after the contract has been made, it may be discharged by impossibility of performance, or by frustration. Since there is a relationship between these various doctrines, we deal with them later when we discuss discharge by impossibility or frustration.[71] Here we are concerned particularly with the way in which various theories of contract, especially meeting of minds theory, have generated mistake doctrines.

A puzzle for meeting of minds theory arises where the parties make a mistake, not about the existence of the subject-matter of the contract, but about its characteristics. For example, suppose that A sells a painting to B, both parties mistakenly assuming that it is a genuine Constable when it is actually a reproduction. How is contract law to treat such a mistake? In English law, the solution to this puzzle was found in the Aristotelian distinction between substance and quality. As Lord Atkin said in the leading case of *Bell v Lever Bros*[72] what is required is a:

---

[69]   (1864) 2 H & C 906.
[70]   *Scott v Coulson* [1903] 2 Ch 249.
[71]   See section 11 below.
[72]   [1932] AC 161, 218. The respondents in this case had paid a substantial sum to the appellant as compensation for terminating a

'mistake of both parties . . . as to the existence of some quality which makes the thing without the quality essentially different from the thing as it was believed to be'.

The principle is easier stated than applied. In *Sherwood v Walker*,[73] for example, a cow thought barren was sold for slaughter for $80. In fact, she was with calf and worth between $750 and $1,000. The contract was held void for mistake. By contrast in *Wood v Boynton*[74] where a girl sold a stone the size of a canary's egg to a jeweller for $1, and it subsequently turned out to be a diamond, it was held that the contract was not void. In the English case of *Nicholson & Venn v Smith Marriott*[75] Hallett J was prepared to hold (obiter) that Charles I table napkins were essentially different from Georgian ones. In truth, the difference between quality and substance is a distinction without a difference. The decision in *Sherwood v Walker*, however, might be justified on the basis that the price and other circumstances indicated that the substance of the contract was one commercial category, ie a cow for slaughter, whereas it belonged to another category, ie a cow for breeding. In other words, the risks that the parties intended to exchange at formation were within one commercial category, but the goods belonged to another.

(iv) A mistake on the part of one party as to the terms of the contract which is known to the other

Meeting of minds theory taken to its logical conclusion ought to entail that if A, a private seller, sells B a car which A knows is a 'lemon', but B thinks is a good bargain, the contract should be void. In fact, provided A has taken care not to make any misrepresentation about the car, but has left B to make his own mistake, the contract is valid. Given that the effect of applying the doctrine to this situation would cut a substantial swathe through the principle of caveat emptor, clearly some means had to be found of limiting its application.

contract for services, which they could have terminated for breach. In fact the substance/quality distinction is to be found in Pothier.
[73]   (1887) 33 NW 919.
[74]   (1885) 25 NW 42.
[75]   [1947] 177 LTR 189.

In the famous case of *Smith v Hughes*[76] the defendant, a racehorse trainer, wanted old oats, but the plaintiff, a farmer, delivered new oats. The defendant refused to pay, and refused to accept further deliveries. The plaintiff sued for the price of the oats delivered, as well as for damages for the defendant's refusal to accept further deliveries. The jury found in favour of the defendant. On appeal, however, it was held that the judge had misdirected the jury. Assuming that the plaintiff had not described the oats that he was offering for sale as 'old' oats, the judge had advised the jury that they should nevertheless find for the defendant if they thought that the defendant mistakenly assumed that he was contracting for old oats, and the plaintiff was aware of the defendant's mistake.[77] The defect in this direction, however, was that it failed to discriminate between two kinds of mistake: a mistake as to the terms of the contract, as opposed to a mistake as to the nature of the oats themselves. Only if the defendant's mistake was of the former kind was there a good defence.

The distinction between these two kinds of mistake is fine but important.[78] If the defendant misunderstood the terms of the contract, and the plaintiff realised this, then the plaintiff could not hold the defendant to the contract (as the plaintiff understood it). However, if the defendant simply mistook the nature of the oats that he had agreed to buy, even though the plaintiff seller realised this, the plaintiff could hold the defendant to the contract. It is axiomatic within classical law that the seller has no duty to disclose to the buyer facts which are material to the buyer (such as the nature of the oats), but which do not directly concern the terms of the contract.

Smith v Hughes might be interpreted as an application of the (subjective) meeting of minds theory: the plaintiff

---

[76]   (1871) LR 6 QB 597.

[77]   This rather complicated question seems to derive from William Paley's *The Principles of Moral and Political Philosophy* (London, 1809 edn) p 126 et seq. Paley cites the example of the tyrant Temores who promised the inhabitants of Sebastia that, if they surrendered to him, no blood would be shed. In the event, Temores kept his promise by burying the inhabitants alive. Not surprisingly, Paley considered this exploitation of a known misunderstanding to be wrong. He therefore proposed that promises should be interpreted in the sense in which the promisor believed that the promisee accepted the promise: ibid p 126.

[78]   Cf Roger Brownsword 'New Notes on the Old Oats' (1987) 131 Sol Jnl 384.

intended to sell new oats, but the defendant intended to buy old oats. However, two aspects of *Smith v Hughes* suggest another interpretation. First, there seems to be a good deal of emphasis on the plaintiff realising that the defendant had made a mistake; and, secondly, in the textbook canon of leading cases it is regarded as an authority for the 'objective approach' in contract.

In *Smith v Hughes* Blackburn J articulated an 'objective' approach to contractual intention in the following terms:

> 'If, whatever a man's real intention may be, he so conducts him-
> self that a reasonable man would believe that he was assenting
> to the terms proposed by the other party, and that other party
> upon that belief enters into a contract with him, the man thus
> conducting himself would be equally bound as if he had
> intended to agree to the other party's terms.'[79]

There are a number of ways of interpreting the 'objective approach. However, the most plausible view is that the approach actually involves an amalgam of objective and subjective tests. As John Cartwright explains in a helpful analysis:[80]

> '[If] A and B are not in actual agreement on the existence and
> terms of their contract, A may still be able to assert that there
> is a contract, on his terms, if he can show that:
>
> (1)   B's conduct was such that a reasonable man would think
>   that B was consenting to A's terms; and
>
> (2)   A in fact so understood B's conduct.'

In other words, the test of B's intention is objective but A's ability to hold B to an objective interpretation is qualified by A's subjective understanding. Accordingly, if in *Smith v Hughes*, the objective interpretation of the buyer's conduct was that he had agreed to buy oats irrespective of whether they were new or old oats, then the seller would be able to hold the buyer to the contract provided that the seller was unaware of the buyer's mistake (ie provided that the seller was unaware of the buyer's subjective understanding of the contractual terms).

---

[79]   (1871) 6 LR QB 597, 607.
[80]   *Unequal Bargaining* (Oxford University, 1991) pp15–16.

8. THE TERMS OF A CONTRACT

The terms of a contract are either express, or implied; and, according to the classical view, contractual terms – whether express or implied – divide into conditions or warranties. The basic ground rules are: (1) terms may not be implied where this would be inconsistent with the express terms of the contract; (2) the standard remedy for breach of any term, whether express or implied, condition or warranty, is an action for damages; and (3) breach of a condition, whether express or implied, gives the innocent party the option of withdrawing from the contract.

(i) Express terms

Express terms are those which the parties have expressly agreed on (whether in writing, or simply by word of mouth). Unfortunately, it is not always clear what contractors have expressly agreed upon. In particular, it is not always clear whether representations made by one of the parties in negotiating the agreement form part of the contract. Representations made by one party to the other can have a number of legal consequences. In the first place, they may give rise to liability which is independent of liability on the contract subsequently entered into. This liability can be in tort, for negligent misstatement[81] or fraud,[82] or under the Misrepresentation Act 1967.[83] Secondly, they may render the contract liable to be rescinded in equity.[84] Finally, they may become terms of the contract, and render the party who made the representation liable for either breach of condition or breach of warranty. The significance of the classification of terms as conditions or warranties has already been mentioned and it is a matter to which we will return shortly.[85] Here, we are concerned only with the circumstances in which representations may become terms.

The modern doctrine of breach of warranty has its an-

---

[81]   *Hedley Byrne & Co Ltd v Heller & Partners Ltd* [1964] AC 465.
[82]   The facts which must be established to give rise to this tort were laid down in *Derry v Peek* [1889] 14 AC 337.
[83]   Section 2(1).
[84]   Eg *Leaf v International Galleries* [1950] 2 KB 86 – though the right to rescind had been lost by lapse of time in that case.
[85]   See p 45 below.

cestry in the action for deceit, under which a representation was not actionable as a warranty unless it were averred as such, which, in effect, makes the intention of the representor the crucial consideration.[86] Another approach to the problem is to take an entirely objective 'fly on the wall' viewpoint:[87] what to outward appearances is the bargain between the parties? The most defensible approach at the present day echoes a view put forward by the eighteenth-century philosopher William Paley,[88] and asks what the representor, as a reasonable person, ought to have understood the representee to understand by the statement. If a statement is made about something which the representee (as the representor appreciates) would imagine to be within the representor's knowledge, then the representation becomes a term of the contract. Thus, in *Couchman v Hill*[89] the plaintiff asked whether a heifer had been served, and was assured by the vendor that it had not been. It was held that the assertion was a term of the contract. By contrast, in *Oscar Chess Ltd v Williams*[90] the seller, a private individual with no particular expertise in cars, and known by the plaintiffs (a garage) to be such, sold a car to the plaintiffs as a 1948 model. It was in fact a 1939 model, though the seller honestly believed it to be a 1948 model (the 1939 and 1948 models of this car were identical). It was held that the representation as to the year was not a term of the contract: it is not reasonable for garages to rely on private sellers for matters which are within the expertise of a garage.

(ii) Implied terms

Parties contracting in a particular line of business will often not spell out the terms of their contract in fine print, because by established custom in the trade, or by long mutual dealings,[91] they assume they are contracting on certain usual

---

[86]   *Chandelor v Lopus* (1603) Cro Jac 4.
[87]   See Spencer (1973) CLJ 104.
[88]   1743–1805. His *The Principles of Moral and Political Philosophy* (1785) was staple student reading for many years. The analysis adopted by the court in *Smith v Hughes* (pp 39–40) appears to derive from this work.
[89]   [1947] KB 554.
[90]   [1957] 1 WLR 370. See also *Harlingdon & Leinster Enterprises Ltd v Christopher Hull Fine Art Ltd* [1991] 1 QB 564.
[91]   See *Hillas & Co Ltd v Arcos Ltd* [1932] All ER 494.

terms. It may also be obvious from the nature of the transaction that certain terms must be assumed to apply. Thus
if a buyer purchases a new camera at full market price, it
may reasonably be supposed that the buyer expects it to
work. As was said in an early case, it must not be supposed
that the buyer purchased the goods to throw them on a
dunghill.[92] Accordingly, the Sale of Goods Act 1979, and
other statutes,[93] imply terms into a contract, eg that goods
must be of satisfactory quality, and fit for the purposes for
which they are sold.[94] Other terms may be implied in a
similar way to give business efficacy to a contract. In *The
Moorcock*[95] it was held to be an implied term of a contract to
moor a ship at a jetty where it was known that ships would
settle on the bottom at low tide, that the bottom of the berth
was safe for this to happen.

The classical view was that terms should be implied only
if the implication was clearly a necessary articulation of the
parties' general intention. In the twentieth century, this
restrictive view was challenged by the view that terms could
be implied if they were reasonable. Since modern judges are
prepared to disallow unreasonable express terms, freedom
of contract notwithstanding, the idea that terms might be
implied on the basis of reasonableness might have been
expected to have gained acceptance. However, in *Liverpool
City Council v Irwin*,[96] the House of Lords took the opportunity to reassert the classical view. In *Irwin*, the contracts in
question were tenancy agreements for flats in a tower block.
The block deteriorated seriously because of vandalism, but
the tenancy agreements contained absolutely no obligations
of repair on the part of the Council. Although the House of
Lords held that there was an implied obligation on the part
of the Council to take reasonable care to keep the block in
reasonable repair and usability, it was emphasised that the
implication rested on necessity. Moreover, the House held
that, on the facts, the Council had complied with their contractual obligations.

---

[92]   *Jones v Bright* (1829) 5 Bing 533.
[93]   In particular the Supply of Goods and Services Act 1982, and the
Supply of Goods (Implied Terms) Act 1973.
[94]   See eg Sale of Goods Act 1979, s 14(2) (as amended by s 1(1) of the Sale
and Supply of Goods Act 1994) and s 14(3).
[95]   (1889) 14 PD 64.
[96]   [1977] AC 239.

(iii) Classification of terms

Traditionally, as we have said, the terms of a contract were either conditions, any breach of which entitled the innocent party to terminate the contract and sue for damages, or warranties a breach of which entitled the innocent party to sue for damages, but not to rescind. In *Hong Kong Fir Shipping Co v Kawasaki Kisen Kaishi Ltd*[97] the Court of Appeal held that there are many terms which at the outset are neither conditions nor warranties, but an intermediate category a minor breach of which will only amount to a breach of warranty, but a serious breach of which will allow the innocent party to rescind. The attraction of this flexible approach is that it allows the court some leeway in dealing with those cases where the so-called 'innocent party' is obviously using a trivial breach to slide out of a contract it no longer finds commercially advantageous.[98] So attractive has this notion proved that even where the parties have called a term in a written contract a 'condition', it is not certain that the courts will construe it literally as such.[99]

9. TERMS EXCLUDING OR RESTRICTING LIABILITY

A party frequently wishes to modify the liability imposed on it by the general law. Thus in contracts of carriage it has long been the practice to limit the carrier's liability, because it is cheaper for the cargo owner to insure the goods, than for the carrier to take out insurance to cover goods of unlimited value. Limiting the carrier's liability therefore reduces freight charges, and cuts the cost of insurance. Sometimes liability is limited by statute, as in the Carriage of Goods by Sea Act 1971, which implements the Hague/Visby Rules, an international convention. Sometimes it is by a signed contractual document which is given effect to on the principle of *L'Estrange v Graucob* mentioned above, or by an unsigned document, of whose terms either the consignor is aware, or sufficient notice of which has been

---

[97] [1962] 2 QB 26.
[98] See *Cehave NV v Bremer Handelgesellschaft MbH* [1976] QB 76; and see further ch 6.
[99] *L. Schuler AG v Wickman Machine Tool Sales* [1974] AC 235.

given.[100] These principles of incorporation are of general application, not being merely confined to contracts of carriage.

Although it is arguable that in strict theory the exclusion clauses incorporated into a contract, whether by a standard form or by a 'one off' negotiated writing, are a way of defining the obligations of a party under a contract,[101] in fact the courts have rarely approached the matter in that way. They have tended to look at the contract apart from the exemption clauses to determine the obligations of the parties – the exemption clauses then operate, if at all, as defences to allegations of breaches of those obligations. Today, such contracting out is generally regulated by the Unfair Contract Terms Act 1977 (UCTA) and, in the case of consumer contracts, by the EC Directive on Unfair Terms in Consumer Contracts[102] (implemented in the United Kingdom by the Unfair Terms in Consumer Contracts Regulations 1994).[103] Prior to UCTA, there was some authority that such clauses were also subject to a doctrine which held that if the party seeking to rely on the clause had broken it in a fundamental way, such breach put an end to the contract so that the exemption clause could not be relied on. The House of Lords, however, finally put an end to this doctrine in *Photo Production v Securicor Transport Ltd*.[104] In that case, the night patrolman supplied by Securicor deliberately started a small fire in the plaintiff's premises. The fire got out of control and destroyed the factory. The House of Lords held that the patrolman's act was not a fundamental breach preventing Securicor's reliance on its contractual exemption clauses. It was simply a matter of construction whether the

---

[100]   *Parker v South Eastern Rly* (1877) 2 CPD 416. As to the history of carrier exclusions prior to this case see Adams 'The Standardisation of Commercial Contracts or the Contractualisation of Standard Forms' (1978) 7 Anglo-American Law Review 136.

[101]   For example, if I want to sell just the black horses in my stable (which contains both black and white horses), then I can contract to sell either 'the black horses in my stable', or 'all the horses in my stable except the white ones' – see Coote *Exception Clauses* (London, Sweet & Maxwell, 1964).

[102]   Council Directive 93/13/EEC, OJ No L 95/29 21.4.93. See ch 8.

[103]   SI 1994/3159 (into force on 1 July 1995). See Roger Brownsword and Geraint Howells, 'The Implementation of the EC Directive on Unfair Terms in Consumer Contracts – Some Unresolved Questions'' (1995) Journal of Business Law 243.

[104]   [1980] AC 827.

exemption clauses applied to the loss which had occurred. In the event, the House held that the clauses did so apply. Whilst this might seem perverse, it must be realised that many such clauses in commercial contracts are intended to allocate insurance risks, and to help obviate double insurance. The uncertainties created by the doctrine of fundamental breach made that objective difficult to attain.[105]

10. ESTOPPEL AND WAIVER

A party may be held unable to rely on an otherwise valid and enforceable contractual term because of his or her conduct. Where one party has led the other to believe that he or she will not enforce its legal rights against the other it may be estopped from enforcing those rights, at least until it has given reasonable notice to the other.[106] For example, in the celebrated *High Trees* case, a landlord company agreed that its tenant company should pay only half the agreed ground rent on a block of flats in wartime London so long as there were problems about letting the flats. Although the landlord company's promise to reduce the ground rent was not supported by consideration, it was estopped from recovering the full ground rent so long as the terms of its undertaking applied. This important topic is dealt with in Chapter 4.

11. IMPOSSIBILITY AND FRUSTRATION

Parties can undertake absolute obligations if they so choose. As Holmes said, you can promise it will rain tomorrow if you wish, and will have to pay damages if it does not.[107] Indeed, insurance contracts are precisely of that character. On the

---

[105] See *Harbutt's 'Plasticine' Ltd v Wayne Tank and Pump Co Ltd* [1970] 1 QB 447 and its aftermath *Wayne Tank and Pump Co Ltd v Employers' Liability Assurance Co* [1974] QB 57.
[106] The famous principle derived from *Central London Property Trust Ltd v High Trees House Ltd* [1947] KB 130. An alternative doctrine leading to a similar result is common law waiver – see *Tool Metal Manufacturing Co Ltd v Tungsten Electric Co Ltd* [1955] 2 All ER 657.
[107] *The Common Law* (Little Brown & Co, 1880) p 273.

other hand, in many commercial contracts it is reasonable to suppose the parties do not intend an absolute obligation. Thus in *Taylor v Caldwell*[108] the defendants agreed to let[109] their music hall to the plaintiffs for four days. The hall was unfortunately burned down without the fault of either party before the letting commenced. It was held that the events which had occurred had 'frustrated' the contract, thus discharging the defendants from liability for failing to provide the plaintiffs with the hall. In the so-called 'coronation cases' this principle was extended to relieve the hirers of rooms to view the coronation of Edward VII from their obligation to pay for them when the coronation was cancelled due to the king's illness.[110]

In some ways mistake and frustration are two sides of a coin. If specific goods have perished without the knowledge of the parties at the time the contract is made, it is void for mistake,[111] but if they perish afterwards, it is void for frustration.[112] Both doctrines are fairly limited in their fields of application. Thus in *Amalgamated Investment and Property Co Ltd v Walker*[113] the plaintiffs had agreed to buy a property for redevelopment. They were told truthfully by the defendants that it was not a listed building, but the day after they had signed the contract the Department of the Environment informed the defendants that the building would be listed with effect from the following day. This reduced the value of the building from £1,710,000 to about £210,000. It was held that because at the date the contract was made, it was not listed, it could not be void for mistake, for, as explained above, mistake is concerned only with events occurring prior to formation. It was also held that the contract was not frustrated. For, following the guidelines set down in the leading modern case, *Davis Contractors Ltd v Fareham UDC*,[114] this was simply a case of a market fluctuation – and, as Lord Radcliffe famously remarked in that case, 'it is not hardship or inconvenience or material loss itself which calls the principle of frustration into play'.[115]

---

[108]   (1863) 3 B & S 826.
[109]   Strictly this was a licence, not a letting.
[110]   See eg *Krell v Henry* [1903] 2 KB 740.
[111]   Sale of Goods Act 1979, s 6.
[112]   Ibid s 7.
[113]   [1976] 3 All ER 509.
[114]   [1956] AC 696.
[115]   At p 729.

12. REMEDIES FOR BREACH

In common law systems, the standard remedy for breach of contract is damages, not specific performance. Specific performance will only be awarded where damages are an inadequate remedy. Similarly, subject to express reservation, the right to withdraw for breach tends to be restricted to cases where damages would not be an adequate remedy.

Where damages are to be awarded for breach of contract, the traditional basis for compensation is the so-called expectation measure. What this means, as Baron Parke explained in *Robinson v Harman*,[116] is that the law tries to put the innocent party 'so far as money can do it, . . . in the same situation . . . as if the contract had been performed'.[117] Over the years, this simple principle has not always proved straightforward in its application. For example, in the recent case of *Ruxley Electronics and Construction Ltd v Forsyth*,[118] the courts had to apply the expectation measure in calculating the compensation due to a client for a contractor's failure to build a swimming pool in accordance with the specification. Whereas the contract specified that the pool should have a maximum depth of 7 ft 6 in, the contractors built a pool with a maximum depth of only 6 ft 9 in. Although this did not decrease the market value of the pool, it interfered with the client's ability to use the pool for diving. How, then, was the client to be put in the same position as if the contract had been performed? Was the client to be paid compensation for the loss of amenity, the loss of opportunity to use the pool for diving (estimated at some £2,500)? Or, should the client receive such damages as would enable him to employ a contractor to cure the defect in the pool (estimated at some £21,560)? The Court of Appeal ruled in favour of the latter measure but the House of Lords reversed this in favour of the former measure.[119] This may be compared with the American case of *Peevyhouse v Garland Coal and Mining Co*,[120] where on similar facts, the majority also preferred to restrict the plaintiff to compensation for the

---

[116] (1848) 1 Exch 850.
[117] At p 855.
[118] [1994] 3 All ER 801.
[119] [1995] NLJR 996, (1995) Times, 3 July.
[120] 382 P 2d 109 (1962).

'difference in value' (some $300) rather than allow the much more expensive 'cost of cure' (some $29,000).

Clearly, the events to be compensated by the award of damages must have been caused by the defendant's breach, but the classical law does not deem it sound policy to hold the defendant liable for all losses so caused. One way of limiting the defendant's liability is to require the plaintiff to take reasonable steps to minimise his loss (the doctrine of mitigation).[121] Another way is to disallow certain consequential losses as 'too remote'. In the leading case of *Hadley v Baxendale*[122] the defendants (ancestors of the carriers Pickfords) were sued for the loss of profit due to a mill being stopped because of the defendant's late delivery of a shaft. Clearly the loss was caused by the defendant, but they had no reason to suppose that the plaintiff's mill would be stopped if they delayed in delivering the shaft. It was held that the defendants were liable only for losses flowing naturally, that is in the ordinary course of things, from the breach, or for those losses which might be supposed to have been in the contemplation of the parties at the time the contract was made. Today these two 'limbs' of the rule in *Hadley v Baxendale* are usually run into one. In *Victoria Laundry v Newman Industries*[123] it was suggested that the defendant was liable for losses which were reasonably foreseeable, which is the test of remoteness applied in the tort of negligence. But different considerations necessarily apply in determining whether damage is too remote in the case of a breach of contract, than in the case of negligence. To signal this, the House of Lords in *The Heron II*[124] attempted a number of formulations of the contractual test (such as the loss having to be 'not unlikely' to flow from the breach) in order to emphasise that the reasonable man in contract is not as long-sighted as the reasonable man in tort. In that case the defendants were to carry a cargo of sugar to Basrah. It arrived in Basrah nine days late, by which time the market had fallen. Did the defendants have to compensate the plaintiff for this drop? It was held that the defendants, had they thought about it, must have realised that the cargo would be sold on arrival, and that market prices fluctuate.

---

[121]   See eg *Payzu Ltd v Saunders* [1919] 2 KB 581.
[122]   (1854) 9 Exch 341.
[123]   [1949] 2 KB 528.
[124]   [1969] 1 AC 350.

The loss was therefore not unlikely, and consequently, the defendant was liable for the loss. On the other hand, provided the type of damage is not unlikely, it does not matter that its extent is unexpectedly great and thus unlikely. Thus, in a later case, where a storage bin for pig nuts was supplied with the ventilator accidentally left sealed, so that the contents went mouldy, it was held that the defendant was liable for the many pigs which died, since some illness was not unlikely if the pigs were fed mouldy nuts, though perhaps not such serious illness as that which occurred.[125]

13. FREEDOM OF CONTRACT AND SANCTITY OF CONTRACT

Having sketched the main contours of contract doctrine, it is as well to conclude this introductory overview by highlighting the focal importance for the classical law of the ideas of 'freedom of contract' and 'sanctity of contract'.

The central tenet of freedom of contract is that the law should set a framework for parties to make their own exchanges. After all, it is reasonable to assume that if the parties freely agree to an exchange, they both regard the transaction as making them better off (as the economists would say, the transaction is 'Pareto optimal'). Obviously, this reasoning does not hold good where a transaction is conducted at gunpoint or is induced by deception. However, after regulating for fraud and coercion, and any illegality, the philosophy of the classical law is to let the parties make such exchanges as they see fit. It follows that it is no part of the classical law that there should be an equivalence or balance in the exchange (consideration, as the textbooks put it, need not be 'adequate'); nor does the classical law offer relief against harsh or unconscionable terms, or anything of that kind. Similarly, within the bounds of public policy, the will of the contractors is sovereign. Accordingly, within the classical law, the contractors are permitted to displace terms implied by statute, and the courts are reluctant in the extreme to imply terms unless it is perfectly clear that the implication accords with the unstated intentions of the contractors.

---

[125] *Parsons v Uttley Ingham & Co Ltd* [1978] QB 791.

If contractors can slide out of their agreed commitments, the marketplace will be dominated by instant exchanges, by cash not credit, by actual performance not promised performance. In order to set a secure transactional framework, the classical law seeks to uphold the ideal of sanctity of contract. Apart from making available to innocent parties a strong array of remedies (including damages based on lost expectation), contract law closes off excuses that might be raised by contractors who are tempted to shirk their obligations. Thus, the objective theory of agreement blocks appeals by contractors to their subjective states of mind; and the restrictive interpretations of the doctrines of mistake and frustration block easy escape routes from onerous contracts.

Without doubt, the classical model has a certain elegance and an obvious theoretical coherence. Indeed, one might wonder how it could ever run into difficulty – even less might one understand how it could be written off by many modern commentators as inappropriate and irrelevant. However, as we proceed through our discussion of the key issues, it will become apparent that contracting practice does not always conform to the classical set-piece, that the expectations of commercial contractors are not static, that the classical model did not reckon with the emergence of a mass market in consumer goods and services, and that modern judges are peculiarly susceptible to considerations of fairness and reasonableness.

Part II

Key issues

Chapter 3

The classical model and contract in practice

Introduction

In Chapter 2 we outlined the key doctrines of the classical law of contract, hinting in our concluding comments at some of the problems to which it gives rise. In this chapter, we will consider two phenomena, each of which has proved troublesome for the classical model.

First, we will look at the emergence of the standard form of contract (and, concomitantly, the trend in certain areas of economic life, away from contract to status).[1] In modern times, standard forms (or more specifically 'adhesion contracts')[2] have tended to be associated with the potential for sharp practice in the mass consumer market – car dealers, holiday operators, insurance companies, and the like, disowning liability on the basis of small print standard provisions which the consumer has not fully appreciated are part of the agreement. However, if we put standard forms into historical perspective (as we do in the first part of this chapter), we find that they are not a distinctively twentieth-century phenomenon. Moreover, we find that the original intent behind the use of standard form limitations was perfectly respectable. Unfortunately, by the time that standard

---

[1]   See Rehbinder 'Status Contract and the Welfare State' (1971) 23 Stanford LR 941.
[2]   Ie pre-formulated stipulations in which the offeror's will is predominant and the conditions are dictated to an undetermined number of acceptants not the individual party: see Saleilles *Déclaration de Volonté* (1901) p 229. This definition is expanded by Planiol et Ripert Vol 6 (2nd edn) p 136.

form exemptions came to be seen to represent the unacceptable face of freedom of contract, the classical law had missed the opportunity to regulate the incorporation of unreasonable provisions in a coherent, overt, and straightforward way. Indeed, it is characteristic of the classical law that it either distorts, or ignores, lines of authority in order to maintain its consistency, as a result of which, far from assisting in the solution of the contractual problems to which the modern world has given rise, it actually gets in the way of trying to solve them.

Secondly, we will explore the tendency, particularly in certain commercial fields, towards so-called 'relational' contracting.[3] Sometimes, this term is used as a corrective to the view (implicit in the classical model) that contracting takes place in a realm free of social relationships and values – contract, as it were, in a social vacuum. Hence, as Ian Macneil puts this point:

> 'It is thus a mistake to think of "net utilitarian advantage" [as per classical contract theory] in its outside-of-society context involving fictional maximisers of individual utility, equally powerful or not. In the real world there are only enhancers of individual utility immersed in relations creating countless contramotives. Exchange is virtually always *relational* exchange, that is, exchange carried on within relations having significant impact on its goals, conduct, and effect.'[4]

At other times, the term 'relational' signifies that a contract is 'long-term'.[5] In this sense, relational contracting indicates that performance runs over an extended period of time (such as would be the case with, say, a construction contract, or a charter-party) and is to be contrasted with a contract that is more or less an instant exchange (such as a purchase of goods in a shop). At yet other times (and most distinctively), however, commentators use the term 'relational' to signify something different to an ongoing relationship forced on the

---

[3]   Seminally, see Ian R. Macneil 'The Many Futures of Contract' (1974) 47 Southern California Law Review 691, and 'Contracts: Adjustments of Long-Term Economic Relations under Classical, Neo-Classical and Relational Contract Law' (1978) 72 Northwestern University Law Review 854.

[4]   Ian R. Macneil 'Exchange Revisited: Individual Utility and Social Solidarity' (1986) 96 Ethics 567, 577.

[5]   See eg John Bell 'The Effect of Changes in Circumstances on Long-term Contracts' in Donald Harris and Denis Tallon (eds) *Contract Law Today* (Oxford, Clarendon Press, 1989) p 195.

parties by the nature of the particular (long-term) contract. The emphasis here is not on whether the performance is long-term or short-term, but on the fact that the contractors are not economic strangers; typically, they deal with one another regularly and, indeed, their businesses may be integrated. In the second part of this chapter, we consider one particular species of relational contracting, the so-called 'requirements contract'. As we shall see, the classical model is as much out of kilter with relational contracting as it is with standard form adhesion contracting.

1. STANDARD FORM CONTRACTS

Standard form contracts can give rise to more than one kind of difficulty. Commonly, the problem is that one party dictates the terms of the contract by imposing its standard conditions. This can occur in both commercial and consumer contracting. Where it does so occur, it gives rise to concerns about both the reality of the agreement as well as the fairness of the transaction. Another problem altogether, however, is presented where both (commercial) contracting parties seek to dictate terms through their own standard forms (this setting up the so-called 'battle of the forms'). Here, the concern is not so much about the fairness of the contract. Rather, the difficulty is that the parties' dealings do not relate to an agreement in any straightforward sense – thus leaving the courts to make the somewhat uneasy choice between either declaring there to be no contract, or constructing from the exchange of documents a set of terms to govern the transaction. In this part of the chapter, we will consider both of these problems.

(i) From status to contract and back again

Sir Henry Maine famously remarked that the development of all societies hitherto had been from status to contract.[6] By this he meant that in early societies a person's rights and duties in relation to others would depend upon their

---

[6]   *Ancient Law* (London, John Murray 1930) ed Pollock, p 182.

position in that society. So, for example, in classical Roman society slaves could not change their status by contracting with their masters.[7] Their rights were entirely determined by the law. Similarly, in feudal societies a person's position on the feudal ladder determined his rights and obligations vis-à-vis his feudal overlord, and any tenants below him. As society develops, however, most of its citizens come to enjoy the right to make what bargains they choose – status gives way to contract.[8] In modern mass consumer markets, though, we find elements of a de facto return to status. At one level, modern legal systems increasingly differentiate between different classes of contractors (private, consumer, and commercial), discriminating positively in favour of those who contract as consumers. At another level, the increasingly widespread use of the standard form contract in modern times can be seen as reintroducing status in place of contract.[9] For example, if you wish to send goods by train in this country, you can do so only on the terms imposed by British Rail (or its successors). If you want to send goods by sea, you will have to accept the terms subject to which the bill of lading is issued. Sometimes these standard terms are statutory, as in the case of those governing contracts for the international carriage of goods by rail and sea,[10] sometimes they are contractual. It is the rise of the latter type of contract which is of interest to us here, rather than those imposed by statute (which are mostly in furtherance of our obligations under international conventions). However, similar exigencies which led to those conventions, led contractors in the first place to impose their own standard terms.

The increasing use of standard forms prompted the famous American writer, Karl Llewellyn, to write:

[7]   Their master could choose to free them by the process known as 'manumission', but that process entailed no contract.
[8]   Of course, no society enfranchises its entire population. For example, we restrict the contracting powers of groups such as bankrupts, minors, and persons mentally disordered, so that a status element remains in relation to these groups.
[9]   See Kessler (1943) 43 Col LR 629, 640–1.
[10]   For rail carriage, the current terms are to be found in the International Transport Conventions Act 1983 giving partial effect to the Convention Concerning International Carriage by Rail. For sea carriage, outward voyages from this country are subject to the terms imposed by the Carriage of Goods by Sea Act 1971, implementing the Hague/Visby Rules.

'The problem is: when a contract ceases to be a matter of dicker, bargain by bargain and item by item and becomes in any field or any outfit's business or any trade's practice a matter of mass production of bargains, with the background filled in not by the general law but by standard clauses and terms prepared often by one of the parties only – then what? One "what" is clear: the presuppositions of our general law no longer maintain in such a situation. Those presuppositions can be stated somewhat as follows: (1) The general law is adequately specialized, and is detailed and balanced to fill in with moderate adequacy any gaps which the parties leave open in their bargaining. (2) Any particular or specialized terms the parties are interested in they will bargain about. (3) Almost any particular clause included in a deal represents the parties' joint judgment as to what they want; and this alone is ground enough for letting it, for the deal in hand, displace and replace the general law. But when contracts are produced by the printing press, with the fountain pen used not for recording thought but for authentication, the adequacy of the general law for filling the gaps in the conscious bargain is flatly negatived, in the view of the party preparing and ordering the form pads . . . The contract is a block-contract, for one side (or both) to take or leave'.[11]

The presuppositions of the general law are those of the classical law of contract, of a bargain negotiated between two individuals, dickering term by term. In reality, as one writer observed: 'The contracting still imagined by courts and law teachers as typical, in which both parties participate in choosing the language of their entire agreement, is no longer of much more than historical importance: 99 per cent of all contracts now made are standard form contracts.'[12] If we ignore everyday contracts for the sale of goods, this on the whole is true.

The 'form pad', as Llewellyn calls it, is a necessity in modern commerce. The need for such standard forms arises for a number of reasons. First, standard forms save time and trouble in bargaining. In many cases bargaining would be impractical, and even if individually bargained, the terms would be the same.[13] Secondly, standard forms simplify internal administration and facilitate planning, thereby

---

[11]   (1939) 52 HLR 700, 703, reviewing Prausnitz *The Standardization of Commercial Contracts* (1937).
[12]   Slawson (1971) 84 HLR 529; Friedmann *Law in a Changing Society* p131.
[13]   Prausnitz *Standardization* p143.

effecting a reduction in administrative costs[14] and cutting overheads by obviating double insurance.[15] The problem with the use of 'form pad' contracting arises when it is used by parties enjoying sufficient power in the market to insist that their terms, set out in their printed form and favourable to themselves, govern their contractual relations.[16] We will argue that the problems which were to be encountered in the present century with such contracts arose largely because of the way in which they were fitted into the classical model, rather than because of rigid adherence to a doctrine of freedom of contract – that, indeed, it was the imperatives of a theory which in its origins had nothing to do with laissez faire economic theory which caused the difficulties.

The story of how the standard form contract came to be fitted into the classical model begins in the eighteenth century. By the mid-eighteenth century, the common carrier,[17] by virtue of his profession as a common carrier, ie, someone whose business it is to carry for persons generally, was considered to be insurer of the goods entrusted to him for carriage, and was liable for their loss or damage irrespective of fault, unless the loss occurred through act of God, or of the King's enemies. In other words, his status as a common carrier determined his liability. As the industrial revolution got under way, larger and larger numbers of bank notes needed to be moved around the country. These bank notes were contained in packages which, although of small size, were of high value. They were easily stolen – and stolen they were. In consequence, the carriers' liability as insurer came to be ruinous. It would appear that at some time prior to 1769 one or more of the leading carriers had consulted counsel, probably Lloyd Kenyon the future Chief Justice, as to what was to be

---

14   Ibid, ch I, part II; Llewellyn loc cit; Wilson (1965) 14 ICLQ 172, 176; Johnston [1967] JBL 133.
15   LC Wkg Paper No 439 para 20 – this was the preliminary study which eventually led to the Unfair Contract Terms Act 1977.
16   See Planiol et Ripert vol 6 (2nd edn) p136 – ie the 'form pad' becomes a 'contract of adhesion'.
17   As the anonymous author of *Strictures upon the Unfounded and Illegal Claims of the Common Carriers* (Wm Phillips, London, 1800) wrote: 'carriers are the great channel of communication between the consumer and vendor of every article of life'.

done.[18] He appears to have advised, on the basis of Lord Coke's notes to *Southcote*'s case,[19] that the carriers should make a special acceptance simply to keep the goods as they would keep their own. Indeed, Coke had justified the imposition of the insurers' liability on the basis that it was open to the carriers to do this.[20] Accordingly, carriers began to display a notice to the effect that they would not be answerable for the loss of goods above £5[21] unless their value were declared and the carriage paid for pro rata. The efficacy of these notices was upheld in the case of *Gibbon v Paynton*.[22]

There followed a period in which these notices were generally upheld, though it was not clear whether this was on the basis of a contract, or a special acceptance modifying the terms of the bailment.[23] Sometimes the notices operated merely to limit the carriers' liability to £5, more usually they were in the form mentioned above. There was an important procedural difference from the consignor's point of view between the two forms: the former, limitation type of notice, did not need to be pleaded in the declaration,[24] whereas the latter type did because proof by the

---

[18]   See the evidence given by Horne, a leading carrier, in the Report of the House of Commons Committee on the Regulation of Charges for Conveyance and Porterage 1825.

[19]   (1601) 4 Co Rep 83b.

[20]   A curious justification, for as Gould J observed in the great case of *Coggs v Bernard* (1703) 2 Ld Raym 909, to make a special acceptance is a thing that no man living who is not a lawyer would think of – his brother Powell J went further and observed that many lawyers would not know the difference!

[21]   This became the usual form: the notice used in *Gibbon v Paynton* (below) simply said that the coachman would not be liable for 'money or jewels or other valuable goods'.

[22]   (1769) 4 Burr 2298.

[23]   In either case, in principle, assent by the consignor was probably necessary, but it must be borne in mind that the parties to the action were incompetent as witnesses, consequently the problem for the carrier was to adduce sufficient evidence as to the prominence of the notice from which the court might infer assent – Leslie *Law of Transport by Railway* (2nd edn) p 23. A third view, that the notices operated to limit the common carriers' profession, was expressed by Erle J in *M'Manus v Lancashire and Yorkshire Rly Co* (1859) 4 H & N 327, 329.

[24]   Because the declaration without it contained an allegation of the entire act or duty to be done by the carrier, see *Clarke v Gray* (1805) 6 East 563. The declaration in modern terminology is the Statement of Claim.

defendant of this (latter) form of notice would bar the action.[25] For the reasons given above, the use of both forms of notice could be justified. However, some carriers began to extend their notices so that they excluded liability altogether.[26] Some writers have seen the fact that the courts upheld this extension as an indication of the increasing emphasis on the contractual basis of liability,[27] the upholding of the extension being an indication of the increasing importance of the doctrine of freedom of contract. But freedom of contract did not logically entail that the carriers' printed terms *automatically* should prevail rather than the common law terms which would otherwise govern the carriage. Indeed, one of the reasons why the courts probably upheld the extension was the fact that the consignor could in theory insist on carriage on common law terms,[28] so that if they were not insisted on, by implication the consignor assented to the carriers' terms. Moreover, when the courts came increasingly to insist on evidence that the notices had been 'brought home' to the consignor[29] this lent colour to the view that if the necessary steps had been taken the consignor was assenting to the terms.[30]

These developments are a remarkable anticipation of the problems which were to be experienced in the mid-twentieth century with exemption clauses in standard form contracts. Furthermore, just as the courts in the modern cases were often reluctant to hold that the exemption clauses would

---

[25]   *Latham v Rutley* (1823) 2 B & C 20; *Chitty on Pleadings* (5th edn, 1831) vol 2, p 356, na.

[26]   *Maving v Todd* (1815) 1 Stark 72; *Leeson v Holt* (1816) 1 Stark 186. The notice in the latter case stated 'all packages . . . are to be entirely at the risk of the owner as to damage, breakage, etc'.

[27]   E. G. M. Fletcher *The Carrier's Liability* (London, Stevens, 1932) p 73.

[28]   *Jackson v Rogers* (1683) 2 Shaw 327.

[29]   In *Clayton v Hunt* (1811) 3 Camp 27 it was said that the notice in the office ought to be in such large characters that no person delivering goods there could fail to read it without gross negligence. See also *Butler v Hearne* (1810) 2 Camp 415. These cases are an interesting anticipation of Lord Denning's 'red hand' test, as articulated in *J. Spurling Ltd v Bradshaw* [1956] 1 WLR 461, 466: 'Some clauses I have seen would need to be printed in red ink on the face of the document with a red hand pointing to it before the notice could be held to be sufficient.'

[30]   It must be recalled, as noted above, that the consignor as plaintiff was not competent as a witness.

exclude liability in negligence,[31] so also were early nineteenth century courts.[32] There was, however, an important difference between the ostensible reasons for the courts in the early nineteenth century being reluctant to hold that liability for negligence was excluded, and the reasons given by judges in the twentieth century, and this is significant in underlining the effect of the ideology of classical contract law. It is likely that the courts in the early nineteenth century were operating on a principle of public policy which could be traced back to the sixteenth century, namely that if a carrier refused to carry unless exempted from liability for fault, the promise was void.[33] By contrast, in the twentieth century the courts had to pretend that it was a principle of construction that a clause would not exclude liability for negligence unless negligence was the only liability to which the clause could relate.[34] Some of these early cases also illustrate the modern distinction between negligence in performing the contract of carriage, and deviation. A carrier deviating from the agreed route, or mode of carriage would not be protected by any exemption clause.[35]

The next phase in the common carriers' saga was the conversion of their notices into the beginnings of the adhesion contract[36] which was to take up so much judicial time a century later. This conversion was a result of the Carriers Act 1830.

Because of the uncertainties which had arisen through

---

[31]   See *White v John Warwick & Co* [1953] 2 All ER 1021; *Hollier v Rambler Motors (AMC) Ltd* [1972] 2 QB 71.

[32]   *Beck v Evans* (1812) 16 East 244; *Bodenham v Bennet* (1817) 4 Price 31; *Smith v Horne* (1818) 8 Taunt 144; *Birkett v Willan* (1819) 2 B & Ald 356; *Batson v Donovan* (1820) 4 B & Ald 21; *Sleat v Fagg* (1822) 5 B & Ald 342; *Wright v Snell* (1822) 5 B & Ald 350; *Newborn v Just* (1825) 2 Carr & P 76; *Riley v Horne* (1828) 5 Bing 217.

[33]   *Doctor and Student* ed Barton, Second Dialogue c 39, p 261 'yf he wolde percase refuse to carye yt onelesse promyse were made vnto hym that he shall not be charged for noo mysdemeanour that sholde be in hym that promyse were voyde. For it were agaynste reason and agaynste good maners'. See Fletcher *The Carrier's Liability* p 192.

[34]   *Alderslade v Hendon Laundry* [1945] KB 189. See also the cases mentioned in n 31 above.

[35]   G. F. Jones *Treatise on the Law Concerning the Rights and Liabilities of Common Carriers* (Butterworth, London, 1827) p 13 citing *Ellis v Turner* (1800) 8 TR 531; *Garnett v Willan* (1821) 5 B & Ald 53; *Jones v Willan* (unreported); *Sleat v Fagg* (1822) 5 B & Ald 342.

[36]   Ie preformulated stipulations in which the offeror's will is predominant: see n 2 above.

the capricious operation of their notices, especially the difficulty of convincing the court that they had been 'brought home' to the consignor,[37] the carriers petitioned the House of Commons to introduce legislation. The result was the Act of 1830. The preamble recites the frequent practice of bankers and others of sending parcels of great value in small compass, by public conveyance, whereby much valuable property was rendered liable to depredation, and through failure to notify the value the carriers had become exposed to unavoidable risks, and sustained heavy losses. Thereafter, where parcels of the specified nature (eg bills, notes, gold, coin) were delivered to a carrier, the value and nature had to be declared, if it exceeded £10. Section 1 of the Act provided accordingly. Section 2 provided that the carrier might lawfully demand an increased rate of carriage for such parcels according to a tariff which was to be prominently displayed in the carrier's offices. Section 4 provided that, thereafter, no public notice should affect the liability of the carrier. Section 6, however, went on to provide that the Act should not affect any special contracts made between the carrier and other parties for the conveyance of goods. The construction placed on these last two sections was crucial to subsequent developments.

In the first place it was held that the terms of acceptance printed on tickets were special contracts within section 6, and not public notices prohibited by s 4 of the Act.[38] Secondly, it was held that such special contracts could exclude liability even for gross negligence. The way in which this latter interpretation was reached was as follows. In *Hinton v Dibbin*[39] parcels of silk, whose value according to s 1 of the Act should have been declared and paid for, were delivered to a carrier with no declaration of their contents or value. The parcels were lost, and the plaintiff sued alleging gross negligence. It was held that the protection afforded by section 1 was absolute, and doubted whether there was any

---

[37]   It must be remembered that such cases were still tried by civil juries, which would be likely to contain customers of the carriers.

[38]   *Palmer v Grand Junction Rly* (1839) 4 M & W 749; F. Walford *Summary of the Law of Railways* (London, Blenkarn, 1845). The practice of printing the terms on a receipt such as a ticket had been suggested as early as 1817 by Lord Ellenborough in *Kerr v Willan* (1817) 6 M & S 150.

[39]   [1842] 2 QB 488.

intelligible difference between gross negligence and negligence. At all events, s 1 protected the carrier from liability for anything short of felonious conduct.[40]

The next step was, in effect, to grant the same protection to the carriers in respect of cargoes which were not listed in section 1 because in 1830 they could not have been carried. As Shelford wrote in the third edition of his *Law of Railways:*[41]

'Prior to the establishment of the railways the courts were in the habit of construing contracts between individuals and carriers, much to the disadvantage of the latter. By the introduction of the railways, a new description of property is carried, and many articles are now transferred from one place to another which had not commonly been carried before. Sheep and other cattle are now ordinarily carried upon railways, and even horses, by means of which the conveyance of goods was effected, are now themselves the subject of conveyance. With reference to this new state of things, railway companies have been allowed to make agreements for the purpose of protecting themselves against the new risks and dangers of carriage to which they are in modern times exposed, and such agreements have been deemed legal by the courts.'

Another factor in this development was the more rigorous rules of pleading introduced by the Hilary Rules of 1834.[42] We have already seen that a notice of the type which disclaimed liability for loss of the goods above £5 in value needed to be pleaded in the declaration, otherwise, if proved by the defendant, the declaration would be bad for variance. The solution was for the plaintiff, as a fall-back position, simply to add a count to the declaration pleading the notice.[43] The Hilary Rules, however, prohibited the pleading of more than one count on the same cause of action. In *Wyld v Pickford*,[44] Parke B held that the carrier was competent to limit his liability because he was entitled to insist by common law on the full price of carriage. If such price was

---

[40] An interpretation supported by s 8 which provided that nothing in the Act should protect the carrier from the felonious acts of any servant in his employ, nor protect *such servant* (emphasis supplied) from liability for loss or injury by his own personal neglect or misconduct.

[41] Butterworth, London, 1853, p 488.

[42] 4 Wm IV reg 5 founded on 3 & 4 Wm IV c 42 s 1.23.

[43] See *Chitty on Pleadings* (5th edn, 1831 vol 2) p 356 – only a notice which operated as an exemption clause needed to be pleaded, a limitation of damages clause did not (see p 61 above).

[44] (1841) 8 M & W 443.

not paid, he was entitled to insist on his own terms. These terms operated by way of special contract. To the objection that it was not alleged by the defendant that the plaintiff had assented to the terms of any such contract, he pointed out that the plaintiff was in a difficulty: he could not enforce the defendant's obligation as common carrier, because he was not willing to pay for the price of carriage beforehand, and if he sued on a bailment on special terms, it could only be on the defendant's special terms.[45] In the event, however, the plaintiff succeeded on an allegation of conversion through misdelivery, against which in modern times it has also been held that an ordinary exemption clause will not protect.[46] The dilemma in which the rules of pleading placed the plaintiff can be seen in a number of cases.[47]

A further factor was the undeveloped state of the law of agency. In *Walker v York & North Midland Rly Co*[48] the railway company sent a person to serve particulars of new terms of carriage on the fish merchants of Scarborough (including the plaintiff consignor). Effectively, the terms provided for a reduced rate of carriage for fish but with the company accepting no liability. The plaintiff informed the person that he did not accept the new terms. Nevertheless, it was held that the new terms were binding unless (a) the plaintiff signified his disapproval, and (b) the railway company acquiesced in it – which was something of an impossibility given that none of the company's representatives at the place of consignment had authority to accept the goods on any other terms. As Coleridge J. summed up the situation:[49]

---

[45]   Pp 458–9. The effect of failing to plead the special terms was that if they were proved, the declaration would be bad for variance. On the other hand if they were pleaded, that left the plaintiff only with such arguments as eg that they did not protect against negligence (possibly sustainable in respect of goods not covered by the Carriers Act on the basis of the earlier case-law but risky). Counsel had therefore the difficult choice to make as to whether the plaintiff was more likely to get away with the jury holding that there had been no special contract.

[46]   *Alexander v Railway Executive* [1951] 2 KB 882; *Sze Hai Tong Bank Ltd v Rambler Cycle Co Ltd* [1959] AC 576 (PC).

[47]   *Shaw v York & North Midland Rly Co* [1849] 13 QB 347; *Austin v Manchester, Sheffield & Lincolnshire Rly Co* [1851] 16 QB 600; *Chippendale v Lancashire and Yorkshire Rly Co* (1851) 21 LJ (QB) 22; *Great Northern Rly Co v Morville* (1852) 21 LJ (QB) 319; *Carr v Lancashire & Yorkshire Rly Co* (1852) 7 Ex 707.

[48]   (1853) 2 E & B 750.

[49]   Ibid at p 763.

'I think that, when [the plaintiff] afterwards brought his goods and sent them at the reduced rates, it was sufficient evidence that he assented to the terms. It is true that, on the same day, he grumbled at those terms: but, as this was addressed only to the station master, who had, as the plaintiff knew, no power to vary them, I think it goes for nothing.'

Walker's case and these others led to great public disquiet. The result was the passing of the Railway and Canal Traffic Act 1854. This Act made the railways liable for loss in respect of carriage of goods.[50] Contracting out was allowed, but the contract had to be signed by the consignor, and as finally construed, the terms had to be reasonable.[51] The burden of showing this rested on the railway companies.[52]

The final stage of this saga took place in the period between the 1854 Act and *Parker v South Eastern Rly Co*,[53] which is the leading modern authority on the incorporation of unsigned terms into a contract. The power of tradition can be seen in the rejection in that case of newer doctrines such as meeting of minds theory. *Parker*'s case is very much a reassertion of the old law – the 1854 Act not applying to goods left in railway cloakrooms,[54] nor to through journeys involving foreign railways,[55] nor of course to other modes of transport. It was, thus, in cases outside the Act that the modern law finally emerged.

From long practice the railways limited their liability for luggage left in their cloakrooms to £10. Some cases, following the old tradition, held that merely by accepting the ticket with the notice of the conditions the plaintiff assented to them.[56] However, a new development created a problem for this older view. From 1851 the parties to actions in England and Wales had become competent as witnesses. For the first time therefore the plaintiff might deny knowledge of, or assent to, the conditions. This actually happened in the

---

[50]   It was originally proposed that it should apply to the carriage of passengers also, but in the event it applied only to goods.

[51]   *Peek v North Staffordshire Rly Co* (1863) 10 HL Cas 473.

[52]   Ibid.

[53]   (1877) 2 CPD 416.

[54]   *Van Toll v South Eastern Rly Co* (1862) 31 LJ (CP) 241.

[55]   *Zunz v South Eastern Rly Co* (1869) LR 4 QB 539.

[56]   *Van Toll v South Eastern Rly Co* (1862) 31 LJ (CP) 241 per Byles J; *Zunz v South Eastern Rly Co* (1869) LR 4 QB 539, 544 per Cockburn CJ.

Scottish case of *Henderson v Stevenson*.[57] If a contract was supposed to require a meeting of minds, there was now a real problem. Lord Chelmsford and Lord O'Hagan held that the plaintiff must indeed have assented to the terms. Lord Chelmsford and Lord Hatherley also suggested that the ticket was a mere receipt, ie the contract was complete before the ticket was handed over.[58] This latter view was, of course, a logical consequence of the new doctrine of offer and acceptance which we outlined in Chapter 2. Lord Cairns, by contrast, thought that the ticket *was* the contract. At all events, the court in *Parker v South Eastern Rly Co* settled for a compromise view, albeit at the expense of doctrinal tidiness.

That case involved the standard £10 notice printed on a cloakroom ticket. This bore on its face 'For conditions see back'.[59] The notice was also displayed on a placard hung up in the cloakroom. Apart from the difference in the nature of the service provided, the close resemblance to the circumstances of the carriers' cases is obvious. Mellish LJ, in his famous judgment, pointed out that if a person signs a written agreement, he is bound by it, in the absence of fraud, and it is immaterial that he has not read the contents. However, in the case of unsigned writings, he held that it could not be laid down as a matter of law that the plaintiff was bound, or that he was not bound, if he did not know the ticket contained conditions. If what the railway company did was sufficient to inform people in general that the ticket contained conditions, the particular plaintiff ought not to be in a better position than other persons on account of his exceptional ignorance, stupidity or carelessness. Provided sufficient was done to give notice of the conditions to persons generally, the railway company was entitled to assume that the person receiving the ticket would understand that it contained conditions. Bramwell LJ, possibly thinking of the case-law on the 1854 Act, asserted that there was an implied understanding that there was no unreasonable condition in the ticket.[60]

Sir Frederick Pollock appeared as counsel for the plaintiff

---

[57]   (1875) LR 2 Sc & Div 470.
[58]   See also the American case of *Hibbard v Eerie RR Co* 15 NY 455 (1856).
[59]   See *Harris v Great Western Rly Co* (1876) 1 QB 515.
[60]   See also *Watkins v Rymill* [1883] 10 QBD 178.

in *Parker*. His views of the state of the law after it are therefore of some interest. In the second edition of his book
Principles of the Law of Contract, after pointing out that the
tendency of earlier cases had been to hold that the special
conditions contained in notices were binding, and the strong
opposite tendency shown in *Henderson v Stevenson*, he
suggested that the result of *Parker*[61] was that it was a question of fact in each case whether the notice given was
reasonably sufficient. If it was, a person entering a contract
would be deemed to assent to the special terms, but this
assent was probably subject to an implied condition that the
terms were fair and reasonable.[62]

Parker, then, settled the law governing the incorporation
of unsigned terms. The leading modern authority on signed
terms is *L'Estrange v Graucob*.[63] That case relied on Mellish
LJ's dictum in *Parker*, though the rule that by signing a
written contract you are generally estopped from denying
assent to its terms was obviously long established.
Parliament, after all, in the Railway and Canal Traffic Act
1854, had thought the requirement of signature by the consignor to be a safeguard for the public, and there were
generations of experience deriving from the Statute of
Frauds, and the rules governing bills of exchange and
promissory notes.

What was curious in the twentieth century was that, given
the need for standard form contracts, and given the reasonably satisfactory rules for the incorporation of standard
terms worked out in the cases discussed above, the courts
did not police them. Bramwell LJ's important caveat in
Parker – that it was implicit that standard form conditions
should not be unreasonable – went largely unheeded. Why
was this?

To give the usual answer – 'Because of the ideology of freedom of contract' – is to beg the question. The real puzzle is
why, in the light of the artificial rules incorporating terms
about which the vast majority of contractors had no real
knowledge, the terms once incorporated came to enjoy a
parallel status with the dickered terms. In the first place, it
must be remembered that the incorporation rules were

---

[61]   And of *Harris v Great Western Rly Co* (n 59 above).
[62]   Pollock *Principles of the Law of Contract* (2nd edn, 1878) pp 30–31.
[63]   [1934] 2 KB 394.

worked out in the context of contracts for the carriage or storage of goods, and special considerations apply to those. As was discovered in the eighteenth century, it is difficult for a carrier to cover at a reasonable cost all the goods consigned to him for an unlimited amount. The result of requiring this would be to drive up freight rates so that consignors of goods of small value would still have to pay the same substantial insurance element as those consigning goods of large value. The same argument applies to contracts to store goods. It is economically far more sensible to limit the carrier's, or other bailee's, liability to a relatively small specified amount, and to put the onus on the owner (who after all knows the value of the goods consigned or otherwise bailed) to take out insurance cover. For this reason international carriage of goods by road, sea, rail and air, are all governed by conventions whose objective is to achieve limitation of the carriers' liability.[64]

However, the relative abstraction of classical contract law did not permit distinctions to be made between categories of contracts: carriage and hire purchase for example. Starting from its propositions that all contracts entailed offer and acceptance, and a meeting of minds, and so on, it proceeded to assume that if the rules governing incorporation had been complied with, both parties had assented to the standard terms, and their minds had met. This in turn created an obvious logical problem in going on to hold that the terms were unreasonable. Thus, in the case of hire purchase contracts, the hirer in the nature of things does not become the owner of the goods until all the instalments have been paid, and the option to purchase has been exercised. Consequently, if a clause were inserted in the contract to the effect that if the customer failed to pay promptly any particular instalment the goods could be repossessed by the owner, it would be effective even though almost all the instalments had been paid. In the 1920s and 1930s many people found that they could not meet their hire purchase commitments, and 'snatch backs' pursuant to clauses of this sort became common. This

---

[64]   For road carriage it is the CMR Convention, for sea either the Hague Rules or the Hague/Visby Rules, for rail the Convention Concerning International Rail Carriage, and for air the Warsaw Convention and Amended Convention.

situation was not remedied until the Hire Purchase Act 1938[65] – significantly, explicit contract differentiation being introduced by statute rather than the common law.

No distinction was made between consumer contracts and commercial contracts. Some legal systems, such as France, have long since distinguished between commercial transactions, subject to the *Code de Commerce* and the *tribunaux de commerce*, and other transactions. Now it must be admitted that in French law the division of labour between the *Code Civil* and the *Code de Commerce* is not particularly rational, but at least the germs of a good idea are there. A similar distinction might have grown up in England had not the Court of Admiralty, which handled mercantile disputes in the sixteenth century, had its wings clipped due to the tendency to associate the civil law which it administered with the Royalist cause in the run up to the civil war.[66] At all events, both commercial and non-commercial disputes came to be decided by the common law courts, which applied to them the same general law of contract (except in the exceptional cases which had been absorbed from the old law merchant, such as the rules governing bills of exchange and promissory notes).[67] The consequences of this lack of differentiation can be seen in the well-known case of *Thompson v London, Midland and Scottish Rly Co.*[68] In that case, the plaintiff, who could not read, asked her niece to buy her a return excursion ticket from Darwen to Manchester. On the face of the ticket was printed 'Excursion, For conditions see back'; on the back were the words 'Issued subject to the conditions and regulations in the company's time-tables and notices and excursion and

---

[65] The transaction had to be within the specified financial limits, however, to fall under the control of the Act. See Borrie and Diamond *The Consumer Society and the Law* (4th edn, 1981) p 159 et seq. For an economic analysis of this question see ch 8.

[66] See B. Levack *Civil Lawyers in England 1603–1641* (Oxford University Press, 1973). The ideological link between the civil law and absolutism, and the common law and Parliament is reflected in the following century in the dispute concerning the Massachusetts Court of Admiralty which occurred just before the American Revolution. The House of Representatives resolved that 'the extension of the powers of the Court of Admiralty within this province is a most violent infraction of the right of trial by juries' – Holdsworth *Select Essays in Anglo-American Legal History* vol I, essay 9.

[67] Which did not fit at all well into the classical contractual model.

[68] [1930] 1 KB 4.

other bills'. The excursion bills referred to the conditions in the company's timetables (which had to be purchased), and these conditions provided that excursion ticket holders should have no right of action against the company in respect of any injury. The plaintiff slipped whilst alighting at Darwen, where the platform was short, and she was injured. It was held that the conditions governed. Lord Hanworth MR said:[69]

> 'The railway company is to be treated as having made an offer to intending travellers that if they will accept the conditions on which the railway company make the offer they can be taken at suitable times, on suitable days and by indicated trains from Darwen to Manchester and back at a price slightly reduced from the common price; but upon certain conditions which can be ascertained, and of the existence of which there can be no doubt, for they are indicated clearly upon the ticket which is issued.'

Now it appears that the Court of Appeal in this case probably thought the exclusion of liability reasonable, but in spite of citing Bramwell LJ's dictum that there is an implied understanding that the conditions must be reasonable, the issue was not addressed directly. Moreover, the criteria by which the court appeared to think the clause reasonable were appropriate to a commercial case, but surely not to one involving a private individual, a consumer as we would now say. In fact the question of the reasonableness of terms was only rarely addressed directly in any case prior to the Unfair Contract Terms Act 1977, which imposed a statutory requirement of reasonableness on, inter alia, exclusion clauses in consumer contracts.[70]

Instead, when the modern courts began to develop hostility to the exclusion of liability in consumer cases, they resorted to a number of less overt devices to avoid giving effect to conditions they appear to have thought unfair in the particular case.[71] Thus, in *Karsales (Harrow) Ltd*

---

[69]   Citing with approval Swift J's dicta in *Nunan v Southern Rly Co* [1923] 2 KB 703, 707.

[70]   See eg the remarks of Lord Denning MR in *Gillespie Bros & Co Ltd v Roy Bowles Transport Ltd* [1973] QB 400, 415–417; and see further ch 8.

[71]   See eg the discussion in Roger Brownsword 'Remedy-Stipulation in the English Law of Contract: Freedom or Paternalism?' (1977) 9 Ottawa Law Review 95.

v Wallis,[72] the defendant wished to purchase on hire purchase a car he had inspected and found in good order and condition. The hire purchase contract contained a term that 'no condition or warranty that the vehicle is roadworthy or as to its condition or fitness for any purpose is given by the owner or implied therein'. The car was delivered with its cylinder head broken, its valves burnt and two pistons broken. Denning LJ said:[73]

'It is necessary to look at the contract apart from the exempting clauses to see what are the terms, express or implied, which impose an obligation on the party. If he has been guilty of a breach of those obligations in a respect which goes to the very root of the contract, he cannot rely on the exempting clauses.'

This doctrine (or doctrines) of the fundamental term or fundamental breach[74] was to enjoy a notorious vogue until finally laid to rest in *Suisse Atlantique Société d' Armement Maritime SA v NV Rotterdamsche Kolen Centrale SA*,[75] and *Photo Production Ltd v Securicor Ltd*,[76] sometimes with startling results[77] because the issue of the reasonableness of the terms in the context of the particular case was not addressed directly, and commercial cases were subjected to the same treatment as consumer cases.

In *Thornton v Shoe Lane Parking Ltd*[78] the Court of Appeal employed another strategy, blocking the incorporation of the defendants' standard conditions. There, the plaintiff had driven into the defendants' car park which had a machine at the entrance which dispensed a ticket automatically. The ticket referred to the defendants' standard terms. It was held, however, that the contract had already been formed by the time the plaintiff received the

---

[72]   [1956] 2 All ER 866.
[73]   Ibid at p 869.
[74]   It was never entirely clear whether there were two doctrines or one: see generally Brian Coote *Exception Clauses* (London, Sweet and Maxwell, 1964); and David Yates *Exclusion Clauses in Contracts* 2nd edn (London, Sweet and Maxwell, 1982) ch 6.
[75]   [1967] 1 AC 361.
[76]   [1980] AC 827.
[77]   See *Harbutts Plasticine Ltd v Wayne Tank and Pump Co Ltd* [1970] 1 QB 447 – and its sequel *Wayne Tank and Pump Co Ltd v Employers' Liability Assurance Co* [1973] 3 All ER 825.
[73]   [1971] 2 QB 163.

ticket.[79] Consequently, he could not be affected by a term
exempting liability for personal injury. Interestingly,
though, with statutory regulation of unreasonable exemptions on the near-horizon, the Court of Appeal in *Thornton*
all but rediscovered Bramwell LJ's caveat in *Parker*. For,
the Court expressed the view that, even if the ticket were
issued prior to the formation of the contract, it still would
not suffice to incorporate a swingeing exemption clause of
the sort the defendants claimed to benefit from. The point
was that, if the defendants wished to incorporate unreasonable terms by notice, then exceptional steps must be
taken to alert their customers to this risk. Although the
Unfair Contract Terms Act has rendered this doctrinal
rediscovery less significant than it otherwise might have
been, it remains a useful rider to the rules on incorporation. Thus, in the post-UCTA case of *Interfoto Picture
Library Ltd v Stiletto Visual Programmes Ltd*,[80] the Court of
Appeal relied on this aspect of *Thornton* to disallow a
standard term that was unusually onerous and that was
not clearly flagged by the party seeking to rely on it. In
short, in both *Thornton* and *Interfoto*, we see the makings
of a doctrine of 'unfair surprise' in relation to standard
form provisions, on the basis of which the classical law
might be brought into alignment with modern contracting
practice.

Another strategy was to construe clauses narrowly, so
that, as noted above, negligence was held not to be excluded
unless it was the only head of liability to which the term
could apply. The avenues for negligence actions could also
be kept open by a strict application of the privity doctrine.

[79] By contrast, in *Zunz v South Eastern Rly Co* (1869) 4 LR 4 CP 539, 544
Cockburn CJ said: 'However harsh it may appear in practice to hold a
man liable by the terms and conditions which may be inserted in some
small print upon the ticket, which he only gets at the last moment after
he has paid his money, and when nine times out of ten he is hustled
out of the place at which he stands to get his ticket by the next customer, . . . still we are bound on the authorities to hold, that when a
man takes a ticket with conditions on it he must be presumed to know
the contents of it, and must be bound by them.' Of course, to the extent
Cockburn CJ seems to be suggesting that merely taking a ticket suffices, his views must be modified in the light of the views expressed in
Parker v South Eastern Rly Co (1877) 2 CPD 416 discussed above.
[80] [1989] QB 433.

For example, in *Adler v Dickson*,[81] an injured passenger was held able to side-step the shipping line's exemption clause by suing the negligent master and boatswain of the vessel. And in *Scruttons Ltd v Midland Silicones Ltd*[82] negligent stevedores were held to be unprotected by the clauses in the contract of carriage purporting to exempt them from liability in accordance with the Hague Rules. Arguably *Scruttons* is a case where the court reached the wrong result,[83] this time because it approached a commercial exemption clause with the same hostility as one in a consumer contract. The great weakness underlying these stratagems, however, was the failure to address head-on the issue of reasonableness – that is, the failure to address explicitly the question of whether particular standard terms truly were 'standard' (and, thus, in line with reasonable expectations), or whether they were exceptional and seriously out of line with reasonable expectations.

Moving forward to the present, we find that contract, in relation to both doctrine and practice (and especially with regard to consumer contracting), has to a considerable extent given way to status. For, a large portion of everyday contracting takes place on standard terms which are not negotiated, or negotiable, but which are subject to control by the courts under the Unfair Contract Terms Act 1977 (and, more recently, the Unfair Terms in Consumer Contracts Regulations).[84] By explicitly distinguishing between commercial and consumer contracts, and by conferring on the courts a discretion to review contractual terms on the grounds of reasonableness, the legislation may seem a rational response to a long-standing problem. Certainly, before arriving at this position, the courts had to engage in some heroic manipulation of contract doctrine, paying lip service to the classical model, but covertly exerting substantive regulation over standard form provisions. As we shall emphasise in due course, this was one of the great (formal) irrationalities of the twentieth century.[85]

---

[81]   [1955] 1 QB 158.
[82]   [1962] AC 446.
[83]   See ch 5.
[84]   SI 1994/3159, implementing the EC Directive on Unfair Terms in Consumer Contracts (Council Directive 93/13/EEC, OJ No L 95/29 21.4.93).
[85]   See further chs 8 and 10.

(ii) The 'battle of the forms'

A problem to which the widespread use of standard forms inevitably gives rise is the 'battle of the forms'. Each party obviously wants its self-serving standard terms to govern, but how is the law to determine which terms should prevail? The problem with the classical theory is that it resolves the dispute rather like a game of tennis. As Lord Denning pointed out, criticising it, in *Butler Machine Tool Co Ltd v Ex-Cell-O Ltd:*[86]

> 'In some cases the battle is won by the man who fires the last shot. He is the man who puts forward the latest terms and conditions: and, if they are not objected to by the other party, he may be taken to have agreed to them. Such was *British Road Services v Arthur Crutchley & Co Ltd*[87] per Lord Pearson; and the illustration given by Professor Guest in *Anson's Law of Contract* where he says that "the terms of the contract consist of the terms of the offer subject to the modifications contained in the acceptance".[88] That may, however, go too far. In some cases, however, the battle is won by the man who gets the blow in first. If he offers to sell at a named price on the terms and conditions stated on the back and the buyer orders the goods purporting to accept the offer on an order form with his own different terms and conditions on the back, then, if the difference is so material that it would affect the price, the buyer ought not to be allowed to take advantage of the difference unless he draws it specifically to the attention of the seller. There are yet other cases where the battle depends on the shots fired on both sides. There is a concluded contract but the forms vary. The terms and conditions of the parties are to be construed together. If they can be reconciled so as to give a harmonious result, all well and good. If the differences are irreconcilable, so that they are mutually contradictory, then the conflicting terms may have to be scrapped and replaced by a reasonable implication.'

In *Butler* itself, the Court of Appeal purported to apply a traditional offer and acceptance approach, thereby allowing the buyer to instate its standard terms against those of the seller who had, so to speak, fired the first shot. The criticism of this kind of approach is that it encourages businessmen to fire salvoes at each other in the hope of firing the decisive

---

[86]   [1979] 1 All ER 965, 968.
[87]   [1968] 1 All ER 811.
[88]   24th edn, 1975, pp 37–8.

shot. That may put a party in an invidious position of either not performing or performing and by implication accepting the other's standard terms, and it allows one party to withdraw even though the other might by then have substantially performed.[89] On the other hand, the main criticism of Lord Denning's approach is said to be that it will not discourage the firing of salvoes, that virtually any term can affect the price, and that terms are difficult to categorise.[90] In practice, however, it is unlikely that *any* rule will have much effect on the way in which businessmen operate. Fundamentally, what is wrong with Lord Denning's approach is that, like section 2-207 of the American Uniform Commercial Code,[91] it conflates the problem as to whether an 'acceptance' differing from the terms of the offer should amount to a rejection, with the problem as to whether there is a contract at all. In many cases it is reasonable to suppose that a differing 'acceptance' is not a rejection.[92] Going on to the next step and recognising that there is a binding contract is something quite different, however. As Professor Waddams points out with reference to Article 2-207, there

---

[89] See Duesenberg and King *Sales and Bulk Transfers under the Uniform Commercial Code* (1966) §3-02; Nordström *Law of Sales* (1970) pp 92–3, 100.

[90] Rawlings [1979] MLR 715.

[91] Section 2-207 of the UCC provides:
> (1) A definite and seasonable expression of acceptance or a written confirmation which is sent within a reasonable time operates as an acceptance even though it states terms additional to or different from those offered or agreed upon, unless acceptance is expressly made conditional on assent to the additional or different terms.
> (2) The additional terms are to be construed as proposals for addition to the contract. Between merchants such terms become part of the contract unless:
> (a) the offer expressly limits acceptance to the terms of the offer;
> (b) they materially alter it; or
> (c) notification of objection to them has already been given or is given within a reasonable time after notice of them is received.
> (3) Conduct by both parties which recognizes the existence of a contract is sufficient to establish a contract for sale although the writings of the parties do not otherwise establish a contract. In such case the terms of the particular contract consist of those terms on which the writings of the parties agree, together with any supplementary terms incorporated under any other provisions of this Act.

[92] *Stevenson v McLean* (1880) 5 QBD 346.

is a basic contradiction in holding that a definite expression of acceptance is an acceptance, even though it states terms additional to or different from those offered.[93]

Lord Denning's approach does, however, have the implication that each case is to be considered on its facts: that the mechanical application of offer and acceptance theory is not the right approach. Although this approach has been criticised by adherents of the classical view (at least, as anything other than an exceptional expedient),[94] it has been supported more recently by the Court of Appeal in *G. Percy Trentham Ltd v Archital Luxfer Ltd*.[95] There, the battle of the forms lay between a main contractor and a sub-contractor, between whom there was 'no orderly negotiation of terms' but rather a 'jockeying for advantage' with the parties 'inching towards finalisation of the transaction'.[96] In a robust judgment, Steyn LJ argued that the courts 'ought not to yield to Victorian times in realism about the practical application of rules of contract formation'.[97] Thus, where a transaction had been fully performed, as was the case in *Trentham*, one should recognise that a contract could come into existence, and be performed, even if the ingredients of the transaction could not be precisely analysed in terms of offer and acceptance. This surely is the only sensible approach to the problem. A detailed analysis of the facts of any given case will frequently, if not usually, point to a solution. It may, for example, be apparent in a 'one shot' deal that the parties had in fact contracted with one another before any standard forms came on the scene ie from an identifiable time both parties had started to behave as though they were contracting with one another, suggesting that from their point of view, the outlines of the deal were sufficiently filled out from that time. In that case the standard terms could be ignored.[98] In other cases, there may have been a course of dealing between the parties which may point to the basis on which it is reasonable to suppose they were contracting with respect to the deal in

---

[93]   *Law of Contracts* 2nd edn (1984) p 63 et seq.
[94]   See especially Lord Diplock in *Gibson v Manchester City Council* [1979] 1 All ER 972, 974.
[95]   [1993] 1 Lloyd's LR 25.
[96]   Ibid, at p 26.
[97]   Ibid, at p 29.
[98]   As in *Olley v Marlborough Court Ltd* [1949] 1 KB 532.

hand.[99] In some cases the counter-terms may be meaning-less, or trivially different. In such cases they can be ignored, especially where the problem is that a party is apparently attempting to seize on a breach of such a term as a way of escaping from a contract.[100]

Where the court is satisfied that effect should be given to 'a proposed deal which in commercial understanding has in fact been closed'[101] a distinction between important and unimportant terms might be drawn in a *particular* case, the emphasis being on the particular case. Terms which affect the primary obligations under the contract will generally be fundamental, but not necessarily so (eg in sale of goods, stipulations as to time of payment are not generally of the essence).[102] On the other hand, terms which affect only the secondary obligations under a contract, such as arbitration clauses,[103] will generally not be of the essence, but may be in a particular case. Limitation of damages clauses intended to allocate insurance cover may be tested against the insurance arrangements in fact operated by the parties.

Where the parties are not agreed on the essential terms of the contract, the only solution is to hold that no contract exists. Any recovery thereafter has to be based on restitution as in *British Steel Corpn v Cleveland Bridge Engineering Co Ltd*.[104] The facts of *Cleveland Bridge* are somewhat complicated, but can be simplified as follows. The plaintiffs, BSC, had manufactured 137 special steel castings for the defendants. The defendants had refused to pay for them, and when sued by BSC, counter-claimed for late delivery and for delivery in the wrong sequence. The defendants claimed that the contract had been entered into on their standard terms, under which BSC would be liable for con-sequential loss. BSC claimed that any contract was governed by their standard terms, which excluded liability for consequential loss. Goff J's analysis of the facts

---

[99]   See *British Road Services v Arthur Crutchley & Co Ltd* [1968] 1 All ER 811; *Kendall v Lillico & Sons Ltd* [1969] 2 AC 31.

[100]   *Clive v Beaumont* (1848) 1 De G & S 397; *Nicolene v Simmonds* [1953] 1 QB 543.

[101]   UCC Art 2-207.

[102]   Sale of Goods Act 1979, s 10.

[103]   *Brogden v Metropolitan Rly Co* (1877) 2 App Case 666.

[104]   [1984] 1 All ER 504. More controversially, the basis of recovery might be argued to be detrimental reliance (see n 105 below).

suggested that the fault for the failure to reach agreement on the terms of a formal contract was the defendants', and it would be quite unfair to hold BSC bound by the defendants' terms. He allowed BSC to recover on a *quantum meruit* (for the value of both the castings delivered and the preparatory work) and dismissed the defendants' counterclaim. In so holding, Goff J affirmed the principle that where work is done by A at the request of B prior to the drawing up of a formal contract (perhaps, as in *Cleveland Bridge* itself, on the basis of a letter of intent), and where the formal contract is never in fact drawn up, then A may recover a reasonable sum from B (on a *quantum meruit*) for the work done – moreover, it seems that this sum may relate to work which would not have had to be paid for had the formal contract been entered into.[105] At all events, by adopting a flexible approach, Goff J appears to have produced a satisfactory result in this particular case.[106]

2. THE TREND TOWARDS RELATIONAL CONTRACTING

It is now something of a truism that the classical law takes the one-off exchange as its paradigm – for example, a motorist purchasing petrol from a garage that he deals with on only the one occasion. However, much modern contracting is relational, with performance being extended over a period of time, or with the contractors being economically related, or with both temporal extension and economic integration being involved to some degree. For example, in *The*

---

[105]   *William Lacey (Hounslow) Ltd v Davis* [1957] 1 WLR 932; *Sanders & Foster v A Monk Ltd* (6 February 1980, unreported); *OTM Ltd v Hydranautics* [1981] 2 Ll Rep 211. This principle departs from the normal restitutionary principle of unjust enrichment, and seems rather to reflect compensating detrimental reliance. The benefit conferred on the defendants in *Cleveland Bridge* was only a benefit, after all, in the sense that the work was done *for* the defendants. See further *Regalian Properties plc v London Dockland Development Corpn.* [1995] 1 All ER 1005.

[106]   See Simon Ball, 'Work Carried Out in Pursuance of Letters of Intent – Contract or Restitution?' (1983) 99 LQR 572; and William Howarth, 'Contract, Reliance and Business Transactions' (1987) Journal of Business Law 122. See further ch 4 (s 4) for discussion of the larger issue raised by the *BSC* case of how far a contractor is to be protected with regard to pre-contractual reliance.

Eurymedon,[107] the dispute arose in the context of a complex of sales and carriage contracts, it being a feature of this complex not only that perfomance was temporally extended but also that two of the principal litigants were companies within the same corporate group (namely, a parent company and its wholly-owned subsidiary). Faced by a classical model of contract that obstructed a commercially convenient resolution of the dispute, Lord Wilberforce was moved to remark:

> 'It is only the precise analysis of this complex of relations into the classical offer and acceptance, with identifiable consideration, that seems to present difficulty, but this same difficulty exists in many situations of daily life, eg sales at auction; supermarket purchases; boarding an omnibus; purchasing a train ticket; tenders for the supply of goods; offers of rewards; acceptance by post; warranties of authority by agents; manufacturers' guarantees; gratuitous bailments; bankers' commercial credits. These are all examples which show that English law, having committed itself to a rather technical and schematic doctrine of contract, in application takes a practical approach, often at the cost of forcing the facts to fit uneasily into the marked slots of offer, acceptance and consideration.'

Lord Wilberforce might also have said that the classical model unrealistically presupposes a precise instant when the contract is formed – a snapshot taken at this time showing all the ingredients of formation coalescing in just the right pattern.

Now, one of the ingredients for contractual formation, as we saw in Chapter 2, is that the terms of the contract should be certain, that the parties' rights and liabilities for the future are fully determined, and that these matters are settled *at the point of formation*.[108] In many relational commercial situations, however, the parties are simply not in a position to anticipate every facet of performance at the moment of formation. Accordingly, they may wish to leave some matters 'to be agreed' during the performance of the contract. For example, in *F & G Sykes (Wessex) Ltd. v Fine Fare Ltd*,[109] the parties entered into a five-year agreement

---

[107] *New Zealand Shipping Co Ltd v AM Satterthwaite and Co Ltd* [1975] AC 154, 167.

[108] See p 28.The classical law, as Ian Macneil (see n 111 below) has put it, requires full 'presentation' of terms.

[109] [1967] 1 Lloyd's Rep 53.

under which the plaintiffs would supply broiler chickens (through nominated growers) to the defendants. In the first year of the agreement, the number supplied each week would be not less than 30,000 and not more than 80,000, and thereafter 'such figures as may be agreed between the parties'. The agreement having run for over a year, the defendants cancelled, and the plaintiffs sued for breach. A classically-minded court would undoubtedly have held that the agreement failed for want of certainty. However, the plaintiffs were fortunate in having the case heard before a progressive Court of Appeal. The philosophy of the Court was well put by Lord Denning MR:[110]

> 'In a commercial agreement the further the parties have gone with their contract, the more ready are the Courts to imply any reasonable term so as to give effect to their intentions. When much has been done, the Courts will do their best not to destroy the bargain. . .[W]hen an agreement has been acted upon and the parties, as here, have been put to great expense in implementing it, we ought to imply all reasonable terms so as to avoid any uncertainties. In this case there is less difficulty than in others because there is an arbitration clause which, liberally construed, is sufficient to resolve any uncertainties which the parties have left.'

In other words, the Court was prepared to be as flexible with the law as the parties needed to be flexible with their agreement.

The contract in *Sykes v Fine Fare* was a requirements contract. The flexible framework offered by such contracts has an obvious utility. For example, motor manufacturers characteristically buy a large number of components from independent manufacturers. The rationale for this is partly that if demand falls, the motor manufacturer is not left with a large inventory of components. However, the manufacturer cannot, for obvious reasons, know exactly how many components it will need over a period of a year, say. Consequently it cannot make a contract, eg for 5,000 radiators. On the other hand, in a very short term, say a week, it may have a fair idea as to how many units it will need. Consequently, it makes very good sense to make a contract in the form that the component maker will supply as many

[110]   Ibid, at pp 57–58.

units as the motor manufacturer should order up to a certain number at a particular price over a twelve-month
period, but that the motor manufacturer is not bound to
order any particular number.[111]

How, though, are the features of requirements contracts
to be forced into the classical template? One possible analysis of this situation is that the component manufacturer is
making a continuing offer, which the motor manufacturer
accepts each time it places an order for the quantity of components it needs. This is indeed the standard analysis given
in the textbooks.[112] The problem with it, however, is that
unless there is consideration for the offer to remain open, it
can be revoked at any time.[113] In point of fact, however, such
authority as there is tends to support the view that such
transactions are actually contracts. The significance of this
is that the supplier cannot withdraw before the end of the
stipulated time.[114]

In *Great Northern Rly Co v Witham*[115] the defendant had
promised to supply the plaintiff with stores at fixed prices
for a period of twelve months 'in such quantities as the
company's storekeeper might order from time to time'. An
order sent by the plaintiffs was not executed and the plaintiffs sued for the difference between the contract price and
the price of purchasing their requirements elsewhere. It
was held that the defendants were liable, a result consistent
with the traditional analysis because if the defendants'
promise were simply an offer it had not been withdrawn at
the time the plaintiff accepted it by placing an order. In fact,
however, neither of the judges who gave reasoned judgments (Keating and Brett JJ) was prepared to express a
definite opinion on the question of whether the defendants
could have withdrawn before the order was placed. In an

---

[111]   See Macaulay 'The Standardised Contracts of the United States
Automobile Manufacturers' 7 Enc of Int Comp L Ch 3; Macneil 'The
Many Futures of Contract' (1974) 47 So Cal LR 691.

[112]   See eg Cheshire Fifoot & Furmston *Law of Contract* (12th edn, 1991)
p 47.

[113]   *Routledge v Grant* (1828) 4 Bingham 653. The Law Revision Committee
recommended abrogation of this rule – Sixth Interim Report (1937)
p 31, but it was never acted on.

[114]   See John N. Adams, 'Consideration for Requirements Contracts'
(1978) 94 Law Quarterly Review 73.

[115]   (1873) LR 9 CP 16.

earlier case, *Burton v Great Northern Rly Co*,[116] the plaintiff had undertaken to provide wagons and horses to convey all the merchandise that the defendants might present to him between Hatfield and Ware at 5s per ton for twelve months. After five and a half months the defendants declined to send any more goods to the plaintiff. Parke B held:[117]

> '[T]here was no breach of contract; because the notice does not amount to a refusal to perform the *contract* [emphasis supplied], but is merely an intimation that from a certain day the defendants would cease to have any goods for the plaintiff to carry.'

He suggested it would be a parallel case if a person agreed to purchase all the wine he needed during the year from a wine merchant and gave up drinking after six months, or a tradesman agreeing with a carrier in similar terms to the contract in question, and giving up his business before the end of the term. The interesting thing about these examples is that they avoid the question as to what would have happened if the customer or the tradesman had taken their custom elsewhere. Again, therefore, the case conveys the impression that the judge considered that there was a contract between the parties. Other cases support the same view. In *Re Gloucester Municipal Election Petition*[118] the offer was to supply certain goods to a Council as required at specified prices over a twelve-month period. This offer was accepted. The issue was whether this was a contract with the Council which disqualified the supplier, a councillor, from office. Darling J held that there was a contract, though he thought that there was an obligation on the Council's part to order the relevant goods from the councillor if they were required. On orthodox theory, of course, the surrender on the part of the Council of its freedom to order elsewhere could amount to consideration for keeping the offer open. It is also arguable that something less than a contract in the technical sense should have sufficed to disqualify the councillor having regard to the policy behind the rule. Again, in *Percival v LCC Asylums and Mental Deficiency Committee*[119] a not dissimilar contract was thought to be valid by Atkin J.

---

[116]   (1854) 9 Exch 507.
[117]   Ibid, at 513–514.
[118]   [1901] 1 KB 683.
[119]   (1918) 87 LJKB 677.

In that case the supplier sued because the Committee had failed to order up to the scheduled amount. It was held that on the true construction of the contract the defendants were not bound to order any of the scheduled goods, but the suppliers were bound to deliver if ordered. There were, Atkin J said, three sorts of contract to be distinguished: (1) where the purchasing body undertakes to buy all the specified material from the contractor; (2) where there is no obligation to give any order at all, but if the purchasing body does so, the contractor is under a duty to supply; and (3) where, although the parties are not bound to any specified quantity, yet they bind themselves to buy and pay for all the goods that are in fact needed by them.

The result in *Percival* could of course have been reached on an orthodox continuing offer analysis. Cases which could only be decided on the basis that a contract existed would be where the supplier repudiated before the specified time, and before an order had been placed, or where the other repudiated before the end of the specified time. The latter situation arose in *Ruffy, Arnell and Baumann Aviation Co Ltd v R.*[120] In 1916 the suppliants entered an agreement with the War Office for the duration of the war under which the suppliants' aviation school would take only pupils sent by the War Office at £100 each, the War Office reserving the right to decide the capacity of the school, and to withdraw pupils at any time. In June 1918 the War Office gave one month's notice of termination. The war did not end until 11 November 1918, and consequently, the War Office had purported to terminate the agreement prematurely. McCardie J, alluding to the fact that it had been argued (somewhat faintly) that the transaction constituted only a revocable offer, held that there was a binding contract between the parties. He said: 'In my humble view the matter is so clear as to dispense with a statement of reasons for my opinion'.[121] The suppliants accordingly recovered damages for general inconvenience.[122]

Whilst it cannot be said that either the decision in *Re Gloucester Election Petition* or in *Ruffy, Arnell and Baumann* is of the highest authority, we would suggest that this line

---

[120]   (1918) 126 LT 573.
[121]   Ibid, at p 577.
[122]   This was assessed at £250.

of cases taken as a whole does provide some support for the view that such requirements contracts, which lack altogether on one side any obligation either positive or negative, are binding, and are not merely continuing offers by the supplier. This view can also be supported from the Privy Council decision in *R v Demers*.[123] That was a Canadian case in which the respondent had agreed to execute printing orders for the Government of Québec at stated prices for a number of years. The Government stopped sending work, and the respondent sued (in other words, the situation was similar to that in *Burton v Great Northern Rly Co*). Their Lordships were prepared to assume that there was a good and valid contract, though the Government had committed no breach of it.

If the agreements in these cases were contracts, the classical view of consideration cannot be maintained – at least, not without some considerable manipulation. However, consideration is undoubtedly a requirement of a common law contract. If, though, we abandon the classical exchange theory of consideration and adopt a test based on legitimate expectation, there is no difficulty. As we saw in the previous chapter, that view is consistent with the common law doctrine of consideration as it existed before the nineteenth century.[124] It is also arguably the one upon which the Court of Appeal decision in *Williams v Roffey Bros & Nicholls (Contractors) Ltd*[125] can be best supported.

In spite of the prevalence of requirements contracts there have been relatively few reported cases concerning them (as the above discussion should have made apparent). This suggests that requirements contracts do not often give rise to litigation, or at least to litigation that finds its way into the mainstream court system (and particularly the Appeal Courts). Why is this? Given the relational background to many requirements contracts, two rather different explanations may be suggested. First, where disputes arise, litigation may be avoided because in this type of contracting, the party who is the supplier is usually relatively small and the purchaser a substantial organisation from whom

---

[123]   [1900] AC 103.
[124]   See generally Simpson *A History of the Common Law of Contract* (Oxford University Press, 1975).
[125]   [1990] 1 All ER 512. See further ch 4.

the supplier would hope to continue to get orders. The effect of the supplier terminating the continuing offer (if such it is) before the agreed term had run would be to decrease the likelihood of getting further orders from the same purchaser. In practice, in a wide range of commercial contracting, non-legal sanctions (particularly, the threat of loss of future business) are often far more important than legal sanctions.[126] Secondly, where the relationship is rather more evenly balanced, the parties may co-operate in finding an acceptable solution to their disputes.[127] To the extent that the classical law is treated as marginal to the activities of some relational contractors, who settle their disputes in a spirit of compromise and give-and-take, we might conclude that the inadequacy of the law does no real harm. However, there is a further possibility which grounds some cause for concern. This is that some contractors' interests might need the law for their proper protection, and yet the contractors fight shy of litigation because they fear that wholly inappropriate classical contract principles will be applied to the resolution of the dispute.[128] As we will see in the next chapter, the classical law's attachment to an exchange theory of contract gives rise to precisely such a concern.

---

[126]   See Stewart Macaulay, 'Non-Contractual Relations in Business' (1963) 28 American Sociological Review 55, and 'Elegant Models, Empirical Patterns, and the Complexities of Contract' (1977) 11 Law and Society Review 507; and Hugh Beale and Tony Dugdale, 'Contracts Between Businessmen: Planning and the Use of Contractual Remedies' (1975) 2 British Journal of Law & Society 45. As a very broad generalisation, for example, the construction industry is fairly litigious, as is the insurance industry (hence the large body of case-law on international carriage contracts). Export and import buyers and sellers are also fairly litigious.

[127]   See further ch 9.

[128]   Cf Oliver Williamson, 'Transaction-Cost Economics. The Governance of Contractual Relations' (1979) 22 Journal of Law and Economics 233.

Chapter 4

The classical paradigm: exchange and expectation

Introduction

Two of the cornerstones of the classical model, as we saw in Chapter 2, are the exchange theory of consideration and the expectation measure of damages. The exchange theory entails that the law of contract will not protect a promisee's interests unless the promise forms part of a bargained-for exchange. This is so, irrespective of whether the promisor seriously intended the promise to be relied on, and irrespective of whether the promisee has actually relied on the promise. On the other hand, where the classical law recognises contractual interests, the expectation measure offers full protection to the promisee by calculating damages on the basis that the promisee should be put into the same position as if the promise had been performed (again, irrespective of whether the promisee has actually relied on the promise).

Critics of the classical model maintain that, whereas the exchange model unduly restricts the potential protective effects of contract law, the expectation measure has a tendency to overcompensate. In other words, the critics argue that the protective scope of contract law is too narrow but that its remedial regime, where it applies, is too strong.[1] In this chapter, we will concentrate on the first part of this criticism, looking particularly at two common situations – pre-contractual reliance and adjustment of long-term contracts – where the exchange theory runs into difficulties.

---

[1] Patrick Atiyah is a leading advocate for this view. Seminally, see eg Patrick Atiyah, 'Promises, Obligations and the Law of Contract' (1978) 94 Law Quarterly Review 193; and for Atiyah's critical reflections on the

1. CONTRACTUAL INTERESTS

In their celebrated article, 'The Reliance Interest in Contract Damages',[2] Lon Fuller and William Perdue identified three interests as falling within the protective realm of contract law. These interests were: the restitution, the reliance, and the expectation interest. The restitution interest arises out of a benefit conferred upon A by B, in circumstances where A would be unjustly enriched if B were not to be compensated for the value of the benefit so conferred. For many years, the protection of such an interest was regarded as 'quasi-contractual' but, with the development of an independent law of restitution, this interest has its own legal division.[3] The reliance interest arises where B relies to his detriment on A's promise. Provided that the relationship between A and B constitutes an exchange, the law of contract has no difficulty in compensating for B's detrimental reliance. However, the protection of the expectation interest is par excellence the function of contract law. The expectation interest arises where A fails to perform as promised and the relationship between A and B constitutes an exchange. Quite simply, B's expectation interest is to be put into the position that he would have been in had A performed as promised.

Although Fuller and Perdue's analysis focuses on the relationship between the interests of transactors and the measurement of damages in contract law, it has become a rallying point for the argument that detrimental reliance *of itself* should be a ground for providing a remedy.[4] In other

expectation measure of damages, see 'Executory Contracts, Expectation Damages, and the Economic Analysis of Contract' in *Essays in Contract* (Oxford, Clarendon Press, 1986) 150. But cf Melvin Eisenberg 'The Bargain Principle and its Limits' (1981-82) 95 Harvard Law Review 741, 785–798.

[2]   (1936) 46 Yale Law Journal 52.

[3]   In Goff and Jones *Law of Restitution* 4th edn (London, Sweet and Maxwell, 1993) p 3, three main classes of restitution interest are recognised: (1) where the defendant has acquired a benefit from the act of the plaintiff; (2) where the defendant has acquired a benefit from a third party for which he must account to the plaintiff; and (3) where the defendant has acquired a benefit through his own wrongful act.

[4]   See Atiyah 'The Move from Agreement to Reliance in English Law and the Exclusion of Liability Relating to Defective Goods' in Donald Harris and Denis Tallon (eds) *Contract Law Today* (Oxford, Clarendon Press, 1989) p 21.

words, the argument is that, where B relies to his detriment on A's promise, B should be able to recover compensation even though A's promise does not form part of an exchange with B. The standard example in support of this argument is the well-known American case of *Hoffman v Red Owl Stores Inc.*[5]

In *Hoffman*, the Red Owl Stores was a franchise network. The plaintiffs, wanting to open a Red Owl Store, approached the defendant with a view to acquiring a franchise. The plaintiffs were encouraged to believe that they would be given a franchise for a particular store and, with the defendant's knowledge, they sold their house and existing business and moved to the town in which the new store was to be situated. In doing so, they incurred considerable expenditure. Shortly before they were due to open the new store, however, the defendant told the plaintiffs that they were not after all going to be given the franchise for the agreed 'up-front' payment, and the deal fell through. Now, had the franchise contract (which is a written document of some complexity, signed by both parties) been entered into, and had the defendant then refused to proceed, then clearly the plaintiffs would have been entitled to damages. The damages would have represented the profits that the Hoffmans expected to make out of the contract. Characteristically, a franchise will be for a fixed term of years, five or ten, and the franchisee will be provided by the franchisor with a projection of the profits which it can reasonably be expected the particular outlet will make. Accordingly, if the projection was, say, $100,000 net profits over a five-year period, awarding the Hoffmans that sum would protect both their expectation and their reliance interest, because they would have had to incur some reliance expenses anyway in acquiring the franchise. The legal difficulty facing the Hoffmans, however, was that they had not entered into a franchise contract with the defendant, and in consequence they did not have a straightforward action for breach of contract.

The basis of the Hoffmans' claim for compensation was not that they had a contract with the defendant, but that it would be unfair if they were not compensated for the

[5]   133 NW 2d 267 (1965).

substantial expenditure incurred in reliance on the expectation induced by the defendant that they would be granted a franchise. Drawing on paragraph 90 of the *American Restatement of Contracts* (2nd edn) the court found in favour of the Hoffmans. According to paragraph 90:

> 'A promise which the promisor should reasonably expect to induce action or forbearance on the part of the promisee . . . and which does induce such action or forbearance is binding if injustice can be avoided only by enforcement of the promise. The remedy granted for the breach may be limited as justice requires.'

The implications of *Hoffman* and para 90 are fairly stark for the classical theory of contract. If detrimental reliance is to be a sufficient condition for the law to be made available to protect one's interests (ie if exchange is no longer a necessary condition), then as Grant Gilmore famously declared we are witnessing the death of contract.[6] In England, however, as we shall now see, the erosion of the exchange model has been rather less dramatic.

2. ESTOPPEL AND THE EXCHANGE MODEL

In *Hoffman v Red Owl Stores Inc*, the American court showed itself willing to protect the Hoffmans against their reliance on the defendant in what was *a pre-contractual situation*. Equally, we can be sure that the court would have protected the Hoffmans if their reliance on the defendant had arisen *after the contract had been formed*. Suppose, for example, that the Hoffmans, having entered the franchise agreement, experienced difficulty in making their franchise payments to the franchisor because the business proved less profitable than expected; and that the franchisor, having promised that the Hoffmans could make reduced payments for a specified period, then reneged on the promise. Even though, in this hypothetical situation, the franchisor's promise would not form part of an exchange, we can be sure that the Hoffmans' reliance on

---

[6]   Grant Gilmore *The Death of Contract* (Columbus Ohio, Ohio State University Press, 1974).

the promise would not go unprotected. So much for American contract law, but how would an English court treat such acts of reliance? Would reliance-based claims, argued in *contract*,[7] be struck out as disclosing no reasonable cause of action (or no defence), or would the courts find a way of responding to the perceived unfairness of leaving the relying party unprotected?

According to Corbin, there is ample support in English law for the view that 'an informal promise may be enforceable by reason of action in reliance upon it, even though that action was not bargained for by the promisor and was not performed as an agreed exchange for the promise'.[8] This, Corbin contends, 'is demonstrated by the decisions of the courts of common law from the very beginnings of the action of assumpsit, by the decrees of the courts of equity making a very flexible use of the doctrine of "estoppel", and by the judgments of the modern courts using the formless and all-inclusive "civil action".'[9] Within the modern law, however, support for Corbin's reading of English law would most readily be identified with the development of the doctrine of equitable estoppel, as seminally articulated by Denning J in the *High Trees*[10] case.

(i) Equitable estoppel

The emergence of the *High Trees* principle is one of the more curious episodes in the modern history of the law of contract. The plaintiffs leased a block of flats in London to the defendants in September 1939. However, as a result of the war and fear of bombing, people moved out of London, and the defendants found that the flats became

---

[7]   For the possibility of such protection grounded in the *tort of negligence*, see *Box v Midland Bank* [1979] 2 Lloyd's Rep 391; and for an (unsuccessful) attempt to argue for such protection based on *restitution*, see *Regalian Properties plc v London Dockland Development Corpn* [1995] 1 All ER 1005.

[8]   *Corbin on Contracts* (St Paul, Minn: West Publishing Co, 1963) para 194.

[9]   Ibid.

[10]   *Central London Property Trust v High Trees House* [1947] 1 KB 130. Corbin also saw a flexible use of the doctrine of estoppel in *Fenner v Blake* [1900] 1 QB 426; *Re Wickham* [1917] 34 TLR 158; and *Re Porter (William) & Co Ltd* [1937] 2 All ER 361.

difficult to sub-let. In January 1940, therefore, the plain-tiffs agreed to accept half rent. No term was set on this reduction. By the end of the war in May 1945 the flats were again full. The plaintiffs were by now in receivership, and the receiver claimed that he was entitled to the full rent originally agreed for the property from January 1940 to date, and for the future. To test the legal position, he sued for the full rent for the last two quarters of 1945. Denning J took the view that the agreement of January 1940 was intended to operate only during the exceptional conditions created by the war, which had ceased to exist by the last two quarters of 1945. Accordingly, the plaintiff was entitled to full rent for those quarters. Denning J also expressed the opinion, however, that had the plaintiff sought to recover for the period 1940–45, then the claim would have failed on the ground of equitable estoppel. In reaching this con-clusion, Denning J had to surmount two difficulties. In the first place, the defendants had given no consideration in the classical sense in return for the plaintiff's promise: they had simply paid less rent. Secondly, the doctrine of estoppel was generally understood to relate to misrepre-sentations as to existing facts, not promises as to the future (such as the landlords' promise to reduce the ground rent).

Estoppel *in pais* was in fact a rule of evidence.[11] The bizarre case of *Freeman v Cooke*[12] is a good illustration of the operation of this doctrine. The defendant, a sheriff, had a writ of execution against the goods of Joseph and Benjamin Broadbent. Benjamin Broadbent's brother William was also in difficulties, and expecting a writ of execution. Apparently unaware of his brother's problems, William removed his goods to his brother Benjamin's house. When the sheriff's officers arrived at Benjamin's house, with the writ against Benjamin, William assumed they had come to seize his (William's) goods. He therefore told them that the goods on the premises were Benjamin's, and they were promptly seized. Since in fact they were William's, the seizure was prima facie wrongful. Parke B eventually held that the seizure was unlawful, but only because William, when he realised the true situation, had tried to explain matters to the officers. Nevertheless, but for this fact, Parke B would

---

[11]   Hence 'pais' or 'pays', the people out of whom a jury is taken.
[12]   (1848) 2 Ex 654.

have held the seizure lawful. He cited the rule in *Pickard v Sears*[13] which states:

'Where one, by his words or conduct, wilfully causes another to believe in the existence of a certain state of things, and induces him to act on that belief, or to alter his own previous position, the former is concluded from averring against the latter a different state of things as existing at the same time.'

Parke B explained 'wilfully' as follows:[14]

'By the term "wilfully" . . . we must understand, if not that the party represents that to be true which he knows to be untrue, at least, that he means his representation to be acted upon and it is acted upon . . . and if whatever a man's real intention may be, he so conducts himself that a reasonable man would take the representation to be true . . . and did act upon it as true . . . the party making the representation would equally be precluded from contesting its truth.'

Parke B also held, in accordance with long-established precedent, that such an estoppel did not need to be specially pleaded by the defendant.[15]

Estoppel was supposed therefore to relate to representations of fact. The leading authority for this proposition was the House of Lords decision in *Jordan v Money*,[16] though it must be conceded that the distinction between statements of fact and promises is not at all clear cut.[17] In that case the plaintiff had led the defendant to believe she would not enforce a bond for a sum of money which she held against him. In reliance upon this, the defendant had got married. The plaintiff's conduct could actually have been interpreted as either, 'I have abandoned the bond' (which looks like a statement of fact), or 'I will not enforce it' (which looks like a promise). The House of Lords, however, took it as a promise not to enforce the bond, and held for the

---

13   (1837) 6 A & E 469.
14   (1848) 2 Ex 654, 663.
15   Citing Wms Saund Vol 1 p 326, n 2. See Vaughan Williams's edition 1871 vol 1, n (d). The reason for this was presumably that it was a rule of evidence, though estoppel could be pleaded if the defendant wished to do so.
16   (1854) 5 HLC 185.
17   On the related point which arises out of some decisions on the Trade Descriptions Act 1968, see *R v Sunair Holidays Ltd* [1973] 2 All ER 1233; and *British Airways Board v Taylor* [1976] 1 All ER 65.

plaintiff.[18] This decision had been followed in *Citizens'
Bank of Louisiana v First National Bank of New Orleans*,[19]
and obviously presented a problem for giving effect to a
promise of the sort given by the landlords in the *High Trees*
case. Denning J, however, distinguished *Jordan v Money*
on the ground that the promisor had made it clear that she
did not intend to be legally bound by her promise, an interpretation which, with due respect to the learned judge, it
is difficult to extract from the report.[20] He went on to refer
to another line of authority, not involving cases of estoppel
in the strict sense, but which involved promises intended
to be binding, intended to be acted upon, and in fact acted
upon. They did not go so far as to give a cause of action in
damages for breach of such a promise, but the courts had
refused to allow the party making the promise to act inconsistently with it. The cases involving this principle were
Hughes v Metropolitan Rly Co,[21] *Birmingham and District
Land v London and North Western Rly Co*,[22] and *Salisbury
(Marquess) v Gilmore*.[23] Each of these cases involved detrimental reliance on the part of the promisee. For example,
in *Hughes v Metropolitan Rly Co*, the tenant under a lease
had the obligation to repair the premises. In October 1874
the landlord gave the tenant six months' notice to repair. If
the tenant failed to comply with this, the lease would be
forfeited. In November, the landlord began negotiations
with the tenant for the sale to the tenant of the reversion

---

[18]   The fact that this case involved a bond is important, and failure to
appreciate the significance of this, has led to the rule being generalised
beyond its proper field of application (rather in the same way as the
rule in *Pinnel*'s case – see p 103). For a critique along these lines, see
Atiyah *Consideration in Contracts* (Australian National University
Press) 50–8; Spencer Bower and Turner *Estoppel by Representation* 3rd
edn (1977) pp 31–5.
[19]   (1873) LR 6 HL 352.
[20]   The key to the decision appears to be the fact that there *was* a contract between the parties, forgiveness of the bond being promised in
consideration of the defendant's marriage. However, that contract was
unenforceable because it was not evidenced in writing as required by
the Statute of Frauds – and the House was not minded to encourage
estoppel to be employed as a means of avoiding the Statute. See Atiyah,
'Consideration: a Restatement' in *Essays on Contract* (Oxford,
Clarendon Press, 1986) pp 234–5.
[21]   (1877) 2 App Cas 439, 448.
[22]   (1888) 40 Ch D 268, 286.
[23]   [1942] 2 KB 38, 51.

of the lease. These negotiations were broken off on 31 December 1874. Because of the negotiations, the tenant had taken no steps to carry out the repairs. On the expiry of the six months, the landlord purported to forfeit the lease. The House of Lords held that the opening of negotiations amounted to a representation by the landlord that, as long as they continued, the notice would not be enforced. Consequently, the six months did not begin to run until the negotiations had been broken off.

Although the result in each of these three cases was formulated as an equitable principle, in point of fact, each could have been explained on the basis of the simple proposition which seems to underlie many common law cases of waiver, namely that you cannot take advantage of a self-induced non-performance of a contract.[24] Denning J, however, chose to rely on the equitable principle, possibly because he thought that a common law waiver of rights was revocable (ie the rights could be resumed by notice); so that after due notice the landlords in *High Trees* could have claimed the full rent for the period of the war – a view which, if he held it, we will argue was mistaken. Denning J, moreover, arguably went further than the existing equitable authorities in two respects. In the first place it had seemed that detrimental reliance was necessary, in the sense that the promisee must have altered his situation for the worse in reliance on the promise, a proposition affirmed by the Privy Council in *Emmanuel Ayodeji Ajayi v R T Briscoe (Nigeria) Ltd*.[25] Yet it was difficult to see how the defendants in *High Trees* had relied on the plaintiffs' promise to their detriment: they had simply paid less rent. It was sufficient according to Denning J, however, that the defendants had acted on the promise – a position he affirmed in *W J Alan & Co v El Nasr Export and Import Co*.[26] Secondly, he took the view that the plaintiffs' rights were extinguished, and not merely suspended.

As a result of these views, if they were correct, English law had apparently managed to reach the position that rights might be extinguished by a promise, even in the absence of detrimental reliance. However, English law had also

---

[24]   See Adams (1972) 36 Conv 245.
[25]   [1964] 3 All ER 556.
[26]   [1972] 2 QB 189.

determined that rights could not be created by reliance on a promise, however detrimental, unless pursuant to a contract (supported by consideration in the classical sense).[27] This latter restriction on the scope of the *High Trees* principle was set out in the important case of *Combe v Combe*.[28] There, a wife had started divorce proceedings against her husband, who promised her £100 per annum as maintenance. No order for maintenance was made by the court. No payments were made, and the wife sued on the promise. Byrne J, at first instance, gave judgment for the wife on the basis that the husband's promise had induced the plaintiff to forbear from applying for a maintenance order. As Byrne J understood the recently enunciated *High Trees* principle, a promisee who relied on a promise seriously given by a promisor could hold the latter to his word (irrespective of whether the relationship between the promisor and the promisee could be analysed as a bargained-for exchange). However, the Court of Appeal, of which Denning LJ was by now a member, held that Byrne J had misinterpreted the *High Trees* principle. The principle was of limited scope: it did not create new causes of action where none existed before; it did not displace the need for consideration where a promisee sued on a promise; in short, the doctrine was available only 'as a shield, not as a sword'.[29]

(ii) Common law waiver

In *Woodhouse A C Israel Cocoa Ltd SA v Nigerian Produce Marketing Co Ltd*[30] Lord Hailsham expressed the view that the line of cases beginning with *High Trees* needed to be reduced to a coherent body of doctrine. It is difficult to quarrel with this view. However, if we are to evaluate the reception of reliance-based protection into English contract law, we need to broaden our field of inquiry to include the doctrine of common law waiver.

In *W J Alan & Co Ltd v El Nasr Export and Import Co*[31] Lord

---

[27]   Cf *Jordan v Money* above.
[28]   [1951] 2 KB 215.
[29]   Ibid, at 224 (Birkett LJ).
[30]   [1972] AC 741, 758.
[31]   [1972] 2 QB 189.

Denning MR asserted that common law waiver was merely an instance of the general principle that:

> 'If one party, by his conduct, leads another to believe that the strict rights arising under the contract will not be insisted upon, intending that the other should act on that belief, and he does act on it, then the first party will not afterwards be allowed to insist on the strict legal rights when it would be inequitable for him to do so.'[32]

In fact, Lord Denning MR was not the first person to argue that common law waiver could be subsumed under a number of other principles. In *Waiver Distributed*,[33] John S Ewart argued that all that is usually spoken of as waiver was 'referable to one or other of the well-defined and well-understood departments of the law, election, estoppel, contract and release'. Whilst it must be admitted that the term 'waiver' has been used loosely to cover a variety of situations which might more accurately be described by some other term, Ewart perhaps overstated his case. We would argue that there is an area properly described as waiver which is referable to common law principles.

The first of these common law principles is the proposition stated above, that a person cannot be permitted to take advantage of a self-induced non-performance of a contract. Consider, for example, the situation in *Plevins v Downing*.[34] There, the defendant had purchased from the plaintiffs a quantity of pig-iron to be delivered by a certain date. On that date the plaintiffs had made short delivery, as a result of which non-performance they were in breach. When the balance was forwarded, the defendants refused to accept it. The plaintiffs sued for non-acceptance. It was held that, as the plaintiffs had not shown that they had withheld delivery in consequence of a request by the defendants, and had not been ready and willing to perform, the action must fail. It is quite likely that the defendants, having been left short at the time when the iron should have been delivered, had secured the amount they needed elsewhere. Clearly, it would have been unfair to have permitted the sellers to have dumped the balance of the iron on the buyers at their convenience. Equally, though, *had the short delivery been at the buyers'*

---

[32]   Ibid, p 213.
[33]   Harvard University Press (1911).
[34]   (1876) LR 1 CPD 220.

request, it would have been unfair to have held the sellers liable for non-performance or to have allowed the buyers to cite the short delivery as a ground for subsequent non-acceptance.[35]

We can see, therefore, that this type of waiver has two principal aspects: first, where a party by his waiver causes a non-performance and then tries to sue on it; secondly, where a party by his waiver causes non-performance, and then tries to set it up as a defence.[36] An example of the first would be a case where a buyer of goods tells the seller who is ready and willing to perform, not to deliver on the delivery date, and then tries to sue for non-delivery. An example of the second would be where the buyer of goods tells the seller who is ready and willing to perform, not to deliver on the delivery date, and then refuses to accept at a later date setting up the non-delivery on the original date as a defence.[37]

There is scarcely anything remarkable in the proposition that a party cannot take advantage of a self-induced non-performance, indeed it is common sense. In another group of waiver cases, however, we find one side acquiescing in, rather than encouraging or inducing, non-performance. For example, in *Ogle v Earl Vane*,[38] the defendant contracted to sell to the plaintiff 500 tons of iron, delivery to extend to 25 July. Owing to an accident at his works, the defendant did

---

[35]   But, would the sellers be liable for non-performance if, having acceded to the buyers' request for short delivery, they refused to deliver when subsequently given notice by the buyers asking for delivery of the balance? Such a question arose in *Tyers v Rosedale and Ferryhill Iron Co* (1875) LR 10 Ex 195 where the defendants had contracted to deliver iron to the plaintiffs by certain instalments. At the request of the plaintiffs, however, several instalments were delivered short. The plaintiffs then demanded delivery of the balance, but the defendants refused. The Court of Exchequer Chamber held that they were liable to deliver the balance. To the suggestion that the plaintiffs were at fault in not being ready and willing to receive the full instalments, Blackburn J said (at p 197) the answer was, 'We were ready to receive the iron when you were ready to deliver it, but we requested you not to require us to receive it, and you consented'. For other cases illustrating the same principle, see eg *Hickman v Haynes* (1875) LR 10 CP 598; and *Levey v Goldberg* [1922] 1 KB 688.

[36]   Here there is no question of the party in whose favour the waiver was made suing on the *promise*; he sues on the original undertakings. This important distinction has misled some writers: see [1963] CLJ 222.

[37]   As in the case of *Hickman v Haynes* (1875) LR 10 CP 598.

[38]   (1868) LR 3 QB 272.

not deliver on that date. Between August and February the plaintiff and defendant negotiated about the matter and in February the defendant finally defaulted. Damages were assessed having regard to the (higher) market price of iron in February, not July. Willes J said: 'the plaintiff's right to purchase was carried over from July by the defendant requesting forbearance and the plaintiff assenting to the request'.[39] How is this to be explained? In principle, in relation to such acquiescence cases, two lines of explanation may be relevant. According to the first line of explanation, the apparent breach (associated with the initial act of non-performance) may be shown, on more careful analysis, to be no actionable breach at all. If, for example, a seller is apparently bound to deliver goods by a certain date, but defaults in this, and the default is ignored by both parties who behave as though no default has occurred, one inference is that the delivery date was merely a declaration of intention binding in honour only, and not intended to have any legal effect. Alternatively, it might be that certain excusing circumstances obtained such that the non-performance was not actionable as a breach. This kind of explanation, however, adds nothing to the jurisprudence of waiver. To bring waiver into the analysis, we need to look to a second line of explanation – an explanation which, by contrast, treats the initial act of non-performance as an actionable breach. On this account, when the innocent party, instead of acting on the breach, acquiesces in the situation, there is a waiver of rights. Essentially, such acquiescence encourages the contract-breaker to believe either that the innocent party is prepared to excuse the breach[40] or that certain remedial options are not to be exercised. The signals generated by the innocent party's acquiescence (and the concomitant waiver) could be quite complex (and confusing). For example, let us suppose that an initial breach is repudiatory, giving the innocent party the option of putting an end to the contract. If the innocent party takes no remedial action, what is the contract-breaker to make of the acquiescence – that the innocent party is excusing the breach, that the innocent party is not excusing the breach but is waiving all remedies, or that the innocent

---

[39]   At p 280.
[40]   Or, even to treat the non-performance as a non-breach.

party is not excusing the breach but is electing (at least for the time being) to keep the contract alive? Whilst each factual situation will give rise to its own interpretive difficulties, it seems an elementary principle of fairness that the innocent party, having acquiesced in the breach, should not be permitted to exercise a remedial option as though no such waiver had occurred.[41]

(iii) The doctrinal basis for modification of contracts

To the extent that the modern law is moving towards the evolution of a separate doctrine of modification of contracts,[42] such a doctrine must as far as possible be based on coherent and comprehensible principles. From *High Trees* onwards, Lord Denning attempted to articulate such principles under the umbrella doctrine of equitable estoppel. As we have remarked, however, the scope and coherence of equitable estoppel remains problematic. Would it be more rational, therefore, to look to common law waiver as the basis for a modern doctrine of modification?

How would the *High Trees* case be decided under the common law doctrine of waiver? We suggested above that a reason why Denning J chose the route he did was because he thought that under the common law doctrine the landlords could have resumed their right to full rentals after notice. Could they? In the first place, it needs to be borne in mind that a covenant to pay rent can be broken in one of two ways: by failing to pay on the day stipulated,[43] or by not paying at all. If the landlord in *High Trees* had said 'Do not pay the full rent on the date it is due, pay 50% then and 50% six months later', he could not have complained about non-payment of the full rent on the due date, but he could complain and take action if the second instalment were unpaid. He did not induce that non-performance. In this case the action is for non-payment of the sum of money due, not for non-payment on the date specified in the lease. The breach induced by the landlords in *High Trees* however was

---

[41] See below for our discussion of the illustrative case of *Charles Rickards Ltd v Oppenhaim* [1950] 1 KB 616.
[42] *Panchaud Frères SA v Etablissements General Grain Co* [1970] 1 Lloyd's Rep 53, 59 (per Winn LJ). And see section 3 below.
[43] *Green's* case (1582) Cro Eliz 3.

of the second sort, for it produced a total non-payment of a part of the rent. In such circumstances, could the unpaid rent subsequently be recovered? Suppose that a landlord wanting to be rid of a tenant holding under a lease, told the tenant, an ignorant layman, that he would reduce the rent, so that the amount foregone would build up to a considerable sum of money after a period. Now, such a landlord surely could not use an action to recover this sum as a way of recovering possession of the property, in effect saying 'Yes, I did agree to take a reduced rent but this promise is not binding on me therefore the tenant must take the consequences if he did not pay the rent reserved by the lease'? The landlord is the author of the default in respect of which he is attempting to take action. To the argument that the landlords in *High Trees* only reduced the rent because the tenant was in financial difficulties, it may be responded that a party is not prevented from saying he is ready and willing to perform, merely because he is short of money. Courts do not generally enquire into financial incapacity. Even bankruptcy does not generally entitle a party to repudiate.[44] A party *required* to pay the full rent, might, after all, have been able to raise it in a number of ways. All that matters at the end of the day is that the creditor *freely* assents to the debtor's non-performance.

The importance of assent being free is highlighted by the reasoning of the Court of Appeal in *D & C Builders v Rees*.[45] There, the plaintiff builders who were in financial difficulties, were in effect forced to accept a lesser sum from the defendant clients in settlement of their bill for building works, by the threat that if they did not accept it, they would get nothing. It was held unanimously that the builders were able to recover the balance of the sum due. For the majority of the court, the issue was straightforward. Although the builders had promised to take a lesser sum in settlement of the defendants' account, the defendants had given no consideration for this concession. Moreover, in the absence of a doctrine of economic duress[46] to protect the builders against the coercive tactics of the defendants, this was not a case for relaxation of the consideration requirement.

---

44 *Brooke v Hewitt* (1796) 3 Ves 253.
45 [1966] 2 QB 617.
46 It will be recalled that the doctrine of economic duress was not developed in England until the late 1970s. See ch 2.

Taking a different approach to the majority (but concurring in the outcome of the case), Lord Denning MR confirmed a suggestion that he had made in the *High Trees* case, that in principle the doctrine of equitable estoppel must protect debtors who rely on concessions made by their creditors. However, the equitable nature of this protective principle entailed that it was not available to the debtor defendants who had, after all, unfairly pressurised the creditor builders into making their concession.

Suppose, though, that the builders in *D & C Builders v Rees* had freely agreed to accept a lesser sum in satisfaction of the clients' debt. If modification of contracts were to be based on the doctrine of common law waiver (or, indeed, on equitable estoppel), the clients would have a good defence should the builders subsequently seek to recover the balance of the original debt. In other words, the logic of common law waiver (as of equitable estoppel) is that free acceptance of a lesser sum would be a good defence to a claim for a larger sum owed under a contract. Yet, this is supposedly contrary to the ancient rule in *Pinnel*'s case,[47] a rule upheld in the late nineteenth century by the House of Lords in *Foakes v Beer*.[48] Mrs Beer had obtained a judgment against Dr Foakes for £2,090. Dr Foakes asked for time to pay, and the parties agreed in writing that he could pay £500 at once, and the balance by instalments. If he did so, Mrs Beer agreed not to claim interest on the judgment (which she was entitled to). Dr Foakes paid as agreed, but Mrs Beer nevertheless claimed interest. It was held that she was entitled to claim this. *Pinnel*'s case, properly understood, however,

---

[47]   (1602) 5 Co Rep 117a.

[48]   (1884) 9 App Cas 605. In fact, historically, the key feature of *Pinnel*'s case was that it concerned a bond. The rule may seem draconian, but it was a restricted rule applying specifically to penal bonds (see generally, Simpson, 'The Penal Bond with Conditional Defeasance' (1966) 82 LQR 392). The action on a bond was debt *sur obligation* and, until the nineteenth century, this remained the only form of action to enforce a debt due under a deed. In *Cumber v Wane* (1721) 1 Strange 426, however, the law appears to have taken a wrong turning in applying *Pinnel*'s case out of context, where the action was *indebitatus assumpsit* and the debt did not, it would seem, arise out of a penal bond. Regrettably, in spite of the discussion of *Cumber v Wane* in *Foakes v Beer*, the House did not pick up this error, and the true intent of *Pinnel*'s case was misread (see Simpson loc cit pp 404-405). On this ground, it can be argued, *Foakes v Beer* was founded on a misreading of the precedents.

turned on rather a technical point. The issue in that case, which involved a bond,[49] was whether or not the defence of satisfaction of the debt lay. Satisfaction required an accord or agreement,[50] supported by fresh consideration. Agreement to do what one was already bound to do could not constitute fresh consideration.[51] In *Foakes v Beer* the House of Lords met the defendant's argument that an agreement, unsupported by consideration, barred the plaintiff's action, by applying a rule developed in the context of the action of debt *sur obligation*, and misapplied to the action of assumpsit. We would suggest that a more sustainable argument for a defendant in a similar situation to Dr Foakes would be that it was Mrs Beer's conduct which had induced the very non-payment about which she was complaining.[52]

This reading provides an explanation of the case of *Buttery v Pickard*,[53] which is a little difficult to explain in terms of *promissory* estoppel. As in the *High Trees* case, the landlord in *Buttery v Pickard* agreed to accept a reduced rental, in that case up to October 1941, when the tenant had the option to terminate a fourteen-year lease. She did not terminate, but continued to pay the reduced rent, gradually increasing it to the full amount due in 1944. The landlord sued for the arrears accruing since October 1941. Humphrey J, citing *Fenner v Blake*,[54] described it as 'an ordinary case of estoppel, the landlord having said in terms to his lessee 'You need not pay more than 15s a week' and the tenant having acted on it. But the tenant did not act on any promise of the landlord in not terminating her lease, since the promise to accept a reduced rent, by its terms, was to last only until October 1941.[55] What had happened was that the tenant had tendered the reduced rent, and the landlord had accepted it as before. In other words, the landlord freely acquiesced in the very act about which he was now complaining. But if the doctrine of equitable estoppel is based on a *promise*

---

[49] See n 48 above for an explanation of the significance of this.
[50] *Peytoe*'s case (1611) 9 Co Rep 77b.
[51] *Stilk v Myrick* (1809) 2 Camp 317: see below.
[52] See below for a further line of argument.
[53] (1945) 174 LT 144.
[54] [1900] 1 QB 426.
[55] The landlord's solicitors had specifically stated that the reduced rent was not to apply in what they called 'the option period' beginning in October 1941.

intended to be acted upon, and in fact acted upon, it is difficult to apply it to the events which had occurred, for the simple reason that there was no promise by its terms covering the relevant period. Fairly clearly, in *Buttery v Pickard*, it was the landlord's acquiescent *conduct* that founded the estoppel.[56]

This explanation also fits quite well with the decision in *Tool Metal Manufacturing Co v Tungsten Electric Co (No 1)*.[57] The plaintiffs (TMMC) had given the defendants (TECO) a licence to import, use and sell certain patented alloys. The licence was to last from 1937 to 1947. In return for this licence, TECO were to pay 'compensation'[58] for sales in excess of a stipulated quota, when the alloys were not obtained from TMMC.[59] After the outbreak of war, TMMC agreed to forego this compensation, a new agreement between the parties being envisaged after the end of hostilities. Negotiations broke down on this new agreement, and TECO sued TMMC alleging fraud and breach of an agreement to end compensation. TMMC counter-claimed for compensation from the end of the war. TECO's action was dismissed. TMMC's counter-claim was also dismissed on the ground that insufficient notice had been given that they were resuming their rights. The rights were held to be suspended on the principle of *Hughes v Metropolitan Rly Co*,[60] and *Birmingham and District Land v London and North Western Rly Co*.[61] The requirement of acting can certainly be found in this case, for TECO had continued to operate under the licence, which they were not bound to do, on the basis of TMMC's promise. The rights could also have been held to be suspended, however, on the basis that TMMC had induced the non-performance. In fact, however, it is something of a puzzle to know why the court needed to deal with

---

[56]   Cf Lord Denning's reflections in 'Recent Developments in the Doctrine of Consideration' (1952) 15 MLR 1, for a sharply drawn distinction between the cases involving *promises* and those involving *conduct* on the part of the representor.

[57]   (1955) 59 RPC 108.

[58]   Ie a royalty. It was presumably referred to as 'compensation' for tax reasons.

[59]   A provision which it would be highly inadvisable to include in a patent licence at the present day having regard to EU competition law.

[60]   (1877) 2 App Cas 439.

[61]   (1888) 40 Ch D 286.

this issue at all, for on the pleadings, TMMC seem to have admitted that their rights were suspended for some period at least.[62] Be that as it may, it is interesting that, in the second action between the parties,[63] Romer LJ used the analogy of a licence to occupy land in relation to the notice necessary to resume TMMC's legal rights. There is implicit in this analogy the view that if a person gives someone a licence to come on to his land, and then tries to sue in trespass, he will fail. The case of a patent licence would be similar.

Whilst, in view of the accepted orthodoxy, there may be seen to be difficulties about applying a theory of free waiver of contractual rights to the payment of a sum of money due under a contract, we would argue that there are no reasons of policy for not doing so. The objection most likely to be made is the 'floodgates' argument: that it would encourage debtors who were seeking to evade their obligations to claim that what was paid on account was in fact short payment induced by the creditor.[64] However, in order to succeed in the defence, the debtor would have to show: (a) that he was ready and willing to perform; and (b) that the reason why he did not perform was because of the creditor's free assent to the modification in respect of which the creditor is now complaining. Provided that the condition of free assent is stringently applied, as in *D & C Builders v Rees*, then the law is perfectly capable of protecting creditors who are in effect blackmailed into accepting lesser sums, in place of the larger ones they are owed.

To summarise, once an act of non-performance has been induced, it can never thereafter be the subject of an action. On the other hand, if the act is of a continuing or repeated nature, as in *High Trees* or *Tool Metal Manufacturing*, reasonable notice that a party is again expected to perform according to the original terms of the contract will have the effect that the 'waiving' party is no longer inducing the non-performance about which he is complaining. On the other hand, in the case of waivers of the kind where one side acquiesces in the other's non-performance, notice may be simply one of the factors which will determine when a contract has finally been breached. Thus, in *Charles*

---

[62]   See [1963] CLJ 222.
[63]   [1954] 2 All ER 28, 41.
[64]   See Stoljar 3 U Queen LJ 356.

Rickards v Oppenhaim,[65] the defendant had ordered from the plaintiffs a motor car to be delivered in seven months, which would have been by 20 March 1948. The car was not delivered by that date, but the defendant did not cancel the contract. He asked for delivery in time for Ascot 1948. It was not delivered in time for Ascot. Finally, since he required the car in time for his holidays in August, he wrote on 29 June saying that he could not accept delivery after 25 July 1948. Delivery was tendered in October, and the defendant refused to accept the car. Finnemore J held that time was of the essence of the contract, but that this condition had been waived by the defendant. However, the letter of 29 June made time again of the essence. Alternatively, it might be argued that the real agreement was for delivery in a reasonable time, delivery in seven months being a sort of target. There had to come a point, however, where the plaintiff's late delivery amounted, first, to a breach, and then to a repudiatory breach. Taking all the facts together, including the defendant's letter of 29 June, that latter date was 25 July.

(iv) Synthesis

The doctrinal response to the problems presented by the modification of contracts has been quite remarkably complex, not least perhaps because it has been elaborated around the margins of classical consideration theory. Thus, in England, over and above the doctrine of common law waiver, we find the *High Trees* principle – a principle of uncertain scope and application – being developed. This, surely, is a prime example of too many doctrines chasing too few ideas.

If we stand back from the complexity of the case-law, two principles of fair dealing stand out. First, if one party, A, at A's own instigation, induces or encourages fellow contractor, B, to deviate from the agreed contractual performance, then A should not be able to take advantage of B's non-performance. Secondly, if one party, A, freely agrees to fellow contractor B deviating from the agreed contractual performance, then A should be bound by the modification so freely agreed. In all cases falling under either of these principles,

---

[65]   [1950] 1 KB 616.

B's non-perfomance will have been authorised in advance by A.[66] As we have seen, however, there is another kind of modification. In some cases, B's non-performance is not authorised in advance by A.[67] Nevertheless, A acquiesces in B's non-performance. Accordingly, a third principle of fair dealing is this: where B's non-performance has not been induced, encouraged, or freely agreed to in advance by A, but A none the less freely and knowingly acquiesces in B's non-performance, then A should be permitted to exercise contractual rights and remedies in relation to B's non-performance only in so far as this is consistent with giving fair effect to A's waiver of rights. If the law is to be rational, it needs to incorporate these principles clearly and explicitly; and, to this extent, it scarcely matters whether the doctrinal vehicle is common law waiver or equitable estoppel – although, given the antecedents of the *High Trees* principle, common law waiver might have provided a more secure foundation for a doctrine of modification of contracts.

Finally, although the case-law on equitable estoppel underlines the need for reliance, there is a notorious ambivalence about whether the reliance must be detrimental. Moreover, there is a subtle shift in the location of reliance if one compares the inducement and encouragement cases with the acquiescence cases. In the former, the act of non-performance is the expression of reliance; in the latter, however, non-performance precedes reliance (which is, so to speak, passively induced by the acquiescence). This prompts the thought that the deeper justification for the basic principles of fair dealing is not so much actual reliance (whether detrimental or otherwise) as legitimate expectation.

---

[66]   Cf Lord Denning, n 56 above, at p 5:

> Where one party deliberately promises to waive, modify or discharge his strict legal rights, intending the other party to act on the faith of the promise, and the other party actually does act on it, then it is contrary . . . to good faith, to allow the promisor to go back on his promise.

[67]   A point emphasised in Tony Dugdale and David Yates, 'Variation, Waiver and Estoppel – A Reappraisal' (1976) 39 MLR 680.

3. *WILLIAMS V ROFFEY BROTHERS AND NICHOLLS:* A NEW PRAGMATISM?

In *The Proodos C*,[68] the parties had agreed a price for the carriage of some trucks by sea. When the carrier arrived at the port where the trucks were to be unloaded, he demanded that the price be increased (otherwise the trucks would not be unloaded). In order to get the trucks unloaded, the owner reluctantly agreed to pay an additional sum. Subsequently, at an arbitration of the matter between the parties, the arbitrator ruled that, in principle, the truck owner was bound by his promise to pay an additional sum – such, the arbitrator held, was the effect of the doctrine of equitable estoppel. On appeal, it was held that the arbitrator had made an elementary mistake. The *High Trees* principle, as famously declared in *Combe v Combe*, is available only as a defence, not as a cause of action.[69] If the carrier were to succeed, consideration would have to be shown.

Could the carrier in *The Proodos C* show consideration? According to the classical exchange theory, a contractual cause of action arose only where an agreement existed supported by consideration moving from each party, in the sense of the price for which the promise of the other party was bought. It followed that there could be no consideration if all that the plaintiff gave, or promised to give, in return for the defendant's promise, was the performance of an obligation imposed on him already. Thus, as we have seen, in *Stilk v Myrick*[70] following the desertion of two members of the crew of a sailing ship, the master had promised the remaining members extra wages if they would work the vessel home shorthanded. They sailed the vessel home, but were not given the extra wages, and they sued. Following the earlier case of *Harris v Watson*[71] Lord Ellenborough denied the plaintiff's claim. However, whereas Lord Kenyon CJ had based his decision on public policy (that to allow the claim would encourage sailors to blackmail the masters of vessels for extra wages), Lord Ellenborough preferred to base his decision on the absence of consideration. Now it is quite

[68] *Syros Shipping Co SA v Elaghill Trading Co, The Proodos C* [1981] 3 All ER 189.
[69] See *Combe v Combe* [1951] 2 KB 215.
[70] (1809) 2 Camp 317, p 27 above.
[71] (1791) Peake 102.

possible that Lord Ellenborough was not using the term 'consideration' in the sense that that term is used in modern textbooks, but rather in the older sense of having regard to the circumstances in which a promise was made in determining whether or not to enforce it.[72] Nevertheless, the case came to be cited for the 'somewhat obvious rule, that there is no consideration if all that the plaintiff does is to perform, or to promise the performance of, an obligation already imposed upon him by a previous contract between him and the defendant'.[73] Applying this obvious rule, the carrier in *The Proodos C* must fail – and, given the coercive circumstances in which the carrier extracted the promise from the truck owner, this answer seems both obvious and right.

Yet, in many contractual situations, it makes perfectly good sense for a party to promise an extra reward in return for the other party performing what he is already obliged to do. Provided that the promise is given freely, it is irrational for the law to obstruct the enforcement of the promise by insisting on the classical requirement of exchange (particularly in the light of the development of an independent doctrine of economic duress). Having greater regard for commercial considerations than for classical theory, in the landmark case of *Williams v Roffey Bros and Nicholls (Contractors) Ltd*,[74] the Court of Appeal held that a promise by A to carry out his existing contractual obligations to B may count as good consideration in relation to a promise freely given by B to pay A an additional sum for the performance of those obligations.

The facts of *Williams v Roffey* were as follows. The defendants were main contractors employed by Shepherds Bush Housing Association Ltd to refurbish 27 flats in a block of flats in London. The defendants engaged the plaintiff to carry out the carpentry work, this comprising the carpentry work on the roof of the block and the first and second fix carpentry work in the flats themselves. The contract price for the work was £20,000, with an implied term, as the judge ruled, providing for interim payments at reasonable intervals. Before the sub-contract work was completed, however, the plaintiff ran into financial difficulties, partly, so the

---

[72]   See p 26.
[73]   *Cheshire, Fifoot and Furmston: Law of Contract* (12th edn, 1991) 90.
[74]   [1990] 1 All ER 512.

judge found, because the work had been under-priced and partly because of the plaintiff's inadequate supervision of his men. At the material time, the plaintiff had completed the roofing work, the first fix to all 27 flats, and he had substantially completed the second fix to nine of the flats. The defendants, fearing that the carpentry work would not be completed on time, and facing an agreed damages clause[75] in the main contract should it overrun, promised to pay the plaintiff an additional sum of £10,300. This extra money was to be paid at the rate of £575 for each flat on which the carpenty work was completed. In the light of this agreement, the plaintiff proceeded with the work. However, with the carpentry work on 17 flats substantially completed, he ceased working.

On these facts, the trial judge held that the plaintiff was entitled to £5,000, made up as follows: (i) £2,200 as a reasonable proportion of the outstanding money on the original £20,000 contract; and (ii) £2,800 in respect of the additional sums promised (calculated as eight flats at £575 each (£4,600) less deductions for minor defects and incomplete items). Given that the defendants had actually paid only £1,500 of this, the plaintiff was within his rights to cease work and to recover a net sum of £3,500.

The defendants, on appeal, contended that the promised additional payments were not recoverable because: (i) the payments were due only on full, not merely substantial completion of the work; and (ii) the promise was not supported by consideration. The Court of Appeal unanimously rejected these contentions. It is the way in which they approached the second contention which is of interest to us here.[76]

Given the long-standing interpretation of *Stilk v Myrick* in the standard textbooks which we set out above, how could the plaintiff be entitled to recover any part of the additional payments? It might be argued that in *Stilk v Myrick* the promise was gratuitous, or that the promisor derived no benefit, but these lines of argument seem to be

---

[75] The judgments refer to the relevant clause as a 'penalty' clause. Although it is commonplace in the construction industry to talk about the contractor being liable to 'penalties' for late completion, we assume that the clause in question was simply a liquidated damages clause.

[76] For comment on the first contention, see John N. Adams and Roger Brownsword 'Contract, Consideration and the Critical Path' (1990) 53 MLR 536, 538.

question-begging and unconvincing. The better answer, and
the one most explicitly adopted by Purchas LJ[77] must be that
Stilk v Myrick was a case involving what would now be recognised as economic duress.[78] Even if we accept, however, that
there was no economic duress involved in *Williams v
Roffey*, the question remains, what consideration did the
plaintiff provide?

Building on the analogous cases of *Ward v Byham*,[79]
Williams v Williams[80] and *Pao On v Lau Yiu Long*,[81] Glidewell
LJ summarised the legal position as follows:[82]

'(i)   if A has entered into a contract with B to do work for, or
         to supply goods or services to, B in return for payment by
         B; and,
(ii)   at some stage before A has completely performed his oblig-
         ations under the contract B has reason to doubt whether
         A will, or will be able to, complete his side of the bargain;
         and
(iii)   B thereupon promises A an additional payment in return
         for A's promise to perform his contractual obligations on
         time; and
(iv)   as a result of giving his promise, B obtains in practice a
         benefit, or obviates a disbenefit; and
(v)   B's promise is not given as the result of economic duress
         or fraud on the part of A; then
(vi)   the benefit to B is capable of being consideration for B's
         promise, so that the promise will be legally binding.'

But, in the light of (iv), what practical benefit did accrue to
the defendants? And, what are the implications of the

---

[77]   At pp 525–26.
[78]   This is in conformity with the views expressed by Lord Kenyon CJ in
        giving the reasons for his decision in *Harris v Watson* above.
[79]   [1956] 1 WLR 496. In *The Alev* [1989] 1 Lloyd's Rep 138, 147, Hobhouse
        J rejected the contention that cases like *Ward v Byham* showed that
        performance of an existing duty constituted good consideration. Yet,
        in the light of the developing doctrine of economic duress, he indicated
        that there was no warrant to refuse to recognise an item as consider-
        ation 'even though it may be insignificant and even though there may
        be no mutual bargain in any realistic use of that phrase'.
[80]   [1957] 1 WLR 148.
[81]   [1980] AC 614.
[82]   [1990] 1 All ER 512, 521–22.

decision for gratuitous promises by creditors to take lesser payments in settlement of their debts?

Counsel for the defendants in *Williams v Roffey* conceded that the promise to pay additional sums secured some practical benefit. In particular, it improved the chances of the plaintiff continuing to work which, in turn, meant that the defendants might avoid having to pay liquidated damages to the Housing Association for late completion, and might avoid the inconvenience and expense involved in engaging another carpenter to complete the sub-contract work.[83] Given that the carpentry work was on the 'critical path of the defendants' global operations',[84] this all seems perfectly plausible. The point is that the defendants, guided by economic imperatives, preferred to cut their losses rather than gain a Pyrrhic victory by standing on their legal rights. And, in coming to terms with this commercial reality, in adopting what Russell LJ called 'a pragmatic approach to the true relationship between the parties',[85] the Court was surely absolutely right.

Consider, however, the implications of this decision for the rule that payment of a lesser sum cannot afford a defence to a claim to the larger sum owed under the original obligation. Let us take Glidewell LJ's six propositions, and amend them to encompass such a situation:

1. if A has entered into a contract with B to do work for, or to supply goods or services to, B in return for payment by B; and
2. at some stage before B has completely performed his obligations under the contract, A has reason to doubt whether B will, or will be able to, complete his side of the bargain (ie whether B will be able to pay); and
3. A thereupon promises B that, in return for B's promise to pay such a sum, he will accept a lesser payment from B; and
4. as a result of giving his promise, A obtains in practice a benefit, or obviates a disbenefit; and

---

[83] For the risks involved in a main contractor having to find a new sub-contractor, see *Percy Bilton Ltd v Greater London Council* [1982] 2 All ER 623.
[84] [1990] 1 All ER 512, 523.
[85] Ibid.

5.   A's promise is not given as the result of economic duress or fraud on the part of B; then

6.   the benefit to A is capable of being consideration for A's promise, so that the promise will be legally binding.

We would argue that the logic of *Williams v Roffey* is that in such a situation the creditor, A, should be held to his promise. If this is correct, the courts will have to reconsider *Foakes v Beer*,[86] in which it will be recalled the House of Lords upheld the modern interpretation of *Pinnel*'s case,[87] namely that a promise by a creditor to accept payment of a lesser sum in settlement of a debt does not bar the creditor's right to recover the balance of the original debt. In fact, soon after *Williams v Roffey*, in the case of *Re Selectmove Ltd*,[88] the Court of Appeal was expressly invited to apply this logic.

The question in *Re Selectmove* arose out of an alleged promise made by the Inland Revenue that it would allow Selectmove Ltd to pay off tax arrears at a rate of £1,000 a month. At first instance, the judge rejected the company's argument that this promise bound the Revenue. He held that, in the absence of any consideration moving from the company to the Revenue for this concession, the point was closed by *Foakes v Beer*. On appeal, counsel for the company put it to the Court of Appeal that, in the light of the reasoning in *Williams v Roffey*, the point could no longer be regarded as settled. To this, Peter Gibson LJ (giving judgment on behalf of the Court) responded:[89]

> 'I see the force of the argument, but the difficulty that I feel with it is that if the principle of *Williams'* case is to be extended to an obligation to make payment, it would in effect leave the principle in *Foakes v Beer* without any application. When a creditor and a debtor who are at arm's length reach agreement on the payment of the debt by instalments to accommodate the debtor, the creditor will no doubt always see a practical benefit to himself in so doing. In the absence of authority there would be much to be said for the enforceability of such a contract. But that was a matter expressly considered in *Foakes v Beer* yet held not to constitute good consideration in law. *Foakes v Beer* was not

[86]   (1884) 9 App Cas 605.
[87]   (1602) 5 Co Rep 117a.
[88]   [1995] 2 All ER 531.
[89]   At p 538.

even referred to in *Williams'* case, and it is in my judgment impossible, consistently with the doctrine of precedent, for this court to extend the principle of *Williams'* case to any circumstances governed by the principle of *Foakes v Beer.* If that extension is to be made, it must be by the House of Lords or, perhaps even more appropriately, by Parliament after consideration by the Law Commission.'

For the present, then, pragmatism must give way to the authority of precedent, leaving the law in a somewhat contradictory state. The point is that, whether you are dealing with a creditor in difficulty or a debtor in difficulty, it is often good commercial sense to make a financial adjustment – and, in the absence of fraud or duress, it seems only reasonable that the law should recognise such adjustments to the parties' original contractual obligations. By hanging on to *Foakes v Beer* and its remnants of the exchange theory, the Court of Appeal has missed the opportunity presented by *Williams v Roffey* to keep contract law closer in touch with commercial practice.

4. PRE-CONTRACTUAL RELIANCE

In *Hoffman v Red Owl Stores*,[90] the Wisconsin court deployed paragraph 90 of the *Restatement* to protect the Hoffmans' pre-contractual reliance. In the famous Australian case of *Walton's Stores (Interstate) Ltd. v Maher*,[91] the High Court turned to the doctrine of estoppel to protect the pre-contractual reliance of Maher (who had demolished a building and started redeveloping the site in expectation of a contract with Walton's). In Canada, in the *Canamerican Auto*[92] case, the idea of a preliminary (collateral) contract was employed[93] in order to protect the pre-contractual

---

[90]   26 Wis 2d 683 (1965).
[91]   (1988) 76 ALR 513.
[92]   R *v Canamerican Auto Lease and Rental Ltd* (1987) 37 DLR (4th) 591.
[93]   Here, the court took its lead from the Canadian Surpeme Court decision in *R in Right of Ontario et al v Ron Engineering and Construction Eastern Ltd* (1981) 119 DLR (3d) 267. In the *Ron Engineering* case (where tenders had been invited for the construction of a water and sewage plant), the Supreme Court said that the 'integrity of the bidding system must be protected where under the law of contract it is possible to do so' (per Estey J at 273).

reliance of a company bidding for car rental concessions at nine major Canadian airports – the company having put in an unnecessarily high bid in reliance on its understanding that concessions would be awarded to the highest bidders.[94] Finally, in the landmark Dutch case of *Plas v Valberg*,[95] the Supreme Court developing its concept of good faith ruled that, in principle, pre-contractual dealings can move through three stages: (1) an initial stage (when parties are free to break off negotiations, and no compensation is available); (2) a continuing stage (when, although negotiations may be broken off, compensation for reliance expenses must be paid); and (3) a final stage (when negotiations cannot be broken off without violating good faith and compensation is payable not only for reliance expenses, but also, if deemed appropriate, for expectation losses). In *Plas* itself, expectation damages were awarded to a construction firm which had been led to believe 'unofficially' that its tender for the building of a municipal swimming pool would be accepted by the council.

Clearly the jurisprudence of pre-contractual reliance is well developed in many legal systems. In England, however, protection of pre-contractual reliance is inhibited by a number of factors. Above all, given that there is not yet an exchange, the classical law does not recognise pre-contractual dealings as a site for contractual remedies – *a fortiori* where the parties cover their dealings with the rubric

---

[94]   The Federal Court of Appeal compensated Canamerican for their reliance losses (the margin of their overbidding), but rejected their claim for expectation losses as too remote.

[95]   Hoge Raad 18 June (1982) Nederlandse Jurisprudentie 1983, 723 (note CJH Brunner). Cf, too, the similar Australian case of *Sabemo Pty Ltd v North Sydney Municipal Council* [1977] 2 NSWLR 880, where (at 902-903) Sheppard J said:

> '[W]here two parties proceed upon the joint assumption that a contract will be entered into between them, and one does work beneficial for the project, and thus in the interests of the two parties, which work he would not be expected, in other circumstances, to do gratuitously, he will be entitled to compensation or restitution, if the other party unilaterally decides to abandon the project, not for any reason associated with bona fide disagreement concerning the terms of the contract to be entered into, but for reasons which, however valid, pertain only to his own position and do not relate at all to that of the other party.'

Cf stages (2) and (3) of the *Plas v Valberg* conceptualisation of the developing pre-contractual relationship.

'subject to contract'.[96] Even remedies for misrepresentation (which necessarily occur in pre-contractual settings and which, by definition, require reliance by the misrepresentee) have a somewhat uneasy relationship with the main body of contract law. At all events, in English law, there is no simple equivalent to paragraph 90 of the *Restatement*; the principle of promissory estoppel was developed in the context of modification of existing contracts and it has only exceptionally (and controversially) been applied in pre-contractual settings; and the civilian doctrine of good faith has not yet been embraced by English law.[97] Despite these inhibitions, as the important case of *Blackpool and Fylde Aero Club v Blackpool Borough Council*[98] shows, the English courts are capable of being resourceful in protecting pre-contractual interests.

In the *Blackpool* case, the defendants, who owned and managed Blackpool airport, raised revenue by granting concessions to operators to use it. The plaintiff club was granted the concession in 1975, 1978 and 1980. Shortly before the plaintiff's last (1980) concession was due to expire, the Council sent an invitation to the plaintiff to tender for the new concession to the club. The Council also sent invitations to six other parties. The invitations stated that the tenders were to be submitted in the envelope provided, that they were not to bear any name or mark which would identify the sender, and that tenders received after 12 noon on 17 March 1983 would not be considered. The plaintiff's

---

[96]   Thus, in *Regalian Properties plc v London Dockland Development Corpn* [1995] 1 All ER 1005 at 1024, we find Rattee J saying:

> 'I appreciate that the English law of restitution should be flexible and capable of continuous development. However, I see no good reason to extend it to apply some such principle as adopted by Sheppard J in the *Sabemo* case [see note 95 above] to facts such as those of the present case, where, however much the parties expect a contract between them to materialise, both enter negotiations expressly (whether by use of the words "subject to contract" or otherwise) on terms that each party is free to withdraw from the negotiations at any time. Each party to such negotiations must be taken to know. . .that pending the conclusion of a binding contract any cost incurred by him in preparation for the intended contract will be incurred at his own risk in the sense that he will have no recompense for those costs if no contract results.'

[97]   See further ch 7.
[98]   [1990] 3 All ER 25. Cf the somewhat similar scenario in *R v Canamerican Auto Lease and Rental Ltd* (1987) 37 DLR (4th) 591.

tender was put in the Town Hall letter box at 11 am on 17 March, but the box was not emptied as it was supposed to be. As a result, the plaintiff's letter was incorrectly recorded as having been received late, and it was not considered when the relevant committee met to award the concession. The concession in the event was awarded to another tenderer. When the mistake came to light, the Council at first proposed to hold another round of tenders, but the tenderer to whom the concession had been awarded threatened legal proceedings, and the Council decided to honour its contract with them. The plaintiff sued alleging a breach of warranty on the part of the defendants to the effect that if the tender were received by the deadline, it would be considered along with the others. The Court of Appeal unanimously upheld the decision of the court at first instance that the defendants were liable for a breach of contract.

Four arguments were presented on behalf of the defendants. First, it was argued that the invitation to tender was not an offer, merely an indication of a willingness to receive offers.[99] Secondly, it was said that it did not follow from the statement that late tenders would not be considered, that timely tenders would be. Thirdly, it was contended that a contract should not be implied merely because it was reasonable to do so.[100] Finally, it was argued that there was a distinction between reasonable expectation and contractual obligation,[101] and that '[t]he court should not subvert well-understood contractual principles by adopting a woolly pragmatic solution designed to remedy a perceived injustice on the unique facts of [the] case'.[102]

The first submission did not really present any difficulty. Relying on Bowen LJ's famous test in *Carlill v Carbolic Smoke Ball Co*[103] (ie how would the ordinary person construe the tendering arrangements?), counsel for the club argued that the ordinary interpretation of the position was as follows:

---

[99]   See *Spencer v Harding* (1870) LR 5 CP 561; *Harris v Nickerson* (1873) LR 8 QB 286; *Rooke v Dawson* [1895] 1 Ch 480.
[100]   *Liverpool City Council v Irwin* [1977] AC 239; *Heilbut Symons and Co v Buckleton* [1913] AC 30.
[101]   Cf *Lavarack v Woods of Colchester* [1966] 3 All ER 683, 690 (per Diplock LJ).
[102]   [1990] 3 All ER 25, 29 (per Bingham LJ).
[103]   [1893] 1 QB 256, 266.

'[T]he Council might or might not accept any particular tender; it might accept no tender; it might decide not to award the concession at all; it might not consider any tender received after the advertised deadline; but if it did consider any tender received before the deadline and conforming with the advertised conditions it would consider all such tenders.'[104]

The Council's second submission, however, was clearly correct. Simply because late tenders would not be considered, it did not follow that conforming tenders would be considered. Thus it was open to the Council to argue that the correct implication was merely that conforming tenders *might* be considered. Moreover, this interpretation of the tendering arrangements was backed by the council's further (third) submission that a reasonableness test should be eschewed (ie that classical principle should prevail over modern pragmatism). Responding to these arguments, Bingham LJ observed:

'[W]hat if, in a situation such as the present, the Council had opened and thereupon accepted the first tender received, even though the deadline had not expired and other invitees had not responded? Or if the Council had considered and accepted a tender admittedly received well after the deadline? Counsel answered that although by so acting the Council might breach its own standing orders, and might fairly be accused of discreditable conduct, it would not be in breach of any legal obligation because at that stage there would be none to breach. This is a conclusion I cannot accept, and if it were accepted there would in my view be an unacceptable discrepancy between the law of contract and the confident assumptions of commercial parties . . . [W]here, as here, tenders are solicited from selected parties all of them known to the invitor, and where a local authority's invitation prescribes a clear, orderly and familiar procedure . . .the invitee is in my judgment protected at least to this extent: if he submits a conforming tender before the deadline he is entitled, *not as a matter of mere expectation but of contractual right*, to be sure that his tender will after the deadline be opened and considered in conjunction with all other conforming tenders or at least that his tender will be considered if others are.'[105]

---

[104] [1990] 3 All ER 25, 30.
[105] Ibid, emphasis supplied. Cf the analysis in PP Craig, 'Legitimate Expectations: A Conceptual Analysis' (1992) 108 Law Quarterly Review 79.

On closer inspection, these remarks might seem to gloss over a number of potentially important distinctions, in particular between intentional and unintentional violation of the principles of good tendering practice, and between holding the Council contractually bound to consider all conforming tenders, as opposed to holding the Council so bound *only if any tenders were considered*. However, for Bingham LJ's purposes, such nice points were largely immaterial. Quite simply, the critical question was whether tenderers reasonably assumed that the Council would observe certain ground rules in dealing with the tenders; if they did, then appropriate contractual warranties would be implied in line with their expectations.[106]

Bearing in mind the Council's fourth submission, we should be careful to note the limitations of the *Blackpool* case as a precedent for the recognition of pre-contractual interests. First, the court clearly treated the case as exceptional. For instance, Stocker LJ observed that it constituted 'one of the fairly rare exceptions to the general rule expounded in the leading cases of *Spencer v Harding . . .* and *Harris v Nickerson*'.[107] More importantly, a good deal of emphasis was placed on the particular features of the tendering arrangements. Since it would not otherwise be self-evident that these features had any special significance, by underlining their materiality the court made it easy for future judges to distinguish the case if so desired. Second, the evidence of the parties' expectations was unusually strong. In particular, the fact that the Council (when its erroneous recording of the club's tender as late was appreciated) was prepared to contemplate a re-run of the tendering process was indicative of its own understanding of the rules of the game. Third, in the light of *Murphy v Brentwood District Council*[108] and analogous

---

[106]　Cf *Harvela Investments Ltd v Royal Trust of Canada (CI) Ltd* [1986] AC 207, which, somewhat curiously, was not cited in the *Black-pool* case. In *Harvela*, a reasonable expectation on the part of the tenderers was that referential bids would be excluded. Thus, the offer (inviting bids) was subject to an appropriate implied qualification. In the *Blackpool* case, essentially the same reasoning was applied except that, in a sense, it was carried one step further – not merely to read an implied qualification into an express offer, but actually to imply the offer itself.

[107]　(1873) LR 8 QB 286.

[108]　[1990] 2 All ER 908. See also *Department of the Environment v Thomas*

cases,[109] we can be fairly confident that the club would not have succeeded in its negligence action. This might encourage the argument that, in pre-contractual situations, the law of contract should not be extended to give remedies otherwise denied in negligence.[110] It is perfectly possible therefore that the pragmatism of the *Blackpool* case will find itself limited by classical habits of thought, possibly fortified by modern thinking about the relationship between contract and tort.

5. RELIANCE AND EXPECTATION

Once we move from classical exchange-based notions of consideration, the key to the enforcement of informal express promises may be seen as (i) reasonable actual reliance by the promisee, (ii) reasonable expectation by the promisor of reliance by the promisee plus actual reliance by the promisee,[111] (iii) reasonable expectation on the part of the promisee, or (iv) reasonable expectation by the promisor that the promisee will take the promise seriously. Arguably, (i) and (ii), which we can term the 'reliance principles', amount to the same thing – actual reliance by the promisee (under (i)) only being judged reasonable where the promisor reasonably expects such reliance. Similarly, it is arguable that (iii) and (iv), which we can term the 'expectation principles', amount to the same thing – expectation by the promisee (under (iii)) only being judged reasonable where the promisor reasonably expects that the promisee will take the promise seriously. What is beyond argument, however, is that (actual) reliance principles are not the same

Bates and Son [1990] 2 All ER 943. The effect of *Murphy* is to put further pressure on contractual techniques for achieving just and sensible results. Generally, this calls for a less schematic approach to questions of formation (cf. Lord Wilberforce's oft-cited remarks in *The Eurymedon*, above at p 81). A specific pressure point here is the doctrine of privity of contract: see ch 5.

109   See especially *D & F Estates Ltd v Church Comrs for England* [1989] AC 177.

110   For the recently influential idea that, in contractual situations, the law of negligence should not be extended to give remedies otherwise denied in contract, see especially Lord Scarman's observations in *Tai Hing Cotton Mill Ltd v Liu Chong Hing Bank Ltd* [1986] AC 80, 107.

111   Cf par 90 *Restatement* 2d above.

thing as expectation principles. Whilst this may seem obvious, this important distinction is clouded by the fact that the decisions in many cases which lie at the fringes of traditional contract theory (eg those dealing with promissory estoppel, pre-contractual dealings, collateral contracts, and the like) are compatible with both the reliance and the expectation principles. Consider, for example, the old case of *Aldwell v Bundey*[112] (which the *Blackpool* case might well have referred to). There the defendant announced a race to be held in a rowing regatta with a first prize of £150. The plaintiffs, who appear to have been professional oarsmen (professional rowing being a major sport at the time), procured a boat, went into training, put in their entry before the stipulated date, and paid their entry fee for the advertised race. However, as the plaintiffs stood on the start with two other entrants, the defendants informed them that the race was cancelled, to be replaced by another event carrying only a £100 prize. The plaintiffs refused to row, and sued. Distinguishing *Harris v Nickerson*,[113] the court held that the defendants' cancellation of the race amounted to a breach of contract.[114] Whilst this decision could be explained on the basis of the plaintiffs and other entrants having reasonably (and detrimentally) relied on the defendants' announcement, it could equally be argued that the defendants were required to keep their word because the plaintiffs had formed a reasonable expectation that the race would be held as announced.

Once the expectation principles have been separated from the reliance principles, the most striking implication of the former is that an express, but informal, promise may be treated as contractually binding even though there has been no actual reliance by the promisee. For example, if A promises to pay B £1,000, A's promise is contractually binding if B reasonably expects A to keep his word. Furthermore,

---

[112]   (1876) 10 SALR 118, 248. Cf also *Jenkins v Knipe* (1885) 11 VLR 269 (Aust).

[113]   On the basis of the rule that an auctioneer's authority to sell may be withdrawn at any time up to the fall of the hammer.

[114]   The plaintiffs recovered only their reliance expenses (viz, their expenses in training and preparing for the race and the cost of procuring a boat). No damages were awarded for the loss of their chance of winning. In disentangling reliance principles from expectation principles, it is important, as we have emphasised, not to confuse their use in formation contexts with their application to remedial questions.

as the many cases discussed in this chapter highlight, the expectation principles (in this respect just like the reliance principles) do not have to be restricted to express promises. In exchange relationships, and proto-exchange dealings, expectations are formed, sometimes but not always on the strength of express promises, and provided such expectations are reasonable, they are contractually enforceable. Whilst to some this may seem like the slippery slope to indeterminate liability to an indeterminate number, it can be said in favour of the expectation principles that they simply return to the older theory of consideration, that they recognise the overriding importance of the doctrine of intention to create legal relations, that they open the way for judicial review of due process in contracting (which is especially welcome in the context of tendering), and that they reflect more faithfully contracting parties' perceptions of their obligations.

6. CONCLUSION

The exchange theory of consideration makes it difficult for the classical law to respond flexibly to the changing needs and expectations of contractors, particularly commercial contractors. In this chapter, we have reviewed these difficulties in the context of both pre-contractual reliance and contractual modification.

In principle, the law could meet these new challenges by founding itself on a theory of expectation or on a theory of reliance. Generally, in so far as English law has responded to the challenges of modern contracting, it has tended to base itself on reliance. This is certainly the case with Lord Denning's bold attempt to mould the doctrine of equitable estoppel into a vehicle for the regulation of contractual modification – an attempt that, whilst certainly laudable, pays scant regard to precedent and that might have been better served by employing the common law doctrine of waiver. More recently, a new pragmatism is evident in both *Williams v Roffey* and the *Blackpool* case. Although *Williams v Roffey* retains traces of the exchange theory, by continuing to require some benefit to the promisor, it all but abandons the classical model in favour of an expectation basis for the enforcement of freely agreed contractual modifications. Similarly, one could explain the *Blackpool* decision on the grounds of some kind of exchange-based collateral contract. However, this would distort the court's approach which explicitly appeals to commercial expectation as the basis for holding the Council to its advertised ground rules.

The new pragmatism of *Williams v Roffey* and the *Blackpool* case is encouraging. However, as *Re Selectmove* reminds us, the classical model is always liable to retard the progressive development of the case-law. If the law of contract is to become more rational in this area, it must shake off the inhibitions of the exchange model; it must respond to the questions raised by pre-contractual dealings and contractual modifications in an open way, putting subterfuge behind it; and, rather than taking actual reliance to be the basis of contractual obligation, we suggest that legitimate expectation should be adopted as the unifying base on which to found the modern law.

Chapter 5

Third party questions

Introduction

A key issue for any regime of contract law concerns the standing of third parties in relation to contracts. In particular, is it open to a third party to sue on a contract made for its benefit? For the classical law, building on meeting of minds theory and adopting the exchange model of consideration, third parties were necessarily strangers to contracts. In consequence, the classical law espoused a strict doctrine of privity of contract according to which: (1) a person could not take the benefit of a contract to which that person was not a party; and (2) a person could not be burdened by a contract to which that person was not a party.

The beginnings of the privity doctrine can be traced to *Williams v Everett*,[1] but the leading case of the nineteenth century is *Tweddle v Atkinson*.[2] In that case, the plaintiff's father, and his prospective father-in-law, mutually agreed to pay sums of money to the plaintiff on his marriage. The plaintiff duly married, but the father-in-law died before his portion of the money had been paid. It was held that the plaintiff could not recover the money, even though the agreement had expressly provided that the plaintiff should have the right to sue on it. Wightman J said:[3]

> '[I]t is now established that no stranger to the consideration can take advantage of a contract, although made for his benefit.'

---

[1] (1811) 4 East 582; see AWB Simpson *History of the Common Law of Contract* (Oxford University Press, 1975) pp 475–85.

[2] (1861) 1 B& S 393.

[3] Ibid at p 398.

To the extent that the court in *Tweddle v Atkinson* assumed that the privity doctrine was a corollary of the consideration requirement, its reasoning was open to challenge. For, whilst the consideration requirement determines *which class of promises* is enforceable, the privity doctrine determines *who* can enforce a promise.[4] These are distinct matters and it does not follow that a third party's lack of consideration should preclude a right to enforce a promise. As fate would have it, though, the chances of exposing such a fallacy in *Tweddle v Atkinson* were reduced by counsel's apparent concession that the privity doctrine represented the general rule in contract law.[5] One might, therefore, have expected the authority of *Tweddle v Atkinson* to be relatively short-lived. However, in 1915, in *Dunlop Pneumatic Tyre Company v Selfridge & Co Ltd*,[6] the House of Lords ringingly declared that the privity doctrine was one of the cornerstone principles of English contract law. From that point onwards, the story of privity (as with so much else of English contract law in the twentieth century) has been one of intrigue and subterfuge as judges have wrestled with the perceived inconvenience and injustice occasioned by the classical law.

In this chapter, we will consider a range of third party issues associated with the privity doctrine. Our contentions are twofold: first, that contract law would be rendered more rational if the problems created by a rigid privity doctrine were to be more openly addressed; and, secondly, that third party principles, like the doctrine of consideration, should be revised to take account of the legitimate expectations of parties involved in transactions.

1. PRIVITY IN COMPARATIVE PERSPECTIVE

When English law unequivocally reaffirmed the privity principle in *Dunlop v Selfridge*, this set a lead to be followed in a number of common law legal systems – for example, in

---

[4]   See eg Hugh Collins *The Law of Contract* 2nd edn (Butterworths, London, 1986) p 288.
[5]   See R. Flannigan 'Privity: The End of an Era (Error)' (1987) 103 Law Quarterly Review 564.
[6]   [1915] AC 847.

both Canada[7] and Australia,[8] a strict privity doctrine took root. Elsewhere, though, particularly in the United States, a less strict approach had survived, with an explicit third-party beneficiary rule being applied.[9] Moreover, the experience of all legal systems, Common Law and civilian, has been that it is remarkably difficult to maintain a strict line on privity.[10]

In recent times, the critics of the privity doctrine have begun to gain the upper hand. Sometimes, this has led to legislative relaxation of the doctrine, a well-known example of this being the New Zealand Contracts (Privity) Act 1982. At other times, the courts have addressed the need for reform in a head-on fashion. Here, two Commonwealth cases stand out as significant: the decision of the High Court of Australia in *Trident General Insurance Co Ltd v McNiece Bros Pty Ltd.*,[11] and that of the Canadian Supreme Court in *London Drugs Ltd v Kuehne and Nagel International Ltd.*[12]

In the *Trident* case, the question was whether McNiece, a contractor employed by Blue Circle, could rely on an insurance policy written by Trident for Blue Circle. The policy was to cover Blue Circle and all its subsidiaries, contractors and sub-contractors involved in specified construction contracts. Although McNiece was within the category covered, it was not directly in contract with Trident. Despite this lack of privity, the majority of the High Court ruled in favour of McNiece. In the words of Toohey J:[13]

'[W]hen a rule of the common law harks back no further than the middle of the last century, when it has been the subject of constant criticism and when, in its widest form, it lacks a sound

---

[7]   See eg *Greenwood Shopping Plaza Ltd v Beattie* (1980) 111 DLR (3rd edn) 257.

[8]   See eg *Wilson v Darling Island Stevedoring & Lighterage Co Ltd* (1956) 95 CLR 43.

[9]   See the famous decision of the New York Court of Appeals in *Lawrence v Fox* 20 NY 268 (1859).

[10]   For the erosion of the privity principle in French law, see Barry Nicholas, *The French Law of Contract* 2nd edn (Oxford, Clarendon Press, 1992) p 169 et seq.

[11]   (1988) 165 CLR 107. See FMB Reynolds, 'Privity of Contract, the Boundaries of Categories and the Limits of the Judicial Function' (1989) 108 Law Quarterly Review 1.

[12]   [1993] 1 WWR 1.

[13]   (1988) 165 CLR 107, 170–171.

foundation in jurisprudence and logic and further, when that
rule has been so affected by exceptions or qualifications, I see
nothing inimical to principled development in this Court now
declaring the law to be otherwise in the circumstance of the
present case.'

But what precisely were the circumstances in the *Trident*
case? Essentially, it was the intention of both Trident and
Blue Circle that the benefit of the insurance policy should
extend to those involved with Blue Circle as contractors and
sub-contractors on the work sites in question. McNiece was
sufficiently identified as one of those involved, and it could
be expected to arrange its business in the light of the background insurance cover. The merits clearly were with
McNiece. Moreover, in their joint majority judgment, Mason
CJ and Wilson J cautioned against resorting to traditional
mechanisms (such as estoppel) as a means of dealing with
the worst excesses of the privity doctrine:[14]

> 'In the ultimate analysis the limited question we have to decide
> is whether the old rules apply to a policy of insurance. The injus-
> tice which would flow from such a result arises not only from its
> failure to give effect to the expressed intention of the person
> who takes out the insurance but also from the common inten-
> tion of the parties and the circumstance that others, aware of
> the existence of the policy, will order their affairs accordingly.
> We doubt that the doctrine of estoppel provides an adequate
> protection of the legitimate expectations of such persons and,
> even if it does, the rights of persons under a policy of insurance
> should not be made to depend on the vagaries of such an intri-
> cate doctrine. In the nature of things the likelihood of some
> degree of reliance on the part of the third party in the case of
> the benefit to be provided for him under an insurance policy is
> so tangible that the common law rule should be shaped with
> that likelihood in mind.'

Whilst these majority judges agree that privity should be
openly relaxed in the circumstances, one can detect some
uncertainty about the precise basis for revision of the
doctrine. Is it the 'intention of the parties', 'legitimate expectation', or perhaps 'actual reliance' that is critical? This
important question is one to which we will have to return.

More recently, in the *London Drugs* case, the Canadian
Supreme Court has followed the example of *Trident* by

[14]   Ibid at pp 123–124.

openly relaxing the privity doctrine in the particular circumstances of the dispute presented to the court. The facts of *London Drugs* were as follows. Pursuant to a warehousing contract, London Drugs delivered a transformer to Kuehne and Nagel for storage. Section 11(b) of the contract provided:

> 'The warehouseman's liability on any one package is limited to $40 unless the holder has declared in writing a valuation in excess of $40 and paid the additional charge specified to cover warehouse liability.'

Instead of making the appropriate declaration and paying the additional charge, London Drugs included the transformer in its own all-risks insurance cover. The transformer was unloaded safely enough. However, when London Drugs gave the order for the transformer to be loaded up for delivery to their new factory, two of Kuehne and Nagel's employees negligently damaged the transformer by attempting to lift it with forklift trucks. The transformer toppled over, occasioning damage of nearly $34,000. London Drugs sued, inter alios, both Kuehne and Nagel (in contract and in negligence) and the two careless employees (in negligence).[15]

The trial judge, Trainor J, having found that the two employees were negligent, and having ruled that Kuehne and Nagel's liability was limited to $40 (in accordance with section 11(b) of the warehousing contract), declared that the main issue was whether the negligent employees were entitled to invoke section 11(b) to limit their liability.[16] Whilst Trainor J had some sympathy for the employees' submission (that they, too, should be shielded by section 11(b)), he ruled that the employees were liable to London Drugs for the full amount of the loss.[17] On appeal to the British Columbia Court of Appeal, this sympathy for the employees was translated into hard legal support by a variety of indirect

---

[15] London Drugs also sued the manufacturers of the transformer. This part of the claim failed at trial, however, it being held that the manufacturers were not negligent in manufacturing and packaging the transformer.

[16] (1986) 2 BCLR (2d) 181, [1986] 4 WWR 183.

[17] Cf *Muller Martini Canada Inc v Kuehne and Nagel International Ltd.* (1990) 73 DLR (4th) 315, where Isaac J refused, on materially similar facts, to allow employees the benefit of the limitation clause in the warehousing contract.

stratagems.[18] However, when the case reached the Supreme Court, a more direct approach was preferred. According to Iacobucci J, who delivered the majority opinion:[19]

'Except for a rigid adherence to the doctrine of privity of contract, I do not see any compelling reason based on principle, authority or policy demonstrating that this Court, or any other, must embark upon a complex and somewhat uncertain "tort analysis" [ie the indirect approach] in order to allow third parties such as the respondents to obtain the benefit of a contractual limitation of liability clause, once it has been established that they breached a recognized duty of care. In my view, apart from privity of contract, it is contrary to neither principle nor authority to allow such a party, in appropriate circumstances, to obtain the benefit directly from the contract (ie in the same manner as would the contracting party) by resorting to what may be referred to as a "contract analysis".'

As in the *Trident* case, the central issue in *London Drugs* was whether the particular circumstances were appropriate ones in which to relax the privity doctrine. The majority had little doubt that the circumstances were eminently appropriate:[20]

'When all the circumstances of this case are taken into account, including the nature of the relationship between employees and their employer, the identity of interest with respect to contractual obligations, the fact that the appellant knew that employees would be involved in performing the contractual obligations, and the absence of a clear indication in the contract to the contrary, the term "warehouseman" in s 11(b) of the contract must be interpreted as meaning "warehousemen". As such, the respondents are not complete strangers to the limitation of liability clause. Rather, they are unexpressed or implicit third party beneficiaries with respect to this clause.'

On this basis, the court held that there should be a general exception to the privity doctrine where: (1) a limitation of liability clause, either expressly or impliedly, extends its benefit to the employees (or employee) seeking to rely on it; and (2) the employees (or employee) seeking the benefit of

---

[18]   See John N Adams and Roger Brownsword 'More Answers than Questions: The *London Drugs* Case' (1991) 55 Saskatchewan Law Review 441; also 'Privity of Contract – That Pestilential Nuisance' (1993) 56 Modern Law Review 722.

[19]   [1993] 1 WWR 1, 25.

[20]   Ibid at p 52.

the limitation of liability clause were acting in the course of their employment and were performing the very services provided for in the contract between their employer and the plaintiff (customer) when the loss occurred.[21]

In England, the Law Revision Committee, in its Sixth Interim Report in 1937, recommended a limited relaxation of the privity doctrine (along with abolition of the consideration rule). However, the Second World War intervened, the Committee's recommendations got shelved,[22] and in *Midland Silicones Ltd v Scruttons Ltd*[23] the privity doctrine was again affirmed by the House of Lords. Thereafter, however, the tendency has been for the highest courts to express severe reservations about the doctrine. Thus, in *KH Enterprise (cargo owners) v Pioneer Container (owners): The Pioneer Container*,[24] an appeal to the Privy Council from the Court of Appeal of Hong Kong, we find Lord Goff saying:[25]

> '[S]o far as English law and the law of Hong Kong are concerned, a technical problem faces shipowners who carry goods . . . where there is no contractual relationship between the shipowners and certain cargo owners. This is because English law still maintains, though subject to increasing criticism, a strict principle of privity of contract, under which as a matter of general principle only a person who is a party to a contract may sue upon it. The force of this principle is supported and enhanced by the doctrine of consideration. . . How long these principles will continue to be maintained in all their strictness is now open to question.'

Lord Goff's comments were not entirely speculative, for in 1991 the Law Commission provisionally recommended that a legislative scheme should be enacted relaxing the privity doctrine.[26] With this provisional proposal set to be hardened

---

[21] Ibid at p 50.
[22] See J. Beatson, 'Reforming the Law of Contracts for the Benefit of Third Parties: A Second Bite at the Cherry' (1992) Current Legal Problems 1.
[23] [1962] AC 446.
[24] [1994] 2 All ER 250. See Phang (1995) 58 MLR 422.
[25] Ibid at pp 255–256. See, too, Lord Goff's comments in *White v Jones* [1995] 1 All ER 691, 705.
[26] Law Commission Consultation Paper No 121. For a rather different concern arising from the doctrine of privity of contract (in this case, a concern with the so-called 'privity trap' which involves the continuing obligations of original tenants under leases), see Rights and Duties of Landlords and Tenants: A Consultation Paper (Lord Chancellor's Department, March 1995).

into a firm recommendation, we can say that the future of the privity doctrine is at the top of the reform agenda.

Having thus set the general scene, our next step is to analyse rather more carefully the various questions implicated in the privity debate. After that, we can consider the appropriate basis for reform – whether the law is best organised around a test based on the intentions of the contracting parties (such as the Law Commission recommends) or a test based on legitimate expectation or actual reliance.

2. PRIVITY QUESTIONS

In our introductory remarks, we identified two general privity questions: whether a person can sue on a contract made for his benefit, but to which he is not·a party; and whether a person can be prejudiced by a contract to which he is not a party. In point of fact, there are four basic privity questions involved here:

1.   can a person enforce a contract to which he is not a party? (We will call questions of this sort P1.)
2.   can a person set up a defence based on the terms of a contract to which he is not a party in order to answer a claim brought by a person who is a party to the relevant contract? (P2)
3.   can a contracting party set up a defence based on the terms of his own contract in order to answer a claim brought by a person who is not a party to the relevant contract? (P3)
4.   can a contracting party enforce his own contract against a person who is not a party to the relevant contract? (P4)

According to the doctrine of privity, each of these questions must be answered in the negative. To answer P1 and P2 in the affirmative would be to allow a third party to take the benefit of a contract to which he was not a party; to answer P3 and P4 in the affirmative would involve burdening a person under a contract to which he was not a party.

(i) Distinguishing the privity questions

Although each of the four privity questions set out above is distinct and requires separate analysis, English law has sometimes blurred the distinctions. This can be seen by the way in which the leading modern case *Dunlop Pneumatic Tyre Company v Selfridge & Co Ltd*,[27] which involved a P1 question, has been cited in decisions involving other privity questions. In *Dunlop v Selfridge*, the plaintiffs had sold some tyres to motor factors, under a contract which provided for resale price maintenance. The factors resold to Selfridge with the proviso in that contract that Selfridge would not resell at less than the stated price, and that if they did so, they would pay to Dunlop £5 per tyre as compensation.[28] Selfridges sold tyres to their customers at less than the stated price, and Dunlop sued them. Accordingly, Dunlop were seeking a benefit under the contract between the factors and Selfridges. It was held by the House of Lords that Dunlop could not sue on this contract. Viscount Haldane said:

> '[In] the law of England certain principles are fundamental. One is that only a person who is a party to a contract can sue on it. Our law knows nothing of a *jus quaesitum tertio* arising by way of contract. Such a right may be conferred by way of property, as, for example, under a trust, but it cannot be conferred on a stranger to a contract as a right to enforce the contract *in persona*.'[29]

Half a century later, this view was expressly approved by the House in *Scruttons v Midland Silicones*.[30] This case posed, however, P2 and P3 questions. A drum of chemicals had been shipped aboard a vessel belonging to the United States Lines under a bill of lading which limited the liability of the carriers to $500. Obviously, between the plaintiff and the carriers this limitation of liability was binding (as it was intended to be pursuant to the Hague Rules to which at the time both the USA and the UK adhered). The carriers employed the defendants as stevedores to unload the

---

[27] [1915] AC 847.
[28] It should be noted that, today, such resale price maintenance is generally outlawed under both UK and EU law.
[29] Ibid at p 853.
[30] [1962] AC 446.

chemicals in London. That contract expressly provided that
the stevedores should have the benefit of the limitation
clause in the bill of lading (an agreement also in accordance
with the intention of the Hague Rules). The drum was damaged during unloading. This raised a P2 question: were the
stevedores able to claim protection under the terms of the
carriage contract, which purported to bestow protection on
them? It also raised a P3 question: were the stevedores,
when sued by the cargo owners, able to take advantage of
the limitation of liability for which they had contracted
with the carriers? The majority of the House of Lords held
that the stevedores' defence must fail on either basis. Lord
Reid said:

> 'Although I may regret it, I find it impossible to deny the exis-
> tence of the general rule that a stranger to a contract cannot in
> a question with either of the contracting parties take advantage
> of provisions of the contract, even where it is clear from the con-
> tract that some provision in it was intended to benefit him . . .
>   The actual words used by Lord Haldane in the *Dunlop* case
> were made the basis of an argument that, although a stranger
> to a contract may not be able to sue for any benefit under it, he
> can rely on the contract as a defence if one of the parties to it
> sues him in breach of his contractual obligations – that he can
> use the contract as a shield though not as a sword. I can find
> no justification for that. If the other contracting party can pre-
> vent the breach of contract well and good, but if he cannot I do
> not see how the stranger can. As was said in *Tweddle v Atkinson*,
> the stranger cannot "take advantage" from the contract.'[31]

Accordingly, the majority took the view that the *Dunlop* principle, expounded in relation to a P1 situation, extended
directly to one involving a P2 question and indirectly to one
involving a P3 question.

P1, P2 and P3 questions often arise in conjunction with
each other. For example, suppose that A has a contract with
B, and B has a contract with C, then A claims against C on
the basis of the contract made between B and C (P1);[32] C
seeks to defend on the basis of the protective provisions in
the contract between A and B (P2);[33] C also seeks to plead
against A protective provisions in the contract between B

---

[31]   Ibid at p 473.
[32]   *Dunlop v Selfridge* [1915] AC 847.
[33]   *Midland Silicones v Scruttons* [1962] AC 446, to the extent that the
        defendant stevedores sought to rely on the limitations in the bill of
        lading.

and C (P3).[34] Question P4, however, tends to arise in isolation, and in a somewhat different context. Typically, it arises where B, having contracted with A to grant A certain rights concerning goods owned by B, sells those goods to X. If X fails to respect A's rights, may A seek a remedy against X on the basis of the contract made between A and B? In *Port Line Ltd v Ben Line Steamers Ltd*,[35] which is generally regarded as the leading authority on this type of question, Diplock J adopted an orthodox approach. In that case the plaintiffs had chartered a ship from its owners for thirty months. The owners then sold it to the defendants who immediately chartered it back to the original owners. This charter contained a provision that it was to cease if the ship were requisitioned. There was no equivalent clause in the plaintiff's charter. The ship was requisitioned, and the plaintiffs sued the defendants for the compensation they had received in respect of the requisitioning. The question as to whether or not the defendants were bound to hand over the money to the plaintiffs turned, inter alia, on the question as to whether when the defendants bought the ship they were bound by the terms of the plaintiff's charter (of which they knew, though they did not know its terms in detail). Diplock J held for the defendants. He said:

> 'There was no privity of contract between the plaintiffs and the defendants. On what ground, therefore, can they assert against the defendants all or any of the contractual rights they had against [the original owners], or any statutory rights which they would have had against [the original owners] by virtue of the existence of such contractual rights?'[36]

The plaintiffs had argued that they could found their claim on the Privy Council decision in *Lord Strathcona Steamship Co v Dominion Coal Co*[37] which similarly involved the sale of a chartered vessel by its original owners. The charterer in that case obtained an injunction against the ultimate purchaser of the vessel (who again had bought with notice of the charter), to prevent that purchaser acting otherwise

---

[34] *Midland Silicones v Scruttons* [1962] AC 446, to the extent that the defendant stevedores sought to rely on the limitations in their own contract with the carrier.

[35] [1958] 2 QB 146.

[36] Ibid at p 164.

[37] [1926] AC 108.

than in accordance with the charter-party. Diplock J, however, observed of this decision:

> 'The difficulty I have found in ascertaining its ratio decidendi, the impossibility which I find in reconciling the actual decision with well-established principles of law, the unsolved and, to me, insoluble problems which that decision raises combine to satisfy me that it was wrongly decided.'[38]

In short, the result of these decisions appears to be that English law 'officially' answers each of the four privity questions in the negative. In spite of this, as we have already indicated, it would not be quite accurate to say that English law is fully committed to the privity rule, for a number of departures from it are recognised both in theory and in practice.

(ii) Exceptions to the privity rule

In relation to P1 questions, there is a tension between the principle laid down in *Dunlop* and the 'neighbour' principle laid down in *Donoghue v Stevenson*.[39] In the latter case a friend bought a bottle of ginger beer for the plaintiff at a café. She drank some of it, then refilled her glass, at which point a decomposing snail allegedly popped out of the opaque bottle. As a result, she became ill, and sued the manufacturers. Now, assuming the ginger beer to have contained a snail,[40] the manufacturers would clearly be liable to the person to whom they supplied it under a contract of sale. But the plaintiff was a third party to that contract of sale (as, indeed, she was a third party to the contract of sale between the café proprietor and the plaintiff's friend). According to the *Dunlop* principle, the plaintiff could acquire no benefit under that contract because she was a third party to it. Yet according to the principle laid down in *Donoghue*, the plaintiff might recover against a manufacturer in respect of physical injuries suffered as a result of the manufacturer's negligence. So long as *Dunlop* is restricted to claims for purely economic loss, and *Donoghue* is restricted to claims other than for purely economic loss (and, we might add, so

---

[38]   [1958] 2 QB 146, 168.
[39]   [1932] AC 562.
[40]   It was later found that it did not, but that finding of fact does not affect the legal principles laid down in the case.

long as a rational distinction can be drawn between the two kinds of loss), the principles do not compete with one another. However, once third parties are permitted to recover in tort in respect of economic losses, as they are in the case of negligent misstatements,[41] the question of the relationship between contractual and tortious principles is raised. This tension came graphically to the fore following the case of *Junior Books Ltd v Veitchi Ltd*.[42] In that case the plaintiffs were permitted to recover in respect of the economic losses they suffered when their factory was closed due to the negligent laying of some flooring by sub-contractors. In effect, therefore, the plaintiff was permitted to recover from the sub-contractor in respect of the sub-contractor's breaches of the duties it owed under its contract with the main contractors. As Walton J observed in *Balsamo v Medici*:[43]

> 'If the [*Junior Books*] principle does not have some certain limits, it will come perilously close to abrogating completely the concept of privity of contract.'

At least so far as P1 questions are concerned (which were the only questions involved in the case), this must be true. On this question, doctrinal orthodoxy has been restored by the House of Lords' decision in *Murphy v Brentwood Corpn*,[44] which has effectively overruled *Junior Books*. Nevertheless, *Donoghue v Stevenson* remains good law, and it must be recognised that (negligent) breaches of contract leading to physical injury to the plaintiff (or damage to the plaintiff's property) provide an exception to the general rule that P1 questions are answered in the negative.

With regard to P2 questions, and the closely related P3 questions, the doctrinal orthodoxy of *Scruttons* co-exists with a number of counter-doctrines, three of which merit particular mention. These are: the principle of vicarious immunity, the principle of special acceptance in bailments, and the doctrine of the contractual setting.

The principle of vicarious immunity is illustrated by the case of *Elder Dempster Ltd v Paterson Zochonis & Co Ltd*.[45]

---

[41] The seminal case is *Hedley Byrne and Co Ltd v Heller and Partners* [1964] AC 465.
[42] [1983] 1 AC 520. See, too, *White v Jones* [1995] 1 All ER 691.
[43] [1984] 2 All ER 304, 311.
[44] [1990] 2 All ER 908.
[45] [1924] AC 522.

In that case the House of Lords held that the owners of a vessel were entitled to rely on the limitations contained in a bill of lading issued pursuant to a contract between the cargo owners and the charterers of the vessel, when they (the owners of the vessel) were sued by the cargo owners in respect of damage caused by bad stowage. In other words, a P2 question was answered in the affirmative.

The doctrine of special acceptance in bailments long pre-dates the emergence of the modern law of contract and the privity principle.[46] In *Morris v C W Martin & Sons Ltd*[47] Lord Denning MR said:

> 'Now comes the question: can the defendants [sub-bailees] rely, as against the plaintiff [the owner of a mink stole deposited with a furrier for cleaning] on the exempting conditions [in the contract between the plaintiff and the furrier] although there was no contract directly between them and her? There is much to be said on each side. On the one hand, it is hard on the plaintiff if her just claim is defeated by exempting conditions of which she knew nothing and to which she was not a party. On the other hand, it is hard on the defendants if they are held liable to a greater responsibility than they agreed to undertake . . . The answer to the problem lies, I think, in this: the owner is bound by the condition if he has expressly or impliedly consented to the bailee making a sub-bailment containing those conditions, but not otherwise.'[48]

The particular privity questions posed in *Morris v Martin* were both P2 and P3: could the sub-bailees rely on the terms either of the head contract between the plaintiff and the furrier, or of the sub-contract between the furrier and themselves, to limit their liability? Lord Denning's dictum is equally applicable to both of these questions, and answers them in the affirmative. He had also articulated the same 'consent' principle in his dissent in *Midland Silicones*.[49] In

---

[46]   It derives primarily from Coke's notes to *Southcote*'s case (1601) 4 Co Rep 83b, see p 18 above. See Adams, 'The Standardisation of Commercial Contracts or the Contractualisation of Standard Forms' (1978) 7 Anglo-American Law Review 136.

[47]   [1966] 1 QB 716.

[48]   Ibid at p 729.

[49]   [1962] AC 446, 488: 'But if you look at the *Elder Dempster* case with the spectacles of 1961, then there is a way in which it can be supported. It is this: even though negligence is an independent tort, nevertheless it is an accepted principle of the law of tort that no man can complain of an injury if he has voluntarily consented to take the risk of it on himself . . . So in the case of through transit, when the shipper of goods

short, the effect of the consent principle – recently endorsed by the Privy Council in *The Pioneer Container*[50] – is that irrespective of whether the exempting terms are contained in the contract with the plaintiff, or in the contract between the sub-bailee and the bailee, a plaintiff who has assented to the terms will be bound by them.

Finally, in cases such as *Southern Water Authority v Carey*[51] and *Norwich City Council v Harvey*[52] we find an exception to the privity rule emerging in the idea of the 'background contractual setting' – an idea, moreover, which much influenced the Canadian Supreme Court in the *London Drugs* case. In *Carey* it was held, inter alia, that a sub-contractor could answer a claim for negligence brought by the plaintiffs by relying on the terms of a contract between themselves and the main contractor. The contract with the main contractor was in standard form, and although the sub-contractors owed a duty of care to the plaintiffs, the plaintiffs' predecessors, by accepting the limitations contained in that standard form (which was the basis on which the sub-contractors had contracted also), had specified the area of risk they had chosen to accept. In section 5 below, we suggest that situations such as those found in the vicarious immunity, sub-bailment, and contractual setting cases, share a number of common characteristics which justify placing them in a special category which we call 'network contracts'.

So far as P4 questions are concerned, although *Port Line* represents the orthodox approach that a person cannot be held to the terms of a contract to which he is not a party, there is contrary authority of some respectability. In *De Mattos v Gibson*,[53] Knight Bruce J said:

consigns them "at owner's risk" for the whole journey, his consent to take the risk avails the second carrier as well as the first, even though there is no contract between the goods owner and the second carrier. Likewise in the *Elder Dempster* case the shipper, by exempting the charterers from bad stowage, may be taken to have consented to exempt the shipowners also.'

[50] [1994] 2 All ER 250. See also *Singer v Tees and Hartlepool Authority* [1988] 2 Lloyd's Rep. 164, 167, where Steyn J discusses *Morris v Martin* and points out that none of their Lordships in *Scruttons* disagreed with Lord Denning MR.

[51] [1985] 2 All ER 1077.

[52] [1989] 1 All ER 1180.

[53] (1858) 4 De G & J 276.

'Reason and justice seem to prescribe that, at least as a general rule, where a man by gift or purchase acquires property from another, with knowledge of a previous contract lawfully and for valuable consideration made by him with a third person to use and employ the property for a particular purpose in a specified manner, the acquirer shall not, to the material damage of the third person, in opposition to the contract and inconsistently with it, use and employ the property in a manner not allowable to the giver or seller.'[54]

Attempts to rely on the *De Mattos* principle have been made in a variety of contractual contexts, most famously (and most successfully) in *Lord Strathcona Steamship Co v Dominion Coal Co*, where the Privy Council apparently applied the principle in holding that the defendant was not free to ignore the terms of a charter-party of which he was aware when he bought the vessel. Although it is possible to reconcile the decision in this case with that in *Port Line*, on the basis that at the relevant time the defendant in the latter case had no knowledge of the plaintiff's rights under the charter-party, the authorities clearly evince differing approaches to P4 questions. Quite what the *Lord Strathcona* approach amounts to is a moot point.[55] It might be an application to personalty of the *Tulk v Moxhay*[56] principle governing restrictive covenants on land. It may be an illustration of the tort of inducing a breach of contract.[57] On the other hand, it may be an independent principle. Whatever the correct interpretation of the principle, its modern use in P4 situations is pretty limited: for, as Hoffman J has tellingly remarked in the recent *Ural Caspian* case, the principle 'does not provide a panacea for outflanking the doctrine of privity of contract'.[58]

(iii) Established exceptions

Doctrinal departures from the privity principle are only part of the story. A wide range of exceptions to the principle exist,

---

[54] Ibid at p 282.
[55] See eg *Swiss Bank Corpn v Lloyds Bank Ltd* [1979] Ch 548.
[56] (1848) 2 Ph 774.
[57] See *Lumley v Gye* (1853) 2 E & B 216. In this case, the defendant will not be liable unless he has actual knowledge of the contract, whereas under the *Tulk v Moxhay* principle, constructive knowledge suffices.
[58] *Law Debenture Trust Corpn plc v Ural Caspian Oil Corpn Ltd* [1993] 2 All ER 355, 362.

both under statute,[59] and under the common law. The most
significant feature of the common law exceptions is the way
in which well-established legal institutions, basically
agency, trust, and implied contract, can be used to circum-
vent the doctrine.[60] Thus, in *Pyrene Co Ltd v Scindia
Navigation Co Ltd*,[61] a carrier was held able to rely on the
terms of the carriage contract made between himself and the
consignee of the goods, to resist a claim made by the seller
of the goods (ie this was a P3 case). One rationalisation of
this decision is that the consignee acted as the seller's agent
in dealing with the carrier.[62] However, the most dramatic
modern example has been Lord Wilberforce's open invitation to the courts to outflank *Scruttons* by employing the
device of the implied contract.[63] In *The New York Star*[64] he
stated that the significance of the Privy Council's earlier
decision in *The Eurymedon*[65] was to establish the principle
that stevedores could take advantage of protective terms in
contracts of carriage, notwithstanding the fact that they
were not parties to those contracts. In that case, it was held
that the bill of lading amounted to an offer to the stevedores
who were employed to unload a vessel. Thus, in consideration of the stevedores accepting the offer by undertaking the

---

[59]   See eg s 11, Married Women's Property Act 1882; s 14(2), Marine
       Insurance Act 1906; Defective Premises Act 1972; Consumer
       Protection Act 1987; s 2, Carriage of Goods by Sea Act 1992 (replacing
       s 1, Bills of Lading Act 1855 – see Bradgate and White (1993) 56 MLR
       188).
[60]   In the light of recent case-law, we should also include in this list the
       employment of the so-called rule in *Dunlop v Lambert* (1839) 6 Cl &
       Finn 600, 7 ER 824. This rule (which relates to a situation where A
       contracts with B, but it is understood that A is actually contracting for
       the benefit of C) exceptionally allows A to sue B to recover the losses
       which C has actually suffered (A then being accountable for the dam-
       ages to C). The significance of this rule has been highlighted recently
       by *Linden Gardens Trust v Lenesta Sludge Disposals Ltd* [1994] AC 85
       and *Darlington Borough Council v Wiltshier Northern Ltd* [1995] 11
       Const LJ 36. Generally, see *White v Jones* [1995] 1 All ER 691,
       708–710.
[61]   [1954] 2 QB 402.
[62]   See GH Treitel *The Law of Contract* 8th edn (London, Sweet and
       Maxwell, 1991) pp 558–559.
[63]   The implied contract device might also be used to rationalise the
       decision in *Pyrene v Scindia*; see Treitel, ibid.
[64]   *Port Jackson Stevedoring Pty Ltd v Salmond & Spraggon (Australia) Pty
       Ltd* [1980] 3 All ER 257.
[65]   *New Zealand Shipping Co Ltd v A.M. Satterthwaite & Co Ltd* [1975] AC
       154.

unloading operation, the cargo owner extended to them the benefit of the exemptions in the bill of lading. Now this solution being based on orthodox contract theory left open a number of potential difficulties. What for example would happen if the stevedores were unaware of the terms of the bill of lading? However, the commercial correctness of the decision, particularly in that it gave effect to the clear intentions of the international conventions governing the terms contained in bills of lading, made it undesirable that courts should too closely concern themselves with niceties about the formation of contracts in this context. Accordingly, Lord Wilberforce observed of *The Eurymedon*:

> 'The decision does not support, and their Lordships would not encourage, a search for fine distinctions which would diminish the general applicability, in the light of established commercial practice, of the principle [in effect, of vicarious immunity].'[66]

Or, to put this point less obliquely, the device of the implied contract bridges the gap between traditional contract doctrine and the exigencies of commercial practice, but the use being made of the device will not stand up to strict orthodox analysis. It would be wise, therefore, not to look too closely.

3. PRIVITY, FAIRNESS AND CONVENIENCE

Adjudication in contract cases involves a complex resolution of tensions.[67] In the case of privity questions, these tensions are particularly acute. On the one hand, the demand for consistency exerts a strong pull towards the orthodox privity authorities, while, on the other hand, the demand for convenience often invites a deviation from the orthodox approach. In consequence of this latter demand, as we have indicated already, we find the law pulled in different directions as the strict privity approach is modified both by doctrinal statement and by subversive judicial practice. Clearly, this is an unsatisfactory state of affairs.

If we were to legislate answers to the first three privity

---

[66]   [1980] 3 All ER 257, 261.
[67]   See Adams and Brownsword 'The Ideologies of Contract Law' (1987) 7 Legal Studies 205; and generally *Understanding Contract Law* 2nd edn (London, Fontana, 1994).

questions, what ideals should we aspire to? We would suggest that there are three criteria which would need to be satisfied. First, the law should be clear, coherent and predictable in its application. Secondly, it should avoid commercial inconvenience (for we are largely concerned with commercial contracting). Finally, it should avoid injustice and anomaly. Undoubtedly, judged by these standards, the present state of English law is seriously deficient. It is unpredictable, its commercial inconvenience is notorious, and it has a tendency to produce unjust results. On this latter point we might quote Sir Robert Megarry VC's well-known remarks in *Ross v Caunters*:[68]

> 'If this is right [that a beneficiary under a will has no claim against the negligent solicitors who drew it], the result is striking. The only person who has a valid claim [the deceased] has suffered no loss, and the only person who has suffered a loss has no valid claim.'

If then the privity doctrine fails under these criteria, why does English law continue to cling to it? Might it be that although the present regime is unsatisfactory, it is a lesser evil than any alternative would be? Is it in fact possible to devise a better regime? We will take these questions in turn, dealing here with the question as to whether the present regime is fairer than any alternative which might be devised, and in the next section with the Law Commission's proposals for reform.

There are two lines of argument which can be made in defence of the privity principle on the grounds of fairness, the first of which appears in Crompton J's judgment in *Tweddle v Atkinson*. After stating the same consideration argument as Wightman J, he continued:

> 'It would be a monstrous proposition to say that a person was a party to the contract for the purpose of suing upon it for his own advantage, and not a party to it for the purpose of being sued.'[69]

This argument appears to have two aspects: either it is an argument that the third party should not be permitted to

---

[68]   [1979] 3 All ER 580, 583. Again, in the recent similar case of *White v Jones* [1995] 1 All ER 691, at 702, Lord Goff, citing Sir Robert Megarry VC's remarks, emphasised that it was of 'cardinal importance' that practical justice should be done.

[69]   (1861) 1 B & S 393, 398.

sue because there is no reciprocity between him and the defendant; or it is an argument that the third party should not be assisted in getting something for nothing. We will consider each of these in turn. The first amounts to saying that the reason why the third party cannot sue one of the parties to the contract is because the parties to the contract cannot sue the third party. But the parties to the contract on the facts of *Tweddle v Atkinson* seem to have been quite happy with a possible third party suit, because they expressly assented to it in their contract. Moreover, the parties to the contract in that case could sue each other, and yet it is not obvious what direct advantage they got from the contract. Following Crompton J's logic we could just as well say that it was monstrous that the plaintiff's father-in-law should be a party to the contract for the purpose of being sued by the plaintiff's father, but not for the purpose of taking any direct advantage from it. The other aspect of the argument is that it is unfair for the third party to get something for nothing. Certainly, on the facts of *Tweddle v Atkinson* the plaintiff stood to get something for nothing, in the sense of benefiting from an exchange to which he had made no contribution. However, this scarcely constitutes an argument for saying that the third party should derive no assistance from the courts when one party to the contract breaks his word. The effect of permitting the promisor to break his word, in fact, is that the *promisor* gets something for nothing. Not only does the party who breaks his word get something for nothing, he has done something morally wrong in breaking his word, which the plaintiff has not. The something for nothing argument then can be applied both to the plaintiff and to the defendant – minimally, we could say, on that score, the scales of justice are evenly balanced, and perhaps even that they are tilted in the plaintiff's favour by the defendant's default.

The second argument is as follows. Under English law a gratuitous promisee cannot sue. If I am promised a gift by a person, who fails to fulfil his promise, I have no remedy. Why then should a gratuitous third party be treated more favourably? Certainly, if a promisor promises a gratuitous promisee that he will confer a benefit on a third party, neither the gratuitous promisee, nor the third party can sue, and in this situation it would be unfair if the third party were in a better position than the gratuitous promisee. But this is not the situation which concerns us. We are concerned with the situation where two parties have a binding contract. Here we are asked to deny the third party a right, not because the promisee, who is a party to the contract, has no right (which clearly he has), but because the third party would have no right if he were a gratuitous promisee. Between the contracting parties, and the third party, it is clearly fair that the third party should have a remedy, because that is what the contracting parties intended.[70] It might also be said, however, in support of this argument, that if the promisor had promised the third party a benefit directly, but gratuitously, the third party (who of course in this situation is not a third party at all) would have had no remedy. Why, then, should he have a remedy where the promise is not made to him directly, but via an enforceable promise made to another party? But this is simply putting the same argument a different way. There is a material difference between the situation where the promise is entirely gratuitous, and the situation where it is only gratuitous vis-à-vis the third party. If, on the other hand, this is simply another version of the 'something for nothing' aspect of Crompton J's argument, we have already met this with the reply we gave above.

Accordingly, there is no deep-seated objection to the relaxation of the privity rule, and the question largely resolves itself into whether or not a better regime can be devised, which will satisfy the criteria we set out above.

4. DUAL INTENTION AS A BASIS FOR REFORM

Reform of the privity rule has been a major project for the Law Commission in recent years. The Commission had earlier looked at the rights of buyers of goods carried by sea, and recommended reform of the Bills of Lading Act 1855.[71]

---

[70] Of course, there is the question as to what might happen if one of the contracting parties wanted to release the other from his contractual obligations. Would it be fair in such a case to hold that other to his contractual obligations on the ground that the third party did not want to release him? We consider the question of variation and cancellation below, in section 6, but the issues raised by release do not undermine the thrust of the argument in the text.

[71] Sale of Goods Forming Part of a Bulk (1993) Law Com No 215; Rights of Suit in Respect of Carriage of Goods by Sea (1991) Law Com No 196 – leading to the Carriage of Goods by Sea Act 1992.

Their work in this connection, together with a more cautious judicial approach to the question of tort liability for economic loss,[72] suggested that a re-examination of the privity rule would be timely. The result has been a Consultation Paper, *Privity of Contract: Contracts for the Benefit of Third Parties*.[73] The Commission agree that there are the four basic privity questions which we have used as an organising scheme above, and that English law at present, in general, answers all four questions in the negative.[74] They conclude provisionally that the law should be reformed (by legislation), and make four principal substantive recommendations:

1. A person will, in principle, be able to sue on a contract to which he is not a party, but which was made for his benefit (provided that the dual intention test is satisfied)[75] ie subject to this test P1 questions will be answered in the affirmative.

2. A person will be able to rely on defences based on a contract to which the plaintiff, but not himself, is a party (provided again that the dual intention test is satisfied) ie subject to this test P2 questions will be answered in the affirmative.

3. Other things being equal, a person will be able to rely on defences based on a contract to which he, but not the plaintiff is a party (on the ground that if the plaintiff takes the benefit of such a contract, he also has to take the burden) ie other things being equal, P3 questions will be answered in the affirmative.

4. A person will not, however, be able to enforce his own contract against a third party, ie P4 questions will continue, in general, to be answered in the negative. The Law Commission's reason for this is that a person should not be permitted to impose on a third party a contract with which that third party 'has nothing whatever to do'.

The 'dual intention' test, which is central to the Commission's proposed scheme, has two limbs:

---

[72]   See *Murphy v Brentwood District Council* [1990] 2 All ER 908, and ch 4.
[73]   Law Commission Consultation Paper No 121 (1991).
[74]   Paras 2.3 and 2.4.
[75]   See below.

(a)   the contracting parties must have intended that the third party 'should receive the benefit of the promised performance'; and,

(b)   they must have intended 'to create a legal obligation enforceable by [the third party]'.[76]

The basis of this test is 'to allow a remedy to the third party when to do so would give effect to the intentions of the contracting parties'.[77] It will be noted that the test figures explicitly only in answers to P1 and P2 questions. Its relevance to P3 questions is not expressly dealt with in the recommendations – hence our 'other things being equal' caveat in relation to the Commission's P3 proposal.

In order to develop a critique of these recommendations it is necessary to distinguish single contract situations from those where there are multiple contracts – as for example in the case of construction contracts (where there will be sub-contractors and sub-sub-contractors) but also chains and strings of contracts such as one finds in sales. We will consider these situations in turn.

(i) Single contract situations

There is little problem with the dual intention test in P1 situations, such as in *Tweddle v Atkinson*. In that case, it will be recalled, the father and father-in-law clearly intended to benefit the plaintiff. Under the Law Commission's proposals, the plaintiff would win, thereby giving effect to the intention of the contracting parties.

P2 questions will be uncommon in single contract settings, but it seems reasonable that a defendant third party should be able to rely on a defence contained in a contract between the plaintiff and a fellow contractor, if this was the intention manifested by the latter contractors.

P3 situations are a little more difficult. The question here is whether the defendant can rely on a provision in a contract between himself and a third party, vis-à-vis the plaintiff. Two situations need to be distinguished. In the first, the defendant and the third party have simply purported to deprive the plaintiff of some right. They cannot be

---

[76]   Para 5.10.
[77]   Para 5.11.

permitted to do this,[78] for the very reason that the Law
Commission give for continuing to answer P4 questions in
the negative – the defendant is trying to impose on the plaintiff a contract with which he 'has nothing whatever to do'. In
the second, however, the defendant and the third party have
purported to confer on the plaintiff some right, but the
enjoyment of this benefit is subject to a condition. Surely,
here it would be wrong to permit the plaintiff to take the benefit, without subjecting him to the condition? This indeed is
the Law Commission's reasoning. However, on closer analysis, this proposition can be seen to be a corollary of the
Commission's recommendation to relax the privity rule in
relation to P1 questions. We can expand the Law
Commission's reasoning in relation to P3 questions of this
type as follows:

(a) a third party will be permitted to sue on a contract
     made for his benefit if the dual intention test is satis-
     fied;
(b) but if the contracting parties intended that the third
     party should take the benefit, only subject to certain
     conditions, the third party will be permitted to enforce
     the contract only subject to these conditions.
     Accordingly, to this extent, the dual intention test is
     relevant to P3 questions.

(ii) Multiple contracts

The dual intention test works nicely with single contract P1
questions. However, as we have seen, much of the modern
case-law arises in complex contractual settings involving
multiple linked contracts. Elsewhere, we have suggested
that some of these complexes of contracts should be treated
as 'networks' (in which the privity rules would be relaxed).

---

[78] For example, in *Haseldine v Daw* [1941] 3 All ER 156, a contract
between the owner of a block of flats and a firm of engineers (employed to maintain the lift at the flats) purported to exclude the
engineers' liability to third parties for injuries sustained while using
the lift. Clearly, to permit the engineers to rely on this contractual provision against a visitor to the flats, injured while using the lift, would
be unfair; and the court ruled that a third party could not be so
prejudiced.

Network contracts would be defined as follows:[79]

1.   A network contract is a contract forming part of a set of contracts.
2.   The set of contracts has the following characteristics:
     (i)   there is a principal contract (or, there are a number of principal contracts) within the set giving the set an overall objective;
     (ii)   other contracts (secondary and tertiary contracts, and so on) are entered into, an object of each of which is, directly or indirectly, to further the attainment of this overall objective; and,
     (iii) the network of contractors expands until a sufficiency of contractors are obligated, whether to the parties to the principal contract, or to other contractors in the set, to attain the overall objective.

Building contracts and contracts for the carriage of goods are paradigm examples of network contracts, as are many credit and financing arrangements. In each of these cases, it is possible to discern a common underlying purpose, so that we can say that the set of contracts as a whole comprises a single network. How far can we apply the Law Commission's proposals in relation to P1, P2 and P3 in contractual networks? Could, for example, the consignor of goods (A), who delivered them to a carrier (B), for transport to a particular destination, sue directly a sub-contractor (C) employed by B for one leg of the journey? On the Law Commission's proposal on P1, the answer is: 'only if the dual intention test is satisfied in relation to B and C's contract'. But, in this type of situation, the specific intention of B and C does not seem particularly relevant. We could if we like find the intention to benefit the plaintiff implicit in the overall purpose of the network, but we should not need to search further than this.

What about P2 questions: can C rely on the exemptions

---

[79]   Adams and Brownsword 'Privity and the Concept of a Network Contract' (1990) 10 Legal Studies 12, 27. Cf Lord Mustill's remarks about the significance of contractual networks (as excluding the recognition of delictual duties) in *White v Jones* [1995] 1 All ER 691, 721. And for an analogue of networks, see the concept of 'groups of contracts' as developed in French law by the first *chambre civil* of the *Cour de cassation*: see Barry Nicholas, *The French Law of Contract* 2nd edn (Oxford, Clarendon Press, 1992) 172–7.

contained in the contract between the consignor (A) and the carrier (B)? Again, according to the Law Commission, this would depend on the intention of A and B. Here, the result seems right. Thus in *The New York Star*[80] it was clearly the intention of the contracting parties to exempt the sub-contracting stevedores from liability, and no doubt insurance had been arranged on this basis. Giving effect to that intention without the need to resort to tortuous and dubious legal reasoning seems correct.

P3 questions are a little more difficult. Can C, if sued by the consignor (A), rely on exempting conditions in the B/C contract? It would appear that the Law Commission's intentions are, as noted above, that if the consignor (A) sues C for breach of the B/C contract, A cannot take the benefit of that contract without taking the burden of any exemptions contained in it. But, to the extent that this situation entails a P1 question, the Law Commission should also require an intention on the part of B and C to benefit the consignor, and what we said above in relation to this question applies again here. What happens, however, if the consignor sues C in negligence, as he is entitled to do in respect of physical damage to the goods? In this situation, the Law Commission's reasoning for subjecting the consignor to the exempting conditions cannot apply. The right answer would appear to be that the consignor (A) should only be prejudiced by the exempting conditions in the B/C contract, if that was the intention manifested in the *consignor/carrier* (A/B) contract.

To summarise: our approach to network contracts differs from the Commission's in two important respects. Whereas, in relation to P1 questions, the Commission would require the dual intention test to be satisfied, we contend that in network contracts the intention to benefit the plaintiff is implicit in the overall purpose of the network, and there should be no need to search further. In relation to P3 questions, whereas the Commission supposes that the justification for fixing the plaintiff (A) with the burdens contained in the B/C (defendant) contract is that the plaintiff is seeking to take the benefit of that contract, we say that this reason is insufficient. The plaintiff may, for example, sue in negligence. The only justification for fixing the plaintiff with

---

[80]   [1980] 3 All ER 257.

the burden of the exempting conditions is that the plaintiff agreed to this in the plaintiff/B contract.

In the case of network contracts, the intentions of the two principal contractors are crucial for the resolution of P2 and P3 situations. Whether the plaintiff (A) sues the defendant (C) for breach of the contract between the defendant and B, or in negligence, the defendant's right to rely on exclusionary terms contained either in the plaintiff/B contract, or in the defendant/B contract, ought to depend, we suggest, on the following presumptions of intent:

(a) where the principal contractors agree that a particular contractual provision in the principal contract shall apply for the benefit of a named subsidiary contractor, or class of contractors, then it is to be assumed that they also intend to create an enforceable right in favour of that named subsidiary contractor, or class of contractors;

(b) where the principal contractors agree that contractual provisions in a subsidiary contract shall apply for the benefit of a named subsidiary contractor, or class of contractors, then it is to be assumed that they also intend to create an enforceable right in favour of that named subsidiary contractor, or class of contractors; and

(c) it is to be assumed that network contractors intend that the benefit of any agreed exclusion or limitation clauses shall be available to employees or agents of the relevant contractors in relation to claims arising out of their performance of their network obligations.[81]

Many network contracts are made on standard forms common to a particular trade or industry. The terms of these forms are well known to those working in the particular trade or industry. Accordingly, a possible strategy which could be adopted in any legislative reform of this area might be to permit the insertion in these forms of a statutory notice. This would be a statement to the effect that the terms were binding not only on the original

---

[81] This responds to the difficulties exposed by the *London Drugs* litigation, see above. See, also, *Muller Martini Canada Ltd v Kuehne and Nagel International Ltd* (1990) 73 DLR (4th) 315; and see Adams and Brownsword (1991) 55 Saskatchewan Law Review 441.

contractors, but also on those performing under them. The onus of a sub-contractor seeking to show that he was not bound by the terms of such a form would be heavy: in fact, little short of an estoppel would prevent the form from being relied on.

(iii) Chains and strings

Clusters of contracts do not necessarily form networks. In particular, it is arguable that simple chains (or strings) of contracts, as with contracts for the sale or supply of goods, should be distinguished from networks (and, thus, should be subject to the usual privity rules). On the Law Commission's proposed dual intention test this would mean that a third party would be permitted to sue on a contract in a chain only where the parties to that contract had the requisite intention. This, however, might be thought to be unfairly restrictive in at least two cases.

First, it is arguable that where a chain of contracts forms an integrated set, then it should be treated as if it were a network. For example, if a dealer is a recognised outlet for a particular manufacturer's products (say, the manufacturer's motor cars, or electrical goods), with the goods being supplied to the dealer through a distribution system controlled by the manufacturer, then it is artificial to treat the chain as so many discrete contracts. Moreover, it is arguable that consumer purchasers should be regarded as being in direct contract with any contractors in the chain.[82]

Secondly, even if end purchasers do not normally have any option other than to sue the immediate contracting party in the chain, we might wish to relax the privity restriction where it is not possible to work liability back along the chain. In such circumstances, it is arguable that the purchaser should be permitted to leapfrog over the first defendant.[83]

---

[82] For proposals in favour of such relaxation of privity, see the European Commission's Green Paper on Guarantees for Consumer Goods and After-Sales Services (COM (93) 509, November 15, 1993). See Stephen Weatherill, 'Consumer Guarantees' (1994) 110 LQR 545.

[83] Cf Deryck Beyleveld and Roger Brownsword 'Privity, Transitivity, and Rationality' (1991) 54 Modern Law Review 48.

We will reconsider these matters shortly in the context of our discussion of an alternative approach to the relaxation of privity.

5. LEGITIMATE EXPECTATION

The Law Commission bases its proposals for the relaxation of privity on the intention of the contracting parties. On this view, the primary concern is to hold the contracting parties to their freely assumed commitments. This, however, is not the only candidate as the basis for reform. Instead, one might focus on legitimate expectations (or justifiable reliance) or on actual reliance by the third party.

Whilst actual reliance has its supporters,[84] it is a concept that presupposes justifiable reliance (ie reliance that would be justified). After all, we cannot suppose that actual reliance should be given any weight unless it is also justifiable reliance. It follows that justifiable reliance is certainly a necessary condition for enforcement of a promise; but the question is whether justifiable (but not actual) reliance is a sufficient condition. If justifiable reliance is not both a necessary and a sufficient condition, we must distinguish between the case where a third party could justifiably have relied (but has not actually relied) and the case where there has been actual reliance which is also justified. Although this all requires more careful analysis,[85] it seems to us that the logic of these conceptual relationships is that it is justifiable reliance that grounds the obligation, while actual reliance serves simply as a measurement of the claim. Since justifiable reliance is equivalent to legitimate expectation, we will persist with our contention that legitimate expectation is the key to

---

[84] Generally, see ch 4; seminally, see the discussion in P. S. Atiyah 'Contracts, Promises, and the Law of Obligations' in *Essays in Contract* (Oxford, Clarendon Press, 1986) p 10.

[85] Cf the relatively advanced state of the conceptual analysis of the concept of legitimate expectation in the field of administrative law: see eg P.P. Craig, 'Legitimate Expectations: A Conceptual Analysis' (1992) 108 Law Quarterly Review 79 (in the light of which, note particularly the distinction between legitimate expectations based on representation or conduct and legitimate expectations linked to protected interests).

contractual obligation and consider how this would work in relation to the privity doctrine.[86]

The Law Commission considered a test based on justifiable and reasonable reliance, but rejected it on the ground that it would 'raise the possibility of an unacceptable volume of litigation and leave promisors open to liability to a potentially indeterminate class of third parties'.[87] To the extent that such a test would by-pass the intention of the contracting parties, this would, of course, be a serious objection. However, where the reliance is supported by the intention of the contracting parties, it is hardly open to this criticism. In other words, in certain, though not necessarily all, settings, the justifiable reliance test requires the intention of the contracting parties to be taken into account.

How would a justifiable reliance test best be implemented? Again, we believe that it is necessary to distinguish single contract settings, multiple contracts, and chains and strings.

(i) Single contract situations

We can divide single contract situations into two categories: those where the contracting parties are under no prior obligation to any third party, and those where there is a prior obligation. In cases falling into the first category, no third party can have any legitimate expectation that the contractors will make a contract for its benefit. A third party can only legitimately expect such a benefit once the contractors have indicated that their intention is to confer such a benefit. In other words, the dual intention test is the correct way of implementing not only the basic intention principle, but also in this particular context, the justifiable reliance principle. In the second category of cases, where one, or both, of

---

[86]   Cf *Darlington Borough Council v Wiltshier Northern Ltd* [1995] 11 Const LJ where Steyn LJ said (Lexis Transcript):

> 'The case for recognising a contract for the benefit of a third party is simple and straightforward. The autonomy of the will of the parties should be respected. The law of contract should give effect to the reasonable expectations of contracting parties . . . Moreover, often the parties, and particularly third parties, organise their affairs on the faith of the contract. They rely on the contract. It is therefore unjust to deny effectiveness to such a contract.'

[87]   Op cit para 5.9.

the contracting parties is already indebted to the third party, the third party may well be thought to have a legitimate expectation of a benefit being conferred, such expectations being independent of the contractors' intentions, and of themselves providing a justification for the enforcement of the promise in favour of the third party.

(ii) Multiple contracts

What we defined as 'network contracts' above provides a convenient shorthand for the situation we find in a number of the leading privity cases. In our view, such contracts call for a special regime, rather in the same way as building schemes have their own rules in the context of restrictive covenants on land. The contracts in a network are all dedicated to a common purpose, a purpose which is the very rationale for the contracts coming into existence.

We suggested above that it would be a mistake to be over-enthusiastic in applying the dual intention test in these contexts. Instead, the focus should be on the agreement made between the principal contractors. Sometimes the dual intention test would produce results which were identical to our proposal, but sometimes, as we have said already, it would not. In particular, whereas our proposed network rules would give the principal contractors the right to sue down the network irrespective of contrary stipulation by any sub-contractor, the dual intention test would make the principal contractors' right to enforce sub-contracts contingent on the intentions of the sub-contractors. This, we believe, is incompatible with our overriding principle of protecting legitimate expectations. Quite simply, the aggregate of the particular benefits promised by the sub-contractors is the benefit promised by the principal contract. Accordingly, there seems no reason why the legitimate expectations (or justifiable reliance) of the principal contractor should vary depending upon whether one is viewing the promised benefit from the point of view of the principal contract, or from that of the sub-contract.

The legitimate expectation principle is equally applicable whether the principal is suing a sub-contractor, or a sub-contractor the principal. An example of this latter situation would be where the sub-contractor seeks to sue the client, who engaged the principal contractor, for non-payment.

Applying the legitimate expectation principle, each sub-contractor must have the right to enforce that part of the principal contract represented by the particular sub-contract work. But, the liability of the client could not be more extensive vis-à-vis the sub-contractor, than vis-à-vis the principal, so that rights of counter-claim and set-off would be pleadable against the sub-contractor. Indeed, in order to produce a fair result in network situations, inter-pleader would be needed, so that the issues between the various parties could be dealt with at the same time.

(iii) Chains and strings

The commonest contracts of this sort are sales of goods, which characteristically are sold down the line, producer to distributor to dealer to consumer. Although the privity rule has been relaxed to some extent by the Consumer Protection Act 1987, giving consumers direct claims where products are unsafe, this does not fully satisfy a test based on legiti-mate expectation. As we have said already, if we focus on legitimate expectations, we have some ground for permitting a consumer to 'leapfrog' over his immediate supplier to the manufacturer where the chain breaks down. Also, where the chain is integrated, there are grounds for permitting direct claims on manufacturers' warranties, the contractual effect of which is somewhat uncertain at present.[87a] Sometimes, they are not discovered until after the goods have been purchased and taken home, and on basic prin-ciples, one cannot accept an offer of which one has no knowledge. Giving legal effect to such warranties per se would be a good way of cutting the Gordian knot of the privity problem in this field.[88]

[87a] For proposals for reform of the law on manufacturers' guarantees, see DTI Consultation Paper, 20 February 1992.

[88] It would also obviate having to deal with the difficult question as to whether a component manufacturer should be liable to the consumer. See eg *Goldberg v Kollman Instruments* 191 NE 2d 81 (1963) where the court had to confront the question as to whether the manufacturer of a defective altimeter should be liable to the passengers of an aeroplane that it had caused to crash. The problem arises because the airframe manufacturers, who in such a case are not at fault, can bear the costs of insurance, but the small instrument manufacturer cannot.

(iv) Variation and cancellation

Where the contracting parties have reserved the right to vary or cancel, the Law Commission implies that they should be free to exercise their right irrespective of any expectation or reliance by a third party.[89] This view is consistent with the Commission's dual intention principle, under which it is the intention of the parties which is fundamental. Presumably, if the contractors have misled the third party, they might be estopped from asserting the variation, but subject to this, they must be free to vary.

Where the parties have not reserved the right to vary or cancel, the Commission declares that its aim is to 'achieve a balance between the interests of the contracting parties (and their creditors) and those of the third party'.[90] Consistently with this aim, two 'extreme' views are rejected: the Scottish view that contractors have no right to vary or cancel, and the opposite view that contractors retain the full right to vary or cancel. In the Commission's view, this narrows down the choice to the Australian rule which curtails the right to vary or cancel once the third party has adopted or accepted the contract, or the New Zealand rule which curtails the right once the third party has materially altered its position in reliance on the contract. Given the logic of the Commission's dual intention test, however, it is difficult to see why it should be concerned with either of these matters. On the other hand, these matters would be relevant to a system based on our suggested principle of legitimate expectations.

Our principle would lead to the following general guidelines in relation to variation or cancellation:

1. Where the contracting parties have reserved the right to vary or cancel, and this fact is known to the third party, they are free to vary or cancel at will.
2. Where the contract expressly excludes the right to cancel (whether unilaterally or by mutual agreement between the contractors), the contract by definition precludes cancellation (irrespective of whether the third party has been notified of this, and irrespective of

[89] See para 5.27 but also (iii) in para 5.31.
[90] Para 5.29.

whether the third party has acted in reliance on the contract).
3.   Where the contract expressly excludes the right to vary, then the contract by definition precludes variation (irrespective of whether the third party has been notified of this, and irrespective of whether the third party has acted in reliance on the contract).[91]
4.   Where the contracting parties have neither reserved nor abandoned the right to vary or cancel, or where the contract is unclear, there should be a presumption that the right has been abandoned. Accordingly, as soon as the contractors notify the third party of the contract, the right is lost.

(v) Procedural questions

Although the reasons traditionally given for the maintenance of the privity rule do not stand up to close examination, it must be asked whether, apart from the weight of precedent, and other difficulties we alluded to in the previous sections, there are other reasons not made explicit by the judges for maintaining it. One range of questions relates to procedure: if the substantive rules were to be altered, but present procedural rules maintained, could injustices result? In order to answer this question we must look separately at each of the privity situations.

We can start with P1 situations. In a case such as *Tweddle v Atkinson*, no injustice would have resulted from the enforcement of the promise, because each of the parties to the contract had promised severally to confer a benefit on the plaintiff. If, however, they had promised jointly to confer a benefit what would have been the position? The rule that an action against one joint debtor barred proceedings against the other (even if the judgment had proved to be unenforceable against the judgment debtor) was abrogated by section 3 of the Civil Liability (Contribution) Act 1978. Accordingly, one potential source of unfairness has gone.

---

[91]   Assuming that variation and cancellation are distinguishable, where the contract excludes variation, it may still be permissible for the contractors to *cancel* prior to the third party coming to know of the contract. Once the third party is notified of the contract, however, guideline (4) in the text applies to bar cancellation.

The possibility of a single defendant joining the other joint promisor is covered by the possibility of issuing a third party notice in accordance with O.16 r 1 Rules of the Supreme Court. Accordingly, no changes seem to be needed here.

With regard to P2 situations, the defendant's (C's) claim to set up a term in a contract between the plaintiff (A) and B as a defence, necessarily may call into question the precise terms of the contract between the plaintiff and B. Similarly, in P3 situations, the precise terms of the contract between the defendant (C) and B may be called into question. A third party notice joining B can only be issued where there is a question of indemnity between B and the defendant (C).[92] This could arise in P3 situations. The question of indemnity is most likely to crop up in network contracts, and is adequately covered by the existing rules. Most other disputes about the terms of the contract with B, whether in P2 or P3 situations, may be resolved by calling B as a witness and requiring him if necessary to produce any relevant documents.[93]

One potential problem occurs to us, however. In a P2 situation, the plaintiff (A) obviously has no interest in pleading any limitation clause in the contract with B, and the defendant (C) may not know of it. We concluded, however, that the joint intention of the plaintiff and B when they entered into their contract that the liability of the defendant should be limited ought to be sufficient justification for limiting the defendant's liability to the plaintiff. A possible solution to this problem is suggested by the changes which were made when the rule against pleading the title of a third party was abrogated by section 8(1) of the Torts (Interference with Goods) Act 1977. The Rules of the Supreme Court were then amended to require the plaintiff to indorse the writ with the names of other parties claiming an interest in the goods.[94] Similarly, the plaintiff might be required to indorse the writ with particulars of any contract to which he is a party which purported to limit his liability vis-à-vis the defendant. If the plaintiff failed to do this, and the contract came to light during the course of the action, the court would have a discretion to dismiss the action altogether. A special provision

---

[92]   As to indemnities, see ch 8.
[93]   If necessary, under a *subpoena duces tecum*: see O.38 r 14 RSC.
[94]   O.15 r 10A RSC.

of this sort might be preferable to leaving matters to come out in discovery (which is limited to documents and therefore would disclose only written terms), or in replies to interrogatories (if it occurred to the defendant to raise the matter), simply because it would bring into play a crucial factor at the earliest stage in the action, thereby obviating the need to amend pleadings when things came to light at a later stage (something which always causes delays).

Finally, as we have said, the Law Commission is not at present proposing to alter the position in relation to P4 situations. Such litigation as has taken place where the requirement of privity has not been adhered to in P4 cases, has taken place under the existing rules. Accordingly, we do not need to consider this further.

Subject to the suggestion made above, it would appear, therefore, that the present procedural rules are adequate to deal with any possible reforms.

6. CONCLUSION

To leave privity unreformed is to invite further irrationality as ever more ways and means of subverting the doctrine are employed.[95] Given the confidence that judges now display (both in England and the Commonwealth) in tackling privity in an explicit and head-on fashion, there is perhaps less danger than there once was of the law being covertly manipulated.[96] Nevertheless, the Law Commission is surely right in recommending the reform of privity and, moreover, that such reform be dealt with by legislation. What is more questionable is whether the Commission's proposed dual intention test is the right basis for revising the law. Whilst the test will often produce the right outcome, we suggest

---

[95]   Cf Lord Diplock in *The Albazero, Albacruz (cargo owners) v Albazero (owners)* [1976] 3 All ER 129, 137:

'[T]here may still be occasional cases in which the rule [in *Dunlop v Lambert*] would provide a remedy where no other would be available to a person sustaining loss which under a rational legal system ought to be compensated by the person who has caused it.'

[96]   Cf A. Corbin 'Contracts for the Benefit of Third Parties' (1930) 46 LQR 12, 44-45, commenting on the evolution of the trust device from a fiction to an explicit exception to the privity principle.

that, in the final analysis, third party issues (like consideration issues) must be based on the concept of legitimate expectation; and, once legitimate expectation becomes the organising idea, we further suggest that, in complex contractual situations, the idea of networks merits serious consideration.

Chapter 6

Breach and withdrawal

Introduction

In common law jurisdictions, the standard remedial option for an innocent party to a breach of contract is to make a claim for damages. However, in some circumstances, a claim for damages might not satisfy the innocent party's remedial interests. For example, the preferred option for the innocent party might be to require the contract-breaker to perform (ie to claim specific performance), or the innocent party might wish to have the option of withdrawing from the contract. This latter option gives rise to the key issue to be discussed in this chapter: in what circumstances should the law confer upon the innocent party the right to withdraw for breach[1] (that is, the right to discharge itself (and the contract-breaker) from any further primary obligations under the contract)?[2]

---

[1] Note the distinction between 'having the right to withdraw for breach' in the sense of (i) having the option to elect between withdrawal and continuation, and (ii) exercising the option in favour of withdrawal in a valid manner and for valid reasons (or, at least, not for invalid reasons). As will become apparent, this chapter is concerned with the right to withdraw in both these senses.

[2] Cf Lord Diplock's oft-cited dictum in *Photo Production Ltd v Securicor Transport Ltd* [1980] AC 827, 849, to the effect that the expression 'breach of condition' should be reserved for situations where 'the contracting parties have agreed, whether by express words, or by implication of law, that any failure by one party to perform a primary obligation, irrespective of the gravity of the event that has in fact resulted from the breach, shall entitle the other party to elect to put an end to all primary obligations of both parties remaining unperformed . . .'

Broadly speaking, the position in English law is that the right to withdraw will be available where the particular term breached has been designated as a 'condition'[3] (by virtue of legislation, precedent, or express agreement). Such designation apart, however, English law treats withdrawal as an exceptional form of relief, to be available only where damages would not be an adequate remedy. On this basis, the critical question (in the absence of prior determination by law or by agreement) is to identify just when and why damages will not adequately compensate the innocent party for the breach. This sounds straightforward enough. Yet, the question of the right to withdraw for breach has, for some time, been a vexed matter in the English law of contract.[4]

To implement the principle that the right to withdraw for breach should be available only where damages would not be adequate, a familiar litany of tests and approaches has been suggested. Thus, if we follow the traditional classification approach, the test is whether the breach goes to the root of the contract, or whether it strikes at an essential or a fundamental term;[5] if we apply the modern *Hong Kong*[6] approach – at any rate, as it is narrowly interpreted[7] – the

---

3   Cf above, n 2.
4   The matter is vexed at more than one level. Quite apart from any surface doctrinal tensions, there are different views about how far the law should strive for calculability in the face of hard cases (see section 1 below). This is reflected in wholesale judicial disagreements as the law is applied to particular cases. For example, the Court of Appeal reversed Mocatta J in both *Maredelanto Cia Naviera SA v Bergbau-Handel GmbH: The Mihalis Angelos* [1971] 1 QB 164 and *Cehave NV v Bremer Handelsgesellschaft mbH: The Hansa Nord* [1976] QB 44. In the former, Mocatta J was held to have relied mistakenly on the modern *Hong Kong* approach (see below, notes 6 and 7) rather than the traditional classification approach, while in the latter he was held to have wrongly employed the traditional classification approach rather than the modern *Hong Kong* approach. More recently, and not untypically, in *Cie Commerciale Sucres et Denrees v C. Czarnikow Ltd: The Naxos* [1990] 3 All ER 641, on the question of whether a particular term was a condition (giving the buyers the right to withdraw), whereas the arbitrator and the majority of the House of Lords held that it was, Gatehouse J and the majority of the Court of Appeal held that it was not.
5   See eg *Bettini v Gye* (1876) 1 QBD 183, 188.
6   See *Hong Kong Fir Shipping Co Ltd v Kawasaki Kisen Kaisha Ltd* [1962] 2 QB 26. See ch 2, p 45.
7   See Diplock LJ's judgment ibid, at pp 69–72. For a broader approach, in which less emphasis is placed on the actual events following the breach, and more weight is attached to 'the nature of the breach and its foreseeable consequences' see Upjohn LJ ibid, at p 64. See also *Bunge Corpn v Tradax SA* [1981] 2 All ER 513, 543 (Lord Scarman).

question is whether the actual consequences of the breach have deprived the innocent party of substantially the whole benefit of what has been bargained for; while, if we adopt the test proposed by Buckley LJ in the *Decro-Wall*[8] case, the question is whether 'the consequences of the breach [are] such that it would be unfair to the injured party to hold him to the contract and leave him to the remedy in damages as and when a breach or breaches may occur'.[9] In other words, the law suggests a number of criteria for assessing the adequacy of damages: in particular, the importance of the term which has been breached (given the surrounding contractual circumstances and the presumed intentions of the parties),[10] the seriousness of the actual consequences of the breach, and the fairness of denying to the innocent party the option of withdrawal.

If one were to start afresh with this, the key issue surely would be whether the innocent party had *good reasons* for claiming a right to withdraw for breach, rather than settling for damages alone. Whilst it might be argued that this very idea is immanent in the existing law – in the sense that the various tests proposed are precisely attempts to identify situations where the innocent party would have good reasons for claiming a right to withdraw[11] – the fact of the matter is that the existing law fails to take into account, in an explicit and coherent way, the reasons underlying the innocent party's claimed right to withdraw. What this signifies is not merely that the law is indifferent to the existence of good reasons for withdrawal, but also that it has no serious concern with bad reasons for withdrawal.

Such indifference to bad reasons has implications at two

---

8   *Decro-Wall International SA v Practitioners in Marketing Ltd* [1971] 2 All ER 216.
9   Ibid, at p 232.
10   For Bowen LJ's classic articulation of this idea, see *Bentsen v Taylor Sons and Co* [1893] 2 QB 274, 281.
11   For example, in *Bettini v Gye* (1876) 1 QBD 183, 188, it was implied that, in looking at whether a breach of a particular term went to the root of the contract, or rendered performance different in substance from that stipulated for, the question was whether damages would adequately compensate for the breach. This, it might be argued, was simply an elliptical way of saying that, where the breach goes to the root (or cannot be adequately compensated by the payment of damages), then the innocent party has good reason for claiming the option of withdrawal.

levels. First, it yields the settled principle that, *if the innocent party has the right to withdraw for breach*, then it is
immaterial (in the absence of estoppel or the like) that bad
legal reasons have been cited at the time of withdrawal.[12]
Thus, in *The Mihalis Angelos*,[13] for example, the innocent
charterers were rescued from having wrongly relied on force
majeure as a ground for withdrawal by the Court of Appeal
holding that there was actually a breach of condition by the
owners of the vessel. Secondly, and more importantly, it
entails that a breach may be cited as the legal ground
for withdrawal when the innocent party's reasons for seeking withdrawal are wholly unrelated to the breach. In other
words, as Mellish LJ once put it, there is no requirement
that the 'real reason'[14] for seeking release from a contract
should coincide with the cited legal reason for withdrawal.
Accordingly, an innocent party may be permitted to cite a
breach as the legal reason for withdrawal when the real
explanation lies in some collateral economic reason – for
example, when a supplier wishes to withdraw on a rising
market, or a buyer wishes to withdraw on a falling market.
Indeed, *The Mihalis Angelos*, if not quite a case of economic opportunism, was just such a case of collateral
economic motivation, the charterers wishing to escape from
the charter-party, not because of the owners' breach, but
because the supply of apatite (the intended cargo) had been
interrupted by events beyond their control.

Against this background, the main idea of this chapter is
to explore the question of how the law might look if, in the
absence of express legal provision or agreement, the starting point for judging whether damages were an adequate
remedy was a consideration of the innocent party's reasons
for claiming a right to withdraw for breach. In other words,
how might the law look if it adopted a 'reason-centred

---

[12]   See KE Lindgren, JW Carter, and DJ Harland, *Contract Law in
       Australia* (Sydney, Butterworths, 1986) para 1969.
[13]   *Maredelanto Cia Naviera SA v Bergbau-Handel GmbH: The Mihalis
       Angelos* [1971] 1 QB 164.
[14]   In *Shand v Bowes* (1876–7) 2 QBD 112, 115, Mellish LJ observed that,
       if the defendant buyers' contention was accepted, then the conse-
       quence would be 'that purchasers would, without any real reason,
       frequently obtain an excuse for rejecting contracts when prices had
       dropped'. On appeal, however, the House was not impressed by this
       consideration, see *Bowes v Shand* (1877) 2 App Cas 455, 465–466
       (Lord Cairns LCh), and 476 (Lord Hatherley).

regime', taking into account, explicitly and centrally, the innocent party's reasons for claiming a right to withdraw? Fairly clearly, a reason-centred regime would cut across the grain of English contract doctrine in at least two important respects. First, notwithstanding the reluctance of English contract lawyers to get involved with questions of intentionality, the culpability of the contract-breaker – the question of whether the breach was intentional, negligent, or entirely innocent – would be regarded as a material factor in assessing good reasons for withdrawal. Secondly, the distinction between withdrawal *'for breach'* as opposed to withdrawal following breach but *'for collateral economic reasons'*, far from being ignored, would be incorporated as a central doctrinal landmark. Moreover, since it will be contended that a purported withdrawal for breach which has actually been inspired by collateral economic reasons should be disallowed on the ground of bad faith, the reason-centred regime would nudge the English law of contract a little closer to adopting a principle of good faith in the enforcement of contracts. This latter point needs some expansion.

As has been intimated, where an innocent party seeks to withdraw for collateral economic reasons, the attraction of withdrawal is that it releases the party from the prices obtaining under the contract into a market with more favourable prices. Often, the price differential (between the contract and the market) will be very substantial so that large gains are to be made if only the innocent party can escape from the contract. By contrast, if the innocent party is restricted to a remedy in damages for the losses directly occasioned by the breach, no more than quite trivial sums may be recoverable. In many cases, therefore, the position is that the innocent party is not the least bit interested in recovering damages for the breach but sees great advantage in securing withdrawal. Prima facie, therefore, this seems like the perfect example of a situation where damages would not be an adequate remedy and where the innocent party would have compelling reasons for claiming the right to withdraw. However, this glosses over one of the fundamental premises of the reason-centred regime, namely that the right to withdraw for breach is precisely the right to withdraw *for breach*. What the reason-centred regime holds is *not* that the innocent party must have good reasons for preferring withdrawal to damages, but that the innocent party must have good reasons for saying that *the breach* is such that damages simply would not be adequate relief. Where the innocent party is motivated by collateral economic considerations, it is the nature of the market, not the nature of the breach, upon which the innocent party must found an argument that damages are not adequate; and this simply will not do. Accordingly, where the reason-centred regime is in place, good reasons for withdrawal must be interpreted, not as an understandable preference for withdrawal rather than damages, but as reasons which relate the inadequacy of damages to the particular breach.

In this chapter, after reviewing some of the tensions and tendencies in the existing law, a sketch will be presented of a reason-centred regime. We deal first with the kind of reasons which would count as good reasons (prior determination by law or by agreement apart)[15] for having a right to withdraw for breach, and then with the question of pre-classification of terms (or prior determination of the availability of the right to withdraw) by express agreement or force of law. By way of a conclusion, a brief comment will be offered on the rationality of a reason-centred legal regime for withdrawal for breach.

1. TENSIONS AND TENDENCIES IN THE LAW

According to the present law, a right to withdraw for breach of a particular term may arise in one of four ways:

1. the term in question is treated as a 'condition' in the strict sense by either statute or by precedent;
2. the parties have expressly stipulated that the term in question shall be treated as a 'condition' in the strict sense (or, that the right to withdraw has been expressly reserved in the event of a particular breach);

---

[15]   To avoid any misunderstanding, 'good reasons' must be read here as a term of art. Where the innocent party has the right to withdraw by virtue of a statutory provision, precedent, or agreement, there is, of course, good reason (in a broad sense) for claiming the right to withdraw. However, the phrase is used in this paper to point to a further category, the category of good reasons (in a technical sense), of grounds for the right to withdraw for breach.

3. the term in question is to be treated as a 'condition' in the strict sense as a matter of necessary implication in the light of the parties' intentions;[16] or,
4. the consequences of the breach are such as to deprive the innocent party of substantially the whole benefit of the bargain.[17]

Characteristically, when the concept of a 'condition' in the strict sense is explained, it is put as a term, any breach of which gives rise to the right to withdraw, even though the consequences of the breach might be quite trivial.[18] In other words, the relative gravity of the actual consequences of the breach is rendered an irrelevant consideration. In principle, however, it is important to grasp that there is a distinction between a condition so defined and a term any breach of which attracts a peremptory right to withdraw ('peremptory' in the sense that the innocent party, faced with a breach of the particular term, would have the right to withdraw *for any reason*). Such a peremptory right, of course, is not at all co-extensive with a right to withdraw irrespective of the gravity of the actual consequences of the breach. In practice, though, English law tends to elide this distinction, treating the innocent party's reasons for seeking a right to withdraw as irrelevant in all cases, and the actual consequences of the breach as irrelevant where a particular term has been designated as a condition in the strict sense.[19] If reasons are to be retrieved, in line with the general direction of the discussion in this chapter, the distinction between a condition in a strict sense (as currently understood) and a term which

---

[16]   Seminally see *Bentsen v Taylor Sons and Co* [1893] 2 QB 274 and its application in the modern law; see eg the judgment of Kerr LJ in *Transcontinental Affiliates Ltd v State Trading Corpn of India: The Sara D* [1989] 2 Lloyd's Rep 277.

[17]   Seminally see *Hong Kong Fir Shipping Co Ltd v Kawasaki Kisen Kaisha Ltd* [1962] 2 QB 26.

[18]   For example, see *Photo Production Ltd v Securicor Transport Ltd* [1980] AC 827, 849 (above, n 2). Similarly, see *The Naxos* [1989] 2 Lloyd's Rep 462, 478, CA, where Butler Sloss LJ says: 'But if this is a condition, any breach, however trivial, would entitle the party aggrieved to bring the contract to an end.'

[19]   Ie not merely called a 'condition' in the general sense (indicating no more than that a particular provision is a term of the contract): see further *L. Schuler AG v Wickman Machine Tool Sales Ltd* [1974] AC 235.

attracts a peremptory right to withdraw for breach also needs to be recovered.

It is generally recognised that the law on withdrawal for breach betrays a fundamental tension between the traditional classification approach and the modern *Hong Kong* approach. At one level, the problem is that the latter approach may be set up, not as a supplement to the traditional approach, but as a rival starting point. And, indeed, during the 1970s, there was something of a suspicion – fostered by cases such as *The Hansa Nord*[20] and *Reardon Smith v Hansen-Tangen*[21] – that the *Hong Kong* approach was making a take-over bid of just this kind. Accordingly, in *Bunge v Tradax*,[22] the House of Lords was at pains to emphasise the supplementary nature of the consequential approach. The *Hong Kong* approach, as Lord Roskill put it, was not 'directed to the determination of the question which terms of a particular contract are conditions'.[23] However, such formal rationalisation of doctrine cannot settle the tensions which remain as undercurrents in the law. For, quite apart from anything else, the application of the *Hong Kong* approach presupposes that terms are *not* conditions (in the strict sense) and implies a reluctance so to construe terms.

The essential point is that it is in the nature of the traditional approach, where a term may be classified as a condition in the strict sense, that the innocent party may have, unreasonably as it seems, the option of withdrawing (for example, the right to withdraw may arise in circumstances where the breach is quite unintentional or its consequences wholly trivial). Thus, for instance, in *The Chikuma*,[24] the House of Lords ruled that the appellant shipowners were entitled to withdraw their vessel when the respondent charterers, having previously paid the hire punctually, defaulted in a technical and quite minor way on the eighty-first payment. This, as Lord Bridge remarked,

---

[20] *Cehave NV v Bremer Handelsgesellschaft mbH: The Hansa Nord* [1976] QB 44.
[21] *Reardon Smith Line Ltd v Yngvar Hansen-Tangen and Sanko SS Co Ltd: The Diana Prosperity* [1976] 3 All ER 570.
[22] *Bunge Corpn v Tradax SA* [1981] 2 All ER 513.
[23] Ibid, at p 551.
[24] *Awilco A/S v Fulvia SpA di Navigazione: The Chikuma* [1981] 1 All ER 652.

was 'yet another instance of a clause . . . operating to produce what appears to be a harsh result'.[25] Similarly, in *Arcos
v Ronaasen*,[26] which – at least in the context of sale of goods
– is perhaps the most frequently cited illustration of this
point,[27] the buyers were able to reject the timber for breach
of condition even though they could have used it for precisely the intended purpose. Had a consequential test of the
Hong Kong kind been applied, a quite different result would
have been reached in these cases. However, once the law
brings a consequential approach to bear on the question of
withdrawal for breach, it necessarily creates some uncertainty about the availability of the remedy in particular
situations (and, of course, prior case-law becomes much
less helpful). So, to pose the choice in the standard way: the
law can either secure a measure of calculability (by favouring the classification approach) but at the price of some hard
cases, or it can respond to hard cases (by employing the
consequential approach) but at the price of jeopardising calculability, not to mention fairness (given the chill factor
produced by the strictness and, to an extent, vagueness of
the test), and weakening pressure for performance.[28] Thus,
in *Schuler v Wickman*,[29] we find the House famously split

---

[25]   Ibid, at p 656. However, in *Scandinavian Trading Tanker Co AB v Flota
      Petrolera Ecuatoriana* [1983] 2 AC 694, 703, Lord Diplock suggested
      that, seen in the context of a volatile freight market, withdrawal of the
      vessel was not particularly harsh. He said: 'If it [ie the freight market]
      rises rapidly during the period of a time charter, the charterer is the
      beneficiary of the windfall which he can realise if he wants to by sub-
      chartering at the then market rates. What withdrawal of the vessel does
      is to transfer the benefit of the windfall from charterer to shipowner.'
      On the other hand, how plausible is this argument once one recalls
      that freight rates may fall, in which case the 'windfall' lies with the
      shipowner?
[26]   [1933] AC 470.
[27]   *Arcos* is commonly mentioned in the same breath as *Re Moore and Co
      Ltd and Landauer and Co* [1921] 2 KB 519, both cases offering illus-
      trations of apparently harsh results flowing from a particular
      interpretation of s 13 of the Sale of Goods Act 1893 (as it then was).
      However, there is an important difference between the cases. Whereas
      Arcos is a blatant example of collateral economic opportunism (see text
      below), there is no indication in *Re Moore and Landauer* that the buy-
      ers were seeking to escape from the contract in order to buy in a falling
      market (although, quaere, might the buyers have overpurchased?).
[28]   Points strongly made by Megaw LJ in both *The Mihalis Angelos* [1971]
      1 QB 164 and *Bunge v Tradax* [1981] 2 All ER 513, CA, and powerfully
      underlined by Tony Weir (1976) 35 Cambridge Law Journal 33.
[29]   *L. Schuler AG v Wickman Machine Tool Sales Ltd* [1974] AC 235.

over this dilemma, the majority favouring the consequential line, Lord Wilberforce dissenting in favour of general calculability and respect for the parties' express intentions.[30]

To this familiar tale, however, there is a further dimension to be added. It is possible to object to decisions such as those in *The Chikuma* and *Arcos v Ronaasen* on more than one ground. For the moment, let us concentrate on the latter case. As it has already been said, the popular objection to *Arcos* is that it was unreasonable to permit the buyers to reject when they could have used the timber for its intended purpose. However, there is a second line of objection. The fact is that, in *Arcos*, timber prices were falling as a result of which the buyers were keen to find a way out of the contract. Initially, when the shipping documents were tendered, the buyers purported to refuse them on the ground that the timber was not shipped 'during the Summer' as the contract provided. Having argued this without success at the ensuing arbitration, the buyers then purported to reject the timber when it arrived, this time on the ground that it did not correspond with its contractual description. Given that the timber was perfectly suitable for its intended purpose, the buyers were quite plainly looking for a breach in order to realise the economic opportunity afforded by the falling market.[31] In other words, the buyers were not rejecting *for breach* (except in the technical legal

---

[30] But cf *Mardorf Peach and Co Ltd v Attica Sea Carriers Corpn of Liberia: The Laconia* [1977] AC 850 where the House, led by Lord Wilberforce, favoured certainty even if some hard cases might result (see esp Lord Salmon at p 878 and Lord Fraser at p 883).

[31] It can be said, of course, that the question of intended purpose was immaterial since the buyers were rejecting for breach of s 13 of the Sale of Goods Act 1893 (as it then was) (ie for the failure of the timber to correspond with its contractual description). However, this begs the question of how s 13 should be interpreted, in particular how it should be read alongside the s 14 requirements. The point is that a literal interpretation of s 13, as in *Arcos*, can give buyers too easy a way out of contracts: see the observations of Lord Wilberforce in *Reardon Smith v Hansen-Tangen* [1976] 3 All ER 570, 576. To avoid this, one might argue for a less literal reading of s 13, or a blocking clause of the kind recently introduced by s 4 of the Sale and Supply of Goods Act 1994 (which provides, in non-consumer cases, that where the buyer would otherwise have the right to withdraw for breach of the implied terms in ss 13–15, SOGA, this right will not be available where 'the breach is so slight that it would be unreasonable for [the buyer] to reject'), or for some general restriction on the right to withdraw (the latter being the thrust of this chapter).

sense); the sellers' breach was merely a pretext for getting out of the bargain. Now, it would be quite wrong to suppose that the House in *Arcos* was unaware of what was really going on. On the contrary, it can be safely assumed that this feature of the case was perfectly well understood. Crucially, the House saw nothing wrong with the buyers taking advantage of the sellers' breach in this way. Indeed, Lord Atkin said explicitly that he accepted that it was permissible for a buyer to rely on a breach of condition in order to withdraw for collateral economic reasons on a falling market:

> 'If a condition is not performed the buyer has a right to reject. I do not myself think that there is any difference between business men and lawyers on this matter. No doubt, in business, men often find it unnecessary or inexpedient to insist on their strict legal rights. In a normal market if they get something substantially like the specified goods they may take them with or without grumbling and a claim for an allowance. But in a falling market I find the buyers are often as eager to insist on their legal rights as courts of law are to maintain them. No doubt at all times sellers are prepared to take a liberal view as to the rigidity of their own obligations, and possibly buyers who in turn are sellers may also dislike too much precision. But buyers are not, as far as my experience goes, inclined to think that the rights defined in the code [ie the Sale of Goods Act] are in excess of business needs.'[32]

If, however, we take issue with Lord Atkin, the objection to the decision in *Arcos* is not so much that the buyers were allowed to act unreasonably or inefficiently[33] by rejecting goods which they could use, but that they were allowed to reject such goods in order to take advantage of a falling market. In short, the objection is that the buyers acted in bad faith.

More recently, in *The Hansa Nord*,[34] the court faced a particularly striking example of such advantage-taking. There, the buyers, having purported to reject a £100,000 cargo for alleged breach of condition, were able to repurchase the

---

[32]   [1933] AC 470, 480.
[33]   Cf George L. Priest 'Breach and Remedy for the Tender of Non-conforming Goods under the Uniform Commercial Code: An Economic Approach' (1978) 91 Harvard Law Review 960.
[34]   *Cehave NV v Bremer Handelsgesellschaft mbH: The Hansa Nord* [1976] QB 44.

goods indirectly for a mere £30,000, before making use of them for a purpose no different from that intended.[35] Although Mocatta J upheld the Board of Appeal's decision in favour of the buyers, the Court of Appeal ruled that the buyers had no right to reject. To achieve this result, the Court of Appeal held, first, that the goods were of merchantable quality (because, despite their deficiency, they remained fit for their intended purpose); and, secondly, that the contractual provision requiring shipment in good condition was an intermediate (ie *Hong Kong*) term, the consequences of the breach of which in this particular instance did not justify withdrawal. The nub of the decision, however, was the court's perception that it would be wrong to assist the buyers to make a killing of this kind. As Lord Denning MR observed:

> 'It often happens that the market price falls between the making of the contract and the time for delivery. In such a situation, it is not fair that a buyer should be allowed to reject a whole consignment of goods just because a small quantity are not up to the contract quality or condition. The proper remedy is a price allowance and not complete rejection.'[36]

There is more to this, however, than a one-off decision to combat a particularly spectacular example of sharp practice. *The Hansa Nord* takes a stand, not simply against bad faith, but, more generally, against economic opportunism within a contractual relationship. This is epitomised by Roskill LJ's remarks:

> 'In my view, a court should not be over ready, unless required by statute or authority so to do, to construe a term in a contract as a "condition" . . . *In principle, contracts are made to be performed and not to be avoided according to the whims of market fluctuation* and where there is a free choice between two possible constructions I think the court should tend to prefer that construction which will ensure performance, and not encourage avoidance of contractual obligations.'[37]

On this view, contracts – even contracts in the commercial world – are matters of obligation, not vehicles for instrumental economic convenience. In other words, contracting

---

[35]   They used, however, smaller percentages than would have been normal with sound goods.
[36]   Ibid, at p 63.
[37]   Ibid, at pp 70–71.

parties commit themselves, by entering into a contract with one another, to keep faith with the bargain even though more attractive economic opportunities might subsequently present themselves elsewhere. Crucially, even innocent parties in post-breach situations must be seen as having a prima facie obligation to perform rather than to avoid the contract.[38]

In *The Hansa Nord*, the implications of Roskill LJ's view seem to run in only one direction. The courts, as his Lordship says, must be wary of construing terms as conditions in a strict sense if the innocent party is simply citing the breach as a pretext for withdrawal, the real reasons being of a collateral economic kind. However, matters are not quite so simple. Two other considerations need to be borne in mind. First, if terms are rarely construed as conditions in a strict sense, the option of withdrawal will rarely be available, and this may weaken the incentive for would-be contract-breakers to take their contractual obligations seriously. Thus, in the more recent case of *The Naxos*,[39] the majority of the House was concerned that the 'ready for delivery' provision (incorporated into a contract for the sale of sugar on the Assuc Sugar Contract No 2 form) should be construed as a condition in the strict sense lest sellers in such contracts might be encouraged to play the market and compensate their buyers only in

---

[38]   For a time, a parallel line of reasoning was evident in relation to a number of cases where owners of vessels purported to withdraw from charters for breach of the punctual payment condition but, really, for collateral economic reasons: see eg *Empresa Cubana de Fletes v Lagonisi Shipping Co Ltd: The Georgios C* [1971] 1 QB 488, 502-503 (Lord Denning MR), and 505 (Phillimore LJ); and *The Laconia* [1976] 1 QB 835, 848-849, CA (Lord Denning MR) and [1977] AC 850, 874 (where Lord Simon seemed willing to countenance the development of a principle of unconscionability in order to protect charterers against owners taking unfair advantage of late payment when the breach 'might be due to pure accident and might occasion no real detriment to the owners'). However, the general view of the House in *The Laconia* was that the punctual payment provisions should be taken at face value, leaving the owners free to withdraw (see above, n 30). For confirmation of this approach in the context of charter-parties, see *The Chikuma* [1981] 1 All ER 652; and for the House's refusal to apply the idea of forfeiture to protect charterers, see *Scandinavian Trading Tanker Co A.B. v Flota Petrolera Ecuatoriana* [1983] 2 AC 694.

[39]   *Cie Commerciale Sucres et Denrees v C. Czarnikow Ltd: The Naxos* [1990] 3 All ER 641.

damages.[40] Secondly, a presumption against withdrawal, whilst perhaps countering collateral economic opportunism, might be unfair to an innocent party who has perfectly respectable reasons for wishing to withdraw. It follows that any regime which treats contracts as matters of obligation must strive to satisfy two desiderata. On the one hand, it must sift out good reasons for withdrawal from bad reasons, eliminating withdrawal motivated by collateral economic considerations. On the other hand, it must maintain the option to withdraw as a security against non-performance (ie in order to discourage breach). To put this slightly differently, the challenge is to devise a legal regime in which the option to withdraw operates as a security against breach but without this becoming an excuse in post-breach situations for the innocent party to discharge itself from its contractual obligations whenever market conditions so favour.

2. GOOD REASONS FOR THE RIGHT TO WITHDRAW

If the innocent party's reasons for withdrawal were to be treated as a focal consideration, in what circumstances would there be a right to withdraw for breach? Basically, a right to withdraw would be available where it was conferred by legislation or case-law, or where it was so agreed by the parties; but, failing such special provision, the right to withdraw would depend upon the innocent party having good reasons for claiming the option of release from the contract, as opposed to settling for damages. In the next section, we will consider the possibility of peremptory and presumptive rights to withdraw being conferred by agreement or by force of law. Our immediate concern, however, is with the idea of the right to withdraw for good reason.

The fact that there has been a breach of contract raises the possibility that the innocent party might have the right to withdraw. The mere fact of breach, however, is not sufficient reason. Breach warrants compensatory damages, but not necessarily the option of withdrawal. What kind of

---

[40] Ibid, at p 651; and, similarly, at the Court of Appeal stage of the case, see Kerr LJ [1989] 2 Lloyd's Rep 462, 469. See also the observations of Bingham J in *Tradax Export S.A. v Italgrani di Francesco Ambrosio* [1983] 2 Lloyd's Rep 109, 115.

reasons, then, might an innocent party advance to support an argument in favour of the right to withdraw? Without any claim to being exhaustive of possible good reasons, six grounds for the right to withdraw may be suggested as follows:

1. the contract-breaker evinces, through the breach, a lack of commitment to the contract as a source of obligation (eg the breach is intentional/calculating, or fraud/dishonesty is involved);
2. the breach raises concerns about the competence of the contract-breaker (eg the breach involves negligence);
3. the breach, although unintentional and non-negligent, renders performance under the contract radically different from that envisaged at formation;
4. proving (or quantifying) losses flowing from the breach gives rise to difficulties which put the innocent party at risk;
5. the breach gives rise to concern about the contract-breaker's ability to meet future claims; and,
6. the breach gives rise to concern about the innocent party's own ability to perform either the contract in question or another associated contract.

Without arguing the point, let us suppose that an innocent party claiming a right to withdraw for good reason must make out a prima facie case under any one of these heads. Further, let us suppose that the right to withdraw only obtains where the innocent party (i) acts in good faith, and (ii) has reasonable grounds for believing that the particular supporting reason applies.[41] Accordingly, once a prima facie case has been made out, the onus shifts to the contract-breaker to rebut the innocent party's claim. This could be done by showing either a lack of good faith or a lack of reasonable grounds. The former might involve dishonesty or the like, but, crucially, if the innocent party has relied on collateral economic reasons – and, thus, is not seeking

---

[41] This seems a fair position to take. Not to ask for reasonable grounds would put the contract-breaker too much at the mercy of the innocent party's good faith (but possibly mistaken) reading of the situation. On the other hand, given that an unjustified withdrawal exposes the innocent party to a counter-claim by the contract-breaker, it would be unfair to insist on the innocent party having a correct reading of the situation.

withdrawal 'for breach' – this would constitute a lack of good faith and would disqualify withdrawal. With these brief comments on the burden and standard of proof, we can look more carefully at the six suggested good reasons for withdrawal upon which argument would centre – always remembering, of course, that these are possible reasons to be cited *in the absence of a right to withdraw being conferred by legislation, precedent, or agreement.*

(i) The breach evinces a failure to treat performance of the contract as a matter of obligation

It is a jurisprudential commonplace that there is a distinction between treating a requirement as 'obligatory', ie as categorically binding, as opposed to merely conforming with a requirement.[42] In relation to contractual requirements, the difference is that, if one treats those requirements as obligatory, one accepts that they are binding even though one would prefer on occasion to act otherwise. On the other hand, mere conformity with a contract indicates no greater commitment than a willingness to perform so long as it suits. Accordingly, where one enters upon a contract as a matter of obligation, one accepts a special kind of commitment, a commitment to stick with the contract even when it is no longer convenient or advantageous to do so. If this is how contracts are to be regarded – and this is precisely how Roskill LJ's view in *The Hansa Nord* suggests they are to be regarded – then the failure of one side to treat performance as obligatory is a particularly serious matter. Of course, in *The Hansa Nord*, the immediate thrust of Roskill LJ's remarks is that, in post-breach situations, the courts should be slow to grant the innocent party the option of withdrawal. Nevertheless, a failure by the contract-breaker to regard the contract as obligatory indicates a breakdown in the relationship and gives the innocent party good reason for seeking a right to withdraw, for such a failure surely goes beyond a matter of financial redress. Indeed, one might say that treating the contract as obligatory is precisely a condition precedent to the contract continuing in force.

---

[42]   See HLA Hart *The Concept of Law* (Oxford, Clarendon Press, 1961) esp pp 79–88.

The most obvious way in which one side could act inconsistently with this ideal is if the contract is broken intentionally or recklessly with a view to mere convenience or commercial advantage. The same holds for dishonesty or fraud. For example, in *The Mihalis Angelos*, at the date of the charter-party, 25 May 1965, the vessel was 7 or 8 days out of Los Angeles with a cargo to be discharged in Hong Kong. The most optimistic estimate was that the vessel would arrive at Haiphong by 13 or 14 July. Yet, the owners represented that the vessel was expected to be ready by about 1 July. In the event, the vessel did not complete discharging its cargo in Hong Kong until 23 July and, thus, could not have arrived at Haiphong before 27 July. At best, this was a case of wishful thinking, or incompetence, by the owners; at worst it was a case of recklessness or dishonesty. If it was the latter, recklessness or dishonesty, the charterers surely had good reasons for withdrawal.[43]

(ii) The breach raises concerns about the competence of the contract-breaker

Mere incompetence is not incompatible with the very idea of a contract as an affair of obligation. Nevertheless, where there is a negligent breach, the innocent party may argue that damages would not be an adequate remedy. Sometimes, the negligence will raise concerns which fall under one of the other heads for withdrawal. For example, it may raise concerns about the ability of the contract-breaker to satisfy a claim in damages. However, what if the case does not fall under one of these other heads? Can withdrawal be justified where there is a single instance of a

---

[43]   Two qualifications need to be made here. First, the fact that the charterers, in principle, might have had clear grounds for withdrawal should not be equated with their having clear grounds in practice. To state the obvious, the charterers might have had no grounds for believing that the owners had acted dishonestly or recklessly (see text infra). Secondly, if, in fact, the charterers withdrew for collateral economic reasons, their action would be tainted by bad faith (ie they would not have good reasons for withdrawal). A rather nice point would then arise if, subsequently, they found that good reasons were available (eg if they secured evidence indicating that the owners' statement was dishonest).

negligent breach without, as it were, any aggravating features? For example, suppose that in *Schuler v Wickman* the agents had committed just one negligent breach of the visiting provision. Or, suppose that in the *Harbutt's Plasticine*[44] case the contractors' negligent breach had been discovered in time to prevent the conflagration. Would the innocent party have a right to withdraw in such circumstances?

Whilst it makes little sense to accuse a negligent contract-breaker of ignoring its obligations, nevertheless the innocent party may take the view that even one negligent failure is one breach too many. In the hypothesised circumstances of *Harbutt's Plasticine*, for example, the clients surely could argue with some plausibility that they simply could not afford to give the contractors a second chance to burn down the factory. On the other hand, in a case like *Schuler v Wickman*, even allowing for the manufacturers' punctiliousness, one negligent breach perhaps seems insufficient reason for having a right to withdraw. Nevertheless, it cannot be right to license negligent contract-breakers 'to pay or perform' indefinitely, for contracts are, after all, for performance, not for compensation in lieu of performance. Accordingly, in a case of this kind, the appropriate remedy for the innocent party seems to be, not the right to withdraw, but a warning that, if there is a repetition of negligence, the option to withdraw will apply.[45]

Given that the strength of the innocent party's argument in favour of having a right to withdraw for a negligent breach per se is liable to vary from one situation to another, an innocent party wishing to be assured of such a right should be advised to make appropriate express provision in the contract.

---

[44] *Harbutt's Plasticine Ltd v Wayne Tank and Pump Co Ltd* [1970] 1 QB 447.

[45] Ie something along the lines provided for in cl 11 of the distributorship agreement in *Schuler v Wickman*.

(iii) The breach, although unintentional and non-negligent, renders performance under the contract radically different from that envisaged at formation

In *Behn v Burness*,[46] the statement in a charter-party, dated 19 October 1860, that the vessel, the *Martaban*, is 'now in the port of Amsterdam' was held by the Court of Exchequer Chamber to be a condition in the strict sense. Four days before, on 15 October, the vessel was en route to Amsterdam, and expected to arrive within 12 hours given favourable circumstances. However, because of strong gales and the absence of tug power, the vessel was unavoidably prevented from reaching a place of discharge in Amsterdam Docks until 23 October. This seems to have been a case of unintentional, non-negligent breach. Thus, the charterer had no reason to withdraw on the grounds that the owners were failing to treat the charter as obligatory; nor was this a case where a warning would be appropriate. It also appeared that this was not a case where the actual consequences of the breach occasioned any great loss to the innocent party, the lower court applying an embryonic *Hong Kong* approach to deny the charterer the right to withdraw.[47] How, then, should such a case be treated?

One view is that all cases of unintentional breach (without more) should be treated the same. In other words, there should be no distinction between negligent and non-negligent breach. At the root of this view is the point already made that parties contract for performance, not for compensation in lieu of performance. Put this way, it makes no difference whether the non-performance arises from a negligent or non-negligent breach. An alternative view is that the two cases of unintentional breach should be treated differently, at least in relation to the availability of the right to withdraw. For negligent breach, a warning – maybe even withdrawal for feared repetition – is appropriate. For non-negligent breach, warnings and withdrawals on the ground of feared repetition are inappropriate. Instead, the innocent party must make some allowance for the contract-breaker's misfortune and, in the absence of

---

[46]   (1863) 3 B and S 751, 122 ER 281.
[47]   (1862) 1 B and S 877, 121 ER 939.

aggravating factors, must expect to enjoy the option of withdrawal only exceptionally – in short, only where the breach renders performance under the contract radically different.

If, for the sake of argument, this alternative view is followed, it remains to determine just what degree of allowance is to be made. Traditionally, the standard for release is set high. For example, in *Flight v Booth*,[48] Tindal CJ proposed the following test for rescission where a seller unintentionally misstated the character of the property:

> '[W]here the misdescription, although not proceeding from fraud, is in a material and substantial point, so far affecting the subject-matter of the contract that it may reasonably be supposed, that, but for such misdescription, the purchaser might never have entered into the contract at all, in such case the contract is avoided altogether, and the purchaser is not bound to resort to the clause of compensation.'[49]

In the regime outlined here, a 'radical difference' test has been adopted. This seems broad enough to encompass situations like that in *Flight v Booth*, as well as the case of the proverbial innocent party who, having contracted for peas, is delivered a cargo of beans. It would also cover a situation such as that in the *Federal Commerce and Navigation*[50] case where the owners' breach, although based on legal advice, was liable to cause grave damage to the charterers' reputation and ability to trade in grain. On the other hand, it seems fairly clear that the charterer in *Behn v Burness*, although understandably concerned that the vessel should be available as anticipated, did not face a radically different situation as a result of the owners' breach.[51]

If a 'radically different' test is adopted, it may be noted that there is then a certain alignment between the ruling *Davis v Fareham*[52] test for frustration and the test for withdrawal

---

[48]   (1834) 1 Bing NC 370, 131 ER 1160.
[49]   Ibid, at p 377; 1162–1163.
[50]   *Federal Commerce and Navigation Co Ltd v Molena Gamma Inc* [1979] AC 757.
[51]   But, of course, if it is established by precedent that descriptive statements of this kind are to be treated as conditions in the strict sense, then the charterer has the right to withdraw irrespective of whether the breach produced a radically different situation.
[52]   *Davis Contractors Ltd v Fareham UDC* [1956] AC 696 (see Lord Radcliffe, esp at p 729).

for breach, thus achieving something of the symmetry sought after by Diplock LJ in the *Hong Kong Fir Shipping* case.[53] However, this alignment is on a very narrow front. It is not a general equation of the tests for withdrawal for breach and frustration: it is simply an equation where *the breach is unintentional and non-negligent*. To be precise the equation is between the test for that category of excused non-performance which discharges the parties (frustration) and that for a right to withdraw in respect of a non-excused non-performance (breach) which is unintentional and non-negligent.[54]

(iv) Proving (or quantifying) losses flowing from the breach gives rise to difficulties which put the innocent party at risk

In *Bunge v Tradax*,[55] Lord Wilberforce made the point that, if the term was not to be construed as a condition in the strict sense, then the sellers would be confined to a remedy in damages 'which might be extremely difficult to quantify'.[56] This, his Lordship conceded, was a serious objection 'in

---

[53]   [1962] 2 QB 26, 65–66.

[54]   There is a tendency to draw a simple contrast between 'breach' and 'frustration'. It would be clearer, however, if the contrast were between 'breach' and 'excused non-performance'. Within such a scheme, 'breach' would divide into 'breach of warranty' and 'breach of condition' while 'excused non-performance' would divide into 'excused non-frustrating non-performance' and 'excused frustrating non-performance' (ie frustration). Roughly speaking, 'breach of warranty' and 'excused non-frustrating non-performance' would be correlates, as would 'breach of condition' and 'excused frustrating non-performance'. Collateral economic reasons fit into this scheme in two ways: first, where a party fails to perform for such reasons, there can be no defence of 'excused non-performance'; and, secondly, where an innocent party seeks to withdraw, ostensibly for breach of condition, but truly for collateral economic reasons, withdrawal will be disallowed.

[55]   *Bunge Corpn v Tradax S.A.* [1981] 2 All ER 513.

[56]   Ibid, at p 541. Similarly, although in different contractual contexts (respectively, a suretyship contract and a distributorship agreement), in *Ankar Propietary Ltd v National Westminster Finance (Australia) Ltd* (1987) 162 CLR 549, 557, the High Court of Australia accepted that the difficulty of proving damages was a factor which favoured reading the relevant terms as conditions in the strict sense; and, in *Schuler v Wickman* [1974] AC 235, Lord Wilberforce pointed to the difficulties of the manufacturers proving lost sales as a result of the agents' breach of the visiting obligation.

practice'.[57] Now, although it seems to be generally accepted that the difficulty of quantifying damages is a factor weighing in favour of the innocent party having the right to withdraw, it is not immediately obvious why this should be so. After all, the quantification difficulty applies irrespective of whether the innocent party has the right to withdraw.

To appreciate the force of this particular reason, it might be helpful to distinguish between two heads of damages each of which may give rise to difficulties of proof or quantification. First, there are those damages (D1) which relate to the instant breach (B1), the breach in respect of which the innocent party is arguing for a right to withdraw. Secondly, there are those damages (D2) which relate to a feared future breach (B2) should the innocent party be denied the right to withdraw for the instant breach (B1). Where the innocent party's argument in favour of having a right to withdraw hinges upon the difficulty of proving or quantifying future damages (D2), then it is clear how the availability of such a right (at least, if the option of withdrawal is exercised) would overcome the problem (viz, by preventing the occurrence of the breach, B2, which would generate the difficulty). However, it remains unclear why the difficulty of quantifying instant breach damages (D1) should operate as a good reason in favour of having the right to withdraw. In support of the innocent party's claim, it might be argued that, given the quantification problems, the innocent party might not pursue its claim for damages (D1) relating to the instant breach (B1), so that, if the right to withdraw were denied, the breach (B1) would go unremedied. Alternatively, it might be argued that, if the innocent party were able to withdraw from the contract, this would free it to pursue its claim for damages without fear of prejudicing the contractual relationship.

Two other points should be made here. First, if damages are difficult to prove, and if this is known to a potential contract-breaker, then the remedial security against breach (B1) is weakened. To protect the party at risk, the right to withdraw may be needed as additional remedial security. If the parties have not provided for this right, this might be an appropriate case for protective intervention by way of pre-classification of terms (ie ex-ante provision to compensate

---

for a weakness in the ex-post reason-centred regime).[58] Secondly, where damages are known at the outset to be difficult to quantify, this is, of course, just the kind of situation in which liquidated damages clauses are to be encouraged. If the parties have agreed upon a liquidated damages provision, then, irrespective of whether the quantification problem concerns instant breach damages (D1) or anticipated future breach damages (D2), this presumably undercuts the argument in favour of a right to withdraw.

(v) The breach gives rise to concern about the contract-breaker's ability to meet future claims

On occasion, a breach may give the innocent party reason to doubt the contract-breaker's ability to satisfy claims for damages in future (eg where the instant breach gives rise to a particularly big claim, or where a negligent breach implies a more general lack of competence). In such a case, therefore, the justifying reason for having a right to withdraw is that the right, if exercised, will protect the innocent party against the risk of under-compensation in the future. This seems plausible enough.[59] However, it should be emphasised that this is not a licence for withdrawal for late payment. Accordingly, in a case like *Decro-Wall International SA v Practitioners in Marketing*,[60] where the defendants were persistently late in paying for goods received, the right to withdraw would not arise *on this ground* because there was no suggestion that the contract-breakers would fail to meet their financial obligations. Nor, of course, would this head operate as a reason licensing withdrawal for late payment where the motivation was of a collateral economic kind.[61] For, it must be remembered that the innocent party will only have the right of withdrawal where the claim is made in good faith.

---

[58] See further, s 3 of the text.
[59] Though, perhaps an assurance might be the first line of security for the innocent party, cf section 2-609 of the Uniform Commercial Code.
[60] *Decro-Wall International SA v Practitioners in Marketing Ltd* [1971] 2 All ER 216.
[61] Cf *The Laconia* [1977] AC 850, and *The Chikuma* [1981] 1 All ER 652.

(vi) The breach gives rise to concern about the innocent party's own ability to perform either the contract in question or another associated contract

Some contracts may be structured in such a way that, not only is there a clear order for performance, but also particular obligations may not arise unless and until some item in the scheduled performance has been fulfilled.[62] In other words, within the contractual structure, performance of one or more of the terms by one of the parties may be a condition precedent to the other party's obligation to perform a particular term. Analysis of such contracts is relatively unproblematic. However, there may be cases where the contractual provisions, although less formally ordered, are none-the-less linked in such a way that if one side fails to perform as contemplated this will prejudice the other party's ability to perform. For example, in *Bunge v Tradax*, Megaw LJ pointed to such interlocking provisions:

> '[J]ust as the contractual time for delivery of the goods is a condition binding on the sellers, so the contractual time by which the notice has to be given for the purpose of enabling the sellers to perform that condition should be regarded as a condition binding on the buyers.'[63]

Given that there are other devices by which the law might protect the innocent party (eg implying appropriate terms for the benefit of that party), it might be only exceptionally that this will generate questions about the right to withdraw. Nevertheless, if the point does arise, it does not seem unreasonable to give the innocent party a right to withdraw in such a case.

Even if the contractual provisions are not linked for ordered performance, in many commercial contracts the contract itself will be linked to *other contracts*. Thus, performance of contract A, if not a condition precedent for the obligations under contract B to arise, at least bears significantly on a party's ability to perform contract B. In *The Naxos*,[64] one of the factors which persuaded the majority of

---

[62] See Hugh Beale, *Remedies for Breach of Contract* (London, Sweet and Maxwell, 1980) chs 2–3, esp pp 28–34.
[63] [1981] 2 All ER 513, 532.
[64] [1990] 3 All ER 641.

their Lordships to rule that the buyers had a right to withdraw was that the dispute arose in the context of a string of contracts, the buyers having onward commitments to fulfil. Yet, why would damages not be an adequate remedy in a case of this type? In some situations (eg where the sub-sale is for specific goods), the right to withdraw will not assist the buyer;[65] and, in other cases, it may be possible for the original contract-breaker to cover the innocent party's own onward liabilities by paying damages. However, if the right to withdraw would enable the innocent party to perform its onward obligations, then there is perhaps force in the argument that it should enjoy this right in order to maintain its commercial reputation (ie, as a party which meets its obligations). Given that the strength of the innocent party's claim might vary from one situation to another, it may be advisable for the the right to withdraw to be expressly reserved in the contract.

Before moving on, in the next section, to the question of prior classification of terms, it is as well to make two general points which perhaps serve to put the heads of good reasons into better perspective. First, to avoid any misunderstanding, it is worth labouring the point that the so-called 'reason-centred' regime permits the innocent party to argue for a right to withdraw under any one of three general headings: namely, by virtue of prior classification of stock terms by statute or precedent, by virtue of prior classification of a particular provision (or, prior reservation of the right to withdraw) by express agreement, or by virtue of having a 'good reason' as outlined in this section. The good reasons sketched above, therefore, represent only one dimension of the regime. Secondly, the category of good reasons may be regarded as being of a residual nature. The point is that if the innocent party lacks the information to discharge the burden of proof in relation to a particular good reason, it may be advisable to argue for the right to withdraw

---

[65]   In *Re Moore and Landauer* [1921] 2 KB 519, the sellers argued that the buyers should be restricted to a remedy in damages. However, the court treated the possibility that the buyers might have sub-contracted on the basis of cases of 30 tins as telling against the sellers. Whilst the possibility of such sub-contract commitments might be relevant to the specification of 30 tin cases as part of the contractual description, it is not clear how the right to withdraw would assist the buyers to meet their sub-contract commitments.

on the basis of prior classification. Moreover, given possible evidential difficulties facing the innocent party (who may not know, for example, whether the breach was intentional or unintentional, negligent or non-negligent), it may turn out, in practice, that innocent parties who have to rely on the residual good reasons tend to favour reason (3) (rather than (1) or (2)) or (4)-(6) where appropriate.[66] If so, this would not be so very different perhaps from the existing position.

3. PRE-CLASSIFICATION OF TERMS

In the previous section, we concentrated on the kind of reasons which, in the absence of stipulation by statute, precedent, or agreement, might justify withdrawal for breach. In this section, we must consider the policy of the law in relation to pre-classification of terms, paying particular attention to the possibility of having terms pre-classified so that they attract either a peremptory or a presumptive right of withdrawal.

(i) Express agreement

We can deal, first, with cases of express agreement. In the wake of the decision in *Schuler v Wickman*,[67] debate focused on whether it was adequate to stipulate that a particular term was a 'condition', or whether it was necessary to spell out that if a particular term was broken then the innocent party should have the right to withdraw, or even to provide that the right to withdraw applied irrespective of the actual consequences of the breach, and so on. Now, it would be possible, in principle, to develop quite complex conventions about particular forms of words in contracts, with precedents available for each required nuance of meaning. However, for our purposes, the critical questions are: (1) whether as a matter of policy it should be possible to agree to a peremptory right of withdrawal; and (2) whether, if so,

---

[66]   It must also be remembered that, no matter how a reason-centred regime were implemented (ie whether by statute or by judicial innovation) it would take some time for the jurisprudence of the reasons to develop.

[67]   [1974] AC 235. See Brownsword (1974) 37 MLR 104.

any of the standard locutions should be recognised as adequate to confer such a peremptory right. The first of these questions is a matter of principle; the second is a practical matter.

Why should it not be open to the parties, if they so wish, to agree to a peremptory right of withdrawal in respect of a particular provision? Two lines of argument suggest themselves, one contending that such a right would be incompatible with the very concept of contract as an affair of obligation, the other that such a right would be capable of producing injustice.

The conceptual argument starts by underlining the point that the essence of contractual commitment is that the parties place themselves under an obligation to one another. If they agree that it is open to withdraw for collateral economic reasons this surely reduces the transaction to a declaration of convenience (or, as it was commonly said in the context of swingeing exclusion clauses, a mere declaration of intent).[68] However, this objection slides over a crucial qualification. A peremptory right to withdraw for breach is not identical to a right to withdraw (or terminate) at convenience; unlike the latter, the former is necessarily conditioned upon there being a breach of the relevant provision. Accordingly, if both sides treat their transaction as obligatory, and perform to the letter, no right to withdraw for breach – peremptory or otherwise – can arise.[69]

The argument based on fairness fixes on the undeniable fact that, if the parties are permitted to agree to a peremptory right of withdrawal for breach, this could license some pretty harsh outcomes. Recall, for example, the nineteenth-

---

[68]   Classically, see *Suisse Atlantique Société d'Armement Maritime S.A. v N.V. Rotterdamsche Kolen Centrale* [1967] 1 AC 361, 432 (Lord Wilberforce).

[69]   In fact, the conceptual point merits more extensive analysis. The essence of a contract is that the parties put themselves under an obligation to one another. A derivative idea is that a breach should not be cited as a pretext for withdrawal (ie, that collateral economic reasoning should be eschewed by the parties). The argument presupposed by the text is that it is possible for the parties to waive their derivative rights without this undermining the very idea of a contract. However, if the parties were to agree that there should be a right to terminate at will, this might be argued to be incompatible with the idea of a contract – although this is not to suggest, of course, that parties should not be free to agree to such an arrangement.

century American cases, *Norrington v Wright*[70] and *Filley v Pope*,[71] in both of which the American buyers argued that a minor deviation from the contract released them to buy used rails on a falling market. In *Filley*, for example, the sellers shipped the rails from the east coast of Scotland rather than from Glasgow (the contract port of shipment) where no vessels were available. The sellers' initiative thus procured speedier delivery than if there had been strict compliance with the contract. Nevertheless, the court in *Filley*, as in *Norrington*, ruled in favour of the buyers. Even such a robust liberal as Charles Fried is critical of these decisions:

> 'The courts in *Norrington* and *Filley* reached absurd results by assuming that the schedule and departure terms respectively were conditions. They assumed this because they assumed that every term was a condition. They assumed that every term was a condition on the fallacious reasoning that since it was their duty to respect the autonomy of the parties and not to impose obligations upon them that they had not assumed, therefore they must condition all of the buyers' duties to the sellers on strict compliance by the sellers with all of the buyers' terms. But this begs the question. If the buyers and sellers did not intend to treat minor, nonmaterial deviations from the terms of the contract as conditions, it frustrates rather than realizes the will of the parties for the courts to treat them as conditions.'[72]

It will be appreciated, though, that the underlying principle in Fried's critique is that party autonomy should be respected and that the parties' intentions should be realised. Accordingly, if the parties in *Norrington* and *Filley* had intended that the buyers should have a right to withdraw for minor deviations, then it would not be unfair to allow such a right to operate. This line of reasoning applies *a fortiori* if we are considering the possibility of a peremptory right to withdraw for breach. In other words, if in cases of this type, the parties have expressly agreed that the buyer should have a peremptory right to withdraw for breach of the schedule or departure terms, then the seller must have been on notice of the risk and there would be no

[70] 115 US 188 (1885).
[71] 115 US 213 (1885).
[72] Charles Fried *Contract as Promise* (Cambridge, Mass, Harvard University Press, 1981) p 122.

injustice in enforcing the agreement.[73] Of course, it might be said that no seller could possibly agree to such terms unless it found itself in a desperate bargaining position; and there may well be some truth in this. Nevertheless, the problem of coerced 'agreements' is one to be addressed directly, by a doctrine of economic duress, or inequality of bargaining strength, or by a requirement of good faith,[74] not indirectly by a restriction on a peremptory right to withdraw (nor by manipulating a doctrine of presumed contractual intention).[75]

This leaves the practical question of how the parties might signal their intention to confer a peremptory right to withdraw for breach. We can deal with this quite summarily. It certainly would not be sufficient, given present conventions, to label the term as a condition – nor, of course, would it do to say that the right obtained irrespective of the gravity of the consequences of the breach. For at least two reasons, it would be essential to spell out the peremptory right quite explicitly, emphasising that, if the particular term were breached, then the innocent party would be entitled to withdraw for any reason (including for collateral economic reasons). On the one hand, this would begin to familiarise the English legal community with the concept of a peremptory right (this idea not yet having been properly disentangled from the concept of a condition in the strict sense as that concept is presently understood);[76] on the other hand, it would serve to ensure that the parties had fully understood the nature of their agreement.

---

[73]   For the moral underpinnings of this kind of view, see Roger Brownsword 'Liberalism and the Law of Contract', in Richard Bellamy (ed), *Liberalism and Recent Legal and Social Philosophy* (Stuttgart, Franz Steiner, 1989) p 86.

[74]   See ch 7.

[75]   Cf Roger Brownsword 'Remedy-Stipulation in the English Law of Contract – Freedom or Paternalism?' (1977) 9 Ottawa Law Review 95.

[76]   However, it should be noted that clauses allowing for termination at will, or termination for convenience, are by no means unknown (although termination here is not necessarily conditional upon there being a breach). See eg Beale *Remedies for Breach of Contract*, above, n 60, at pp 23–26; and J.W. Carter, 'Termination Clauses' (1990) 3 Journal of Contract Law 90, 94.

(ii) Pre-classification by law

The regime of good reasons, if sound, ensures that the innocent party has proper redress when the question of
withdrawal for breach is addressed in an ex-post fashion.
Moreover, by leaving the parties free to vary this regime by
express agreement, there is always the possibility of their
contracting out of any unwanted features. One might
wonder, therefore, whether it is necessary to regulate the situation any further. In particular, why should there be any
need to pre-classify certain terms by statute or precedent?

As explained already, prior classification of terms as conditions in the strict sense (as we now understand it) can lead
to 'unreasonable' withdrawals, in particular withdrawal for
collateral economic reasons. Clearly, this is a path to be
avoided. One qualification, therefore, must be that pre-
classification does not become a shield for withdrawal based
on collateral reasons. To neutralise this possibility, it simply
has to be provided that where a particular term is pre-
classified as a condition in the strict sense this does *not*
confer upon the innocent party a peremptory right of withdrawal for breach. Rather, it confers, so to speak, *a
presumptive right*, in the sense that the innocent party is
relieved of the requirement of making out a prima facie case
of good reason for having the right to withdraw. What this
would entail would be that the innocent party, once having
established a breach of the relevant pre-classified term,
would then be free to withdraw unless the contract-breaker
could counter by showing collateral economic reasons.
Although this avoids one problem with pre-classification, it
fails to respond to the initial question of why such an ex-
ante strategy is needed at all. In other words, even though
we are granting only a presumptive (not a peremptory) right
of withdrawal, why give the innocent party this advantage?

Three considerations might be advanced in response to
this question. First, as it is commonly said in favour of the
extant classification approach, pre-classification might
render the legal position more certain, more calculable for
both the parties and their advisers. Pre-classification
assists, therefore, with ex-post dispute resolution. This line
of reasoning is perhaps most persuasive in relation to unintentional non-negligent breaches where the proposed test,
the radical difference test, is imprecise. Inevitably, with
such questions of degree, there will be clear cases and

marginal cases. If, by pre-classification, the number of marginal cases can be reduced, this must be to the good.

A second line of argument views pre-classification as a device, not merely to clarify the application of the reasons regime, but equally to protect innocent parties who might lack the resources, whether economic or informational, to make out a case in support of a claimed right to withdraw. In other words, pre-classification is seen as a means of delivering the right to withdraw as a practical remedy to classes of contractors (typically consumers rather than commercial contractors) who otherwise might have difficulty in exercising their paper remedies.[77]

Thirdly, pre-classification might be favoured as a device to secure performance, thereby improving the prospect of the parties treating their contracts as obligatory in both theory and practice. In other words, the *settled* availability of a presumptive right of withdrawal might act as a deterrent against non-performance. And, to pick up an earlier point, this might offer significant remedial security where damages would be difficult to prove. Of course, the threat of withdrawal can be translated into monetary terms, to be put into a cost/benefit calculation alongside anticipated damages for breach. However, what sharpens the deterrent effect with a pre-classified term (bearing a presumptive right of withdrawal for breach) is that the burden of rebuttal lies with the contract-breaker and can be argued only on very narrow grounds. Other things being equal, therefore, the putative contract-breaker must judge that there is little reason why the innocent party should be inhibited from withdrawing.

If pre-classification appeals as a deterrent against breach, one might be tempted to pursue a deterrent strategy independently of the ex-post regime. For example, one might pre-classify as conditions (ie conferring a presumptive right of withdrawal) terms the breach of which do not go to the root of contract. Quite clearly, though, this would be a significant step, for it would enable innocent parties to withdraw in circumstances where they might not otherwise have good reasons for withdrawal. If we suppose that the point of prior classification (with the concomitant presumptive right to withdraw for breach) is either to resolve

---

[77]   Cf Chris Willett (1991) 54 MLR 552.

problematic borderline cases of good reasons or to relieve the innocent party of the burden of eliciting good reasons which it is plausibly assumed to have, then pre-classification cannot be allowed to open the way for withdrawal where it is known that there are not good reasons. On the other hand, it may be argued that such an extension of the right to withdraw can be justified in order to discourage economic opportunism (by would-be contract-breakers) and thereby to advance the principle that contracts should be treated as affairs of obligation. Plainly, there is a tension here which needs to be teased out and resolved.

In fact, the tension is quite complex. Two very general principles have exerted a gravitational force in pulling our thinking towards the idea of a reason-centred regime and the notion that the right to withdraw should be available, prior classification (or reservation) apart, only where the innocent party has good reason. First, there is the principle that, prior classification apart, the right to withdraw for breach should be available only where damages would not be an adequate remedy. This leads directly to the idea that the adequacy of damages is to be judged according to whether, in the light of the breach, the innocent party has good reasons for seeking the right to withdraw. Secondly, there is the principle that contracts, being a matter of obligation, are to be performed. This yields the principle that contracting parties have a duty to eschew economic opportunism, which, in post-breach situations, generates the idea that, prior classification apart, the innocent party should have good reasons for withdrawal. If we act on the first principle (viz, that, prior classification apart, the right to withdraw should be available only where damages would not be an adequate remedy), we need to decide whether prior classification should be regulated, too, by the regime of good reasons. If we think that it should, then there are severe limits on the extent to which prior classification can be used as a deterrent against non-performance. If, however, we think that it should not, then there is no apparent objection to employing prior classification as a deterrent strategy. Turning to the second principle, the fundamental idea is that the law of contract should act against economic opportunism. To this end, prior classification is the law's ex-ante strategy, while the requirement of good reasons is its ex-post strategy. On the face of things, this conception of contract must favour performance as against compensation, so that, in the event of any tension, the ex-ante strategy must have priority. Accordingly, on this interpretation, it would not be inconsistent to employ the right to withdraw extensively as a deterrent strategy. Of course, since we can probably afford to be fairly sceptical about anything more than very general claims concerning the deterrent or incentive effect of a known right to withdraw, the various tensions involved in these principles do not have to be resolved as a matter of urgency. Nevertheless, it has to be conceded that there is considerable unfinished business here.

4. REASONS AND RATIONALITY

Given that no more than a sketch has been offered of what a reason-centred legal regime for withdrawal for breach might look like, there is no warrant for claiming that such a regime would be more rational than the existing law. Nevertheless, in favour of such a regime, it can at least be said that it promises to avoid one form of irrationality – namely, a lack of congruence between the law as declared and the law as administered – which has been particularly prevalent in the English law of contract this century.

Rationality, as applied to legal doctrine, is a complex concept, involving a number of dimensions.[78] To be fully rational, legal doctrine must be *formally* rational (for example, it must not violate the law of non-contradiction);[79] it must be *instrumentally* rational at both a generic level (ie it must be capable in general of guiding action) and a specific level (ie it must be an appropriate means towards a particular end); and it must be *substantively* rational (ie its content must be acceptable relative to some criterion of 'legitimacy').

One significant form of *instrumental* irrationality (at a generic level) arises where legal doctrines proclaim one thing

---

[78]   For full elaboration of the idea, see ch 10.

[79]   Two caveats need to be noted here. First, contradictions in legal doctrine cannot be avoided simply by drawing arbitrary distinctions or by refusing to consider doctrines drawn from different divisions of the law (eg contract and tort). Secondly, contradictions cannot be established simply by pointing to a tension between principles, see Deryck Beyleveld and Roger Brownsword 'Privity, Transitivity, and Rationality' (1991) 54 MLR 48, at 55–56.

but legal officials, while purporting to apply these doctrines, actually act on different, unstated, considerations. Where this happens, there is what Lon Fuller called a lack of congruence between the law in the books and the law in action.[80] In contract, we have seen such covert judicial activity in a number of fields, for example in relation to the protection of consumers against one-sided standard form contracts and sweeping exclusion clauses,[81] and in commercial contexts where the privity doctrine obstructs commercially sensible outcomes.[82] Now, as these examples make clear, the covert considerations relied upon are not necessarily in any sense illegitimate. On the contrary, the judges' real reasons, although not in line with legal doctrine, were perfectly good reasons. The irrationality, then, does not reside at all in judges acting on bad reasons, but in their having to conceal perfectly good reasons behind doctrine which does not yet track such reasons. When we reflect upon this question of congruence in relation to the right to withdraw for breach, it is arguable that legal doctrine no longer tracks the real reasons acted upon by judges. Granted, the disjunction between official doctrine and actual practice may not be quite as marked here as in some other areas of contract, but there is surely evidence enough that the problem exists. Quite apart from conspicuous examples such as *The Hansa Nord*, and the various attempts to protect charterers against opportunistic withdrawals by vessel owners,[83] it is arguable that the rationale of the *Hong*

---

[80]   Lon Fuller, *The Morality of Law* (New Haven, Yale University Press, 1969) pp 81–91. Moreover, it is in the principle of congruence, coupled with the principle of generality, that Fuller identifies the essence of the Rule of Law, see pp 209–210.

[81]   See chs 3 and 8. See, too, eg Brownsword (1972) 35 MLR 179; see above, note 75; and John Adams and Roger Brownsword, *Understanding Contract Law* 2nd edn (London, Fontana, 1994) pp 136–47.

[82]   See ch 5. See, too, eg John Adams and Roger Brownsword 'Privity and the Concept of a Network Contract' (1990) 10 Legal Studies 12, and 'Privity of Contract – That Pestilential Nuisance' (1993) 56 MLR 722.

[83]   Although *The Chikuma* effectively settled that, where the charterer is in breach of the punctual payment clause of the NYPE form of time charter, the owner can withdraw for collateral economic reasons (see above, n 38), later decisions have hinted at a residual protective concern for charterers. For example, in *Afovos Shipping Co S.A. v Romano Pagnan and Pietro Pagnan: The Afovos* [1983] 1 WLR 195, the House construed a 'non-technicality' payment clause in such a way that the

Kong approach is to counter withdrawals based on collateral economic reasons. After all, as Tony Weir has pointed out, in any case where the consequences of the breach are such as to deprive the innocent party of substantially the whole benefit of the bargain, it is a fair bet that the withdrawal is not motivated by economic opportunism.[84] Accordingly, if legal doctrine is to be brought into line with the real considerations guiding judicial determination of the question of withdrawal for breach, the reasons relied upon by the innocent party who seeks withdrawal must be addressed explicitly and incorporated coherently within legal doctrine.

Rationality, to repeat, is a complex concept with a number of facets. It does not follow, therefore, that the elimination of the particular irrationality of a lack of congruence will complete the rationality of the law in relation to the right to withdraw for breach of contract. For instance, it might be objected that the reason-centred regime, having overcome one form of instrumental irrationality, unwittingly replaces it with another. Most obviously, this line of objection will appeal to those who feel that the proposed regime is simply too uncertain to act as a guide to commercial contractors and their advisers. Less obviously, it might also appeal to those who sense that, if collateral economic opportunism is the mischief, then the appropriate cure is simply to introduce a general requirement of good faith,[85] or, less

---

owners' notice of intention to withdraw was invalid. Similarly, in *Antaios Compania Naviera S.A. v Salen Rederierna A.B.* [1985] AC 191 (which Lord Diplock, at p 200, said 'was a typical case of a shipowner seeking to find an excuse to bring a long-term charter to a premature end in a rising freight market'), the House upheld the arbitrators' ruling that the punctual payment clause could not be read as meaning that any breach of the charter-party, however trivial, gave the owners the option of withdrawal.

84   See Weir (1976) 35 Cambridge Law Journal 33.

85   Generally, see ch 7; and, cf section 1-203 of the Uniform Commercial Code which provides for good faith in the performance and enforcement of contracts. Seminally, see E. Allan Farnsworth, 'Good Faith Performance and Commercial Reasonableness Under the Uniform Commercial Code' (1962-3) 30 University of Chicago Law Review 666, and Robert S. Summers '"Good Faith" in General Contract Law and the Sales Provisions of the Uniform Commercial Code' (1968) 54 Virginia Law Review 195. With particular reference to bad faith economic opportunism in the context of breach, see Steven J. Burton 'Breach of Contract and the Common Law Duty to Perform in Good Faith' (1980–81) 94 Harvard Law Review 369.

ambitiously, a good faith – or 'abuse of right' – proviso in relation to the *exercise* of the right of withdrawal.[86] Alternatively, it might be argued that the reason-centred regime is *substantively* irrational because it relies too much on the principle that the right to withdraw for breach should be available only where damages would not be an adequate remedy. In line with this contention, it might be submitted that, provided the innocent party seeks in good faith to withdraw 'for breach', then the right to withdraw should hold without restriction (ie for any breach of any term).[87] Whilst these points are certainly not to be lightly dismissed, it is suggested that a reason-centred regime of the kind proposed at least deserves a second look – and that, while we are having a second look at such a regime, we might do well to consider its potential for regulating withdrawals and 'terminations' across the whole range of contractual contexts.[88]

[86] If the good faith provision merely determined whether the exercise of the option to withdraw was valid, the law determining whether the option was available in the first place could be left unchanged (note the distinction drawn above in n 1).

[87] But, does it make sense to provide for an unrestricted right to withdraw, eg even where there is an unintentional, non-negligent breach which does not render the performance radically different? If not, must we presuppose a duty to support the contractual project, or a duty to co-operate, or something of that kind? Generally, see ch 9; and cf Hugh Collins, *The Law of Contract* 2nd edn (London, Butterworths, 1993) especially ch 13.

[88] Cf Charlotte Villiers, Robert Bradgate, and John Birds (eds) *Termination of Contracts* (London, Chancery, 1995), particularly with regard to discussions of termination of contracts of employment; and see Gwyneth Pitt 'Dismissal at Common Law: The Relevance in Britain of American Developments' (1989) 52 MLR 23, esp at 28–29.

Chapter 7

Good faith

Introduction

Whereas the law of contract in many legal systems – for example, in the American, French, and German legal systems – explicitly requires that the parties should act in good faith,[1] the English law of contract has no such provision.[2] Why is it that English law has declined to adopt an overriding principle of good faith in contracts? One view, the 'pragmatic thesis', as it may be termed, was clearly expressed by Sir Thomas Bingham in *Interfoto Picture Library Ltd v Stiletto Visual Programmes Ltd.*[3] This view holds that, although English contract law has not committed itself to an explicit principle of good faith, it nevertheless succeeds in acting against cases of unfair dealing by one means or another – English law, as Sir Thomas put it, has 'developed piecemeal solutions in response to demonstrated problems of unfairness'.[4] The implication of this view is that, whilst there is no real objection to a good faith requirement, the

---

[1]   See (for the United States) section 1-203 of the Uniform Commercial Code and section 205 of the *Restatement (Second) of Contracts* (1981), which provide for a requirement of good faith in the performance and enforcement of contracts; Article 1134(3) of the French *Code civil*; and section 242 of the German *Bürgerliches Gesetzbuch.*

[2]   See e g Raphael Powell, 'Good Faith in Contracts' (1956) 9 Current Legal Problems 16; J. F. O'Connor, *Good Faith in English Law* (Aldershot, Dartmouth Publishing Company, 1991) ch 3; Roy Goode, 'The Concept of "Good Faith" in English Law' (Centro di Studi e Richerche di Diritto Comparato e Straniero, Saggi, Conferenze e Seminari 2, Rome 1992).

[3]   [1989] QB 433. But cf Sir Thomas's more recent remarks in Philips' claim against BSB and Sky Television: see (1995) 9 The Lawyer 10.

[4]   At 439.

198

English can manage quite nicely without one. There is, however, another view – let us term it the 'repugnancy thesis' – which strikes an altogether more hostile attitude towards a good faith doctrine. Thus, in *Walford v Miles*,[5] where the House of Lords both reasserted the orthodox English view that an agreement to negotiate falls short of a legally enforceable contract and rejected the appellants' invitation to recognise an agreement to negotiate *in good faith* as a legally enforceable contract, Lord Ackner said:

> '[T]he concept of a duty to carry on negotiations in good faith is inherently repugnant to the adversarial position of the parties when involved in negotiations. Each party to the negotiations is entitled to pursue his (or her) own interest, so long as he avoids making misrepresentations. . . A duty to negotiate in good faith is as unworkable in practice as it is inherently inconsistent with the position of a negotiating party.'[6]

The repugnancy thesis, it will be appreciated, is one way of expressing the larger concern, nicely put by Kirby P, that in commercial matters one should not 'substitute lawyerly conscience for the hard-headed decisions of business people'.[7] Now, whilst some may wish to distance themselves

---

[5]   [1992] 1 All ER 453.

[6]   At 460-461.

[7]   *Austotel Pty Ltd v Franklins Selfserve Pty Ltd* (1989) 16 NSWLR 582, 585. Cf Meagher J.A. in the important Australian case of *Renard Constructions (ME) Property Ltd v Minister for Public Works* (1992) 26 NSWLR 234, 275:

> 'In the present case the parties apparently interpreted the concept of reasonableness as involving the balancing "of the interests of the principal against those of the contract" (sic, quaere contractor). There is no possible basis for inflicting such a duty on the principal, and his Honour was correct to repudiate it. There is no reason why the principal should have regard to any interests except his own.'

Similarly, see Wallace JA (dissenting) in the Canadian case of *Re Empress Towers Ltd and Bank of Nova Scotia* 73 DLR (4th) (1991) 400, 409–410:

> 'I have always had difficulty in determining what constitutes "good faith" in contract negotiations. If one of the parties "stubbornly" or "unreasonably" refuses to accept an offer or make a counter-offer, the other party usually categorizes the first person's conduct as "refusing to bargain in good faith." It usually reflects one party's view of the conduct of the other party where that person remains adamant and refuses to move from a bargaining position he or she has adopted . . .
>   In my view, where there is neither fraud nor deceit and one is

from the repugnancy thesis, the pragmatic thesis surely captures a widely held view to the effect that the English law of contract serves well enough without explicitly adopting a requirement of good faith.[8]

This chapter is most directly concerned with the credentials of the pragmatic thesis, the principal contention being that this view is altogether too sanguine. However, it does not follow from this either that the repugnancy thesis is of no interest for present purposes or that it is obviously to be rejected. In fact, the repugnancy thesis – at least, in the context of a case like *Walford v Miles* – serves to draw attention to two important matters. First, it emphasises that the adoption of a good faith requirement constrains the pursuit of self-interest in a way that goes beyond the minimal restrictions of the classical law. The more that good faith impinges on the classical law, the more the ground rules of contract change. Moreover, whilst it might be possible to

simply exercising his or her contractual right to maintain a certain bargaining position, the question of "good faith" does not enter into the issue.'

For the majority in *Empress Towers*, however, the contract implied a duty to negotiate in good faith where the bank-lessees purported to exercise an option to renew at a rent of 'the market value prevailing . . . as mutually agreed between the Landlord and the Tenant'. According to the majority, there was an obligation to negotiate in good faith (with a view to reaching agreement on a market rental rate) and not unreasonably to withhold agreement.

8   Cf S. M. Waddams, 'Pre-Contractual Duties of Disclosure' in Peter Cane and Jane Stapleton (eds) *Essays for Patrick Atiyah* (Oxford, Clarendon Press, 1991) 237, at 253-4. Waddams suggests that, whilst there are, at first sight, attractions in embracing broad concepts such as good faith and fair dealing, this does not always produce expected results. Experience indicates that:

'What is needed is a set of rules sufficiently in conformity with the community sense of morality not to produce results perceived as outrageous, while at the same time preserving sufficient content to be workable and reasonably inexpensive of regular application, and maintaining a fair degree of security of property transfers.'

In the light of this, Waddams concludes that, rather than espousing a general good faith requirement, a 'more effective way of producing honest behaviour is likely to be the adoption of specific rules that, in particular contexts, make honesty the best policy'. Taking this view, English pragmatism would seem a sound approach. And cf the pragmatic English line taken in *Regalian Properties plc v London Docklands Development Corpn* [1995] 1 All ER 1005 with that taken in Australia in *Sabemo Pty Ltd v North Sydney Municipal Council* [1977] 2 NSWLR 880.

interpret a fairly limited good faith requirement as no more than an 'extension' of the classical law, there undoubtedly comes a point at which it is correct to conceive of good faith as 'repugnant' to the classical model of contract as self-interested exchange. Quite where the line is to be drawn between good faith as a mere extension of the classical law and as the harbinger of a radically different model of contract is a matter for debate.[9] However, there is no doubt that the repugnancy thesis rightly identifies the adoption of a good faith requirement with potential sea-changes in contract law. Secondly, the particular issue in *Walford v Miles* centres on good faith in *negotiation* of a contract, rather than good faith in performance or enforcement. Arguably, the distinction between, on the one hand, good faith in negotiation and, on the other hand, good faith in the performance or enforcement of a contract is of considerable significance. To require good faith in the performance or enforcement of a contract is not to require good faith at large; the requirement can be related to the intentions or expectations of the particular contracting parties and, in this sense, good faith can be viewed as a mutually agreed (self-imposed) constraint on the pursuit of self-interest. To require good faith in negotiation, however, is quite another matter. Such a requirement cuts deep into the classical adversarial model – and it is surely no accident that the repugnancy thesis was articulated in the context of a claim for good faith in negotiation.

Turning from the repugnancy thesis, as we have said, the principal contention of this chapter is that the pragmatic thesis is ill-judged. Specifically, it is submitted, *first*, that English contract law would be improved if it were explicitly to adopt a general requirement of good faith – a requirement applying to the performance and enforcement of contracts, but also (at any rate, in principle) to their negotiation (as in *Walford v Miles*); *secondly*, that in adopting such a requirement, a choice must be made between two concepts of good faith, between 'good faith as an exception' (the exception being to a general rule sanctioning wholly self-interested dealing) in contrast with 'good faith as the rule' (the rule being that contracting should be guided by an ideal of other-regarding, or co-operative, dealing); and, *thirdly*, that, although the former concept of good faith might fit more

---

[9] See further ch 9.

readily with both the style and much of the substance of the English common law of contract, there are grounds for thinking that a fully rational law of contract would operate with the latter concept of good faith. If this final submission were to be accepted, one would be committed to adopting a non-adversarial model of contract, repugnant indeed to the classical adversarial model, but a model judged to be rationally superior to its rivals.

These contentions are elaborated in four sections. Section 1 argues that, without an explicit concept of good faith, English law suffers from a simple lack of rationality. The point is that, without such a resource, the law of contract is ill-equipped to deal with cases of bad faith; at best, it can do so only in a back-handed manipulative way; and it disables itself from developing a coherent jurisprudence of bad faith and good faith. In section 2, the distinction between 'good faith as an exception' and 'good faith as the rule' is introduced. Whereas the concept of good faith as an exception belongs within a contractual regime the basic ethic of which is that contractors are permitted to deal in a wholly self-interested way, the concept of good faith as the rule presupposes an essentially co-operative model of contract. Relating the concept of good faith as an exception to Robert Summers's well-known analysis of good faith as an 'excluder',[10] the requirement of good faith is constituted by a number of prohibitions against bad faith; such prohibitions reflect prevailing commercial standards of good and bad faith, and serve to restrain the otherwise generally permissible pursuit of economic self-interest in contract. Similarly, relating the concept of good faith as the rule to the idea, often articulated in opposition to Summers's analysis, that the positive aspect of good faith needs to be accentuated, the requirement of good faith flows from a theory of co-operative dealing, the axiomatic principle of which is that one should respect the legitimate interests of fellow contractors. In section 3, some of the implications and applications of these rival concepts of good faith are explored by focusing on three possible paradigms of bad faith: namely, playing the market, opportunistic re-negotiation, and non-

---

[10]   Robert S. Summers, '"Good Faith" in General Contract Law and the Sales Provisions of the Uniform Commercial Code' (1968) 54 Virginia Law Review 195.

disclosure. The main submission in this section is that the development of a coherent jurisprudence of good faith as the rule is a viable project. In section 4, some opening thoughts are presented on the difficult question of whether there are grounds for adopting one concept of good faith in preference to the other. We suggest: (1) that, if we treat the good faith models as candidates for the default rules of contract, then instrumental-rational considerations seem to be neutral between the rival candidates; but (2) that, if we are guided by liberal-welfarist morality of the kind associated with John Rawls, Ronald Dworkin, and Alan Gewirth,[11] then there are good moral reasons for preferring good faith as the rule rather than good faith as the exception. In short, a good faith requirement needs to be incorporated into English commercial contract law, and it is the concept of good faith as the rule that needs to be adopted.

1. LAW AS A RATIONAL ENTERPRISE

Our first contention is that English contract law would be improved if it were explicitly to adopt a requirement of good faith. The argument for this has nothing to do with harmonisation, with bringing English law into line with contract law in other jurisdictions. Rather, the argument turns on the initial premise that law aspires to be a rational enterprise. This aspiration proceeds on several fronts. At one level, it is a matter of keeping legal doctrine clear and free from contradiction; at another level, rationality is concerned with the effectiveness of law, with whether law regulates as intended; and at yet another level, the quest for rational law is the quest for legitimate law. These aspirations for law apply to all branches of law, including the law of contract.[12]

Attempts to justify the claim that the English law of contract would be more rational (and, thus, improved) if a good

---

[11]   John Rawls, *A Theory of Justice* (London, Oxford University Press, 1972); Ronald Dworkin, *Taking Rights Seriously* (London, Duckworth, 1978); Alan Gewirth, *Reason and Morality* (Chicago, University of Chicago Press, 1978).

[12]   Seminally, see Lon Fuller, *The Morality of Law* (New Haven, Yale University Press, 1969). Specifically in relation to contract, see R. Brownsword 'Towards a Rational Law of Contract' in Thomas Wilhelmsson (ed) *Perspectives of Critical Contract Law* (Aldershot, Dartmouth Publishing Company, 1993) 241.

faith requirement were to be adopted might be developed in more than one way. For example, one might argue that English contract law would be more effective (more instrumentally rational) in regulating commercial dealing if a good faith requirement were incorporated, because this would bring the law more into line with the expectations and understandings of commercial practice.[13] Alternatively, one might appeal to moral considerations (moral rationality) in favour of the adoption of a good faith requirement; and, in section 4 of this chapter, just such an appeal will be employed – although, at that stage, the appeal will be not so much in support of the adoption of an explicit good faith requirement (as against the pragmatic thesis which holds that we can do well enough without such a requirement) but in support of the adoption of one concept of good faith rather than another (namely, the adoption of good faith as the rule rather than good faith as an exception). However, this is to get ahead of ourselves. The immediate task is to support the basic contention that English contract law would be more rational if an explicit requirement of good faith were to be adopted (whether that requirement be good faith as the rule or good faith as an exception); and, for this purpose, the principal rationality consideration is what Lon Fuller identified as the ideal of congruence in the law.[14]

Rationality in any rule-governed system starts with the ideal of congruence, with the ideal that the game should be played according to the declared rules. In the case of law,

---

[13]   Thus, in *Renard Constructions (ME) Property Ltd v Minister for Public Works* (1992) 26 NSWLR 234, 268, Priestley J.A. observed:

> '[P]eople generally, including judges and other lawyers, from all strands of the community, have grown used to the courts applying standards of fairness to contract which are wholly consistent with the existence in all contracts of a duty upon the parties of good faith and fair dealing in its performance. In my view this is in these days the expected standard, and *anything less is contrary to prevailing community expectations*' (emphasis supplied).

See, too, the tenor of Bingham LJ's judgment in *Blackpool and Fylde Aero Club v Blackpool Borough Council* [1990] 3 All ER 25, 30 (and see Adams and Brownsword (1991) 54 MLR 281).

[14]   For Fuller, congruence is one of a number of procedural ideals representing the so-called 'inner morality of law', see Lon Fuller, *The Morality of Law* (New Haven, Yale University Press, 1969) esp ch 2. Among these ideals, however, congruence has a privileged place, constituting the essence of the Rule of Law, see Fuller at pp 209–210.

congruence demands that legal officials, including judges, should apply the law as promulgated. Obviously, this goes right to the heart of the rule of law in relation to the criminal law, but it is crucial, too, in relation to the regulation of transactions. How often are we reminded – not least by the English judiciary – that it is of the first importance that contractors, particularly commercial contractors, should know where they stand? The fact is, however, that calculable rules on paper are no use unless, in practice, such rules are administered as declared.

As we have seen in earlier chapters, the pattern of English contract law in the twentieth century is that calculable general rules from the classical law of the nineteenth century have often been found inappropriate to the modern market place. On the one hand, mass consumer contracting, particularly mass credit purchasing and standard form dealing, has made it hard to hold the line on the canons of the classical law (freedom and sanctity of contract). On the other hand, the classical law ill fits quite a lot of modern commercial contracting: in particular, the model of contract as instant exchange is out of line with long-term contracts, which are often first preceded by extended negotiation and then by ongoing adjustment as performance proceeds. Faced with modern demands for consumer protection, for some measure of protection for reasonable pre-contractual reliance, and for greater flexibility in relation to the ongoing adjustment of contracts, the courts have tended to maintain the rhetoric of the classical law of contract while discreetly qualifying its substance – this has been a noble lie but, in the long run, a practice that has impaired the rationality of the law.

One example[15] of the lack of congruence between the rules as declared and the law as applied has been (and still is) in the area of the exercise of the right to withdraw for breach

[15] Another example is the judicial treatment of 'subject to' clauses, on which see John Carter 'Good Faith and Fairness in Failed Contract Negotiations' (paper delivered at Fourth Annual *JCL* Conference, London, 1993) at pp 11-13. Although Carter does not present the modern treatment of 'subject to' clauses as exemplifying a lack of congruence, he says that 'it would be difficult to refute the argument of a realist that these cases are simply illustrations that, faced with a choice between two interpretations, a court chooses the one which has the effect of *preventing withdrawal from negotiations on a ground not related to the agreed event*' (at 12, emphasis supplied).

of contract. As we suggested in Chapter 6, if English law had a doctrine of good faith in the enforcement of contracts, it would be simple enough to insist that the right to withdraw must not be exercised as a pretext for ulterior economic motives.[16] Of course, this is not to suggest that the English case-law would necessarily have produced radically different results if a doctrine of good faith had been available.[17] However, it is contended that, with a good faith requirement, English law could have avoided an element of irrationality by bringing the paper rules and the real rules into alignment. Instead of having to conjure up ingenious strategies to block bad faith withdrawals, the courts could say quite simply that bad faith withdrawals are not permissible. At once, this would not only achieve congruence, it would direct attention to the real issues raised by opportunistic withdrawals.

Now, if the incorporation of a good faith requirement would facilitate congruence in relation to the law regulating withdrawals for breach of contract, might it not have similar rationality-enhancing effects in other areas of contract law? For example, consider the situation in *Walford v Miles*.[18] There, the Walford brothers, who were negotiating to buy the Miles' business, thought that they had secured the Miles' agreement to negotiate exclusively with them. However, the Miles departed from this understanding by selling the business to a third party. Although the Walfords felt aggrieved by the Miles' conduct, there was no evidence of straightforward bad faith on the part of the latter – there was no evidence, for example, that they were stringing along the Walfords, nor that they withdrew from negotiations with the Walfords simply to take advantage of a more attractive financial offer from the third party. Nevertheless, without an

[16]   Recently, English law has gone some way towards blocking opportunistic rejections in the context of the sale of goods: see s 4 of the Sale and Supply of Goods Act 1994, which prevents commercial contractors from rejecting goods for breach of the implied terms in ss 13–15 SOGA where 'the breach is so slight that it would be unreasonable for [the buyer] to reject them'.

[17]   For one thing, the effect of a doctrine of good faith will depend upon the substantive question of how the seminal idea of 'taking account of the legitimate interests of the other party' is interpreted. In some good faith regimes, there may well be occasions when it is permissible to withdraw from a contract in order to take advantage of changed economic conditions.

[18]   [1992] 1 All ER 453.

explicit good faith requirement, the House's unsympathetic treatment of the Walfords' attempt to construct an enforceable lock-out agreement compares somewhat unfavourably with the treatment of agreements to negotiate in other jurisdictions.[19] Moreover, if there had been a suspicion of bad faith in the case, the House would either have had to turn a blind eye to unfair dealing or, if it had wished to protect the Walfords, it would have had to force the facts to fit the classical mould. As Charles Knapp puts it:

> 'If the law persists in declaring bad faith irrelevant in the negotiation process, the court which is faced with clear bad faith conduct will be forced either to find a complete contract where in the absence of bad faith no such contract would be found, or else to write an opinion in which bad faith conduct is either condoned or ignored. Neither of these alternatives makes for "good law" . . .'[20]

Knapp is surely correct. On the one hand, it cannot be rational to ignore bad faith; on the other hand, neither can it be rational to have judicial inquiries into bad faith distorted and obscured by a conceptual framework which no longer articulates the right issues.

This last point is important: without an explicit requirement of good faith the development of a jurisprudence of good faith is impeded. 'Head-on' engagement with the real question is essential.[21] Consider, for example, the impact that an explicit good faith requirement might have in the

---

[19] See eg the sophisticated handling of this question in *Coal Cliff Collieries v Sijehama Property Ltd* (1991) 24 NSWLR 1; and, see, too, the majority approach in *Re Empress Towers Ltd and Bank of Nova Scotia* (1991) 73 DLR (4th) 400. Generally, see E. Allan Farnsworth, 'Pre-Contractual Liability and Preliminary Agreements: Fair Dealing and Failed Negotiations' (1987) 87 Columbia Law Review 217. Ironically, in the more recent non-commercial case of *Pitt v PHH Asset Management Ltd* [1993] 4 All ER 961, the Court of Appeal has bent over backwards to uphold a lock-out agreement in favour of a prospective purchaser of a residential property.

[20] Charles L. Knapp 'Enforcing the Contract to Bargain' (1969) 44 New York University Law Review 673, 727.

[21] Cf the laudable head-on treatment of the privity question by the Australian High Court in *Trident General Insurance Co v McNiece Bros Pty Ltd* (1988) 80 ALR 574, and most recently by the Canadian Supreme Court in *London Drugs v Kuehne and Nagel International Ltd.* [1993] 1 WWR 1 – on the latter of which see J. Adams and R. Brownsword (1993) 56 MLR 722. Generally, see ch 5.

area of implied terms. Where a contractor suspects that the other side is not playing quite fair, this often leads to a claim formulated as breach of an implied term of co-operation (or something of that sort).[22] For instance, in the well-known case of *Luxor (Eastbourne) Ltd v Cooper*,[23] the respondent agents, having found a party willing to purchase the appellants' cinemas at the asking price, argued that the appellants, by failing to proceed with the sale, had unfairly prevented them from earning their commission. In line with the classical law on implied terms, the agents' claim turned on whether the implication of such a term was necessary (to give the contract business efficacy). Given that the agents' claimed commission (earned in just over a week) was the equivalent, as Lord Russell wryly observed, to the annual remuneration of a Lord Chancellor, it is perhaps not surprising that the House saw little merit on the agents' side. This, however, is hardly the point. The real question in *Luxor* was whether there was any impropriety, any bad faith, on the part of the cinema owners. Such an inquiry, it is submitted, was not facilitated by posing the issue in the classical terms of necessary implication.[24]

A more recent illustration of this lack of rationality in English law is offered by the *Manchester United* case.[25] The dispute in that case involved a contract for the transfer of a football player from one club, Bournemouth, to another club, Manchester United. The transfer fee was some

---

[22]   J F Burrows, 'Contractual Co-operation and the Implied Term' (1968) 31 MLR 390; Hugh Collins, 'Implied Duty to Give Information During Performance of Contracts' (1992) 55 MLR 556. Recently, see (1995) 9 The Lawyer 10 for Philips' claim against BSB and Sky Television.

[23]   [1941] AC 108.

[24]   See, too, Robert Summers's astute observation:

'And surely, how a doctrine is conceptualized can affect the outcome of cases. For example, it seems likely that a judge who thinks in terms of implied provisions will be less willing to enforce duties of good faith than the judge who thinks explicitly in terms of such duties; one who views himself as "implying terms" is more likely to think he is remaking a contract to some extent – something which judges are reluctant to do.'

Robert S. Summers, '"Good Faith" in General Contract Law and the Sales Provisions of the Uniform Commercial Code' (1968) 54 Virginia Law Review 195, 233.

[25]   *Bournemouth and Boscombe Athletic Football Club v Manchester United Football Club* (1980) Times, 22 May (Transcript 1974 B No 1531).

£200,000, the deal being that Bournemouth received an initial fee of £175,000 with the remaining £25,000 to be paid if and when the player scored twenty goals in first-team competitive matches. Before the player had scored this number of goals, there was a change of managers at Manchester United and the player was sold to another club, West Ham United, for £170,000. Bournemouth argued that Manchester United were in breach of an implied term, effectively requiring Manchester United to give the player a fair opportunity to score the goals that would trigger the £25,000 payment. The trial judge having ruled in Bournemouth's favour, a split Court of Appeal[26] dismissed Manchester United's appeal. As in *Luxor*, the Court of Appeal's treatment of this point is structured in the unhelpful language of necessity, business efficacy, and the like, the question of bad faith being mentioned only in the closing sentence of Brightman LJ's dissenting judgment, when his Lordship remarked that the position would be quite different if it had been found that Manchester United had acted in bad faith. Clearly, though, this was a critical question. For, if the management at Manchester United had transferred the player simply in order to avoid the bonus payment, then we can be confident that the Court would have been unanimous not only in treating this as bad faith but also in agreeing that it was necessary to imply a term which would protect Bournemouth against a sale motivated by such a reason. However, the evidence was that the transfer was not motivated by any such reason, but occurred simply because the player did not fit in with the new manager's team plans. Brightman LJ thought that this was a perfectly legitimate reason for the transfer and did not see how a term could be implied which would restrict the manager's discretion in relation to matters of team-building and team-selection. For the majority, however, even a legitimate transfer of this kind defeated Bournemouth's expectation that Manchester United would not unreasonably prevent the additional £25,000 being earned and it was, thus, necessary to imply a term to protect this expectation. In other words, even though there was no dishonesty or transparent bad faith on Manchester United's part, a strong

---

[26] Lord Denning MR and Donaldson LJ, with Brightman LJ dissenting.

duty of co-operation (ie a duty of good faith performance) was necessarily implied.[27]

As it stands, the reasoning in the *Manchester United* case is pretty opaque. At one level, there is an obvious tension between the Court's concern to deliver a reasonable interpretation of the contract and the orthodox view (at the time, only recently re-asserted by the House of Lords in *Liverpool City Council v Irwin*)[28] that terms may be implied only if strictly necessary and not simply because judged reasonable.[29] However, the real problem is the absence from English law of an explicit requirement of good faith in the performance of contracts. Had the Court been able to frame the issue in terms of good faith, there would have been a double improvement in the intelligibility of the judgments. First, it would have been very much easier to focus argument explicitly on the material questions: particularly, whether Manchester United were trying in bad faith to shirk their obligations, and how far the duty of good faith impinged on their freedom to deal with the player in the

---

[27]   To a considerable extent, this parallels John Carter's reading of the modern 'subject to' cases (above n 15), according to which (at p 13):

> 'What stands out in the context of "subject to" clauses is that the courts have in effect recognised a general term implied in law qualifying the express terms. The only debate likely to be raised in any case is the precise scope and content of the (good faith) implication. The courts will not always treat honest decisions as sufficient. Good faith merely requires that the other party's interest be considered. In many cases, more onerous obligations are implied.'

Our point is not simply that the members of the Court of Appeal in the *Manchester United* case were divided along these very lines (the majority placing more onerous obligations on the buyers), but that the absence of an explicit requirement of good faith hampered the articulation and justification of this division of opinion.

[28]   [1977] AC 239.

[29]   This particular tension has been eased somewhat by the development post-*Irwin* of the view that, whereas necessity remains the test in relation to one-off implied terms (terms implied in fact), reasonableness is the standard where sets of model terms are to be implied into identifiable categories of contract (terms implied at law). It follows that reasonable interpretations can be delivered by characterising the agreement in question as an identifiable category (albeit a narrow species) of contract; see eg *Scally v Southern Health and Social Services Board* [1992] 1 AC 294. But this still leaves a rationality deficit, formal doctrinal distinctions failing to correspond to the real questions of good and bad faith.

transfer market.[30] Secondly, it would have been easier for the judges to have explained and explored their differences by relating them to the competing conceptions of good faith underlying their opinions. Of course, it is worth repeating that the adoption of an explicit requirement of good faith would not necessarily generate radically different outcomes. Indeed, the outcome of the *Manchester United* case itself might remain unaltered. However, what would alter would be the transparency and formal rationality of decision-making.

The first step, therefore, is clear. In the interests of rationality, a general requirement of good faith must be explicitly adopted in the English law of contract. Without such a legal resource, the alternative, as Robert Summers emphasises, is unattractive:

> '[Without a principle of good faith, a judge] might, in a particular case, be unable to do justice at all, or he might be able to do it only at the cost of fictionalizing existing legal concepts and rules, thereby snarling up the law for future cases. In begetting snarl, fiction may introduce inequity, unclarity or unpredictability. In addition, fiction can divert analytical focus or even cast aspersions on an innocent party.'[31]

In short, the answer to the question 'Why should the English

---

[30] For example, Lord Denning MR put the hypothetical case of the player doing well (scoring 18 goals in short time) and then another club offering £250,000 for him. If the player was transferred in these circumstances, Lord Denning thought it clear that Manchester United would not be entitled to refuse to pay Bournemouth the £25,000. But, why so? In what sense would this be a bad faith transfer or a breach of good faith? Is the assumption that Manchester United had, by contract, shut itself out of speculative transfer dealings (for a reasonable period)? If so, how does this differ from the lock-out (lock-in) agreement pleaded in *Walford v Miles*? Cf text below pp 232–233.

[31] Robert S. Summers '"Good Faith" in General Contract Law and the Sales Provisions of the Uniform Commercial Code' (1968) 54 Virginia Law Review 195, 198–199. To similar effect see eg Robert S. Summers 'The General Duty of Good Faith – Its Recognition and Conceptualization' (1982) 67 Cornell Law Review 810, 812; and Priestley J.A. in *Renard Constructions (ME) Property Ltd v Minister for Public Works* (1992) 26 NSWLR 234, 266. Generally, on the need for direct and overt treatment of legal issues, equipped with appropriate rules and reasons, see Karl N. Llewellyn, *Book Review* (1959) 52 Harvard Law Review 700, 703; and Barry J. Reiter and John Swan, 'Contracts and the Protection of Reasonable Expectations' in Barry J. Reiter and John Swan (eds) *Studies in Contract Law* (Toronto, Butterworths, 1980) 1, p 4.

law of contract explicitly incorporate an overriding principle of good faith?' is that this would make for transparency, it would serve the ideal of congruence and, where bad faith was in issue, it would help lawyers to keep their eye on the ball. The next steps, however, are altogether more difficult. First, allowing that the idea of good faith is somewhat elusive, is it possible to bring the concept(s) more clearly into focus? And, secondly, if (as will be argued) we are faced with a choice between different concepts of good faith, which one should English law adopt?

2. TWO CONCEPTS OF GOOD FAITH

English lawyers, perhaps not altogether surprisingly, find good faith an elusive concept. For example, in *Central Estates (Belgravia) Ltd v Woolgar*,[32] where the Court of Appeal had to determine for the purposes of the Leasehold Reform Act 1967 whether a tenant's claim to buy the freehold was made in good faith, Phillimore LJ remarked:

> 'Counsel could not help us very much. One said that a claim was not made in good faith when it was made in bad faith. Another said that a claim must be dishonest if it was to be made otherwise than in good faith. It was said that a claim would not be made in good faith if the facts showed it was untrue to the knowledge of the tenant or if the claim was made for some ulterior motive. One counsel said it all depended on "quo animo" the claim was made and another said that motive must be distinguished from intention.'[33]

If this seems somewhat harsh on counsel's efforts, it nevertheless suggests that the English jurisprudence of good faith is fairly primitive. To make any headway with the concept, specifically as applied in the field of contract law, we really need to look elsewhere.

In his seminal discussion of the good faith provision of the UCC, E. Allan Farnsworth distinguishes between two senses of good faith.[34] There is good faith, as in 'good faith purchase'; and there is good faith, as in 'good faith performance

---

[32]   [1971] 3 All ER 647.
[33]   At 650.
[34]   E. Allan Farnsworth, 'Good Faith Performance and Commercial Reasonableness Under the Uniform Commercial Code' (1962–63) 30 University of Chicago Law Review 666.

or enforcement'. In the former sense, good faith connotes a particular (innocent) state of mind, namely one free from suspicion or notice – good faith in the sense of 'the pure heart and the empty head' as Lord Kenyon once put it.[35] In the latter sense, Farnsworth maintains that good faith 'has nothing to do with a state of mind'.[36] Rather, this sense of good faith connotes 'decency, fairness or reasonableness in performance [and] enforcement' and it is linked to the idea of an implied term 'requiring co-operation on the part of one party to the contract so that another party will not be deprived of his reasonable expectations'.[37] Whilst English law has some considerable experience of good faith in the first of these senses, particularly for instance in relation to sale of goods and negotiable instruments,[38] it is good faith in the second sense that is of present concern. In Farnsworth's view, common sense and tradition dictate that a good faith requirement in this second sense should adopt an objective test, preferably making the criterion of good faith 'reasonable commercial standards of fair dealing in the trade.'[39]

Farnsworth's analysis paves the way for a now familiar set of questions concerning the specification of a good faith requirement. First, is good faith to be judged by a subjective or an objective standard, or, indeed, by an inter-subjective standard?[40] Secondly, if good faith is to be judged by an objective standard, what is the reference point for this

---

[35] See *Lawson v Weston* (1801) 4 Esp 56, 170 ER 806.
[36] Farnsworth, above n 34 at 668.
[37] Farnsworth, above n 34, at 669.
[38] See eg J. F. O'Connor, *Good Faith in English Law* (Aldershot, Dartmouth Publishing Company, 1991) pp 39–45.
[39] As per section 2-103(1)(b) of the UCC which has a special merchants' definition of good faith for sales as 'honesty in fact and the observance of reasonable commercial standards of fair dealing in the trade'. Recently, Farnsworth has shown how an objective standard of good faith can operate in conjunction with a subjective approach qualified by various bad faith exceptions, see 'The Concept of Good Faith in American Law' (Centro di Studi e Richerche di Diritto Comparato e Straniere, Saggi, Conferenze E Seminari 3, Rome, April 1993).
[40] See eg Robert Dugan 'Good Faith and the Enforceability of Standardized Terms' (1980) 22 William and Mary Law Review 1, who proposes that, in standard form dealing, the good faith test should focus on whether the drafting party had notice of a legitimate interest or expectation on the part of the non-drafting party which the drafting party then failed to respect.

standard?[41] Thirdly, how far can notions of good faith be
firmed up in the context of contractual negotiation, rather
than in relation to performance or enforcement of contracts?[42] Or, to put this another way, is there a fundamental
distinction between good faith in negotiation and good faith
in performance and enforcement?[43] And, fourthly, to what
extent is it permissible for the contractors to exclude a good
faith requirement (and, if it is permissible, how is exclusion
to be signalled)? Whilst these are all important questions,
they are not the central question. The central question, it is
suggested, has to home in on the nub of bad faith, which
characteristically involves the prioritisation of self-interest.
The essential question raised by a good faith doctrine, as J.
F. Burrows observes, is

> '. . . how far one party will be allowed to put his own selfish inter-
> ests above those of his contractual partner. For when a party
> does something which interferes with the performance of the
> contract, or the benefit the other party hoped to get from it, his
> action is seldom contumacious; he has simply decided that
> some other interest of his own deserves first preference.'[44]

This should not be misunderstood. It is not being suggested
that good faith equates with the duties of a fiduciary, at least
not if this implies that good faith writes self-interest out of
the contract script. What Burrows correctly identifies is that
a good faith requirement impinges upon, or constrains,[45]
purely self-interested dealing. Developing this idea, two
fundamental questions come into view. The first question
concerns the extent to which a good faith requirement constrains self-interest; and the second question is whether a
requirement of good faith is to be interpreted as an exception (or qualification) to a general rule licensing wholly
self-interested dealing, or whether good faith dealing is itself

---

[41]   Cf Powell, above n 2.
[42]   Cf E Allan Farnsworth, 'Pre-Contractual Liability and Preliminary
Agreements: Fair Dealing and Failed Negotiations' (1987) 87 Columbia
Law Review 217.
[43]   Cf Steven J. Burton, 'Breach of Contract and the Common Law Duty
to Perform in Good Faith' (1980–81) 94 Harvard Law Review 369.
[44]   Burrows, above n 22, at 390.
[45]   Or, it might be said, the requirement of good faith 'curtails' rather than
'denies' the right to act in a self-interested way. See John Carter 'Good
Faith and Fairness in Failed Contract Negotiations' (paper delivered at
Fourth Annual JCL Conference, London, 1993) at p 5, citing Paul Finn
'Contract and the Fiduciary Principle' (1989) 12 UNSWLJ 76 at 82-3.

to be the rule. We can consider these two questions in turn.

To what extent does a good faith requirement constrain self-interested dealing? It is sometimes suggested that good faith is a nonsense because it presupposes an altruistic model of contract. Quite likely, an altruistic model would be a nonsense – at least, where the altruistic ground rules applied to *both* contracting parties – since both parties would be falling over backwards in their attempts to prioritise the interests of one another. Moreover, what reason would there be for preferring the altruistic model to a model of unconstrained self-interested dealing in which both sides attempted directly to advance their own interests rather than those of the other side? We can safely assume, therefore, that the altruistic model is not a plausible candidate for a good faith requirement. But, if the altruistic model is rejected, does it follow that good faith presupposes ground rules which require the contractors to give equal weight to one another's preferences? This hints at a co-operative model of contracting, but it is still not quite on the mark. What good faith characteristically requires is that contractors respect one another's legitimate interests, a corollary of which is that a good faith regime necessarily imposes constraints on the pursuit of self-interest. In short, the pursuit of self-interest is permissible only so long as it is compatible with the legitimate interests of others (most proximately, the legitimate interests of one's fellow contracting party, but also the legitimate interests of third parties).

Now, if good faith enjoins respect for the legitimate interests of one's fellow contracting party, the extent of a good faith regime's constraint on the pursuit of self-interest will be determined by the particular conception of legitimate interests with which it operates. The more extensive a party's legitimate interests are taken to be, the greater the constraint imposed by good faith; the less extensive, the less the constraint on the pursuit of self-interest. This generates the obvious, but critical, point that different conceptions of good faith hinge upon different conceptions of legitimate interest.[46]

---

[46] Cf Recital 16 of the EC Directive on Unfair Terms in Consumer Contracts, 93/13/EEC, which provides that the requirement of good faith is satisfied where 'the seller or supplier deals fairly and equitably with the other party whose legitimate interests he has to take into account'. Rather obviously, this begs the crucial question of *which* interests are to be regarded as legitimate.

The second question, it will be recalled, was whether good faith operates as an exception to a general rule sanctioning self-interested dealing or whether good faith itself operates as the rule. Clearly, if we follow Farnsworth's suggestion that questions of good and bad faith should be arbitrated in the light of prevailing reasonable commercial standards, then the contrast between the concept of good faith as an exception and good faith as the rule is something of a distinction without a difference. Where good faith operates as an exception, contractors will be permitted to deal in a wholly self-interested way until they reach the bad faith line as drawn by the commercial community. Where, by contrast, good faith is the rule, contractors will be required to eschew wholly self-interested dealing except in those situations in which the commercial community permits self-interested dealing. Yet, if the community to which these questions are remitted is *one and the same community, with one and the same set of standards*, it surely cannot matter how the question of good and bad faith is posed – the answer will always be based on the community's view of the limits of the legitimate pursuit of self-interest. What follows is that, if the distinction between good faith as an exception and good faith as the rule is to be sustained, one must in effect presuppose two different communities, each with its own model of contract, each with its own contractual ethic, each with its own conception of legitimate interest, each with its own concept of good faith.

But, what kind of hypothetical communities are presupposed here? For example, are we dealing with the kind of contrast that Roberto Unger draws between the merchant community of Venice, in which unadulterated self-interest rules, and the community of Belmont 'in which contracts remain for the most part superfluous'?[47] On the face of it, this is not quite the contrast that we are trying to draw. Good faith as the exception is not co-extensive with the Venetian model of contract, for it disallows at least some forms of bad faith in pursuit of self-interest. The Belmontian model, on the other hand, is not quite what good faith as the rule presupposes. In good faith as the rule, contract remains important and there is no question of the law requiring one

---

[47]   Roberto Unger *The Critical Legal Studies Movement* (Cambridge, Mass, Harvard University Press, 1986) at p 64.

to subordinate one's own legitimate interests to those of other contractors. What we are looking for, therefore, are two concepts of good faith with their concomitant models of contract and community, lying somewhere, so to speak, between Venice and Belmont. Good faith as an exception fits with a model of qualified self-interest; good faith as the rule fits with a model which is organised around a coherent concept of co-operative responsibilities. Whilst these rival good faith conceptions might sometimes converge to generate the same outcomes, their theoretical bases must remain distinct – or, to put this another way, these rival conceptions of good faith are driven by rival conceptions of a contracting party's legitimate interests.

In the light of these abstract specifications, we can begin to discern our two concepts of good faith. Good faith as an exception belongs to a regime in which the general rule licenses contractors to deal in a wholly self-interested manner and in which a party's legitimate interests function as constraints on the licensed pursuit of self-interest. By contrast, good faith as the rule is at the core of a regime in which contract is viewed as a co-operative enterprise, and in which respect for a party's legitimate interests is the general rule – in other words, the general standard for contract is set by the good faith requirement itself. The next step is to try to clarify the nature of each of these concepts of good faith.

(i) Good faith as an exception

The concept of good faith as an exception fits with a neo-classical model of contract. According to the classical view, the social function of contract is not simply to facilitate exchange; contract is a vehicle for maximising economic self-interest. Contractors may legitimately pursue their own interests, prioritising their own interests against those of the other side, subject only to such minimal constraints as those pertaining to fraud and coercion.[48] There are a number of ways of trying to rationalise these restrictions on the unbridled pursuit of self-interest. However, for present purposes, let us suppose that these restrictions are adopted

[48]   See John N. Adams 'The Economics of Good Faith' (1995) 8 Journal of Contract Law I.

because they are widely supported in the commercial community. On this view, a good faith requirement appears as another restriction on the pursuit of self-interest, specifically seeking to restrain the more egregious forms of bad faith condemned at any one time by commercial opinion – or, as Comment a to s 205 of the *Restatement (Second) of Contracts* expresses it, '[good faith] excludes a variety of types of conduct characterized as involving "bad faith" because they violate community standards of decency, fairness or reasonableness'.

This view of good faith also fits with Robert Summers's well-known analysis of the principle as an 'excluder':

> 'If good faith had a general meaning or meanings of its own . . . there would seldom be occasion to derive a meaning for it from an opposite; its specific uses would almost always be readily and immediately understood. But good faith is not that kind of doctrine. In contract law, taken as a whole, good faith is an "excluder". It is a phrase without general meaning (or meanings) of its own and serves to exclude a wide range of heterogeneous forms of bad faith. In a particular context the phrase takes on specific meaning, but usually this is only by way of contrast with the specific form of bad faith actually or hypothetically ruled out.'[49]

It follows, as the mid-century Oxford linguistic philosophers might have put it, that 'bad faith rather than good wears the [trousers]'.[50] If pressed for a coherent underlying concept, Summers would say:

> 'In most cases the party acting in bad faith frustrates the justified expectations of another. . .the ways in which he may do this are numerous and radically diverse. Moreover, whether an aggrieved party's expectations are justified must inevitably vary with attendant circumstances. For these reasons it is not fruitful to try to generalize further. It is easy enough to formulate examples of bad faith and work from them.'[51]

In other words, with good faith as an exception, one might construct a general notion of good faith by reference to the contractors' justified (ie legitimate) expectations or understandings, but this would be no more than a rhetorical gloss; in every case, one would simply be led back to the mosaic of

[49] Summers, above n 10, at 201.
[50] At p 207.
[51] At p 263.

bad faith forms which negatively define the substance of the good faith requirement.

What sort of conduct might be treated as bad faith? In relation to *negotiation*, Summers draws on the American case-law to identify negotiating without serious intent to contract, abusing the privilege to withdraw a proposal or an offer, entering a deal not intending to perform (or recklessly disregarding prospective inability to perform), a seller's non-disclosure of known infirmities in goods, and taking advantage of another in driving a hard bargain, as examples of bad faith. Similarly, in relation to *performance*, he identifies evasion of the spirit of the deal, lack of diligence and slacking off, wilfully rendering only 'substantial' performance, abuse of a power to specify contract terms, abuse of a power to determine compliance, and interference with or failing to co-operate in the other party's performance. In relation to *raising and resolving contract disputes*, Summers's examples of bad faith are conjuring up a dispute, adopting overreaching or 'weaseling' interpretations and constructions of contract language, and taking advantage of another to get a favourable readjustment or settlement of a dispute. And, finally, in relation to *taking remedial action*, Summers cites abuse of a right to adequate assurances of future performance, wrongful refusal to accept the other's performance, wilful failure to mitigate damages, and abuse of a power to terminate, as examples of bad faith.[52]

These examples not only afford a helpful indication of the variety of conduct that might be condemned as bad faith dealing at any particular time, they counter the temptation to equate good faith as an exception with a necessarily restricted concept of a fellow contractor's legitimate interests – and we should be careful, therefore, not to misconstrue Summers's remark that 'a requirement of good faith is a minimal standard rather than a high ideal'.[53] In practice, in certain commercial communities, even with good faith as an exception a high degree of co-operation in contracting may be required. However, this should not blur the essential characteristics of the concept of good faith as

---

[52] At pp 220–52.
[53] Robert S. Summers 'The General Duty of Good Faith – Its Recognition and Conceptualization' (1982) 67 Cornell Law Review 810, 834.

an exception: namely, the starting point for contract is a competitive ethic, which generally licenses self-interested dealing, but which regulates bad faith as identified by the commercial community in the light of its prevailing ideas of legitimate interests. In other words, the degree of co-operation demanded by good faith as an exception depends upon where the particular commercial community happens to draw the line between good faith and bad faith, between the legitimate pursuit of self-interest and the violation of another's legitimate interests.

(ii) Good faith as the rule

If contract is not about the single-minded pursuit of self-interest, what else could it be about? In contrast to the classical model of self-interest, we might imagine a model in which contract is viewed as a vehicle for promoting mutual advantage. A has something that B wants, B has something that A wants; or, A and B both want the same thing but cannot secure it without each other's assistance.[54] Contract is the answer to their problems. In the one case they exchange, in the other case they enter into a co-operative joint venture; but, in both cases, it is of the essence that contractors should attempt to promote their joint interests, and they may not legitimately prioritise their own interests against the protected interests of the other side. Placed in this context, the concept of good faith as the rule becomes the guiding ideal for co-operative dealing. Again, to avoid any misunderstanding, this does not mean that individuals may not pursue their own projects and purposes, nor that each contractor must altruistically endeavour to prioritise the interests of the other side; what it means is that each party must respect the legitimate interests of the other contracting party (as defined by a co-operative ideal of contracting).

Now, if we operate with such a model of contract, the doctrine of good faith is no longer a mere shadow created by a number of bad faith restrictions on the pursuit of self-interest. Instead, as a number of writers have argued (commonly against Summers's 'excluder' analysis) the

---

[54]   Cf Lon L. Fuller, 'The Forms and Limits of Adjudication' (1978-79) 92 Harvard Law Review 353, at 357–62.

positive is to be accentuated.[55] For example, Michael Bayles takes good faith in contract to 'require conduct necessary for the minimal trust rational people need to interact *with a reasonable prospect of it being mutually beneficial*';[56] and Russell A. Eisenberg says:

'Although it is probably an impossible task to frame universal definitions and standards of good faith, it is not at all a difficult task to keep in mind at all times what the *concept* is meant to accomplish, and what it requires of businessmen on a daily basis. It is a concept which has proven viable for thousands of years, and a concept which serves as one of the bases of our civilized society.'

It is the *concept* of the term which must always be stressed and applied, not standardized definitions, refined definitions, analyses of definitions and of terms. Courts and businessmen can deal with, and handle, concepts and understand them and work with them, without getting "hung up" on definitions,

---

[55] See Summers, above n 53, for his assessment of the commentators' reaction to his excluder analysis. Summers clearly takes Steven Burton to be one of his major critics (at 826). However, although Burton rejects Summers' excluder analysis, the sense in which he contends that the positive aspect of good faith should be accentuated is not that far removed from Summers' own analysis (in which basic excluder analysis is glossed with the articulation of relevant criteria of bad faith). According to Burton:

'Preliminarily, let is be clear that both of us [ie Burton and Summers] fully agree that one cannot state a "positive definition" of good faith or bad faith performance. That is to say that there is no one fact or set of facts that is present in all cases of one class or the other as a sign of its membership in the class. One cannot state the necessary and sufficient factual conditions for a finding of good faith or bad faith. Decisions in good faith performance cases therefore cannot be made by a wholly deductive method of reasoning. Excluder analysis takes this view, but adopting this view does not commit one to excluder analysis.' (See Steven J. Burton 'More on Good Faith Performance of a Contract: A Reply to Professor Summers' (1984) 69 Iowa Law Review 497, 508.)

Burton goes on to contend that legal reasoning in good faith cases would be aided, not by drawing up lists of relevant bad faith factors (after the fashion of Summers's analysis), but by a general descriptive technique enabling one to see essential similarities between situations of advantage-taking and the like. Thus: 'Unlike most lists of factors, the general description technique encourages us to focus on complex webs of relationships among the facts' (at 510).

[56] Michael D. Bayles *Principles of Law: A Normative Analysis* (Dordrecht, D. Reidel Publishing Co, 1987) p 189 (emphasis supplied).

classifications, and rules with exceptions which only result in confusion.

The purpose of the term "good faith". . . is to constantly remind the business community that it must act in a just and righteous manner, and that it must transact its business in a moral manner . . .'[57]

Whilst Bayles's benchmark of the interactive requirements of rational people, and Eisenberg's injunction to transact one's business in a moral manner might be interpreted in many ways, they appear to have similar ideas in mind. For Bayles, rational people would adopt legal principles that are acceptable 'from both parties' points of view', principles that would be accepted as reasonable 'whichever party one might be' – and, '[it] is assumed that rational persons could be either party to a dispute or legal case'.[58] Eisenberg, for his part, apparently equates the concept of good faith with such ancient maxims as 'Let the property of thy fellowman be as dear to thee as thine own', 'What is displeasing to thee, that do thou not to others', and 'Thou shalt love thy fellow-man as thyself'[59] – in other words, for Eisenberg, legitimate interests are to be determined by applications of the Golden Rule.

In form, the concept of good faith as the rule distinguishes itself from good faith as an exception by putting the emphasis on good faith itself, rather than on many particular instances of bad faith. In substance, though, the critical question is how one interprets the central concept of a legitimate or protected interest, or how one applies tests such as those proposed by Bayles and Eisenberg. The point is that, in principle, one might interpret legitimate interests rather narrowly (as in the classical model of contract law) or one might take an altogether broader, more protective, interpretation (as in the co-operative model of contract that we are trying to bring into focus). If we are to keep a clear line between good faith as an exception and good faith as the

[57]   Russell A Eisenberg 'Good Faith under the Uniform Commercial Code – A New Look at an Old Problem' (1971) 54 Marquette Law Review 1, 17. In fact, Eisenberg goes on to tie the concept of good faith to 'the framework of generally accepted prevailing business practices' (pp 17–18), which rather clouds his position. However, without this qualification, Eisenberg's observations capture nicely the spirit of good faith as a (non-contingent) moral rule.

[58]   Bayles, above n 56, pp 6–7.

[59]   At p 10.

rule, it is essential to remember that the latter concept pre-supposes a co-operative model of contract, the rules of which are designed to facilitate secure and mutually bene-ficial exchange.[60]

(iii) **Synthesis**

The rival conceptions of good faith, good faith as an excep-tion and good faith as the rule, are generated by two sets of distinctions. First, there is the distinction between two views of the basic ethic of contract, between 'an ethic of self-interest in contract' and 'an ethic of co-operation in contract'. On the former view, contract is seen as a vehicle for self-interested exchange, from which it follows that the ground rules for contracting should facilitate the making of exchanges in which each party is able to advance its own interests (irrespective of the interests of the other party); on the latter view, contract is seen as a vehicle for mutual sup-port and co-operation, from which it follows that the ground rules for contracting should channel the parties towards the making of mutually beneficial exchanges. Secondly, there is the distinction between 'contingency' and 'non-contingency' as this applies to both the making of judgments of good faith (and bad faith) and the specification of a party's legitimate interests. Judgments are contingent in this sense when they depend upon (or are relative to) the standards of a particu-lar contracting community. By contrast, judgments are non-contingent when they are not dependent upon (nor relative to) the standards of a particular contracting com-munity, but are based instead upon some independent theory of legitimate interests and good faith. Thus, whereas contingent judgments of good faith (and bad faith) simply draw on the custom and practice of a particular commercial community, non-contingent judgments of good faith (and bad faith) are not so tied to the actual practice of a particu-lar community.

When these two sets of distinctions (contract as self-

---

[60] Of course, even a clear line in principle cannot avoid some degree of convergence between the two regimes in practice. See eg the remarks of Friedrich Kessler and Edith Fine 'Culpa in Contrahendo, Bargaining in Good Faith and Freedom of Contract: A Comparative Study' (1964) 77 Harvard Law Review 401.

interested exchange/ contract as co-operation, and contingency/non-contingency) are put together, they yield four combinations, as follows: (1) contract as self-interested exchange/contingency; (2) contract as self-interested exchange/non-contingency; (3) contract as co-operation/contingency; and (4) contract as co-operation/non-contingency. The conception of good faith as an exception represents the first of these combinations, and the conception of good faith as the rule represents the fourth. This can be presented diagramatically thus:

	Contingency	Non-Contingency
Contract as self-interested exchange	GOOD FAITH AS AN EXCEPTION	
Contract as co-operation		GOOD FAITH AS THE RULE

In this light, it will be apparent that good faith as an exception and good faith as the rule belong to radically different regimes of contract law. Good faith as an exception bears strong traces of the classical model of contract, the basic ethic of which is to license competitive self-interested dealing. Within this regime, respect for a fellow contractor's legitimate interests prohibits certain forms of fraud and coercion, and the requirement of good faith extends this protection as far as prevailing commercial standards happen to dictate. At minimum, good faith as an exception will do little to extend the protective effects of the classical law but, as Robert Summers' review of the American case-law shows, within a particular commercial community there is no reason why good faith as an exception should not constrain self-interested dealing very extensively indeed. By contrast, good faith as the rule belongs to a diametrically opposed model of contract, a model which not only enjoins co-operative dealing and respect for one's fellow contractors as participants in a transaction that is designed to be mutually beneficial, but also distances itself from the custom, practice, and standards of particular commercial communities.

In good faith as the rule, the line between good faith and bad faith is drawn not by reference to commercial opinion, but by relying on an independent theory of legitimate interests set against an ideal of co-operative dealing.

3. TOWARDS A JURISPRUDENCE OF GOOD FAITH

How far is it meaningful to talk about a jurisprudence of good faith? If we adopt the concept of good faith as an exception, can we do any more than list the specific forms of bad faith condemned by the commercial community at any one time? If we adopt the concept of good faith as the rule, can we develop general principles of good faith from our abstract contractual ideal (co-operation, respect for the legitimate interests of the other party, or the like) which can then be applied to concrete issues of alleged bad faith? In this section, our principal interest is in the latter question which we can address by reflecting on three arguable paradigms of bad faith: namely, playing the market, opportunistic re-negotiation, and non-disclosure. However, before considering these three test cases, a brief answer to the first question is in order.

As it has been formulated, the concept of good faith as an exception does not allow for the development of a jurisprudence of good faith. No developed theory of good faith, no developed theory of legitimate interests is required. In each case, it is simply a matter of asking whether on the particular facts a contractor has acted in bad faith, this being judged according to prevailing commercial conventions. Good faith as an exception thus implies a pragmatic case-by-case approach. So interpreted, therefore, the only 'jurisprudence' associated with good faith as an exception is the work involved in maintaining an up-to-date list of the specific forms of bad faith condemned by the commercial community (or particular commercial communities). However, the concept of good faith as an exception might be applied in a rather different way. Instead of being guided by raw commercial conventions, the law of contract might take as its yardstick of bad faith 'the better commercial opinion' or some such notion. Minimally, this might be a device for settling questions of good faith where the evidence from the commercial community is unclear. However, where 'the better commercial opinion' transforms itself into 'reasonable commercial opinion', there is a parallel transformation in the jurisprudence of good faith. Once the concept of the reasonable commercial person becomes focal, the testimony of commercial persons assumes far less importance, and determinations of the bounds of good and bad faith are driven by ruling (and not necessarily homogeneous) judicial perceptions of 'reasonable' commercial conduct. In the courts, this interpretation of good faith as an exception leads to a jurisprudence of good faith, articulated in terms of reasonableness, anchored only to certain (assumed) paradigm cases of bad faith, and largely taking on a life of its own. In so far as jurists are working in the wake of the decided cases, the jurisprudence of good faith may bear a range of theoretical imprints – for example, jurists may strive to render the case-law coherent, or they may prefer (as in the Critical Legal Studies Movement) to 'deconstruct' the law in one way or another.

The upshot of this is that the concept of good faith as an exception either involves no jurisprudence worth speaking of, or it involves a jurisprudence which teases out some vision of transactional propriety from the decided cases. Whilst the possibility of a jurisprudence of this latter kind is not uninteresting, it is not of immediate concern. For the next task, as we have said, is to consider whether the abstract ideal of co-operative dealing can be connected to concrete issues of good and bad faith.

(i) Playing the market

Contractors may be tempted to play the market during any phase of a contract's life – negotiation, performance, or termination. The pattern is always the same: the contract (under negotiation or actually agreed) represents a particular deal, but it can be made even more attractive (internally, by manipulating performance) or a more attractive deal presents itself (externally); economic self-interest prevails (in bad faith) over contractual commitment.

As we saw in the last chapter, a familiar tale of temptation is to be found in the English case, *Arcos v Ronaasen*,[61] where it was in the buyers' interest to be able to escape from the contract in order to take advantage of falling prices on

---

[61]   [1933] AC 470.

the timber market./ The House of Lords, it will be recalled, applied the rule under s 13 of the Sale of Goods Act 1893 (that correspondence of goods with their description was a condition of sales contracts) and unanimously upheld the buyers' right to withdraw from the contract. The House did not, of course, treat the buyers' exercise of the right to withdraw as subject to an overriding requirement of good faith; but what might have been the position if such a requirement had been invoked?

If, on these facts, the House had employed the concept of good faith as an exception, the question would have been whether the relevant commercial community would have regarded the buyers' rejection as a bad faith withdrawal – and, on the evidence of Lord Atkin's judgment,[62] we can take it that the answer would have been in the negative, with the result that a good faith requirement would not have altered the outcome of the case. What is more, we can probably assume that Lord Atkin would have answered the question in the negative irrespective of whether he had posed the issue in terms of prevailing commercial standards, the better commercial view, or reasonable commercial standards. However, this was a market-individualist judge[63] adjudicating against the background of the timber trade of the inter-war years, and who knows what other judges and other commercial communities might condemn as bad faith at another time and in another place?[64]

If, instead, we suppose that the House had employed the concept of good faith as the rule, the question then would have been whether the buyers' rejection of the timber was compatible with respect for the co-operative ideal of contract. However, there are two rather obvious difficulties with applying such a question to the facts of *Arcos v Ronaasen*. First, given that the sellers were in breach, why should the buyers have to respect their interests? Secondly, even if the buyers were required to respect the interests of the

---

[62] Especially at 480.

[63] Cf a similar adherence to a market-individualist approach by Lord Atkin in another leading case of the 1930s, *Bell v Lever Bros* [1932] AC 161.

[64] But even this commercial community might have condemned as bad faith the practice of the timber suppliers in *Hillas and Co Ltd v Arcos Ltd* (1932) 147 LT 503; which, in turn, might explain the House of Lords' unwillingness to allow the timber suppliers to slide out of their option obligations on the alleged grounds of uncertainty.

sellers, how could they do this when, in the circumstances of the falling timber market, their interests were diametrically opposed?

The answer to the first question is that, as a matter of general principle, a party does not lose the protection of a co-operative contractual regime simply because it happens to be in breach of contract – essentially, breach only involves forfeiture where the contract-breaker evinces a lack of respect for the legitimate interests of the innocent party. To adopt Roskill LJ's terminology in *The Hansa Nord*, contract is a matter of obligation;[65] and, innocent parties must continue to respect the interests of contract-breakers unless the particular breach evinces a failure by the latter to treat the contract as a matter of obligation.[66] One example of such a failure would be if the contract-breaker failed to deal in good faith with the innocent party. Thus, to return to *Arcos v Ronaasen*, we would need to ascertain why it was that the sellers delivered timber that was fractionally out. If, for example, it transpired that the sellers had a conforming consignment ready to be shipped to the buyers when a third party came along and made a better offer for the timber, which the sellers accepted, then the sellers' bad faith would release the buyers from their general duties of good faith dealing with the sellers.[67] Short of something of this sort, however, the sellers would not have forfeited their co-operative rights against the buyers. At all events, assuming that the buyers were not released from their good faith obligations, this raises the second difficulty: how could the buyers give due weight to the conflicting interests of the sellers?

One way of answering this question is given by Steven J Burton's thesis that we find one of the paradigms of bad faith in the illegitimate exercise of contractual discretion. Clearly, when contractors close on a deal, they forego certain options that would otherwise be available for playing the market. Minimally, if A has contracted to buy goods from B, but then C comes along and offers to supply A on more attractive terms, A has foregone the option to buy from C *in*

---

[65] *Cehave NV v Bremer Handelsgesellschaft mbH: The Hansa Nord* [1976] QB 44 at 70-1.
[66] See ch 6.
[67] Given that timber prices were falling, this seems a pretty unlikely scenario.

preference to B and can do so only by breaking the contract with B. However, A's duplicity may not be quite so crude. The contract between A and B may present A with a number of arguable openings (discretions) to escape the deal with B and to take advantage of C's better offer. According to Burton:

'Bad faith performance occurs precisely when discretion is used to recapture opportunities foregone upon contracting – when the discretion-exercising party refuses to pay the expected cost of performance. Good faith performance, in turn, occurs when a party's discretion is exercised for any purpose within the reasonable contemplation of the parties at the time of formation – to capture opportunities that were preserved upon entering the contract, interpreted objectively.'[68]

As Burton emphasises, it is the reasons underlying the exercise of discretion that are critical in distinguishing between good and bad faith. Where discretion is driven by market-playing reasons, there is, at the very least, a suspicion of bad faith.[69] Thus, when the parties contracted in *Arcos v Ronaasen*, they locked themselves into the contractual regime of prices, irrespective of rising or falling markets outside the contract, and the parties' interests must be interpreted in the light of this arrangement. Hence, although the buyers had an undoubted economic interest in rejecting the timber, that interest should be regarded as trumped by the overriding (or protected) interests of the sellers as

---

[68] Burton, above n 43, at 373.
[69] Discussing a 1957 decision of the Ohio Court of Appeals, *Joseph v Doraty* [77 Ohio L Abs 381, 144 NE 2d 111 (Ohio Ct App 1957)] Knapp (above n 20) comments at 699-700:

'If the parties had been asked at the time they signed their agreement whether each regarded himself as free to withdraw *for any reason* – including simply a better deal elsewhere – they both would have have probably disclaimed any such privilege of withdrawal. At least each would probably have disclaimed it in the presence of the other party, which may be a good rule of thumb for questions of this sort.'

Although this is in line with the spirit of good faith, the proposed rule of thumb involves more contingency than can be allowed if good faith is to be the rule. Where good faith is the rule, legitimate reasons for withdrawal are to be determined not by commercial opinion, nor by what the contractors would probably have assented to in one another's presence, but by the compatibility of such reasons with the legitimate or protected interests of one's fellow contractor (interpreted in the light of the co-operative ideal).

determined by the contract. In other words, co-operative contracting does not eradicate situations in which parties have conflicting economic interests; rather, it establishes a particular regime of legitimate interests to which conflicting economic self-interest must yield.

This same pattern can be seen in many other facets of contracting: for example, if a contract between A and B is a requirements contract, and A adjusts his order to B so that he can take goods from C on more advantageous terms – or, if A's contract with B is conditional upon some matter to be dealt with to A's satisfaction (for example, the sale is of a car, subject to A receiving a satisfactory report from an inspecting engineer, and A treats the report as unsatisfactory as a pretext for escaping from the contract with B).[70] A good example of bad faith in the former context is *Orange and Rockland Utilities Inc v Amerade Hess Corpn*,[71] where the parties had a five-year requirements contract for the supply of fuel oil. As the market price for fuel oil more than doubled, the buyers increased their orders until eventually the suppliers refused to make available more than the estimated quantities plus ten per cent. The buyers' action for

---

[70]   Cf eg *Docker v Hyams* [1969] 3 All ER 808, 811, where Harman LJ, reviewing a number of authorities of this kind says:

'[The cases] amount to this, I think, that where the condition is that something is to be done to A's approval or to his satisfaction then he is the judge, and as long as he is honest he need not be reasonable.'

However, it is fairly clear that the requirement of 'honesty' in this context would cover bad faith withdrawals (although cf Handley JA in *Renard Constructions (ME) Pty Ltd v Minister for Public Works* (1992) 26 NSWLR 234, 280). Generally, see John Carter's discussion of the 'subject to' cases, above n 15.

[71]   59 AD 2d 110, 397 NYS 2d 814 (1977). For discussion of this case, see Steven J. Burton 'Good Faith Performance of a Contract within Article 2 of the Uniform Commercial Code' (1981) 67 Iowa Law Review 1, 7–9. Here, and in 'Breach of Contract and the Common Law Duty to Perform in Good Faith' (1980–81) 94 Harvard Law Review 369, Burton elaborates the idea of the 'cost perspective' as a way of operationalising the concept of good faith in relation to the performance of contracts. The basic idea is that, at the time of formation, the parties forego market opportunities that would otherwise be available. The cost of entry into a contract, in other words, is the loss of these market options. To attempt to recapture such lost opportunities by a speculative exercise of contractual discretion is to violate the good faith requirement. Whether a particular action is speculative is to be determined by the (objective) standards of reasonable business persons in conjunction with an inquiry into the (subjective) intentions of the actor.

breach failed, the court holding that the buyers had increased their requirements in bad faith, effectively transforming themselves from fuel oil consumers to energy suppliers by using a fixed price requirements contract for speculative purposes.

In the light of this, we can say that a contracting party has a legitimate interest in having a fellow contractor treat the agreement as a matter of obligation. Mere economic convenience has to be subordinated to the overriding commitments enshrined in the agreement. No doubt, contractors would like to be able both to play the market against the contract (as in *Arcos v Ronaasen*), and play the contract against the market (as in *Orange and Rockland Utilities*), as well as have the contract shield them against the market. But contractors cannot have it all ways. Accordingly, the first aspect of good faith emphasises that entry into a contract is at the same time exit from the market, at least exit from the market for the purpose of speculative advantage-taking. Moreover, this principle applies to the exercise of all options in the performance and enforcement of contracts.

Is it possible to apply this idea, too, in pre-contractual situations? There are any number of ways in which one side can string along the other side during negotiations. For example, A invites B to tender for some work, A having no intention of letting the work or of accepting B's tender; or A encourages B to believe that, although the deal is still technically under negotiation, an upcoming contract is a mere formality, when in fact A has no intention of completing with B; or in such cases, A is in good faith at the start but subsequently changes his mind about dealing with B, but does not notify B to this effect.[72] In such cases A's duplicity may be motivated by various considerations – perhaps a better deal comes along, or A simply gets cold feet, or maybe A takes some perverse pleasure in encouraging an expectation in B which he will then frustrate. If we are operating with good faith as an exception, whether or not such cases are treated as bad faith dealing will depend on happenstance commercial conventions or on judicial interpretations of reasonableness in contracting. However, if we are developing general principles of good faith under the rubric of good

---

[72] See eg *Hoffman v Red Owl Stores Inc* 26 Wis 2d 683 (1965); *Walton's Stores (Interstate) Ltd v Maher* (1988) 62 ALJR 110.

faith as the rule, we must condemn market-playing during negotiation in so far as this is inconsistent with the co-operative ideal. But, of course, this begs the question of whether market-playing during negotiation *is* inconsistent with the co-operative ideal, and this raises the large, and difficult, question of whether a requirement of good faith in performance and enforcement entails a requirement of good faith in negotiation.

On a weak interpretation of the co-operative ideal, there is a clear line to be drawn between good faith in performance and enforcement, and good faith in negotiation. On this view, the reason why market-playing, for example, in relation to performance and enforcement involves bad faith is because this violates the implicit terms of the parties' agreement. Thus, we find Burton himself saying:

> 'In my view, courts generally do not use the good faith performance doctrine to override the agreement of the parties. Rather, the good faith performance doctrine is used to effectuate the intentions of the parties, or to protect their reasonable expectations, through interpretation and implication . . . [It] is hard to see what justifies a court in disregarding the agreement of the parties on grounds of "contractual morality" when the intentions of the parties or their reasonable expectations can be reasonably ascertained . . . [The] decided cases on the whole do not support the view that the good faith performance doctrine incorporates vague requirements of contractual morality into the law of contract performance and breach. Both the UCC and the common-law cases make clear that the parties are free to determine by agreement what good faith will permit or require of them.'[73]

The logic of this (unless the idea of reasonable expectation is to be developed) is that *prior to* the parties reaching agreement (and, thus, setting the parameters of their co-operative obligations), while matters are still at the negotiating stage, there is no restriction on market-playing – the duty to co-operate has not yet taken hold. However, if we take a more robust view, conceiving of the contracting process as an exercise in co-operation, it is by no means implausible to hold that the good faith requirement applies also during the stage of negotiation. Indeed, according to Friedrich Kessler and Edith Fine, the basic civilian position is to require

---

[73]   Steven J. Burton, above n 55, at 499–500.

bargaining in good faith.[74] For, on the civilian interpretation of the principle of good faith:

'Once parties enter into negotiations for a contract . . . a relationship of trust and confidence comes into existence, irrespective of whether they succeed or fail.'[75]

Of course, even allowing that the co-operative ideal might have such implications, it remains to be settled when precisely the negotiating stage commences and what good faith then requires of the negotiating parties. Nevertheless, it is at least plausible to suppose that some forms of market-playing by negotiating parties – for example, if one side were merely to go through the motions of negotiation, knowing that a better offer was available with a third party; or, if a party to a lock-out agreement failed to use best endeavours to finalise the deal because a better deal with a third party was known to be available; or, to take a classroom favourite, if an offeree posted an acceptance and then, in order to play the market, tried to escape by sending a faster retraction of the acceptance to the offeror – are prima facie incompatible with the culture of trust and confidence implicit in the co-operative model of contract and, thus, raise a presumption of bad faith.

(ii) Opportunistic re-negotiation

In the nineteenth-century American case of *Headley v Hackley*,[76] Headley claimed that Hackley owed him over $6,000 for logs. Hackley, knowing that Headley urgently needed the money, paid him only $4,000 and extracted a receipt from Headley apparently discharging the debt. The court held that Hackley had acted in bad faith and that Headley was entitled to full recovery. English contract lawyers will recognise this fact situation at once as similar to that of *D and C Builders Ltd v Rees*,[77] where the Court of Appeal followed the American example by allowing the hard-pressed creditors (the jobbing builders) to recover the

---

[74]   See Friedrich Kessler and Edith Fine 'Culpa in Contrahendo, Bargaining in Good Faith and Freedom of Contract: A Comparative Study' (1964) 77 Harvard Law Review 401.
[75]   At p 404.
[76]   45 Mich 569, 8 NW 511 (1881).
[77]   [1966] 2 QB 617.

balance of the debt against the opportunistic debtor (the client). One can assume that, under good faith as the exception, such sharp practice would be condemned in many commercial communities and by many judges (as inconsistent with standards of reasonable commercial dealing); and under good faith as the rule, there is an obvious violation here of co-operative standards.

Although such bad faith by the debtor has caused little difficulty, bad faith by the creditor (demanding an increased payment) has only recently begun to make its mark on the current debate about the scope of the economic duress doctrine in English contract law. For example, Peter Birks has argued that the criterion for illegitimate pressure should be bad faith in the sense that the threat was 'intended to exploit the plaintiff's weakness rather than to solve financial or other problems of the defendant'.[78] The well-known American case of *Alaska Packers Association v Domenico*[79] provides a clear illustration of such a threat. There, the defendant, having hired seamen to fish for salmon in Alaska, was faced in Alaskan waters with a demand from the seamen that they would not work unless higher wages were paid. Given the short fishing season in Alaska and the unavailability of substitute seamen, the defendant had little choice but to accede to the demand. When the defendant reneged on his promise, it was held that the agreement to pay higher wages was unenforceable (for want of consideration).[80] Whilst this may not dispense with all the difficulties of the economic duress doctrine, it at least picks out one clear case of illegitimate pressure – if the creditor realises that it has the debtor 'over a barrel' and simply seizes on the opportunity to improve the terms of the deal, then this is

---

[78]   Peter Birks, *An Introduction to the Law of Restitution* (revised paperback edn) (Oxford, Clarendon Press, 1989) p183. Birks says:

> 'Since the effect [of the modern cases] is to commit them to impossible and inscrutable inquiry into the metaphysics of the will, they thus secure a concealed discretion to distinguish between reasonable and unreasonable, legitimate and illegitimate applications of this species of independently unlawful pressure [viz, pressure to increase the price on pain of breach of contract]. The simplest and most open course would be to restrict the right to restitution to the case in which the defendant [creditor] sought, *mala fide*, to exploit the weakness of the plaintiff.'

[79]   117 F 99 (9th Cir 1902).
[80]   Cf *Stilk v Myrick* (1809) 2 Camp 317, discussed in ch 2.

bad faith, and other things being equal the debtor will be able to reinstate the original terms.[81]

Whilst some of the economic duress cases fit the pattern of crude opportunism, this is not always the case. For example, in another well-known American case, *Goebel v Linn*,[82] where the plaintiff was unable to fulfil a contract to supply the defendant with ice (because of unusually warm weather), it was held that the plaintiff was entitled to enforce the defendant's promise to pay a higher price. Here, the modification was not opportunistic, but a reasonable response to the plaintiff's dire financial situation which was brought about by the original contract price in conjunction with the unexpected failure of the supply of ice. Again, in the seminal English case of *The Atlantic Baron*,[83] the shipyard's demand for a price adjustment was not a simple attempt to capitalise on the clients' vulnerability. The devaluation of the dollar made the contract less profitable; it was a matter beyond the control of the shipyard; and, had there been no devaluation, the shipyard would not have pressed for an increase in the price. On the other hand, the absence of a fluctuation clause in the contract implied that the shipyard took the risk of a dollar devaluation; and, if the clients had not been quite so vulnerable, they presumably would not have agreed to the shipyard's demand. Whether the relevant commercial community[84] would regard the shipyard's demand as in bad faith (assuming good faith as an exception) is an open question[85] (as it is moot what the commercial community would make of the ice-supplier's

---

[81] For a helpful discussion of the developing law, see Andrew Burrows, *The Law of Restitution* (London, Butterworths, 1993) pp 179–82.

[82] 47 Mich 489, 11 NW 284 (1882).

[83] *North Ocean Shipping Co Ltd v Hyundai Construction Co Ltd: The Atlantic Baron* [1979] QB 705.

[84] Identification of the relevant commercial community will not always be straightforward. Where a contract has connections with more than one commercial community, and where those communities have different ideas about bad faith, which community counts as the relevant one? In *The Atlantic Baron*, for instance, was the relevant commercial community English or Korean?

[85] Cf Steven Fennell and Simon Ball 'Welfarism and the Renegotiation of Contracts' in Roger Brownsword, Geraint Howells, and Thomas Wilhelmsson (eds) *Welfarism in Contract Law* (Aldershot, Dartmouth, 1994) 212. Fennell and Ball argue that, in English law, a 'business standards model' now regulates the critical economic duress issue of whether the particular threat is illegitimate – the test of legitimacy is set by the standards of 'the relevant business community'.

demand in *Goebel v Linn* and, indeed, whether it should be distinguished from the shipyard's demand in *The Atlantic Baron*). However, the question to be asked if we work with good faith as the rule is whether the ice-supplier's or the shipyard's demand could be treated as consistent with respect for the legitimate interests of one's fellow contractor (interpreted in the light of the co-operative ideal).

Good faith as the rule needs to distinguish between crude cases of opportunism (where, say, A demands an upward adjustment of the price having no reason for the demand other than the awareness that he is in a position to exploit B) and cases where the demand is related to a genuine financial difficulty. In the former type of case, the protected interest in having the contract treated as a matter of obligation (as already identified) clearly applies. In the latter type of case, matters are less clear-cut. One needs to take account of a range of factors. Thus, where A seeks to re-negotiate the price (upwards) with B, it might be material to consider whether A knows that B is vulnerable, whether A's difficulty is of his own making, whether B has contributed to A's difficulty, whether the difficulty arises from matters related to the contract, and so on.

The much-debated decision of the Court of Appeal in *Williams v Roffey Bros and Nicholls (Contractors) Ltd*[86] provides a convenient focus for this aspect of good faith. The case, it will be recalled, involved an agreement by a main contractor to pay additional sums to a financially troubled sub-contractor. In a bold decision, the court held that, provided that the promise to pay the additional sums was given without fraud or economic duress, and provided that the promisor derived some practical benefit (or, obviated some practical disbenefit) from the agreement, then the promise was binding. Somewhat frustratingly, however, economic duress was not argued in the case, leaving the sub-contractors with a relatively clear run but leaving the commentators guessing about the outcome of the case had economic duress been pleaded by the main contractors. Let us, therefore, pose this issue, but pose it in terms of good faith. What might have been the outcome of the case if the main contractors had disputed their liability to pay the

---

[86]   [1990] 1 All ER 512. See eg Adams and Brownsword (1990) 53 MLR 536; Halson (1990) 106 LQR 183.

promised additional sums on the ground that the sub-contractors had failed to act in good faith?

The trial judge found that the sub-contractor had got into financial difficulty for two reasons – because the contract was underpriced and because of inadequate supervision of his men. To simplify this discussion, let us suppose that underpricing was the root of the sub-contractor's difficulty. In principle, at the time of contracting, four possible situations might have existed as follows:

1. The sub-contractor realised that the contract was underpriced; the main contractor did not.
2. The sub-contractor and the main contractor both realised that the contract was underpriced.
3. The sub-contractor did not realise that the contract was underpriced; the main contractor did realise that the contract was underpriced.
4. Neither the sub-contractor nor the main contractor realised that the contract was underpriced.

For our purposes, the most instructive scenarios are (1) and (3). Situation (1) looks like a pretty clear case of bad faith by the sub-contractor. For the sub-contractor has won the sub-contract under false pretences, promising to do the work for a certain price but intending to apply pressure for the payment of additional sums in due course. Although the sub-contractor's subsequent financial difficulty might be genuine enough, the demand for extra payment is tainted by the bad faith carried through from the time of tender.

Situation (3) is less straightforward.[87] Assuming that, on these facts, there is no bad faith by the sub-contractor,[88] there are nevertheless two views that one might have about the demand for additional payment, namely:

> (a) it is permissible for the sub-contractor to seek additional payment, but there is no obligation on the part of the main contractor to accede to the sub-contractor's

---

[87] Hugh Collins suggests that there was evidence that the main contractors in *Williams v Roffey* realised that the sub-contractor's price was 'unrealistically low', see *The Law of Contract* 2nd edn (London, Butterworths, 1993) 324.

[88] We can eliminate three examples of bad faith here: (1) the tender was genuine; (2) no attempt is being made to exploit a known vulnerability on the part of the main contractor; and (3) the sub-contractor is not so much threatening breach as predicting the inevitable if additional payment is refused.

demand; if, however, the main contractor agrees to
make additional payment, the promise is binding and
cannot subsequently be recalled on the ground of economic duress;
(b) the sub-contractor's demand is legitimate and the
main contractor has an obligation to make a reasonable
additional payment; a refusal by the main contractor
would violate good faith.

Either of these views might be justified by reference to the
main contractor's initial (bad faith) acceptance of a tender
known to be unrealistic. However, at least in the case of (b),
this presupposes a duty to disclose during negotiations
which, in turn, presupposes a good faith duty to assist one's
fellow contractors (at least, where the difficulties of the latter arise directly from one's own bad faith). Extending this
line of thinking, it is arguable in situation (4) (where there
is no bad faith on either side) that the parties are not only
released from the contract but that the main contractor has
a duty to open the re-negotiations by making a reasonable
offer of increased payment to the sub-contractor.

The re-negotiation paradigm discloses a critical aspect of
co-operative contracting. If good faith as the rule is given its
most robust interpretation, it demands not only that contractors eschew opportunistic advantage-taking, but also
that they offer acts of support and assistance to one another.

(iii) Non-disclosure

Non-disclosure can be a bone of contention either at the
stage of negotiation or during performance of a contract. In
relation to the latter, some striking judicial dicta in the
recent English case-law suggest a remarkably tolerant view
of bad faith silence. For instance, in the *Banque Financière*[89]
case, Slade LJ said:

'The law cannot police the fairness of every commercial contract
by reference to moral principles. It frequently appears with hindsight . . . that one contracting party had knowledge of facts
which, if communicated to the other party, would have protected
him from loss. However, subject to well-recognised exceptions,

---

[89]   *Banque Financière de la Cité SA v Westgate Insurance Co Ltd* [1989] 2
All ER 952, CA; [1990] 2 All ER 947, HL.

the law does not and should not undertake the reopening of commercial transactions in order to adjust such losses.'[90]

Similarly, in *The Good Luck*,[91] the Court of Appeal declined to imply a term for disclosure, May LJ saying that terms were not to be implied on the strength 'of a supposed unhesitating willingness of the particular parties to accept it as a legal obligation merely because they would have recognised it as a moral obligation'.[92]

If English courts are prepared to turn a blind eye to silence during performance of the contract, even where motivated wholly by the non-disclosing party's perception of commercial self-interest, then non-disclosure during negotiation is almost an *a fortiori* case. As Lord Ackner underlined in *Walford v Miles*, the classical view is that contractors may adopt an adversarial role, each side seeking (subject to background restrictions) to maximise its own interests without regard to the interests of the other side. It follows that each side is entitled to play its cards close to its chest, which entails that there is no obligation to disclose information which manifestly is material to the other side. Thus, in the classic case of *Smith v Hughes*,[93] the farmer had no obligation to disclose to the racehorse trainer that the oats he was contemplating purchasing were unsuitable for his needs. As Cockburn CJ put it:

'The buyer persuaded himself they were old oats, when they were not so; but the seller neither said nor did anything to contribute to his deception. He has himself to blame. The question is not what a man of scrupulous morality or nice honour would do under such circumstances. The case put of the purchaser of an estate, in which there is a mine under the surface, but the fact is unknown to the seller, is one in which a man of tender conscience or high honour would be unwilling to take advantage of the ignorance of the seller; but there can be no doubt that the contract for the sale of the estate would be binding . . .'[94]

---

90 [1989] 2 All ER 952, 1013.
91 *Bank of Nova Scotia v Hellenic Mutual War Risks Association (Bermuda) Ltd: The Good Luck* [1989] 3 All ER 628, CA; [1991] 3 All ER 1, HL.
92 [1989] 3 All ER 628, 667 (in the House of Lords [1991] 3 All ER 1, disclosure was held to be required on the basis of an *express* undertaking given by the insurer to the bank). On the other hand, compare *Scally v Southern Health and Social Services Board* [1992] 1 AC 294; and see Collins (1992) 55 MLR 556.
93 (1871) LR 6 QB 597.
94 At 603-604.

Now, if we employ the concept of good faith as an exception, the question is not what 'a man of scrupulous morality or nice honour would do in such circumstances'; the question is whether non-disclosure offends the sensibilities of the particular commercial community (or judicial perceptions of reasonable commercial conduct).[95] By and large, English judges seem to think that commercial people have few scruples about being economical with extrinsic (collateral market-sensitive) information known to be material to the other side. Granted, in the *Interfoto* case, where Sir Thomas Bingham said that the essence of good faith is conveyed by colloquialisms such as 'playing fair', 'coming clean', and 'putting one's cards face upwards on the table',[96] the court applied the modern rules on incorporation to defeat the picture library's undisclosed extortionate standard form provision for late return of the photographs; but this was intrinsic (contract-constitutive), not extrinsic (collateral market-sensitive), information.

Fairly clearly, the recent English approach to the question of non-disclosure during the performance of commercial contracts is inconsistent with the co-operative ideal under-pinning good faith as the rule. It is less clear, however, whether the rugged English view, generally permitting deception by silence during negotiation, is out of line with good faith as the rule. As we have said already, there is room for debate about how far good faith (even under the co-operative ideal) applies to the negotiation stage; and, in the present context, there is certainly room for argument about the precise scope of the good faith disclosure requirement.[97]

Nevertheless, suppose that we took a bold stand: suppose that we declared that, because co-operative dealing pre-supposes acts of support and assistance and because information is critical to making mutually beneficial exchanges, disclosure in negotiation should be the rule rather than the exception. Even so, would it be plausible to treat negotiators as having a duty to share all information

---

[95]   Cf S. M. Waddams 'Pre-Contractual Duties of Disclosure', in Peter Cane and Jane Stapleton (eds) *Essays for Patrick Atiyah* (Oxford, Clarendon Press, 1991) p 237, at 253, who points out that even the drafters of the *Second Restatement of Contracts* (US) did not intend to require disclosure in a case such as that suggested by Cockburn CJ.

[96]   *Interfoto Picture Library Ltd v Stiletto Visual Programmes Ltd* [1989] QB 433, 439.

[97]   Cf John Carter, above n 15.

that might be material to the transaction? Would *all* cards, literally, have to be face up on the table (and, in literally *all* situations)? Would the duty to disclose obtain even if, as Michael Bayles hypothesises, 'the other party's ignorance is due to negligence or sheer stupidity'?[98] If such a disclosure rule seems to take co-operation too far, we might instead adopt a more limited view. For example, we might adopt the civilian view according to which (putting the matter somewhat generally) each party must disclose 'such matters as are clearly of importance to the other party's decision, provided that the latter is unable to procure the information himself and the non-disclosing party is aware of the fact'[99] – and provided, we should add (to take account of Bayles' point), the other party's ignorance is justifiable.[100] However, this would not be the end of our difficulties. Quite apart from the obvious problems of interpretation set by the concept of 'importance' and by the proviso (does 'unable' imply impossibility or something short of that?),[101] there are complex

[98] Bayles, above n 56, at 191.
[99] Cf Friedrich Kessler and Edith Fine 'Culpa in Contrahendo, Bargaining in Good Faith and Freedom of Contract: A Comparative Study' (1964) 77 Harvard Law Review 401, 404-405.
[100] This, it should be emphasised, is a very generalised statement of the civilian position, assuming a no doubt artificial degree of homogeneity (just as one might talk in very general terms about the 'common law' position). According to one commentator, for example, the classical French view actually converged with the English position that pre-contractual silence is not normally actionable, see P. Legrand 'Pre-Contractual Disclosure and Information: English and French Law Compared' (1986) 6 OJLS 322. Over the last three decades or so, however, the positions on either side of the Channel have diverged, the idea of an 'obligation of information' progressively gaining ground in France. Summarising the modern divergence between French and English law in relation to pre-contractual disclosure, Legrand says (at 349):

> 'While French law may therefore be described as positive (there is an obligation of information), solidarist (a party must share certain knowledge with his co-contractor), and concrete (the status of the parties is what chiefly matters), English common law remains more negative (one cannot deceive or misrepresent), individualist (every party must acquire the necessary knowledge for himself), and abstract (every party is deemed to have the same ability to see to his interest).'

[101] It is one thing, perhaps, for a retailer not to tell a customer that identical goods can be purchased nearby at a lower price; but quite another thing for a master of a stricken ship not to disclose to the salvor that the vessel is holed below the water line.

questions concerning possible exceptions to the basic disclosure rule (as, for example, where special efforts have been invested by one party in obtaining the information).[102] In the light of this, we can speculate that *if* good faith as the rule applies to disclosure during negotiation, then the scope of the legitimate interest of one contracting party in having access to information held by the other is probably to be determined by such factors as the materiality of the information,[103] the ability of the former to obtain the information, the efforts made by the latter to obtain the information, whether the latter is a professional dealer (or an undisclosed professional dealer),[104] whether the information is intrinsic (contract-constitutive) or extrinsic (collateral market-sensitive),[105] and so on.[106] We can also state with some confidence that, if good faith as the rule so applies to disclosure in negotiation, then a major chapter in the jurisprudence of co-operative dealing will need to be written.

---

[102] To take Cicero's classic conundrum, would the concept of good faith as the rule require a merchant who arrives first with a cargo of corn in famine-stricken Rhodes, to disclose that other corn suppliers will shortly arrive? Is this an exceptional case, where the incentive effects of permissible non-disclosure might justify an exception to the usual rule requiring disclosure? Generally, cf Anthony Kronman, 'Mistake, Disclosure, Information, and the Law of Contracts' (1978) 7 Journal of Legal Studies 1; and 'Contract Law and Distributive Justice' (1980) 89 Yale Law Journal 472; Barry Nicholas 'The Pre-Contractual Obligation to Disclose Information: English Report' in Donald Harris and Denis Tallon (eds) *Contract Law Today* (Oxford, Clarendon Press, 1989) 166; Roy Goode, above n 2.

[103] As in insurance proposals: see s 18, Marine Insurance Act 1906.

[104] Cf J. Ghestin 'The Obligation to Disclose Information' in Donald Harris and Denis Tallon (eds) *Contract Law Today* (Oxford, Clarendon Press, 1989) 157, at 165 (quoting Ivainer, JCP 1972. I. 2495, nos 37ff):

> 'The technician must enlighten the layman . . . Good faith entails for the professional the obligation to place the layman on his own level of knowledge so that they can deal with each other on an equal footing.'

[105] Even where a welfarist regime, designed to secure a fair distribution of basic resources, is in operation, it is arguable that markets cannot work efficiently without an *uneven* distribution of market-sensitive information. See Hugh Collins 'Disclosure of Information and Welfarism', in Roger Brownsword, Geraint Howells, and Thomas Wilhelmsson (eds) *Welfarism in Contract Law* (Aldershot, Dartmouth, 1994) 97.

[106] Cf P. Legrand 'Pre-Contractual Disclosure and Information: English and French Law Compared' (1986) 6 OJLS 322; and J. Ghestin 'The Obligation to Disclose Information' in Donald Harris and Denis Tallon (eds) *Contract Law Today* (Oxford, Clarendon Press, 1989) 157.

(iv) Summary

This section opened with two questions. The first question was whether, if we adopt the concept of good faith as an exception, we can do any more than list the specific forms of bad faith condemned by particular commercial communities at any one time. The short answer is that we cannot, at any rate, not unless we distance our theory of good faith from local conventions and take as our bench-mark the better commercial opinion, or the reasonable commercial person, or something of that kind. Certainly, the standards of commercial communities may often overlap, so that particular forms of dealing are widely regarded as bad faith, but with good faith as the exception the law is essentially working in the wake of local commercial convention or established paradigms of bad faith. The second question was whether, if we adopt the concept of good faith as the rule, we can develop general principles of good faith from our abstract contractual ideal (co-operation, respect for the legitimate interests of the other party, or the like) which can then be applied to concrete issues of alleged bad faith. The thrust of this section is that this is a viable project. Principles prohibiting market-playing and opportunistic re-negotiation, and enjoining disclosure, can be related to the co-operative ideal and applied to a variety of concrete situations. Moreover, a jurisprudence of substantive regulation of contractual provisions is waiting to be developed once the concept of a party's legitimate expectations is worked out under the co-operative ideal.[107] The keyword, however, is that this jurisprudence is *waiting* to be developed; and if good faith as the exception has better credentials than good faith as the rule, we might conclude that this is a jurisprudential labour that can be safely postponed.

4. WHICH CONCEPT OF GOOD FAITH SHOULD BE ADOPTED?

This long haul has been designed to establish two points. First, it has been argued that the rationality of English contract law would be enhanced if an explicit concept of good

---

[107] Cf chs 8–10. See, too, Dugan, n 40 above.

faith were to be adopted.[108] Secondly, it has been argued that the essential choice lies between a concept of good faith which grafts a number of bad faith exceptions on to a regime of licensed self-interested dealing and a concept which makes co-operative dealing the rule. The question now arises: is there any reason why one of these concepts should be preferred to the other? In this section, we ask whether, relative to considerations of rationality, there are grounds for thinking that the concept of good faith as the (co-operative) rule is to be preferred. The tentative submission is that no such case can be made out on grounds of instrumental rationality but that a case in favour of good faith as the rule may be made out on grounds of moral rationality.

(i) Considerations of instrumental rationality

Contract lawyers, like lawyers in general, assume that law aspires to be a rational enterprise.[109] Whether the law is designed to facilitate or to prohibit, it must be capable of guiding action. Rules need to be clear, results should be calculable, people must know where they stand. What this familiar appeal for certainty and predictability presupposes is that contract law sets a framework which facilitates, rather than hinders, the pursuit of individual projects. At root, there is a model of social beings here which emphasises their individuality, their free choice of aims and life-styles, and the essentially purposive nature of human social existence. In other words, the function of law in general is to establish a supportive infrastructure for human agency; and the function of contract law in particular is to establish a supportive framework for those deals which need to be made if the various projects and plans that individuals have are to be realised.

---

[108]   This argument, it should be said, did not deal with the objection that a contract regime without any kind of good faith requirement would be more economically rational than a contract regime with an explicit (or an implicit) good faith requirement. This point was not addressed because the assumption of the discussion, as conceded by the pragmatic thesis, is that English contract law often seeks out bad faith by one means or another and, to this extent, it already has an implicit good faith requirement. If this assumption were to be dropped, the objection in question would then need to be considered. However, the objection raises far too many issues to be tackled here.

[109]   See s 1 of this chapter.

Any set of contractual ground rules will have a 'default' specification, a set of rules that is to apply in the absence of specific agreement otherwise. In the present context, therefore, the question is whether the function of contract law is better served by a default rule incorporating good faith as an exception or by a default rule prescribing good faith as the rule. In other words, would individuals do better in achieving their purposes if, in the absence of agreement to the contrary, good faith was treated as the exception or as the rule?

It is difficult to see that either option necessarily has better credentials as a matter of certainty or calculability. Where good faith as an exception is the default rule (or, more precisely, where good faith as an exception sets a number of default rules), and assuming knowledge of the legal position, contractors will know that they are entitled to pursue their own interests up to the point where commercial opinion (or, judicial interpretation of that opinion) condemns action as bad faith. They will know, too, that if they wish to displace some or all of the default rules, they may make express provision to this effect. Provided that commercial standards are tolerably well-defined, contractors should generally know where they stand under such a regime. Where good faith as the rule represents the default legal position, and assuming knowledge of the law, contractors will know that, in the absence of express displacement of the default rules, they must respect the legitimate interests of fellow contracting parties (as defined by a contractual regime orientated towards a co-operative ideal). Provided that the jurisprudence of good faith as the rule is tolerably clear, contractors should again know where they stand under such a regime. Of course, if commercial standards are vague, or if judicial employment of the idea of the reasonable commercial person becomes arbitrary and unpredictable, or if the jurisprudence of legitimate interests (within the co-operative model) is unclear, there may be instrumental advantages in adopting one concept of good faith rather than the other; but, subject to such contingent circumstances, there is as yet nothing to indicate which concept is favoured on grounds of instrumental rationality.

Although each concept of good faith may be developed to the point where contractors fully appreciate where they stand, the concepts might nevertheless invite rather different attitudes to contracting. Where good faith as an exception is the default rule, rational contractors might be advised to deal defensively. For, if the default rule has not been re-negotiated, contractors will need to be careful that their interests are protected (in so far as there is a gap between commercial constraints on bad faith and the standard set by good faith as the rule). On the other hand, where good faith as the rule is the default legal position, contractors need be less defensive, and it is arguable that the 'transaction costs' under such a regime are likely to be lower than the equivalent costs under a regime that treats good faith as an exception. To see how this might work, consider the various examples of legitimate non-disclosure cited by Lord Atkin in his seminal speech in *Bell v Lever Bros Ltd*:

> 'A buys B's horse; he thinks the horse is sound and he pays the price of a sound horse; he would certainly not have bought the horse if he had known as the fact is that the horse is unsound. If B has made no representation as to soundness and has not contracted that the horse is sound, A is bound and cannot recover back the price . . . A agrees to take on lease or to buy from B an unfurnished dwelling-house. The house is in fact uninhabitable. A would never have entered into the bargain if he had known the fact. A has no remedy, and the position is the same whether B knew the facts or not, so long as he made no representation or gave no warranty. A buys a roadside garage business from B abutting on a public thoroughfare: unknown to A, but known to B, it has already been decided to construct a bypass road which will divert substantially the whole of the traffic from passing A's garage. Again A has no remedy.'[110]

Now, if we were advising A in any of these situations, and if the default rule was good faith as an exception, and if the commercial community did not treat non-disclosure by B as a case of bad faith, then we should have to advise A to take steps to confirm that the subject-matter of the contract had the qualities he assumed it had, or (failing this) to secure appropriate assurances from B. Rather obviously, this could lead to protracted enquiries on the part of A, extended negotiations, and a good deal of diversion (from the direct pursuit of chosen projects). If, on the other hand, the default position was good faith as the rule, B would have a duty to disclose, thus reducing A's transaction costs. However, there is a complication. Good faith as the rule promises to reduce the costs of contracting only so long as the parties

[110]   [1932] AC 161, 224.

deal according to the rules. If, however, they do not play by the rules, any initial savings in transaction costs might be offset by subsequent remedial costs. Moreover, where breach of good faith as the rule is widespread, parties who are aware of this will incur transaction costs as they revert to a defensive negotiating approach.

These brief reflections suggest that there is no simple argument favouring one concept of good faith to the other on instrumental rational grounds.

(ii) Considerations of moral rationality

If there is no easy arbitration between competing concepts of good faith on instrumental rational grounds, one would hardly expect it to be any the easier to make a reasoned choice on moral grounds. Granted, it might be possible to demonstrate that a particular concept of good faith is in line with a particular moral theory; but this has no persuasive force unless one accepts, first, that rational decision-making should be guided by moral considerations (which amoralists do not accept) and, secondly, that one particular moral theory (the particular moral theory in question) must be employed by all rational persons (which moral relativists, in the final analysis, do not accept).

One way of trying to deal with the sceptics is to argue from criteria such as the Golden Rule or Kant's Categorical Imperative which are taken to express in purely formal terms the features of *any* moral viewpoint. However, such arguments are vulnerable on two fronts. First, they do not respond to the amoralist challenge: amoralists do not dispute what is involved in having a moral position, they dispute that it is necessary to become involved with moral positions at all. Secondly, formulations such as the Golden Rule tend to be compatible with too many different substantive moral theories. In modern liberal theory, for instance, we find writers as diverse as Robert Nozick[111] (on the individualist Right) and Ronald Dworkin and John Rawls (on the welfarist Left)[112] claiming to work in the

---

[111] Robert Nozick *Anarchy, State, and Utopia* (Oxford, Basil Blackwell, 1974).
[112] John Rawls *A Theory of Justice* (London, Oxford University Press, 1972); Ronald Dworkin *Taking Rights Seriously* (London, Duckworth, 1978).

Kantian tradition, specifically by respecting the Kantian moral imperative that one should always treat others as ends and never simply as a means.

Another strategy is to give up worrying about the amoralists and the relativists. Thus, we find in both Dworkin and Rawls an overriding concern to elaborate the implications of a particular set of moral convictions. The task of moral theory, in other words, is not so much to defend being moral or to justify one's particular moral convictions, but to work out what one is thereby committed to and what kind of (idealtypical) moral community would flow from such commitments. Quite possibly, one might be able to distil from an ideal-typical community's moral commitments a fitting doctrine of good faith, but this would obviously vary from one ideal-type to another. If we are not to surrender to the amoralists and the relativists, this kind of strategy will not do. Yet, is there any credible alternative?

The boldest modern attempt to answer both the amoralists and the relativists is to be found in Alan Gewirth's moral theory.[113] In response to the amoralist objection, Gewirth accepts that any non-question-begging attempt to argue for a compelling moral theory must start at a point which does not already take the moral viewpoint for granted. Given that moralists and amoralists are contesting the criteria of rational action, specifically the question of why one ought (as moralists contend) to be moral, and given that such a debate presupposes a community of 'agents' (that is, a community of beings each individually capable of freely choosing and pursuing their own preferred purposes, their own reasons for action), then Gewirth contends that the required non-question-begging starting point is the concept of agency. Whereas the amoralist equates rational action with an agent *effectively* pursuing its (amoral) purposes, the moralist equates rational action with an agent effectively pursuing *legitimate* (moral) purposes. The question is whether an analysis of the concept of agency can demonstrate that agents are *necessarily* committed to moral purposes.

In Chapters 9 and 10, we will sketch Gewirth's argument for the necessity of moral principles, and apply that

[113]   Alan Gewirth *Reason and Morality* (Chicago, University of Chicago Press, 1978).

argument to the general design of contract law. For the purposes of our present discussion of good faith, however, we need only state Gewirth's substantive conclusion. This is that, as between agents, there is a network of rights and duties organised around a supreme moral principle – the Principle of Generic Consistency (the *PGC*), as Gewirth terms it – according to which each agent must respect the freedom and well-being of fellow agents.[114]

If the *PGC* is the criterion of moral rational action, how does this assist with our present attempt to arbitrate between our two concepts of good faith in contract law? Fairly obviously, Gewirth's theory yields an inventory of an agent's legitimate interests and expectations, starting with respect for one's freedom and well-being. It follows that the constitutive rules of contract law must be consistent both with respect for well-being and with taking the parties' transactional freedom seriously. In principle, then, contract law should seek to uphold freely-made agreements even where, as sometimes might be the case, freedom is bad for the contractor's own health. However, contract law still needs default rules which are to apply where the conditions of free agreement do not obtain or where freely-made agreements are incomplete or unclear; and, if contract law is to be consistent with the *PGC*, such default rules must protect a contractor's well-being. This bare statement needs to be elaborated in two important respects.

First, it must always be remembered that Gewirth's concept of well-being does not vary from one agent to another; well-being is constituted by a set of interests which all agents have if they are to function as agents. In other words, whilst each agent will have its own specific purposes (which may or may not dictate that particular contracts are made), these specific purposes are irrelevant to identifying an agent's legitimate interests – or, whilst it is characteristic of agents that they have purposes, the purposes they happen to have are not relevant to characterising their interests (as agents) in freedom and well-being. To this extent, protected legitimate interests in Gewirth's moral theory are independent of an agent's specific purposes at any time. Accordingly, where the default rules for contract build on an agent's legitimate interests in well-being, it is important that such

---

[114] See further pp 313–318 and 345–351.

interests are specified independently of the particular purposes for which an agent has chosen to contract.

Secondly, Gewirth's theory does not merely yield an inventory of legitimate interests (founded in the concept of agency), it yields a *hierarchy* of legitimate interests. An agent's 'basic' interests (basic rights) concern the essential conditions of agency. Correlatively, basic harms include 'whatever adversely affects the necessary preconditions of one's action, as by removing one's life, freedom of movement, physical integrity, or mental equilibrium . . .'[115] At the next tier of the hierarchy, agents have 'non-subtractive' interests (rights), these interests relating to an agent's ability to maintain present levels of purpose-fulfilment. According to Gewirth, non-subtractive harms include:

> 'being lied to, cheated, stolen from, defamed, insulted, suffering broken promises, and having one's privacy violated, as well as being subjected to dangerous, degrading, or excessively debilitating conditions of physical labor or housing or other strategic conditions of life when resources are available for improvement'.[116]

Finally, agents have 'additive' interests (rights) which concern the ability to increase present levels of purpose-fulfilment. The correlative duty requires:

> '[E]ach person [to] refrain from feeling or exhibiting contempt towards others; persons must not be insulted, belittled, or patronized, nor must they be discriminated against on grounds of race, religion, or nationality. Put positively, the duties of such respect require that persons must have toward one another an attitude of mutual acceptance and toleration, including acquiescence in diversity so long as this falls within the limits set by the *PGC*'s duties regarding basic and non-subtractive goods'.[117]

Where agents have conflicting legitimate interests, higher order interests take priority over lower order interests. Thus, in so far as contracting is largely an institution which serves the parties' additive interests, default rules protecting the parties' basic and non-subtractive interests will be consistent with the *PGC*.

How does the choice between the two concepts of good faith look in the light of a Gewirthian interpretation of an

---

[115]　Gewirth, above n 113, at pp 232–3.
[116]　At p 233.
[117]　At p 242.

agent's legitimate interests? Whilst the *form* of good faith as the rule fits well with Gewirthian thinking (in the sense that it presupposes an independent jurisprudence of legitimate interests), it is not immediately obvious that the same can be said about the co-operative ethic which constitutes the substance of this concept of good faith. Given that, following Gewirth, an agent must respect the freedom and well-being of other agents, does this mean anything more than that an agent should eschew fraud and coercion in contracting, and avoid the more egregious kinds of advantage-taking in performance and enforcement? If not, the concept of good faith as an exception might fit better. This, however, overlooks an important ingredient in Gewirth's thinking, namely that agents have a duty not only (negatively) to eschew interference with the freedom and well-being of other agents but also (positively) to support the freedom and well-being of others. Thus, writing in the context of an individual's (agent's) duty to rescue, Gewirth says:

> '[Morality] requires that an agent not only refrain from interfering with his recipients' freedom and well-being, but also that he assist them to have those necessary goods when they cannot have them by their own efforts and when he can give such assistance at no comparable cost to himself.'[118]

If Gewirthian morality inscribes a duty to assist, it is a fair bet that it can be unpacked to yield an ethic of co-operation as the default rule for transactions. Accordingly, if this bet is well-inspired, good faith as the rule seems to have the right moral credentials both as to form and as to substance.

If we pull together these threads of substantive thinking in Gewirth, we have the makings of a theory establishing a scheme of rights and duties for a community of transacting agents. True to the spirit of Gewirth, the substance of the scheme remains independent of any transacting agent's particular purposes, but it is of the essence that the default rules of contract are set so that the well-being of contractors, *qua* contracting agents (ie as agents contracting in order to serve their freely-chosen purposes, whatever those purposes might be), is fully secured. In other words, the default rules must protect those interests which all agents necessarily have in the institution of contract itself – and, ideal-typically, as any reflective agent surely must agree, the

[118]   At p 218.

function of contract is to improve the well-being of *both* parties by facilitating an exchange which operates to their mutual advantage.[119] This does not mean that contracting agents must assist one another to get precisely the same amount of subjective advantage from a particular transaction, but it does mean that contract is not a vehicle for promoting one's own advantage by knowingly subtracting from the pre-contractual state of well-being of the other side. Contract, as James Gordley has argued, is about (roughly equal) exchange, not about gift nor about unintended redistribution of wealth.[120] Or, to put this more explicitly in Gewirthian terms, the default rules of contract law should not license agents to advance their additive interests at the known expense of another agent's basic or non-subtractive interests.

Much of what we have said about the concept of good faith as the rule, straightforwardly, involves non-subtractive interests acting as a constraint on the pursuit of additive interests. For example, where an agreement has been made, the parties have a non-subtractive interest in the benefits exchanged (or to be exchanged) under the deal. Where good faith as the rule condemns attempts by one party to play the market to the disadvantage of the other, or to apply pressure to increase the price, or the like, this can be seen as a principled protection of the non-subtractive interests of the vulnerable party. The case of non-disclosure, too, is instructive. It was suggested earlier that a plausible interpretation of the concept of good faith as the rule is that each contractor is put under a prima facie duty to disclose facts which are known to be material to the other side (at least where the other side cannot reasonably be expected to have access to such facts). The fact that this calls for each side to assist one another, by rectifying known informational deficits, is not an insuperable objection, for the *PGC* enjoins certain acts of positive assistance – in this case, rescuing an agent from ignorance. Moreover, where the only argument

---

[119]   See further, the argument in ch 9. Indeed, according to Dugan (above n 40, at 18 and 47), even in the classical view, the institution of contract is seen as being designed to promote the interests of both parties to the transaction. Certainly, one might attribute this ideal to such classical rhetoric as emphasises free and equal exchange.

[120]   See James Gordley 'Equality in Exchange' (1981) 69 California Law Review 1587, esp at 1622–1625.

in favour of non-assistance (non-disclosure) is that this will enable one agent to improve its position (its additive interests) by knowingly disimproving the position of another agent (the other agent's non-subtractive interests), then this seems to be condemned by the priority rules set by the *PGC*'s hierarchy of interests. It follows that, although the precise circumstances surrounding Lord Atkin's famous examples of permissible non-disclosure in *Bell v Lever Bros Ltd*[121] are rather left to the imagination, his inference that the sellers have no duty to disclose must be highly suspect. After all, to permit such sellers to deal without disclosing the material facts violates the general principle that the ideal-typical function of contract is to enable agents to exchange so that both sides are better placed to fulfil their chosen ends; and non-disclosure in such cases violates the *PGC* by prioritising the seller's additive interests at the expense of the buyer's non-subtractive interests. Subject to any hidden special case exceptional circumstances, therefore, the concept of good faith as the rule seems to be in line with the *PGC* in insisting upon default rules designed to prevent unjust enrichment by non-disclosure.

In sum, although the moral calculation is no easier than the instrumental calculation, and although Gewirth's claims have been vigorously attacked[122] and rigorously defended,[123] it is submitted that there is some considerable encouragement in these resources for believing that the default rules in contract should adopt the concept of good faith as the (co-operative) rule.

5. CONCLUSION

The central contention of this chapter is that English contract law urgently needs an explicit doctrine of good faith to enable it to deal more openly, more rationally, with the many manifestations of bad faith encountered in commercial

---

[121] See text above at p 246.
[122] Notably, see the critical essays in Edward Regis Jr (ed) *Gewirth's Ethical Rationalism* (Chicago, Chicago University Press, 1984).
[123] In addition to Gewirth's own many defensive statements and explanations, see Deryck Beyleveld *The Dialectical Necessity of Morality: An Analysis and Defense of Alan Gewirth's Argument to the PGC* (Chicago, Chicago University Press, 1991).

contracting. Of course, the availability of a good faith provision does not guarantee utilisation, nor the development of an articulate jurisprudence of good faith.[124] Nevertheless, in the absence of such an explicit doctrine, we can be quite sure that the law of contract will muddle through in an unnecessarily irrational way.

Once the case for adopting an explicit requirement of good faith has been made out, the difficult question arises of which concept of good faith should be adopted. The concept of good faith as an exception might have some attraction to English lawyers. It qualifies the classical licence for self-interested dealing only to the extent insisted upon by the commercial community at any particular time; it permits the line between good faith and bad faith to be re-drawn as commercial standards evolve (or as judges make one-off decisions behind the facade of the reasonable commercial person); and it concentrates on concrete cases of bad faith without demanding the development of a theory of legitimate interests or co-operative dealing.[125] In short, the concept of good faith as an exception is consistent with a pragmatic case-by-case approach. By contrast, the concept of good faith as the rule calls for the articulation of a principled jurisprudence involving the development of such key notions as 'legitimate interests' and 'co-operative dealing'. Unless there are good reasons for taking on such a task, there is a temptation to avoid such a theoretical engagement. The position taken in this chapter is that there are good reasons for preferring the concept of good faith as the rule, for it fits with defensible moral theory; and, whilst the theoretical engagement now required is by no means easy, it is unavoidable if the rationality of the law is not simply to be made more transparent but to be put on a firm moral footing.

---

[124]   See eg Robert A. Hillman 'Policing Contract Modifications under the UCC: Good Faith and the Doctrine of Economic Duress' (1979) 64 Iowa Law Review 849; and, for the somewhat bizarre circumstances triggering more active use of article 242 of the BGB, see John P. Dawson *The Oracles of the Law* (Michigan University Press, 1968) 465–75.

[125]   Cf The Hon Mr Justice Steyn 'The Role of Good Faith and Fair Dealing in Contract Law: A Hair-Shirt Philosophy?' (Royal Bank of Scotland Lecture, Oxford, 1991).

Chapter 8

Unfair contract terms

Introduction

According to the classical view, provided that a bargain has been freely made (ie provided that there has been no fraud or duress) between contractors of full capacity, there is no basis for intervening simply because the transaction seems unreasonable or unbalanced, or because particular terms seem unfair or unconscionable, or because there seems to be some inequality of bargaining power between the parties. By contrast, one of the outstanding features of the modern law is that intervention on just such grounds is thought to be appropriate. Sometimes, intervention takes the form of a legislative 'black-list' of certain terms (which are deemed to be unfair or unreasonable and, thus, void); at other times, the law grants reserve powers to the courts to strike out terms that are judged to be unfair or unreasonable (or, on which it would be unfair or unreasonable to allow reliance);[1]

---

[1] One of the most striking examples of such reserve powers is found in section 36 of the Nordic Contracts Act, which (in its Finnish version) provides:

'If a contract or a term thereof is unfair, or its application would be unfair, it may be adjusted or left unapplied. When considering the unfairness the whole content of the contract, the position of the parties, the circumstances when the contract was made and thereafter and other circumstances shall be taken into account . . . Price is to be considered one possible term for adjustment.'

Similarly, judicial reserve powers can be tied to the idea of unconscionable terms. For example, section 2-302 of the Uniform Commercial Code provides:

'If the court as a matter of law finds the contract or any clause of the and, in some legal systems, consumer ombudsmen or the like are authorised to initiate pre-emptive challenges against terms judged to be unreasonable. In England, the leading examples of modern intervention are the Unfair Contract Terms Act 1977 and the Unfair Terms in Consumer Contracts Regulations 1994[2] (implementing the EC Directive on Unfair Terms in Consumer Contracts).[3] Whereas the former combines a black-list with reserve judicial powers, the latter contains an indicative and non-exhaustive list of terms regarded as unfair and it combines reserve judicial powers with the possibility of pre-emptive challenge.

When the tide is running so strongly in favour of intervention in contracts in order to protect contractors, particularly consumer contractors, against standard forms and exclusions, it is easy to assume that the classical view is indefensible. However, it is possible to construct a plausible defence of the classsical approach from more than one theoretical perspective. For example, it is arguable that the function of the law of contract is to establish a stable context within which contractors may exercise their right to autonomy, and that the way to respect the contractors' autonomy is by enforcing the transactional choices that they have actually made – not the transactional choices that judges think that it would be reasonable for the parties to have made.[4] Equally, from an economic welfare-maximising

> contract to have been unconscionable at the time it was made the court may refuse to enforce the contract, or it may enforce the remainder of the contract without the unconscionable clause, or it may so limit the application of any unconscionable clause as to avoid any unconscionable result.'

Seminally, see Arthur Leff 'Unconscionability and the Code – the Emperor's New Clause' (1967) 115 *University of Pennsylvania Law Review* 485.

[2]   SI 1994/3159 (came into force on 1 July 1995).
[3]   93/13/EEC.
[4]   See eg Lord Wilberforce's celebrated dissenting speech in *L. Schuler AG v Wickman Machine Tool Sales Ltd* [1974] AC 235, 263:

> '[T]o call the clause arbitrary, capricious or fantastic, or to introduce as a test of its validity the ubiquitous reasonable man (I do not know whether he is English or German) is to assume, contrary to the evidence, that both parties to this contract adopted a standard of easygoing tolerance rather than one of aggressive, insistent punctuality and efficiency. This is not an assumption I am prepared to make, nor do I think myself entitled to impose the former standard upon the parties if their words indicate, as they plainly do, the latter.'

perspective, it is arguable that it is a mistake to adjust the parties' own freely-struck agreements because such agreements must be the best evidence we have of the parties' own preferences. Moreover, once judges are licensed to make ad hoc adjustments to contracts on such contestable grounds as fairness and reasonableness, decision-making becomes arbitrary and the net effect can be counter-productive.

Clearly, regulation of the substantive fairness of contracts poses a major challenge to the rationality of the law. At one level, the challenge is simply to administer the law as declared, not to exercise a substantive veto covertly. At another level, the challenge is to avoid counter-productive interventions. And, above all, the challenge for the modern law of contract is to articulate a defensible conception of fairness and reasonableness to justify its interventions. As James Gordley has contended:[5]

> 'Many jurists are now pessimistic about the very possibility of discovering general principles or doctrines that can explain the rules of positive [contract] law or the results most people regard as fair. Their pessimism is understandable. The attempt to build coherent doctrine seems to have ended in failure.'

In this chapter, we will consider these matters, first, in relation to the application of the Unfair Contract Terms Act 1977, particularly the application of the Act to commercial contracts, and, secondly, in relation to the interpretation of the Unfair Terms in Consumer Contracts Regulations 1994 (which are restricted to the regulation of consumer contracts and to terms in such contracts that have not been individually negotiated). To begin with, though, we say a little more about the defence of the classical non-interventionist line.

1. THE CLASSICAL ARGUMENT AGAINST INTERVENTION

The classical position, as we have said, may be defended in more than one way. In modern debates, one tends to associate the classical view with free-market economics and so it is not surprising that contemporary exponents of free-market theories argue against intervention – theories of the

---

[5] James Gordley *The Philosophical Origins of Modern Contract Doctrine* (Oxford, Clarendon Press, 1991) 230–1.

minimal State tend to go with theories of a minimal law of contract. In this section, we outline the views of one of the most influential modern law and economics writers, Richard Posner.

In *The Economic Analysis of Law*,[6] Posner argues that it makes poor economic sense for a court to have a general jurisdiction to relieve against unconscionable transactions:[7]

> 'If unconscionability means that a court may nullify a contract if it considers the consideration inadequate or the terms otherwise one-sided, the basic principle of encouraging market rather than surrogate legal transactions where (market) transaction costs are low is badly compromised. Economic analysis reveals no grounds other than fraud, incapacity, and duress (the last narrowly defined) for allowing a party to repudiate the bargain that he made in entering into the contract.'

Duress, it will be noted, is interpreted narrowly by Posner. According to Posner, 'duress' is a term that does not have a well-defined meaning. It is, he says, used in four distinct senses:

1. In its original sense where a contract was entered into under threat of violence (eg the courts would refuse to compel a person to make good a promissory note which he had signed because a knife was held to his throat).
2. A threat of non-performance to compel the other party to accept unfavourable terms (eg where A knowing that B is in a bad financial situation compels B to accept a lesser sum in full and final settlement by threatening that if he does not he will get nothing (and thus face potential bankruptcy)).[8]
3. As a synonym for fraud for example where an illiterate person is tricked into signing a contract thinking it is something else (ie in situations where the defence of 'non est factum' lies). Most cases of abuse of a confidential or fiduciary relationship fall into this category, though they are in reality cases of fraud.[9]

---

[6]   4th edn, ch 4.7.

[7]   Ibid p 116.

[8]   Cf *D & C Builders v Rees* [1966] 2 QB 617. In fact, Posner treats *Alaska Packers Association v Domenico* 117 F 99 (1902) (see our discussion of economic duress in ch 7) as his paradigm for duress in this second sense.

[9]   In the UK, such cases are grouped under the general category of 'equitable fraud'.

4.   Abuse of a monopoly (eg if a ship is sinking and A refuses to bring his tug boat to the rescue unless B the master agrees to very unfavourable terms).

From an economic point of view (which is Posner's concern) intervention in case (1) is unproblematic: the conduct of the threatener has retarded rather than advanced the *free* movement of resources to their most valuable uses – although Posner actually says that the party under threat exercises free will in acceding to the demand, no one supposes that transfers effected at the end of a highwayman's pistol achieve Paretian optimality. Intervention is also justifiable in case (2), which is only a modest extension of (1).[10] Case (3) is in reality fraud and, again, intervention is unproblematic. Finally, intervention in the Bad Samaritan scenario in case (4) is arguably justifiable: for, if the law permits monopoly profits in rescue operations, an excessive amount of resources may be attracted to the rescue business.[11]

Now, in the absence of fraud, incapacity, or duress (as elaborated above), Posner's basic position is that bargains should be upheld. Nevertheless, the modern tendency is to intervene in a broader range of situations, particularly where a transaction involves a large corporation offering to contract only on its standard printed form contract. Here, it is tempting to invoke the analogy of case (1) and conclude that the deal is coercive, especially if the other person is a consumer. After all, if a monopoly situation exists, the consumer will have no alternative but to accept the terms offered. This is precisely the problem of the adhesion contract as it is generally perceived; and, as we saw in Chapter 3, it is by no means a new problem. Indeed, it was a problem that very much exercised the English courts in the early days of the railways and led to the Railway and Canal Traffic Act 1854. The problem here, however, according to Posner, is not duress but monopoly, for if perfect competition existed between those offering equivalent goods or services there would be a direct link between the terms offered and the prices charged. For example, if carrier A were to offer to carry at a low price but on owner's risk terms, and carrier B at a higher price but on full insurance terms, then the consignor

---

[10]   Posner ch 4.2 on the *Alaska Packers* case, above.
[11]   Op cit p 102.

C would decide whether it was a better deal to accept A's terms, and insure the goods himself, or to accept B's offer which in effect includes insurance. Thus, in so far as standard form problems can be explained away as monopoly problems, there is no need for Posner to concede a conscionability clause to the judges.

Many standard forms, however, use fine print and obscure 'legalese' so that it is difficult for the other party (especially consumers) to evaluate the bargain they are being offered.[12] The effect of this is to impose excessive search costs on buyers, which of course is not economically efficient. Posner's response is to suggest that this is a species of fraud rather than an exercise of stronger bargaining power – though in a highly competitive market people might avoid those who insisted on such fine print forms. Again, therefore, it is possible to hold the classical line while regulating the procedural abuse.

It is also, however, a distinctive thread of modern thinking that contractors who are in a weak bargaining position should be protected. As a group, consumers have come to be identified as weak bargainers par excellence. Not surprisingly, therefore, a great deal of consumer protection legislation has been passed in modern times. For instance, s 123 of the Consumer Credit Act 1974 prohibits the taking of a negotiable instrument (other than a bank note or cheque in discharge of any sum payable) under a regulated agreement. The reason for this is that if the buyer defaults and the 'seller' repossesses, the buyer will still be liable to the bank to whom the promissory note has been discounted. Such protective measures, however, may not make economic sense. As Posner points out, the taking of a promissory note reduces the overall cost of credit because it makes collection more certain and collection actions cheaper. In other words some cases of individual prejudice are the price of the wider benefit of lower costs – which, of course, is textbook utilitarian reasoning. Similarly, the practice of 'snatch-back' whereby the 'seller' seizes on a minor default to repossess when he has already received almost the full price is perceived of as unconscionable because the seller thereby

---

[12]   See further John N. Adams 'Unconscionability and the Standard Form Contract' in Roger Brownsword, Geraint Howells and Thomas Wilhelmsson (eds) *Welfarism in Contract Law* (Aldershot, Dartmouth, 1994) 230.

makes a windfall gain.[13] But if the default occurs early the repossessing creditor may incur a loss, because the instalments received and the resale price of the goods may be insufficient to cover their cost, and recovery of the difference from the buyer may be impracticable. In a situation of perfect competition between sellers on credit, limiting windfall gains on late defaults would result in sellers requiring either larger down payments, higher initial payments, or the charging of higher prices in order to cover themselves from losses on early defaults. Again, therefore, an indirect cost is imposed by the legislation on borrowers as a whole.

In commercial contexts, too, economic analysis enjoins a cautious approach to intervention simply on the ground of inequality of bargaining power or unreasonable terms. Posner, indeed, even questions whether the Bad Samaritan example of the ship in distress is quite so self-evidently one requiring intervention. It is a long-established Admiralty rule that in such cases the salvor is entitled only to the reasonable costs of salvage, and the sum agreed to by the master is only evidence of what a reasonable sum might be. Although this solution may prevent the salvage business attracting too many resources, the market could, in principle, produce a satisfactory result because presumably there must be a point where masters would simply choose to abandon their ship and let it sink if the salvor was asking too much. The situation might be different, of course, if human life were at risk.

Whether or not we agree with economic analysis of the kind advanced by Posner, there is no denying that it should give modernists pause for thought before they rush into a programme of protective intervention. For, even if we reject such analysis as ultimately irrational – perhaps because we judge that it rests on utilitarian maximising premises – we cannot afford to ignore the costs directly and indirectly imposed by intervention (together with any alteration in the law's incentive and disincentive effects).

---

[13]   In the UK, this is prohibited by section 90 of the Consumer Credit Act 1974. See, too, s 137 of the same Act, which regulates against 'extortionate credit bargains': for discussion of the use of s 137, see Lionel Bently and Geraint Howells, 'Judicial Treatment of Extortionate Credit Bargains' (1989) The Conveyancer 164, and 'Loansharks and Extortionate Credit Bargains' ibid, at p 234.

2. THE UNFAIR CONTRACT TERMS ACT

As we said in our introductory remarks, the prime example of modern interventionist legislation in England is the Unfair Contract Terms Act 1977 (UCTA). The centrepiece of the Act is s 3. This section regulates contracts made on standard terms and contracts made with consumers (whether or not made on a standard form). In conjunction with s 11 of UCTA, s 3 essentially provides that those terms in such contracts which exclude or restrict liability are to be enforced only to the extent that they are judged to be fair and reasonable terms to have been included in the contract in question. We can evaluate the operation of UCTA in three stages: first, by looking at the way in which English judges have tended to view exclusion clauses in standard forms; secondly, by considering the application of the reasonableness requirement; and, thirdly, by reviewing how the courts have responded to invitations to extend the scope of UCTA to cover two kinds of provision which are common in commercial contracts – indemnity clauses and clauses excluding the right of set-off.

(i) The 'two-stage' approach to standard form contracts

As we saw in chapter 3, an interventionist approach was adopted by many judges, long before any legislation explicitly authorising such intervention had been enacted. In different jurisdictions, the styles of intervention varied. Whereas English judges favoured covert restriction of the scope of individual clauses by a strict interpretation of the incorporation rules, by narrow construction, or by the somewhat conceptually questionable device of fundamental breach,[14] American judges were more robust, flatly denying efficacy to exclusions on grounds of policy (as in the famous case of *Henningsen v Bloomfield Motors*).[15] All of these judicial approaches, however, required the courts to look at the contract apart from the exception clause to see what the rights and liabilities of the parties should be; the exception clause then operated, if at all, as a defence. This

---

[14]   See Coote (1970) CLJ 221 for a list of such devices.
[15]   161 A 2d 69 (1960).

characterisation of exceptions as defences was famously attacked by Professor Coote[16] who argued that exception clauses were simply a way of defining the parties' obligations. For example, Smith might contract to sell all of the white horses in his stable containing black and white horses, or all the horses except the black horses. The two formulations mean the same thing, and are logically no different. Similarly, Jones might say, 'I do not undertake to perform this service with proper care and skill' or 'I will perform this service, but *I do not accept liability for the want of proper care and skill on my part*'. Now, if the italicised words appeared as prominently as the first words in the second statement, or were generally understood and taken as allocative of insurance risks, as might be the case in certain commercial contracts of carriage, Coote's argument (with its classical foundations) might have found some favour with the courts. His argument never did, however, find much favour with the courts, which were always much less consistent in their adoption of classical theory than academic textbook writers. Moreover, although the drafting of UCTA does not unequivocally invite rejection of Coote's approach,[17] the tendency post-UCTA has been to continue with the familiar two-stage approach, ie looking at the contract apart from the exemption clauses, and then applying UCTA to the exceptions (which are regarded, in effect, as defences).[18]

(ii) The application of the reasonableness test

There are several instances where UCTA black-lists terms which purport to contract out of liability vis-à-vis persons who deal as consumers. To this extent, the regulation of exclusions in consumer contracts under section 3 is very much a fail-safe provision. With regard to commercial contracts, however, few provisions are black-listed. It follows that the courts' reading of the reasonableness requirement in the context of commercial contracts is particularly instructive. The ground rules for the application of the reasonableness requirement are laid down in three House of Lords decisions, *Photo Production Ltd v Securicor*

---

[16]   Coote *Exception Clauses* (London, Sweet and Maxwell, 1964).
[17]   For Coote's criticism of UCTA, see (1978) 41 MLR 312.
[18]   See eg *Smith v Eric S. Bush* [1989] 2 All ER 514.

Transport Ltd,[19] *George Mitchell (Chesterhall) Ltd v Finney Lock Seeds Ltd*,[20] and *Smith v Eric S. Bush*.[21]

In the *Photo Production* case, the question was whether Securicor could rely on exclusions and limitations in their contract to provide a night patrol service at Photo Production's factory, when the patrolman had started a fire which had gutted the factory. Lord Wilberforce spelled out a textbook case for non-interventionism:[22]

> 'After this Act, in commercial matters generally, when the parties are not of unequal bargaining power, and when risks are normally borne by insurance, not only is the case for judicial intervention undemonstrated, but there is everything to be said, and this seems to have been Parliament's intention, for leaving the parties free to apportion the risks as they think fit and for respecting their decisions.'

By contrast, in *George Mitchell v Finney Lock Seeds* the House of Lords, if not exactly operating from the opposite viewpoint, at least did not operate with a presumption against striking out terms as unreasonable – rather, the exclusionary terms, even in standard form commercial contracts, should be subject to a balancing test to determine whether, all things considered, they were reasonable. In the event, the House held that it would be unreasonable for the defendant seed suppliers, having supplied defective cabbage seeds to the plaintiff farmer (who had in consequence lost profits of some £61,000), to be permitted to rely on a clause limiting liability to a refund of the price of the seeds (some £201).

In the *George Mitchell* case, the balancing test was complicated by the fact that the reasonableness of the seed suppliers' limitation clause fell to be decided under transitional provisions.[23] According to those provisions, the test was not whether (as UCTA provides) the term was a fair and reasonable one to have been included in the contract, but whether it would now be fair and reasonable to allow reliance on the term 'having regard to all the circumstances of the case'. This proved to be critical to the outcome of the case, for the House took into account the post-breach fact

[19]   [1980] AC 827.
[20]   [1983] AC 803.
[21]   [1989] 2 All ER 514.
[22]   [1980] AC 827, 843.
[23]   See s 55 of the Sale of Goods Act 1979.

that the seed suppliers had attempted to compromise the plaintiff's claim by offering a sum in excess of their limitation. In Lord Bridge's judgment, this showed that reliance on the limitation of liability would not be fair and reasonable – in effect, the seed suppliers' post-breach conduct estopped them from arguing that their limitation set a reasonable compensatory figure.[24]

UCTA's adoption of an 'inclusion' test of reasonableness, rather than a 'reliance' test, was a measured attempt to constrain the reserve powers conferred upon the judges by the Act. In fact, the legislation rejects the English Law Commission's recommendation that the test should be that reliance on the term would be unfair, in favour of the Scottish Law Commission's recommendation that the term should be a fair and reasonable one to be included. For the Scottish Law Commission, the importance of calculability in commercial contracting is not to be forgotten:[25]

'It must be clear or at least determinable from the outset what each contracting party has agreed to do or to give or to abstain from doing. This is not merely a matter of theory but one of great practical importance . . . A contracting party must be in a position to assess his risks before he enters into the contract, not only to facilitate his decision whether or not to insure against the contingencies which the contract involves or to establish an appropriate contingency fund. For the same reasons a solution should be preferred which enables a lawyer to give sound advice to a client who is contemplating entering into a contract. If such advice is not available, there may be unnecessary litigation which would inevitably involve delay and expense.

. . . If the courts were able to pronounce on the reasonableness of an exemption clause in the light of subsequent events, businessmen could not have any reasonable assurance that the essential provisions of certain classes of contracts entered into would be upheld in the future.'

Schedule 2 of UCTA also attempts to structure the balancing test of the kind employed in *George Mitchell* by laying down a number of guidelines for the application of the

---

[24]   Similarly, in *Rees Hough Ltd v Redland Reinforced Plastics Ltd* (1985) 2 Con LR 109, the court took the fact that the defendants had not ordinarily relied on their limitation of liability, to be an admission of the unreasonableness of the clause.

[25]   The Law Commission, Exemption Clauses, Second Report (Law Com No 69) (1975) paras 171 and 174.

reasonableness test.[26] Factors which weigh against the reasonableness of a term include: (a) that the parties are of unequal bargaining strength (where the party in the stronger bargaining position has imposed the term on the party in the weaker bargaining position); and (b) that the supplier is in a monopoly position in relation to the customer – that, for the customer, it is essentially a case of 'take it or leave it'.[27] On the other side, factors which weigh in favour of the reasonableness of a term include: (a) that an inducement is offered for acceptance of the term (eg a price reduction for a limitation of liability); (b) that the customer has other options; and (c) that the customer knows, or ought reasonably to know, about the term. With specific reference to limitations of liability (such as in the *George Mitchell* case), s 11(4) of UCTA provides that the reasonableness of the term shall be determined in the light, inter alia, of how far it was open to the party relying on the limitation to cover himself by insurance. In practice, this narrow reference to insurance can be treated as having a broader relevance; for, bearing in mind the reasoning of the House in the *Photo Production* case, we can assume that, where a contractual term simply tracks sensible background insurance arrangements, this will be a further factor counting in favour of the reasonableness of the term.

Now, if we pause to reflect on the nature of these balancing factors, it is apparent that they do not relate *directly* to the reasonableness of particular terms. Rather, they refer to the context in which a contract has been formed. In fact, by posing questions about equality of bargaining strength, inducements, knowledge, and the like, the guidelines are asking whether the contract resulted from the parties' free agreement. In other words, the application of the regime of substantive regulation represented by UCTA relies very much on procedural questions of a kind which even a

---

[26]   Although the guidelines in Schedule 2 relate explicitly only to the reasonableness test as it arises under s 6 and 7 of UCTA, judicial practice is to regard the guidelines as generally applicable. See eg *Stag Line Ltd v Tyne Shiprepair Group Ltd (The Zinnia)* [1984] 2 Lloyd's Rep 211; *Rees Hough Ltd v Redland Reinforced Plastics Ltd* (1985) 2 Con. LR 109; and *Phillips Products Ltd v T. Hyland and Hamstead Plant Hire Co Ltd* [1987] 2 All ER 620.

[27]   Schedule 2 of UCTA also lists 'whether the goods were manufactured, processed or adapted to the special order of the customer'. Presumably, this factor tends to weigh in favour of the reasonableness of a term.

clear-thinking classical contract lawyer would accept as appropriate. So, how are we to characterise the modern interventionism? Quite simply, the pattern of modern thinking has two dimensions. At one level, some contractual provisions are regarded as wholly unconscionable and black-listed. It does not matter whether there has been free acceptance of such terms – they are unenforceable. So, for example, UCTA black-lists any term which purports to exclude or restrict liability for death or personal injury caused by negligence,[28] and similarly any term in a consumer sales contract which purports to exclude or restrict liability in relation to the statutory obligations concerning the merchantability and fitness for purpose of the goods.[29] At another level, certain kinds of contractual provision are regarded as questionable. They are not wholly unconscionable, but the burden is on those who wish to rely on such terms to show that they are reasonable. To show that they are reasonable, however, it is not a matter of raising fresh substantive considerations. Rather, the emphasis is on the classical question of whether the term was freely accepted – hence the reference to the various procedural factors.[30] Presenting the matter thus, the distinction between the approach in *Photo Production* and that in *George Mitchell* is not so much one concerning outright substantive regulation, but one relating to the procedural issues. In *Photo Production*, the House is ready to assume that commercial contractors enjoy roughly equal bargaining strength and that the terms will have been freely agreed. In *George Mitchell*, however, the House is less ready to make this assumption; it feels the need to take a hard look at the conditions in which the contract was formed (as well as the post-breach circumstances); and it wants to be satisfied that the terms genuinely were the product of free agreement.

The third major post-UCTA decision is that of the House of Lords in *Smith v Eric S. Bush*. In this case, the

---

[28]   Section 2(1).

[29]   Section 6(2).

[30]   As Joseph Raz puts it, 'to be autonomous [in our context, to agree freely] a person must not only be given a choice but must be given an adequate range of choices': see *The Morality of Freedom* (Oxford, Clarendon Press, 1986) p 373. With particular reference to standard form contracts, see the analysis in Todd D. Rakoff, 'Contracts of Adhesion: An Essay in Reconstruction' (1983) 96 Harvard Law Review 1174.

purchasers of a relatively modest house sued the surveyor,
employed by their building society, for negligent preparation
of a survey report on the property. The survey report disclaimed any responsibility, indicating that the purchasers
relied on the report at their own risk. The House, applying
a balancing approach along the lines of that in *George
Mitchell*, held that the disclaimer was unreasonable. The
clause was suspect in the first place because it purported to
exclude liability for a negligent survey, for work which, as
Lord Griffiths put it, surely is 'at the lower end of the surveyor's field of professional expertise'.[31] It was also a
disclaimer very much imposed on the house-purchasers.
They paid their building society the fee to have the survey
carried out (principally for the building society's benefit);
they had no say in negotiating the terms of the survey
contract; and it was unrealistic to expect ordinary house-
purchasers (unlike commercial contractors buying
industrial property or the like) to commission their own survey on the property. Lord Griffiths also indicated that such
a hard case, with catastrophic loss to ordinary people on one
side and insured professionals on the other side, was suitable for relief. Indeed, such a case was almost the paradigm
for holding the professionals liable and allowing them to
spread the loss by marginal adjustment to their fees.

The pattern of the UCTA case-law suggests that the courts
are very much seized of the idea that it is right to intervene
in cases of inequality of bargaining power – even though this
is a concept that is by no means free of difficulty.[32] In
practice, this means that we can expect to find the courts
well-disposed towards exercising their reserve powers in

[31] [1989] 2 All ER 514, 531.
[32] See eg Hugh Beale, 'Inequality of Bargaining Power' (1986) 6 Oxford
Journal of Legal Studies 123; and Spencer N. Thal, 'The Inequality of
Bargaining Power Doctrine: The Problem of Defining Contractual
Unfairness' (1988) 8 Oxford Journal of Legal Studies 17. Thal draws
an interesting distinction between situations where one side is in an
unusually strong bargaining position and situations where one side is
in an unusually weak bargaining position (because of ignorance,
necessity, or the like). At pp 29-30, he says:

'The difference between strength- and weakness-based inequality is
in the scope of the inquiry. An assessment of strength-based
inequality requires an inquiry into the contestability of the market,
whereas an assessment of weakness-based inequality only requires
an analysis of the individual transaction. It is probably for this
reason that issues of strength-based inequality are usually left to the

favour of consumer contractors and relatively weak contractors such as the house-purchasers in *Smith v Eric S. Bush*. The more pressing questions arise, however, where the disputants are commercial contractors who are not obviously of unequal bargaining strength. In such cases, the courts may take the *Photo Production* approach and effectively decline jurisdiction; or, they may follow the *George Mitchell* approach and apply a balancing test, the outcome of which will depend on how easily they are satisfied that the term was freely accepted.[33]

(iii) The scope of UCTA: indemnity and exclusion of set-off clauses

The tension between interventionist and non-interventionist judicial approaches arises not only in relation to the application of the reasonableness requirement, but also in relation to the prior question of whether a particular contractual provision falls within the ambit of UCTA. Such a question has been raised with reference to a variety of terms.[34] In this section, we review judicial treatment of two such kinds of provision, indemnity clauses and clauses which exclude a party's right to set-off.

(a) Indemnity clauses

Indemnity clauses have attracted altogether less attention than exclusions, even though they play an important part in commercial contracts, and even though, as Viscount Dilhorne once said, an indemnity is 'the obverse of an

legislature, as the institution most capable of making inquiry into the contestability of markets, while issues of weakness-based inequality are left to the courts as the body best suited to resolving the fairness of individual transactions.'

[33]   Cf *St Albans City and District Council v International Computers Ltd* (1994) Times, 11 November, where the Council had little option but to accept ICL's limitation of liability because the only two other suppliers were offering identical terms.

[34]   In addition to the cases discussed in the text, see eg *Johnstone v Bloomsbury HA* [1992] QB 333; and *Tudor Grange Holdings Ltd v Citibank NA* [1991] 4 All ER 1. Generally, see Elizabeth Macdonald 'Exclusion Clauses: the Ambit of s 13(1) of the Unfair Contract Terms Act 1977' (1992) 12 Legal Studies 277, and 'Mapping the Unfair Contract Terms Act 1977 and the Directive on Unfair Terms in Consumer Contracts' (1994) Journal of Business Law 441.

exempting clause'.[35] An indemnity may be defined as a clause which operates 'where one contracting party, A, may become liable to a third party, X, and the other contracting party, B, promises to indemnify A'.[36] An indemnity in this form is a way of insuring against third-party claims.[37] Indeed, ordinary contracts of insurance are commonly in this form. In point of fact, however, this is not the only sort of indemnity clause. There is also the reflexive indemnity clause, which requires B, who has successfully sued his fellow (but defaulting) contracting party A, to indemnify A. No doubt it was this type of indemnity clause that Viscount Dilhorne had in mind when he related indemnities to exceptions. Before we consider the treatment of indemnities under UCTA, we can review briefly the way that judges applied the common law to such provisions.

Prior to UCTA, the reported cases involve only insurance indemnities. Typically, the situation is that a third party, X, has recovered damages from A in respect of A's negligence, and A now seeks to recover on a contractual indemnity clause against B (who is not at fault in relation to X's claim). As with exemption clauses, we find some judges more willing than others to regulate commercial agreements. The leading example of an interventionist approach is the House of Lords' decision in *Smith v South Wales Switchgear*.[38] In that case South Wales Switchgear (SWS) were employed to carry out an overhaul at the factory of UMB Chrysler (Scotland) Ltd. During the overhaul, Smith, an electrical fitter employed by SWS, was seriously injured. Smith having recovered substantial damages from the factory owners (for their negligence and breach of statutory duty in failing to take reasonable care for the safety of people working at the site), Chrysler sought to claim from SWS under an indemnity clause in the contract. Although the indemnity was

---

[35]   See *Smith v South Wales Switchgear Ltd.* [1978] 1 All ER 18, 22.

[36]   *Halsbury's Laws of England* 4th edn vol 9, para 363, n 2. See also, Conley and Sayre 'Indemnity Revisited: Insurance of the Shifting Risk' (1971) 22 Hastings LJ 1201.

[37]   Or, exceptionally, to cover the costs of litigation in defending against an unsuccessful third-party claim, see eg *Collins v Harland & Wolff Ltd and Staff Caterers Ltd* [1951] 2 Lloyd's Rep 235, and *Richardson v Buckinghamshire County Council* [1971] 1 Lloyd's Rep 533.

[38]   [1978] 1 All ER 18. See also *AMF International v Magnet Bowling Ltd* [1968] 2 All ER 789; and *Walters v Whessoe Ltd and Shell Refining Co Ltd* [1968] 2 All ER 876.

drafted in very wide terms,[39] the House held that the principles applicable to exemption clauses were applicable to the indemnity clause. Accordingly, the clause did not provide indemnity against the consequences of Chrysler's own negligence unless it expressly so provided, or the words of the clause were sufficiently wide in their ordinary meaning to cover their negligence. Since there was no express reference in the clause to 'negligence', it was held that the clause did not provide Chrysler with a right of indemnity against SWS in the present case.[40]

Although *Smith v South Wales Switchgear* reflects the powerful judicial instinct that contractors at fault should bear responsibility for the losses they occasion, there is the rival instinct that provisions in commercial contracts should be left alone – particularly where indemnities appear (as they often do) in standard form contracts promulgated by trade associations, and widely used by their members. So, for example, in *Gillespie Bros & Co v Roy Bowles Transport Ltd*,[41] the Court of Appeal allowed negligent carriers to enforce an indemnity clause against totally innocent forwarding agents. Lord Denning MR considered that the indemnity, which had the effect of neutralising the decision in *Midland Silicones Ltd v Scruttons Ltd*,[42] made good commercial sense.[43] Thus:

'It has been the common practice of carriers – by land, sea or air – to make conditions limiting their liability to specific sums: and

---

[39] SWS undertook to keep Chrysler indemnified against, inter alia, 'Any liability, loss, claim or proceedings whatsoever under Statute or Common Law (i) in respect of personal injury to, or death of, any person whomsoever, (ii) in respect of any injury or damage whatsoever to any property real or personal, arising out of or in the course of or caused by the execution of this order'.

[40] See also *Canada SS Lines v R* [1952] AC 192. Recently, in *Caledonia (EE) Ltd v Orbit Valve plc* [1995] 1 All ER 174, the Court of Appeal applied the reasoning of *Canada SS* and *Smith v South Wales Switchgear* to hold that the parties had contracted on the basis of a reciprocal indemnity clause, but with each party assuming the risk of its own negligence. The indemnity clause did not explicitly refer to negligence. Moreover, Steyn LJ suggested (at p 185), the reading adopted by the Court conformed with the reasonable expectations of the parties.

[41] [1973] QB 400.

[42] [1962] AC 446 (see ch 5).

[43] It should be recalled that Lord Denning delivered a dissenting speech in the House of Lords in the *Midland Silicones* case.

to leave the goods owner to insure if he wants greater cover. Carriers base their charges – and insurers calculate their premiums – on the footing that the limitation is valid and effective between all concerned. The law should support this course of trade and uphold the limitation. But it has not done so. The effectiveness of the conditions was seriously undermined by the *Midland Silicones* case. So in consequence many efforts have been made to get round the decision. [Indemnity clauses are one such attempt].'[44]

Similarly, in *Wescott v J. M. Jenner (Plasterers) Ltd*,[45] the court held that a negligent contractor, A (who had compensated a third party) could enforce an indemnity against a contractor, B, who was entirely blameless in relation to the third party's injury. Again, the thinking was that this was commercially sound, for contractor B had been put on notice of the indemnity and advised to cover the risk by insuring. If B had insured as advised, the enforcement of the indemnity should not be viewed as shifting the risk from a negligent to an innocent party, but as maintaining the intended alignment between the background insurance arrangements and the contractual allocation of risk.

Turning to UCTA, we find only one section, s 4, explicitly dealing with indemnity clauses. However, s 4 provides only for indemnities in consumer contracts (basically, subjecting such indemnities to the reasonableness test). Are we to conclude, therefore, that UCTA fails altogether to provide for indemnities in commercial contracts?

Although UCTA certainly makes no unequivocal provision for indemnities in commercial contracts, there are two ways of arguing for the inclusion of such clauses. First, one might argue from s 13, which (so far as is material) provides:

'(1) To the extent that this Part of the Act prevents the exclusion or restriction of any liability it also prevents –
    (b) excluding or restricting any right or remedy in respect of the liability, or *subjecting a person to any prejudice in consequence of his pursuing any such right or remedy* . . .'[46]

This section is by no means easy to interpret. However, the natural reading is that it applies to reflexive indemnity

---

[44]   [1973] QB 400, 412.
[45]   [1962] 1 Lloyd's Rep 309.
[46]   Emphasis supplied.

clauses (in both consumer and commercial contracts), but that it does not apply to insurance indemnities.[47] Quite simply, the reason why insurance indemnities seem to fall outside s 13 is that it is a third party X who pursues a remedy (against A), while it is B who is subjected to prejudice. If the section read 'subjecting a person to any prejudice in consequence of the [not "his"] pursuing of any such right or remedy . . .', we might be able to stretch it to include insurance indemnities. Without such wording, however, it seems that s 13 misses out on the most important species of commercial indemnity.

The second way of arguing for the inclusion of commercial indemnities is by focusing on the phrase 'exclude or restrict' liability, which is the way that UCTA (in s 3 and elsewhere) generally signals that it is talking about exclusion clauses. Is it arguable, though, that such a description includes indemnities? Is it not true of indemnities that they, too, exclude or restrict liability? This very point came up for decision in two Court of Appeal cases, *Phillips Products v Hyland*,[48] and *Thompson v T. Lohan (Plant Hire) and Another (J. W. Hurdiss Ltd, Third Party)*.[49] Both cases involved similar fact situations, and the Model Conditions of the Contractors Plant-Hire Association. In *Phillips* the driver of a JCB negligently damaged the hirer's buildings; in *Thompson* the driver's negligence led to the death of Mr Thompson. The drivers in both cases were supplied by the owner of the plant. In both cases the key question was whether or not the owners could rely on clause 8 of the Model Conditions. The (earlier) version of that clause used in *Phillips* provided:

> 'When a driver or operator is supplied by the owner to work the plant, he shall be under the direction and control of the hirer. Such drivers or operators shall for all purposes in connection with their employment in the working of the plant be regarded as the servants or agents of the hirer who alone shall be responsible for all claims arising in connection with the operation of the plant by the said drivers or operators . . .'

The (later) version used in *Thompson* was similar except that

[47]   See Law Commission, Exemption Clauses Second Report, (LC No 69) p 147.
[48]   [1987] 2 All ER 620.
[49]   [1987] 2 All ER 631.

it included an express undertaking as to the competence of the driver supplied by the owner of the plant. In *Phillips* the Court of Appeal held that clause 8 was caught by s 2(2) of UCTA (which provides that clauses purporting to exclude or restrict liability for negligence, where the negligence has not led to death or personal injury, are subject to the reasonableness test). In consequence, the owners could rely on clause 8 only if it satisfied the reasonableness requirement. It was held that the terms having been presented to the hirer in a largely take-it-or-leave-it manner, clause 8 did not pass muster.[50] By contrast, in *Thompson*, it was held that s 2(1) (which, it will be recalled, black-lists any term which purports to exclude or restrict liability for negligence where the negligence has led to death or personal injury) did not apply to clause 8. Nothing turns on the fact that the cases involved different sub-sections of section 2. Both sub-sections regulate contractual terms which 'exclude or restrict' liability in negligence.

In *Phillips* the owners argued that clause 8 was not an exclusion or restriction of liability at all; rather it was an attempt 'to divide and allocate the obligations or responsibilities arising in relation to the contract by transferring liability for the acts of the operator from the plant owners to the hirers'. Delivering the judgment of the court, Slade LJ, however, dismissed this argument:[51]

> 'There is no mystique about "exclusion" or "restriction" clauses. To decide whether a person "excludes" liability by reference to a contract term, you look at the effect of the term. You look at its substance. The effect here is beyond doubt. Hamstead [the owner] does most certainly purport to exclude its liability for negligence by reference to Condition 8.'

Yet, if in a case like *Phillips*, clause 8 fell within the scope of s 2, how could the court in *Thompson* avoid the same conclusion? Nothing seems to have turned on the difference in wording between the respective versions of clause 8, for Fox LJ in *Thompson*, referring to the House of Lords decision in *Arthur White (Contractors) Ltd v Tarmac Civil Engineering Ltd*[52] which also involved the old version of clause 8,

---

[50]   [1987] 2 All ER 620, 626-630.
[51]   Ibid, at p 625.
[52]   [1967] 1 WLR 1508.

described the two versions as 'substantially the same'.[53] The Court distinguished *Phillips* in the following way:[54]

'If one then turns to the present case, the sharp distinction between it and the *Phillips* case is this, that whereas in the *Phillips* case there was liability in negligence by Hamstead [the owners] to Phillips (and that was sought to be excluded), in the present case there is no exclusion or restriction of the liability sought to be achieved by reliance on the provisions of Condition 8. The plaintiff has her judgment against Lohan and can enforce it. The plaintiff is not prejudiced in any way by the operation sought to be established of Condition 8.'

The difference between the cases, in other words, was that in *Phillips* clause 8, if effective, would have denied a remedy to the victim of the negligent act, whereas in *Thompson* the victim's remedy was not affected by the clause. In other words, whilst the owners in *Phillips* sought to rely on clause 8 to exclude liability to the victim, the owners in *Thompson* were not setting up clause 8 for this purpose. Fox LJ said:[55]

'In my opinion, section 2(1) is concerned with protecting the victim of negligence, and of course those who claim under him. It is not concerned with arrangements made by the wrongdoer with other persons as to the sharing or bearing of the burden of compensating the victim. In such a case it seems to me there is no exclusion or restriction of the liability at all. The liability has been established . . . The circumstances that the defendants have between themselves chosen to bear the liability in a particular way does not affect that liability; it does not exclude it and it does not restrict it.'

What these decisions suggest, therefore, is that commercial indemnity clauses, like clause 8, will not be subject to s 2 of UCTA unless such provisions are employed to prejudice the victim's claim to compensation for the negligent act.

On closer inspection, however, this is only one possible interpretation of UCTA. Another reading is that s 2 applies to all commercial indemnity clauses because by transferring the risk to the other party one party necessarily employs an indemnity clause to exclude or restrict his own liability. And, a further possibility is that s 2 has no application at all to commercial indemnity clauses. It seems likely that the Court in *Phillips* assumed that s 2 applies generally to

---

[53]   [1987] 2 All ER 620, 626.
[54]   [1987] 2 All ER 631, 636.
[55]   Ibid, at p 638.

commercial indemnities. This is borne out by the following passage from Slade LJ's judgment:[56]

> 'Certainly there is nothing which leads to the conclusion that a plant-owner who uses the general conditions is not excluding his liability for negligence in the relevant sense by reference to the contract term Condition 8. We are unable to accept that, in the ordinary sensible meaning of words in the context of section 2 and the 1977 Act as a whole, the provisions of Condition 8 do not fall within the scope of section 2(2). A transfer of liability from A to B necessarily and inevitably involves the exclusion of liability so far as A is concerned.'

Note the last sentence of this passage. Slade LJ is arguing that where an indemnity clause transfers risk from A to B this must have the effect of excluding liability 'so far as A is concerned'. This does not address the effect of the indemnity clause from the victim's standpoint; it treats the transfer of risk as an exclusion of liability from A's point of view. If this view is correct, the Court went wrong in *Thompson*. What should have been material in that case was that the owner was attempting to transfer its liability to the hirer by reference to clause 8. Accordingly, s 2(1) should have applied.[57]

Support for the opposite view, that s 2 does not apply to commercial indemnity clauses at all, can be found in Dillon LJ's judgment in *Thompson*. Although Dillon LJ agreed with Fox LJ's reasoning, he was also prepared to accept that s 2 did not apply to commercial indemnity clauses at all, because this would make the specific and rather different treatment of indemnities in s 4 anomalous. Section 4, after all, subjects indemnities in consumer contracts to the test of reasonableness. If s 2(1) applied to commercial indemnity clauses, it would mean that they were subjected to a more stringent regime than consumer contracts, because no question of reasonableness can be raised in relation to s 2(1). This Dillon LJ thought was 'a strong indication' that

---

[56]   [1987] 2 All ER 620, 626.
[57]   In the unreported case of *Paul v Ruddle Bros* (26 April 1985), Michael Turner QC followed this second line. The facts of the case were similar to *Thompson*, in that there was no question of the victim being denied a remedy if the clause were upheld. He considered it reasonable both because the hirer as a regular hirer of plant would have been familiar with it, and because the purpose of Clause 8 is the apportionment of insurance risks, and the action was effectively between the respective parties' insurers.

commercial indemnities are outside the scope of s 2 altogether.[58] The logic of this view is that *Phillips* was wrong,
though Dillon LJ did not specifically say so. Given the
general scheme of UCTA, which of these views is correct?

Although only ss 2 and 4 were discussed in the above
cases, we must not forget the possible application of s 13. It
is certainly arguable that the effect of clause 8 (or similar
clauses) in a case like *Phillips* is precisely to prejudice a person in consequence of his pursuing a remedy for negligence.
It would follow from this that the clause in question (which
is a reflexive indemnity clause) is indirectly drawn into the
regulatory net of s 2. If this argument is accepted, we must
reject Dillon LJ's view that s 2 does not apply to commercial
indemnity clauses at all. Moreover, it obviates the anomaly
on which his views were based, because s 13 treats both
commercial and consumer contracts in the same way.
Reference to s 13 also suggests that Fox LJ's view that s 2
applies to both insurance and reflexive indemnity clauses is
wrong. Although it is possible to read references in s 2 to
provisions which 'exclude or restrict liability' as being
intended to cover both reflexive and insurance indemnity
clauses, this reading would leave ss 4 and 13 overlapping in
a somewhat messy and unsatisfactory way.[59]

This leaves us with the view that s 2 applies to those commercial indemnity clauses which have the effect of excluding
or restricting the victim's claim, as in *Phillips*, but does not
apply in situations of the *Thompson* kind. This is consistent
with the apparent intention of s 13 that reflexive indemnities in commercial contracts should be caught by s 2, but
not insurance indemnities. Certainly this view seems to fit
better with the overall scheme of the Act than either of the
other two views.

Although this analysis invites judges to leave commercial
insurance indemnities outside the range of UCTA, it is no
guarantee that such provisions will be routinely enforced.
Courts wishing to police commercial insurance indemnities
can give UCTA a robust reading to justify intervention; and,
even without UCTA, it must not be forgotten that the

---

[58] [1987] 2 All ER 631, 640.
[59] See further John N. Adams and Roger Brownsword 'Double Indemnity
– Contractual Indemnity Clauses Revisited' (1988) Journal of Business
Law 146, 150–4.

common law resources for intervention remain in place (as *Smith v South Wales Switchgear* confirms).

(b) Exclusion of set-off provisions

In the 1970s, a rash of cases went to the appeal courts in which the dispute centred on the validity of so-called set-off clauses.[60] Generally, these clauses were contained in standard form contracts which were widely used in the construction industry. The gist of a set-off clause is that one contracting party reserves the right to make deductions from payments otherwise due to the other contracting party, such deductions reflecting sums due (or allegedly due) in respect of a counter-claim. In the construction cases, clients were relying on set-off clauses to deduct sums from payments otherwise due to main contractors, main contractors were likewise setting-off against payments otherwise due to sub-contractors, and sub-contractors were setting-off against sub-sub-contractors, and so on. In each case, the counter-claim underlying the set-off would relate to alleged delay or defective work or something of that sort. The effect of the set-off was not, of course, to foreclose any disputes concerning the allegations of delay or defective work; the set-off simply meant that the paying party held on to the money during the contract, leaving the disputed allegations to be contested in arbitration proceedings at the completion of the work. In practice, though, the fact that the payer could hold on to the money set-off was tremendously important, for it often meant that smaller contractors were starved of payment under the contract as a result of which they sometimes experienced serious cash-flow problems (or even became insolvent). In one of the major cases of the period, *Dawnays Ltd v. F.G. Minter Ltd*,[61] the threat to small contractors represented by set-off provisions encouraged the Court of Appeal to take a restrictive approach towards such clauses. Cash-flow, Lord Denning MR famously remarked, was the life-blood of the industry; from which it followed that, unless a right of set-off was expressly and unequivocally reserved, money certified as due to contractors for work done must be paid on time, leaving any disputed

[60]   See, especially, *Dawnays Ltd v F.G. Minter Ltd*. [1971] 1 WLR 1205; and *Gilbert Ash (Northern) Ltd v Modern Engineering (Bristol) Ltd* [1973] 3 All ER 195.
[61]   [1971] 1 WLR 1205.

claims to be settled at arbitration after the completion of the work.

Now, the situation in the 1970s set-off cases has a party in a strong bargaining position seizing on set-off provisions (arguably, sometimes a bit dubiously), with a view to holding on to money when cash is tight. However, we could imagine a very different case. For example, with the recession of the late 1980s, there has been a lot of litigation between franchisors and (relatively vulnerable) franchisees. Commonly, as a franchisor's financial situation deteriorates, it ceases to provide the management and advertising services to which the franchisee is entitled under the terms of the franchise agreement; and the franchisee, in turn, declines to pay the fees otherwise due under the franchise. One such case was *Fastframe v Lohinsky Ltd*,[62] where the franchisee of a picture framing business stopped paying fees to the franchisor, because he felt that he was receiving nothing in return for the fees and because, moreover, the business had ceased to be profitable (partly, so the franchisee alleged, because the franchisor had deliberately diverted away profitable commercial contracts). In such circumstances, one can readily understand the franchisee's reluctance to make the payments normally due under the franchise. As Dillon LJ put it:

> 'In the context of this agreement, with its rather one-sided wording of so many clauses but none the less being intended to produce the development of a franchise service, is it reasonable that all payments to be made to the franchisor are to be made without any set-off whatsoever? In particular, is it reasonable that they must be made without any set-off which is referable to any breach or claimed breach of the franchisor's obligations under the same agreement? I do not think that it is.'

Accordingly, if there had been a set-off provision in the franchise agreement, one would sympathise with the franchisee seeking to set-off against the franchisor. However, in *Fastframe v Lohinsky*, as in the earlier case of *Stewart Gill Ltd v Horatio Myer & Co Ltd*,[63] the dispute concerned not the validity of a set-off provision, but the validity of a clause

---

[62]   Court of Appeal, 3 March 1993 (unreported); for comment, see John N. Adams '"No Deduction or Set-Off" Clauses' (1994) 57 MLR 960. Generally, see Adams and Prichard Jones 3rd edn *Franchising* (London, Butterworths, 1990).

[63]   [1992] 2 All ER 257. See Edwin Peel (1993) 56 MLR 98.

purporting to *exclude* the right to set-off – in other words, in *Fastframe*, the relevant clause purported to exclude any right to set-off on the part of the franchisee. Fairly clearly, UCTA does not regulate set-off clauses but does it cover clauses which purport to exclude set-off? In both cases, the Court of Appeal held that the clauses in question fell within the scope of UCTA (and, indeed, that they failed to satisfy the reasonableness requirement).[64]

In *Stewart Gill*, the contract was for the installation of an overhead conveyor system. When the customers sought to set-off against final payments due under the contract, the contractors argued that set-off was excluded under clause 12.4 of the contract. According to this clause:

> 'The Customer shall not be entitled to withhold payment of any amount due to the Company under the Contract by reason of any payment credit set off counterclaim allegation of incorrect or defective Goods or for any other reason whatsoever which the Customer may allege excuses him from performing his obligations hereunder.'

This clause, however, was held to fall within the ambit of UCTA by virtue of the extended definition of an exclusion given in s 13(1), which provides:

> 'To the extent that this Part of this Act prevents the exclusion or restriction of any liability, it also prevents . . . (a) making the liability or its enforcement subject to restrictive or onerous conditions; (b) excluding or restricting any right or remedy in respect of the liability . . . (c) excluding or restricting rules . . . of procedure.'

The Court of Appeal could have made a plausible case for catching clause 12.4 under paragraph (a), (b), or (c). In fact, reliance was placed on paragraph (b) – set-off being characterised as both a right and a remedy – and, in due course, the court followed suit in *Fastframe v Lohinsky*. Of course, catching clauses (such as clause 12.4) which exclude set-off under s 13 does not settle the issue, for, as we have seen, s 13 indirectly remits the issue to one of the other sections

---

[64]   Cf *Electricity Supply Nominees Ltd v IAF Group plc* [1993] 3 All ER 372, where it was held that a clause in a lease, which purported to exclude the tenant's right of set-off, was not regulated by UCTA. This was because Schedule 1 of UCTA expressly disapplies ss 2–4 of the Act in relation to 'any contract so far as it relates to the creation or transfer of an interest in land'.

of UCTA. It follows that clauses excluding set-off may sometimes be void, but generally they will be subject to the reasonableness test – and, indeed, in both *Stewart Gill* and *Fastframe v Lohinsky* the exclusionary provisions were held to be unreasonable. Even this does not finally settle the issue, for the substance of the matter to which the set-off relates still has to be decided. Nevertheless, the regulation of exclusions of set-off under UCTA is of considerable practical significance: it enables the party setting-off to hold on to the money in the interim and it prevents the claimant (contractor or franchisor) going through to summary judgment.

We thus arrive at a somewhat curious position. Clauses asserting or implying a right to set-off, which in the light of the litigation of the1970s appeared unreasonable, are not regulated by UCTA, but remain regulated by ordinary common law control techniques. On the other hand, as *Stewart Gill* and *Fastframe v Lohinsky* decide, UCTA applies to clauses which purport to exclude the right to set-off. Moreover, on the evidence of these two cases, such exclusionary clauses will fail as unreasonable.[65]

3. THE UNFAIR TERMS IN CONSUMER CONTRACTS REGULATIONS

Where consumers deal on terms that have not been individually negotiated, s 3 of UCTA can catch any exclusions twice-over (once because the exclusions are in a consumer contract, and again if the contract is on the dealer's written standard terms). Such exclusions are valid only if they satisfy the reasonableness test. From the beginning of July 1995, however, the Unfair Terms in Consumer Contracts Regulations[66] (implementing the EC Directive on Unfair Terms in Consumer Contracts)[67] subject provisions of this

---

[65] There is also the possibility, of course, that a clause designed to prevent set-off will be restrictively regulated under ordinary common law principles of construction. For example, in *Connaught Restaurants Ltd v Indoor Leisure Ltd* [1994] 4 All ER 834, the Court of Appeal held that a term in a lease requiring the tenant to pay the agreed rent to the landlord 'without any deduction' was not sufficiently clear to exclude the tenant's equitable right of set-off (where the tenant sought to withhold rent because he suffered severe damage caused by flooding from the landlord's retained part of the building).

[66] SI 1994/3159.

[67] 93/13/EEC.

kind (ie terms in consumer contracts that have not been individually negotiated) to yet a further layer of regulation.[68]

(i) The field of application

The Regulations apply to any term in a contract concluded between a seller or supplier and a consumer where the term has not been individually negotiated.[69] For the purposes of the Regulations, a 'seller' is defined as 'a person who sells goods and who . . . is acting for purposes relating to his business'; a 'supplier' likewise is defined as 'a person who supplies goods or services and who . . . is acting for purposes relating to his business'; and a 'consumer' is defined as 'a natural person who . . . is acting for purposes which are outside his business'.[70] The definition of a 'consumer' makes an interesting comparison with the position under UCTA. On the one hand, the Regulations impose no requirement (equivalent to s 12(1)(c), UCTA) that a party only deals as a consumer where 'the goods passing under or in pursuance of the contract are of a type ordinarily supplied for private use or consumption'. On the other hand, the plaintiff private company in *R & B Custom Brokers Co Ltd v United Dominions Trust Ltd*[71] (which was held to deal as a consumer under UCTA) would not be a consumer under the Regulations.

The onus is on the seller or supplier to show that a term

---

[68]   For discussion of the Directive, see P. Duffy 'Unfair Contract Terms and the Draft EC Directive' (1993) Journal of Business Law 67; Meryll Dean 'Unfair Contract Terms: The European Approach' (1993) 56 MLR 581; Ewoud Hondius 'EC Directive on Unfair Terms in Consumer Contracts: Towards a European Law of Contract' (1994) 7 Journal of Contract Law 34; Hugh Collins, 'Good Faith in European Contract Law' (1994) 14 Oxford Journal of Legal Studies 229; and Roger Brownsword, Geraint Howells, and Thomas Wilhemsson 'The EC Unfair Contract Terms Directive and Welfarism' in Roger Brownsword, Geraint Howells, and Thomas Wilhemsson (eds) *Welfarism in Contract Law* (Aldershot, Dartmouth, 1994) 275.

   On the implementing Regulations in the United Kingdom, the Unfair Terms in Consumer Contracts Regulations, 1994, see Roger Brownsword and Geraint Howells, 'The Implementation of the EC Directive on Unfair Terms in Consumer Contracts – Some Unresolved Questions' (1995) JBL 243.

[69]   Regulation 3(1).

[70]   For all three definitions, see Regulation 2(1).

[71]   [1988] 1 All ER 847.

was individually negotiated (and, thus, beyond the scope of the Regulations).[72] According to the Regulations, a term is always regarded as not having been individually negotiated 'where it has been drafted in advance and the consumer has not been able to influence the substance of the term'.[73] Quite what the reference to advance drafting adds to this definition is unclear, the point being that, if the consumer has not been able to influence the substance of the term, it is already arguable that the term has not been individually negotiated. Even though an individual term may have been negotiated, the Regulations still apply to the rest of the contract if an overall assessment of the contract indicates that it is a pre-formulated standard contract.[74] Similarly, although this is not clear from the wording of the Regulations, it seems that what is intended is that even if part of a *term* is individually negotiated, the test of fairness still applies to the remainder of the term.[75]

Finally, it should also be said that the Regulations, like UCTA, do not apply to a number of excluded categories of contract.[76] The categories excluded under the Regulations and under UCTA by no means coincide and, most significantly, the Regulations (unlike UCTA) apply to insurance contracts.[77]

(ii) The test of fairness

What determines whether a particular term is unfair? The Directive itself, which suffers somewhat from the compromises involved in Euro-drafting, offers only limited guidance on this matter. Some of its Recitals, particularly the

---

[72] Regulation 3(5).
[73] Regulation 3(3).
[74] Regulation 3(4).
[75] See Directive, Article 3(2).
[76] For particulars of these exclusions, see Schedule 1 of the Regulations and Schedule 1 of UCTA.
[77] Although Regulation 3(2), by providing that the 'core' terms of a contract are not to be assessed for their fairness, may well weaken the impact of the Regulations in relation to insurance contracts. See further Elizabeth Macdonald, 'Mapping the Unfair Contract Terms Act 1977 and the Directive on Unfair Terms in Consumer Contracts' (1994) JBL 441; and Roger Brownsword and Geraint Howells, n 68 above.

important Recital 16,[78] are intelligible only to those versed in Euro-speak, and its cornerstone provision on unfairness, Art 3 (now implemented by Reg 4), is open to various interpretations. According to Reg 4(1) (following Art 3(1)), a term is unfair if 'contrary to the requirement of good faith, it causes a significant imbalance in the parties' rights and obligations arising under the contract, to the detriment of the consumer'; and, in Reg 4(3) (following Art 3(3)), reference is made to Sch 2 of the Regulations (an Annex in the Directive) which contains 'an indicative and non-exhaustive list of terms which may be regarded as unfair'. The status of the indicative list is a moot point. It certainly is not a black-list (even though a number of the indicative examples would be void in English law). However, we can assume that it is a kind of grey-list, illustrating some types of terms which involve a significant imbalance of the kind contemplated by Reg 4(1).[79] For present purposes, the pressing question is the interpretation of the general test of fairness in Reg 4(1).

One reading of Reg 4(1) is that a term is unfair if it involves a significant imbalance to the detriment of the consumer. On this reading, when the Regulation says 'contrary to the requirement of good faith', it simply means 'contrary to the requirement of good faith in the sense that the term involves a significant imbalance to the detriment of the consumer'.[80] An alternative reading, however, is that the

---

[78]   This Recital provides: 'Whereas the assessment, according to the general criteria chosen, of the unfair character of terms, in particular sales or supply activities of a public nature providing collective services which take account of solidarity among users, must be supplemented by a means of making an overall evaluation of the different interests involved; whereas this constitutes the requirement of good faith; whereas, in making an assessment of good faith, particular regard shall be had to the strength of the bargaining positions of the parties, whether the consumer had an inducement to agree to the term and whether the goods or services were sold or supplied to the special order of the consumer; whereas the requirement of good faith may be satisfied by the seller or supplier where he deals fairly and equitably with the other party whose legitimate interests he has to take into account.'

[79]   See the comments on the Annex by Dean and Hondius supra. See also the analysis in Roger Brownsword, Geraint Howells, and Thomas Wilhelmsson 'Between Market and Welfare: Some Reflections on Article 3 of the EC Directive on Unfair Terms in Consumer Contracts' in C. Willett (ed) *Unfair Contract Terms* (Edward Elgar, forthcoming).

[80]   For this simple 'definitional' reading, see Stephen A. Smith 'Contract' in Ben Pettet (ed) *Current Legal Problems 1994* (Volume 47: Part One. Annual Review) 5.

reference to good faith is not definitional, but actually sets a first condition for unfairness. On this reading, a term is unfair if: (1) it is procured contrary to the requirement of good faith; and (2) it causes a significant imbalance to the detriment of the consumer. The Department of Trade and Industry, in its consultation document immediately prior to the promulgation of the Regulations, indicated that it had opted for the latter rather than the former reading.[81]

Reg 4(3), in conjunction with Sch 2, provides that in determining whether a term satisfies the requirement of good faith, regard shall be had to the following matters:

(a) the strength of the bargaining position of the parties;
(b) whether the consumer had an inducement to agree to the term;
(c) whether the goods or services were sold or supplied to the special order of the consumer; and
(d) the extent to which the seller or supplier has dealt fairly and equitably with the consumer.

Of these four matters, the first three are taken from the reasonableness guidelines under UCTA, and the fourth reflects an idea expressed in the Recitals to the effect that the requirement of good faith is satisfied where the dealer takes into account the legitimate interests of the consumer.[82] The pattern of the Directive as implemented, therefore, is similar to that under UCTA. Questionable terms are singled out (in the indicative list in the case of the Regulations) and they will be enforced only if the court is persuaded that the consumer freely agreed to the provision – fairness being determined under the Regulations, as under UCTA, in the light of the circumstances prevailing at the time of formation of the contract.[83] Moreover, if the good faith requirement is taken to signal protection against unfair surprise (one of the stock complaints about standard form

---

[81]   See Implementation of the EC Directive on Unfair Terms in Consumer Contracts (93/13/EEC): A Further Consultation Document (Department of Trade and Industry, September 1994), at p 3, where it is said that the test of fairness has three elements (namely, contrary to the requirement of good faith, causing a significant imbalance in the parties' rights and obligations, and to the detriment of the consumer).
[82]   See Recital 16, n 78 above.
[83]   See Article 4.1 and Regulation 4(2).

conditions),[84] then the Regulations will serve to emphasise that free agreement entails *informed* choice.

(iii) Access to justice and the Director General's powers

Whilst the general pattern of the Regulations is not dissimilar to that found in UCTA, it is hardly a mark of rational law-making to create two overlapping, but not co-extensive,[85] jurisdictions. Indeed, it has been rightly said that this is 'likely to produce a situation of nightmarish complexity in an area, that of consumer law, where simple and user-friendly rules should be the order of the day'.[86] However, there is more to user-friendliness than tidy enactment. In practice, it is important that consumers are able to pursue their claims without unnecessary procedural obstruction and inconvenience. Given the difficulties of securing consumer access to justice and the relatively limited effect of individual challenges to unfair terms, Reg 8 (implementing Art 7 of the Directive) opens the way to making important additional provision for pre-emptive challenges to unfair terms.

After some initial reluctance by the Department of Trade and Industry to put in place any machinery for such challenges,[87] the implementing Regulations place a duty on the Director General of Fair Trading to consider complaints that

---

[84] See eg Robert Dugan 'Good Faith and the Enforceability of Standardized Terms' (1980) 22 William and Mary Law Review 1.

[85] See Department of Trade and Industry, Implementation of the EC Directive on Unfair Terms in Consumer Contracts (93/13/EEC): A Further Consultation Document (September 1994), esp pp 3 and 12.

[86] FMB Reynolds, 'Unfair Contract Terms' (1994) 110 Law Quarterly Review 1.

[87] See Department of Trade and Industry, Implementation of the EC Directive on Unfair Terms in Consumer Contracts (93/13/EEC): A Consultative Document (October, 1993). Member states, of course, do not have an entirely free hand in the implementation and application of Directives. National courts are required to interpret national law in the light of the wording and purpose of Directives: see *Marleasing SA v La Comercial Internacional de Alimentacion SA* Case C-106/89 [1990] ECR I-4135. Moreover, since *Francovich and Bonifaci v Italy* Cases C-6, C-9/90, failure to implement a Directive can give rise to liability on the part of the member state to a person suffering damage thereby. However, Directives are binding only (vertically) on the member states to which they are addressed and, thus, cannot be invoked (horizontally) in disputes between private individuals: see eg *Paolo Faccini Dori*

terms drawn up for general use are unfair.[88] Where the Director General judges a term to be unfair, he may proceed for an injunction against 'any person appearing to him to be using or recommending use of such a term in contracts concluded with consumers'.[89] On such an application by the Director General, the court 'may grant an injunction on such terms as it thinks fit'.[90] Alternatively, where it is considered appropriate, the Director General may seek undertakings from the parties concerned about the continued use of the term.[91]

Sadly, such implementing measures are likely to please no one. Contract lawyers will worry that neither the Directive nor the implementing Regulations seem to have fully grappled with the relationship between *ex casu* regulation under Art 3 (Reg 4) and pre-emptive control under Art 7 (Reg 8)[92] – the problem being that pre-emptive control cannot function by reference to the master test of fairness as set by Art 3 (Reg 4). As we have explained, the fate of contractual provisions challenged under Reg 4 turns on whether *in the particular case* the term at issue has been freely agreed to – Reg 4, in other words, is designed for *ex casu* challenges. Since pre-emptive challenges do not occur in the context of any case in particular, it is hard to see quite how the Director General is to judge a term unfair. In effect, he seems to be left to draw up a black-list of his own when this is something that the Directive itself eschews (and

---

    v Recreb Srl Case C-91/92 July 14, 1994. Generally, see Stephen Weatherill and Paul Beaumont *EC Law* (Harmondsworth, Penguin, 1993).

[88] Regulation 8(1).
[89] Regulation 8(2).
[90] Regulation 8(5).
[91] Regulation 8(3).
[92] The Directive, unlike the implementing Regulations, does at least make passing reference to Art 7 elsewhere in its provisions. Thus, Article 4 is expressed to be 'without prejudice to Article 7'; thereby indicating, we assume, that general pre-emptive challenges under Art 7 may proceed notwithstanding that no specific contract has actually been concluded containing the term under challenge – and thereby revealing some awareness of the problematic relationship between Articles 3 and 7. There is also a cross-reference to Art 7 in Art 5 (which requires written contracts to be drafted in 'plain, intelligible language', coupled with the *contra proferentem* rule). The purpose of this cross-reference, which effectively says that the *contra proferentem* rule is not to apply in the context of challenges under Art 7, seems to be to render the term under challenge more vulnerable to being struck out as unfair.

when UCTA itself exercises some restraint in declaring provisions to be black-listed). Moreover, conferring such an open-ended discretion on the Director General invites the objection that the regulation of contracts is to be determined more by administrative fiat than by transparent and accountable decision-making of the kind advocated by the rule of law.[93] On the other hand, the consumer lobby will be less concerned about the breadth of the Director General's licence than about his willingness to use it – for this lobby, the Regulations would have been welcomed as altogether more effective if they had empowered consumer groups to run their own challenges, pre-emptive and *ex casu*.

4. CONCLUSION

Neither UCTA nor the Regulations implementing the EC Directive can be expected to offer an instant resolution to a problem which has existed in our jurisprudence for over two hundred years. The increasing use of standard forms in that period was undoubtedly a concomitant of industrialisation and a concern with economic efficiency. However, the general law was increasingly inadequate for the problems which arose with industrialisation. The persistent way in which the courts have ignored the problems created by monopoly, small print and 'legalese' was bound to usher in legislative reform, particularly when (as in the present century) those problems manifested themselves in the mass consumer market.

How, then, are we to judge the modern rise of reasonableness? Is the adoption of judicial discretion organised around the concept of fair and reasonable terms a rational development? At one level, the enactment of the modern discretions is certainly a rational development, for it enables the courts to regulate contracts openly; no longer do judges have to resort to underhand techniques where they feel the need to intervene on the grounds of fairness and reasonableness. It does not follow from this, however, that the law is any more effective in regulating unfairness in contracts;

---

[93]   The Regulations are unclear as to the jurisdiction of the courts with regard to the Director General's powers. However, we assume that if the Director General applies for an injunction, the courts will not mechanically rubber-stamp his application.

nor does it follow that modern discretionary interventions can be justified – as we saw when we outlined Posner's position at the start of this chapter, there is a powerful case to be made out against ad hoc adjustment of the substance of agreements.

It is difficult to assess whether the modern statutory-based discretions are more effective in delivering desired ends than the old common law techniques. In relation to consumer contracts, there is a litany of well-known difficulties about the effectiveness of private law remedies: customers are easily put off by dealers; they rarely know their rights; they worry about the cost of taking legal proceedings; small claim self-help procedures are not perhaps as helpful as they might be; and so on. Quite simply, if consumers fail to set the legal ball rolling, it matters little whether common law or statutory controls are in place. For this reason, the consumer lobby would argue that the implementation of Art 7 of the Directive (in Reg 8) is far more important than the fine-tuning of Reg 4 (implementing Art 3). In relation to commercial contracts, it is again difficult to take stock of the effectiveness of modern regulation. Commercially-minded judges, like Lord Wilberforce in the *Photo Production* case, caution against intervention: it is more important to commercial contractors to know where they stand (so that they can deal against a predictable legal backcloth) rather than undermining calculability for the sake of the occasional hard case. Indeed, the commercial argument is fortified by cases such as *Phillips* and *Thompson*, where the litigation was driven by the insurers' need to know where they stood. Up to a point, the insurers would not be greatly concerned about the particular outcome of these cases, for they would hold insurance cover for both owners and hirers – in other words, it would be a case of 'swings and roundabouts'; but the overriding concern was to settle the effect of clause 8 of the standard terms.

Finally, there is the question of whether reasonableness discretions, and their modern application, are rational in the sense of being legitimate. Three concluding remarks are in order here. First, the discretions and their application draw very explicitly on the distinction between consumer and commercial contracts – indeed, so much so, that we can talk about a bifurcation in the modern law of contract. To put the matter somewhat crudely, the modern law of consumer contracts is far more protective than the modern law of commercial contracts. Although this distinction fits with a number of intuitions that we might have about inequality of bargaining power and the standardisation of contracts in the consumer market, it is worth pondering whether this bifurcation can be justified. This is a matter to which we will return in Chapter 10.

Secondly, it is arguable that much of the modern intervention can be squared with the silent premise of the non-interventionist case (and of freedom of contract) that agreements should be freely made. Where agreements are not freely made, the case for non-intervention collapses. As we have suggested, one way of reading the development of judicial reserve powers (as under UCTA) is that terms are struck out as unreasonable in just those cases where it is unclear that the agreement in question was freely made. To the extent that modern interventionism strives indirectly to limit enforcement to freely-made agreements, it could be said to be taking freedom of contract seriously. This, of course, does not offer a final justification for intervention; but it shields much of the modern law from the stock non-interventionist objection.[94]

Finally, in so far as the modern law draws up black-lists, it really does seem to impinge on freedom of contract; for the effect of a black-list is to render a particular kind of term unenforceable even though the parties might freely have agreed to it. Of course, the modern law is not unique in condemning particular terms as being against public policy, but 'public policy' should not be confused with a warrant for rational justification.[95] Why, for example, should UCTA black-list terms which exclude or restrict liability for negligence where negligence leads to death or personal injury, but not where negligence does not have such consequences? Likewise, why should UCTA black-list terms in consumer sales contracts (but not in commercial sales contracts) which exclude or restrict the liability of the dealer with regard to the fitness or quality of the goods? Possibly, one

---

[94]   Cf Patrick Atiyah, 'Freedom of Contract and the New Right' in *Essays in Contract* (Oxford, Clarendon Press, 1986) esp at pp 362–3. See, too, the reasoning of Judge Skelly Wright in *Williams v Walker-Thomas Furniture Co* (OC Cir 1965) 350 F 2d 445, one of the leading cases on the unconscionability section of the UCC.

[95]   Cf Roger Brownsword (ed) *Law and the Public Interest* ARSP Beiheft 55 (Stuttgart, Franz Steiner, 1993).

might argue that such provisions are again indirect measures to preserve freedom of contract – that is to say, such measures presuppose that it is implausible that contractors would freely agree to such exclusions or restrictions of liability. On the other hand, one might wish to argue that contractors' freedom is legitimately restricted in this way, just as one might argue that the law of contracts should not enforce agreements for the sale of human organs, or agreements of enslavement, and the like.[96] This raises the key issue of the limits of freedom of contract to which we will return briefly in Chapter 10.

---

[96] But cf eg Michael J. Trebilcock, *The Limits of Freedom of Contract* (Cambridge, Mass, Harvard University Press, 1993) ch 2; and Richard Posner 'Utilitarianism, Economics, and Legal Theory' (1979) 8 Journal of Legal Studies 103, 138–9 (for discussion of a free market in babies and body parts).

Part III

Co-operation and rationality in contract

Chapter 9

Co-operation in contract

Introduction

Our consideration of a number of key doctrinal issues has brought to light a variety of widely acknowledged deficiencies in the classical law – in particular, deficiencies arising from an inflexible exchange model of agreement, and a failure to ensure that the doctrines of freedom of contract and sanctity of contract do not result in unconscionable dealing in the mass consumer market. However, our discussion of the right to withdraw (in Chapter 6) and good faith (in Chapter 7) suggests that there is a deeper problem with the classical law. Essentially, this problem is that the classical law is predicated on a model of competitive (self-interested) dealing when it would be more rational for the law to base itself on a model of co-operation in contract. In this chapter, we distance ourselves somewhat from the particulars of legal doctrine in order to sharpen our understanding of the concept of 'co-operative dealing'.

By taking a harder look at the concept of co-operation, this chapter is not designed to defend the classical model (in the way in which it is usually expounded), but to clarify how the phenomena that we associate with 'co-operative contracting' might stand opposed to the classical model and to identify how they might then relate to the articulation of a rational law of contract. In general terms, what will be highlighted is that there are some serious uncertainties surrounding the concept of co-operation, and that the resolution of these uncertainties is important for various lines of inquiry – particularly for modern attempts to theorise contractual doctrine and the practice of contracting, but equally so for attempts to formulate statements about the rationality of contractors' actions as well as about the rationality of the law itself.

After outlining several of the strands in the co-operative critique of the classical model (in section 1), a number of general questions are raised concerning the concept of co-operation in contract (in section 2) – questions about the criterion of co-operative behaviour, the scope of co-operation, the basis for co-operation, and so on. Such questions defy ready answers. In particular, even if it is agreed that the essence of co-operative dealing lies in the subordination of self-interest to a contractual community of interest, it remains unclear what precisely the co-operative ideal requires of contractors. In short, how are we to determine whether or not particular conduct is compatible with the co-operative ideal? Two responses to this question are outlined (in section 3). One response (a procedural strategy) is to remit specific issues of this kind to the relevant body of commercial opinion, allowing the commercial community to set its own standards of co-operation. Such a response is analogous to one of the ways in which one might operationalise a requirement of good faith in contract.[1] An alternative response (a substantive strategy) is to develop a general theory of a community of interests by analysing the conditions that the institution of contract must possess if it is to be functional as a framework for exchange. One might elaborate this idea in more than one way,[2] but the particular approach outlined here draws on the method employed by Alan Gewirth[3] whose moral theory we have already encountered in Chapter 7. We then sketch (in section 4) a framework for rational law, in the light of which the respective credentials of the procedural and the substantive strategy are assessed. In favour of the procedural strategy, it can be argued that by leaving the contracting community to set its own standards of co-operation, the law would have a reasonable prospect of being effective. However, if practical rationality ultimately hinges on moral legitimacy, then (parallel to our conclusion in Chapter 7 concerning good

---

[1]   Cf our discussion of 'good faith as an exception' in ch 7.

[2]   Cf eg the strategy adopted in Michael D. Bayles *Principles of Law* (Dordrecht, D. Reidel Publishing Company, 1987).

[3]   See Alan Gewirth *Reason and Morality* (Chicago, Chicago University Press, 1978).

faith as the rule) the substantive strategy must have the better credentials.

1. THE CO-OPERATIVE CRITIQUE OF THE CLASSICAL MODEL

According to the classical model, contract is to be conceived of in terms of discrete exchanges freely made by utility-maximising agents.[4] This model invites a variety of articulations. At a doctrinal level, the classical view is that the law of contract does (and, indeed, should) set a regulatory framework for transactions within which contractors are by and large permitted to deal in a self-interested way, even to the point of taking advantage of the ignorance or vulnerability of the other party in order to drive a hard bargain. Correspondingly, at a practical level, the classical model has it that contractors operate as ruthless utility-maximisers, exploiting every opportunity within the law to advance their own self-interest – in the classical market-place, we find the self-regarding merchants of Venice, not the other-regarding citizens of Belmont.[5] Moreover, at both a doctrinal and a practical level, the classical model pre-supposes discrete rather than relational or long-term dealing.

It is widely thought that the classical model of contract, if not quite dead,[6] is certainly discredited – and, as we have said, one of the central reasons for this view is that the classical model is seen as failing to give due weight to the idea of co-operation, both in its account of contract doctrine and in its assumptions about contracting in practice.[7] Thus, critics of the classical model argue that modern contract doctrine regulates (and, indeed, rightly regulates) against one-sided advantage-taking far more systematically than the classical model allows. Not only have consumer

---

[4] We use the term 'agents' here, not in its technical legal sense, but in the conventional philosophical sense of 'individual actors'.

[5] See Roberto M. Unger, *The Critical Legal Studies Movement* (Cambridge, Mass, Harvard University Press, 1986) 64.

[6] See eg Lord Ackner's robust rehearsal of the adversarial view of contract in *Walford v Miles* [1992] 1 All ER 453, 460-461.

[7] See David Campbell and Donald Harris 'Flexibility in Long-term Contractual Relationships: The Role of Co-operation' (1993) 20 Journal of Law and Society 166.

contractors been singled out for special protection by modern contract doctrine,[8] even in commercial contracting, vulnerable parties can seek protection in doctrines such as economic duress, restraint of trade, and unconscionability. Most significantly, the development in many common law jurisdictions (albeit not in England) of an overriding doctrinal requirement of good faith in the performance and enforcement of contracts signals the law of contract's concern with co-operation between contractors.[9]

Turning from doctrine to practice, the classical model again encounters criticism, the objection being that it presents a distorted picture of the actual behaviour of contracting parties. At its strongest, this criticism has it that the classical model even distorts the nature of contracting in the market economy of the nineteenth century. Thus, according to Ian Macneil:

> 'Although the intellectual concepts of the market exchange economy took – and still have – a stranglehold on Western thinking, it is a mistake of incredible magnitude to think that any economy has ever been a market exchange economy in the sense suggested by formal economic analysis, a mistake regularly made by the intellectual right, left, and middle. Market exchange in the utilitarian model is exchange in discrete transactions in which relations between the parties are seemingly assumed not to exist. *This is as empty a social set in a nineteenth-century market economy or modern twentieth-century economy as it is in primitive economies.* Not only has market exchange always been heavily embedded in social relations, but discrete (relatively) exchange patterns have always occupied only limited sectors of market economies as well. Utilitarian theory, with its focus on discrete exchanges, obscures the fact that production and most aspects of distribution have always been carried on almost entirely in ongoing relationships – family in the case, for example, of cottage industry; relatively long-term employment relations in factory, farm, transportation, and office; ongoing relations among capitalists within the corporate structure; and

---

8   See eg Roger Brownsword 'The Philosophy of Welfarism and its Emergence in the Modern English Law of Contract', in Roger Brownsword, Geraint Howells and Thomas Wilhelmsson (eds) *Welfarism in Contract Law* (Aldershot, Dartmouth Publishing Company, 1994) 21 and Thomas Wilhelmsson 'The Philosophy of Welfarism and its Emergence in the Modern Scandinavian Contract Law', 63.

9   See Hugh Collins, *The Law of Contract* 2nd edn (London, Butterworths, 1993) ch 13.

countless others.'[10]

In a similar vein, but underlining the co-operative implications of this relational insight, Stewart Macaulay says:[11]

'Academic writers [in line with the classical model] often make individualistic assumptions. Their theories rest on worlds of discrete transactions where people respond to calculations of short-term advantage. However, people engaged in business often find that they do not need contract planning and contract law because of relational sanctions. There are effective private governments and social fields, affected but seldom controlled by the formal legal system. Even discrete transactions take place within a setting of continuing relationships and interdependence. The value of these relationships means that all involved must work to satisfy each other. Potential disputes are suppressed, ignored, or compromised in the service of keeping the relationship alive.'

In other words, apart from the familiar socio-legalism that contract law, together with the formal machinery of the civil legal system, is largely marginal to much contracting in practice, Macaulay is emphasising here that for many business people co-operation is the name of the (relational) game.

The embryonic modern co-operative model of contract can derive support from at least three academic constituencies. First, jurists will confirm that much contract doctrine and adjudication in contract disputes is guided, overtly or covertly, by co-operative ideals.[12] Secondly, socio-legal commentators will testify to the body of empirical research revealing a high level of co-operative contracting.[13] And, thirdly, law and economics writers will argue that economic rationality often dictates co-operative conduct and that co-operative default rules for contract law may be welfare-

---

[10]   Ian R. Macneil 'Exchange Revisited: Individual Utility and Social Solidarity' (1986) 96 Ethics 567, 591-2 (emphasis added).

[11]   Stewart Macaulay 'An Empirical View of Contract' (1985) Wisconsin Law Review 465.

[12]   See eg Roger Brownsword 'Two Concepts of Good Faith' (1994) 7 Journal of Contract Law 197.

[13]   See eg Stewart Macaulay, 'Non-Contractual Relations in Business' (1963) 28 American Sociological Review 55; 'Elegant Models, Empirical Patterns, and the Complexities of Contract' (1977) 11 Law and Society Review 507; and 'An Empirical View of Contract' (1985) Wisconsin Law Review 465. Similarly, see Hugh Beale and Tony Dugdale, 'Contracts between Businessmen: Planning and the Use of Contractual Remedies'

maximising.[14] Accordingly, a new co-operative model of contract beckons – a model which has it that contractors
actually do deal on a basis of co-operation and trust, that
contract doctrine recognises and promotes such dealing,
and that both doctrine and practice are rational in so
espousing a co-operative approach. Before we embrace this
model, however, we would do well to pause to clarify the concept of co-operation.

2. SOME KEY QUESTIONS ABOUT THE CONCEPT OF CO-OPERATION

When commentators remark – in opposition to the classical
description of contract – that much modern contracting is
characterised by a spirit of co-operation, there is a temptation to nod along with this proposition. Yet, what precisely
is it that we are assenting to? What exactly do the commentators mean when they talk about 'co-operation'? In
what ways do contractors 'co-operate' with one another? Is
'co-operation' a good or a bad thing? Moreover, when contractors 'co-operate', why do they do so? Do they 'co-operate'
because they think that it is prudential (or expedient) to do
so, or are they guided by moral considerations? If 'co-
operative' contracting (and, concomitantly, a contract law of
'co-operation') is underpinned by a moral theory, what kind
of theory is it?

Reflections of this kind prompt a number of important
questions about the concept of co-operation. In particular:

1. What is the criterion of co-operation in contract? How
    do we distinguish between conduct that instantiates

(1975) 2 British Journal of Law and Society 45. And, for 'antagonistic co-operation' between divergent interest organisations, see Bernd Marin, 'Contracting Without Contracts: Economic Policy Concertation by Autopoietic Regimes Beyond Law' in Gunther Teubner and Alberto Febbrajo (eds) *State, Law, and Economy as Autopoietic Systems* (Milan, Guiffrè,1992) p 295.

[14]   See eg Douglas G. Baird, 'Self-Interest and Cooperation in Long-Term Contracts' (1990) 19 Journal of Legal Studies 583; and Michael J. Trebilcock, *The Limits of Freedom of Contract* (Cambridge, Mass, Harvard University Press, 1993). See, too, the development of rational choice theory in David Gauthier, *Morals by Agreement* (Oxford, Clarendon Press, 1986).

co-operation and that which instantiates non-co-operation?

2. What is the scope of co-operation in contract?
3. Is the basis of co-operation prudential or moral?
4. What kind of moral theory could support co-operation in contract?

In this section, we can consider each of these questions in turn.

(i) **What is the criterion of co-operation in contract?**

The modern idea of co-operation in contract lies somewhere between the classical model of self-regarding utility-max-imisation and sheer altruism. On the one side, co-operation is not simply a matter of performing one's part of the bar-gain, or of making it possible for the other side to perform (or to take the benefit of the contract) where, quite literally, some act of co-operation is required. On the other side, co-operation is not a matter of acceding to any demand made by another contracting party. In other words, co-operation lies between the unreserved pursuit of self-interest and the unreserved subordination of self-interest.

Edward Lorenz,[15] in his account of co-operation between machinery producers and their sub-contractors in Lyons, likens the relationship between the contractors to one of partnership:

> 'Partnership clearly implies something more than what is stated on the order form. It is not merely a question of not buying more than you know you can pay for. It seems rather to involve the following: in exchange for improved performance by the subcontractor on quality and delivery, the client firm will make every effort to guarantee a level of work; furthermore, any adaptations to price, quantity and delivery are to be made in a non-opportunistic way by both sides, with full dis-closure of the relevant information. In particular, this implies that the subcontractor will not be unconditionally dropped if a differential in terms of price or quality emerges with respect to - competitors . . .

[15] See Edward H. Lorenz 'Neither Friends nor Strangers: Informal Networks of Subcontracting in French Industry', in Grahame Thompson, Jennifer Frances, Rosalind Levacic, and Jeremy Mitchell (eds) *Markets, Hierarchies and Networks* (London, Sage Publications, 1991) pp 189–90.

To sum up, partnership entails a long-term commitment and reflects a condition of mutual dependency where both client and subcontractor are in a position to influence the other by their behaviour. Partnership is a set of normative rules, determining what behaviour is permissible and what constitutes a violation of trust. The rules are designed to facilitate exchange in a situation otherwise open to exploitation.'

There are some helpful clues in these remarks. Co-operation signals a certain way of relating to a fellow contractor, much as one would expect in a partnership. There is, so to speak, a joint investment in the contract, a mutual dependency, and a reciprocity in performance. Moreover, Lorenz's remarks chime in with a recurrent theme in the literature of co-operation, namely that opportunistic behaviour[16] is to be eschewed. Contractors who relate to one another in a spirit of co-operation simply do not play the market even though they could maximise their utility (at least in the short run) by doing so. Accordingly, the general idea of co-operation is that contractors exercise some restraint in the pursuit of self-interest and accept their share of responsibility for the success of the contract viewed as a joint venture.

If we try to formulate a criterion of co-operation on the basis of these observations, we find that it is not at all straightforward. We can say that we are seeking out the line between conduct that is, and conduct that is not, compatible with the burdens of responsibility and restraint embedded in co-operative dealing – but this is circular and merely restates the question. Nevertheless, it is clear that the concept of co-operation does imply responsibility and restraint, and that it places limits on the prioritisation of self-interest in a way that the classical model does not. Indeed, whereas the classical model sees contract law as a framework for occasional encounters between two parties, each of whom is seeking to maximise its own interests,[17] it is of the essence of the co-operative model that there is, so to speak, a community of interest between contracting parties. This community of interest does not write self-interest

---

[16] As Lorenz puts it (at p 186): 'either reneging on the agreement or using the occasion of unanticipated contingencies to try to shift the distribution of joint profits in one's favour.'

[17] See eg Ian R. Macneil, 'The Many Futures of Contract' (1974) 47 *Southern California Law Review* 691.

out of the contract script, but it serves to regulate the prioritisation of self-interest. *Formally, therefore, the criterion of co-operation is whether self-interested action by a contracting party is compatible with the contractual community of interest.* If action is so compatible it instantiates co-operation; if it is not so compatible, it violates the co-operative ideal.

A formal criterion of co-operation, of course, offers less than a complete answer to our puzzle. To determine whether some particular action is compatible with the co-operative ideal, we need to have some substantive input into the notion of a community of interest. Thus far, we have various suggestions – concerning restraint and responsibility – but we have a long way to go before we have a clear criterion of co-operation and an inventory of its requirements. At this stage, however, we can take the matter no further.

(ii) **What is the scope of co-operation in contract?**

The doctrine of good faith is commonly seen as the most direct way of importing into contract law the idea of co-operation. Indeed, good faith is often equated with an implied term of co-operation.[18] Although good faith provisions, such as s 1-203 of the Uniform Commercial Code, tend to demand good faith in the performance and enforcement of contracts, such provisions are often extended to cover the negotiating stage of a contract.[19] In principle, therefore, the scope of co-operative contracting might run right through the contractual process, from negotiation to termination. Accordingly, an important question to be resolved is how wide a scope the co-operative ideal has.

The co-operative model, as we have seen, likens contract to a partnership, with the parties locked into a relationship for which they each have responsibilities – as contracting

---

[18] See E. Allan Farnsworth, 'Good Faith Performance and Commercial Reasonableness Under the Uniform Commercial Code' (1962-63) 30 University of Chicago Law Review 666; and J. F. Burrows, 'Contractual Co-operation and the Implied Term' (1968) 31 Modern Law Review 390.

[19] See eg P. Legrand, 'Pre-Contractual Disclosure and Information: English and French Law Compared' (1986) 6 Oxford Journal of Legal Studies 322.

partners, the parties have a community of interest, a shared stake in their contract. With regard to the scope of co-operation, this model is open to a number of interpretations, three of which we can label the 'contract-specific interpretation', the 'relational interpretation', and the 'institutional interpretation'.

The *contract-specific interpretation* gives co-operation a narrow compass. This interpretation draws a sharp distinction between, on the one hand, the process of negotiation and, on the other hand, dealings between the parties once negotiations have been brought to a successful conclusion. Once the agreement has been struck, the parties are joined by their contract and it is this contractual union that brings the regime of co-operative rights and obligations into play. Accordingly, on the contract-specific interpretation, the paradigm for co-operation is in relation to performance and enforcement of the contract, the co-operative ideal holding that during the period running from formation through to termination of the contract (but only during this period) self-interest is not to be pursued against the contractual community of interest.

The *relational interpretation* broadens the scope of the contract-specific interpretation in one respect. Generally, a sharp line is drawn (as in the contract-specific interpretation) between negotiation itself and post-negotiation dealings. However, where the parties involved are in a course of regular dealings with one another, this line is to be relaxed and the co-operative ideal is to be regarded as setting the framework for *all* dealings associated with contracting between these particular parties (ie both pre- and post-formation).

The *institutional interpretation* gives co-operation the broadest scope. On this interpretation, the co-operative ideal is not triggered by a specific contractual agreement (as in the contract-specific interpretation), nor is it tied to an ongoing relationship between parties (as in the relational interpretation). Rather, the institutional interpretation treats the co-operative ideal as regulative of *all dealings associated with the contractual process*. There is, therefore, no line to be drawn between negotiation and post-negotiation dealings; and, to this extent, the institutional interpretation is in line with the civilian view that: 'Once parties enter into negotiations for a contract . . . a relationship of trust and confidence comes into existence, irrespective of whether they succeed or fail.'[20] Of course, this leaves unsettled the question of when precisely 'parties enter into negotiations for a contract', but the present interpretation adopts the robust position that it is simply in the nature of the institution of contract that parties should co-operate.

The choice between the contract-specific, relational, and institutional interpretations is just one level of uncertainty concerning the concept of co-operation. Suppose, however, that this particular uncertainty were to be resolved. Suppose, for example, that the institutional interpretation were to be adopted, so that the right to the pursuit of self-interest was to be balanced against, and limited by, the contractual community of interest at all stages of the contracting process. It would then be of central importance to specify the particular requirements of the contractual community of interest. So far as negotiation is concerned, we might speculate that parties should not string along one another, take advantage of another's ignorance, apply undue pressure, simply have regard to their own interests, and the like. Indeed, as Sheppard J put it in the Australian case of *Sabemo Pty Ltd v North Sydney Municipal Council*:[21]

> '[W]here two parties proceed upon the joint assumption that a contract will be entered into between them, and one does work beneficial for the project, and thus in the interests of the two parties, which work he would not be expected, in other circumstances, to do gratuitously, he will be entitled to compensation or restitution, if the other party unilaterally decides to abandon the project, *not for any reason associated with bona fide disagreement concerning the terms of the contract to be entered into, but for reasons which, however valid, pertain only to his own position and do not relate at all to that of the other party.*'

And, with regard to performance, we might speculate that the co-operative ideal prescribes against slacking or shirking, opportunistic manipulation of requirements, obstruction or lack of diligence, and so on.[22] However, the concept of co-operation is destined to remain vague until we

---

20   Friedrich Kessler and Edith Fine 'Culpa in Contrahendo, Bargaining in Good Faith and Freedom of Contract: A Comparative Study' (1964) 77 Harvard Law Review 401, 404. Cf the thinking of the Dutch Supreme Court in *Plas v Valberg* Hoge Raad 18 June (1982), Nederlandse Jurisprudentie 1983, 723 (note CJH Brunner).

21   [1977] 2 NSWLR 880, 902-903, emphasis added.

22   Cf Robert S. Summers, '"Good Faith" in General Contract Law and the Sales Provisions of the Uniform Commercial Code' (1968) 54 Virginia Law Review 195, 220–52.

have developed a non-speculative strategy for filling out its substantive requirements.

(iii) Is the basis of co-operation prudential or moral?

Contractual conduct that is apparently compatible with the co-operative ideal might be accompanied by a variety of mental states, some more reflective than others. Where a contractor reasons that co-operative conduct is something that it 'ought to do' in the circumstances, this 'ought' might be guided by more than one kind of consideration.[23] Whereas some contractors might reason that co-operation will advance their own interests, whether in the short, medium, or long term, whether in relation to a specific fellow contractor or in relation to a broader group of contractors, others might reason that co-operation is morally required.

A change of context, from contract to cycling, might help to clarify the question to be posed here. Suppose that on a particular stage in the Tour de France a group of six cyclists has broken away from the main *peloton*. If the breakaway group can maintain its momentum, there is a good chance that it will not be caught by the *peloton* and that one of the riders in the group will win the stage. To maintain the momentum each of the six riders takes it in turn to lead the group. Now, the conduct of the six breakaway riders, taken at face value, is a clear case of co-operation in what is generally a competitive and wholly self-interested situation. But why do the riders co-operate in this way? One possibility is that they do this purely as a matter of self-interest – they each know that, without taking their turn at the front of the group, they cannot hope to keep clear of the *peloton* and have any chance of winning the stage. Another possibility is that they do this because they think that it would be unfair to accept a tow from the other riders without taking one's turn at the front – in fact, this would be a quite literal example of free-riding. So long as each of the riders takes his turn, the basis on which the 'co-operation' takes place is of little

---

[23]   Peter Vincent-Jones, 'Contract and Business Transactions: A Socio-Legal Analysis' (1989) 16 Journal of Law and Society 166; and 'The Limits of Contractual Order in Public Sector Transacting' (1994) 14 Legal Studies 364.

practical import. There is, however, a theoretical issue here: namely, whether the concept of co-operation should distinguish between the behaviour of the riders where they are motivated by self-interest as opposed to the situation where they take their turn because they believe that this is (morally) the right thing to do.[24]

After this brief detour, we can return to contract. Recall the situation in *Williams v Roffey Bros and Nicholls (Contractors) Ltd*,[25] where the main contractor agreed to pay additional sums to the carpenter sub-contractor who was in financial difficulty. Suppose that we take this at face value and treat the main contractor's promise to pay these additional sums as an act of co-operation. Now, in principle, the main contractor, in reflecting on whether to promise the additional sums, could have reasoned:

> (a) that, if the sub-contractor dropped out of the contract, the costs incurred in replacing him would be greater than if the additional sums were paid; so, in cost/benefit terms promising the additional money looked the better bet; or
> (b) that main contractors have a responsibility towards their sub-contractors, who are part of the same team engaged upon a common project, that risks associated with the project have to be shared, and that where the sub-contractor runs into financial difficulty he has a right to look for support from the main contractor; so, irrespective of cost/benefit calculations, there is an obligation to offer the sub-contractor financial assistance.

The challenge here is not to identify the more plausible account, nor is it to relate the Court of Appeal's 'practical benefit' approach to one of these accounts. Rather, the

---

[24] Cf Ian Macneil, op cit n 10 above, at p 586: 'Thus in the household we find intensely specialised exchange, generating a high exchange-surplus, but taking place in the form of generalised reciprocity, the gift route to solidarity. We may speculate about why this occurs – efficiency, a drive towards altruism, et cetera – but the fact of its occurrence in the prototypical household seems beyond dispute.' The dual thrust of the conceptual discussion in the text is: (i) that the essence of co-operation lies in the reasons for engaging in 'generalised reciprocity'; and (ii) that, unless the reciprocal conduct is backed by the right kind of reason, it is not truly an instance of co-operation. To this extent, speculation about why reciprocal conduct occurs is not exactly an optional matter, and to assume 'the fact of its occurrence' is to beg the fundamental conceptual question.

[25] [1990] 1 All ER 512. See John N. Adams and Roger Brownsword 'Contract, Consideration and the Critical Path' (1990) 53 Modern Law Review 536.

question – as in the cycling example – is whether the main contractor's promise should be characterised as an act of 'co-operation' irrespective of whether it is underpinned by the reasoning in (a) or in (b). In other words, the question is whether the concept of co-operation is co-extensive with such conduct as is compatible with the contractual community of interest *simpliciter*, or whether the essence of co-operation is that the contractual community of interest is regarded as an overriding moral consideration – that is, conduct is not truly co-operative unless it is taken for the sake of the contractual community of interest, irrespective of self-interest (or, more pointedly, even where co-operation is contrary to one's own interests).

To formulate the issue a little more precisely, the above reflections prompt two questions. First, does co-operation presuppose that compliance with the contractual community of interest is treated as a matter of exclusionary reason[26] and, thus, as taking priority over wants, preferences, inclinations and at least short-term self-interest? Secondly, if co-operative conduct implicates exclusionary reason, does it matter whether that reason represents a form of enlightened self-interest or is moral in nature?

Generally, this part of the discussion is more concerned with identifying questions rather than offering answers. However, in relation to these two questions, an answer will be proposed. *The answer is that the concept of co-operation can only serve as a significant theoretical construct if it breaks free from the model of action-guided-by-self-interest which is central to the classical view of contract.* In other words, if a co-operative model is to be employed to detect significant movements in contract law and contracting practice, it must mark something more than the continuing influence of self-interest. It follows that the concept of co-operation certainly implies exclusionary reason. In principle, however, such reason might remain rooted in self-interest (as enlightened longer-term calculations of self-interest generate a prudential kind of exclusionary reason) or it might be moral in nature. Now, it clearly will not do to employ the concept of co-operation wherever one detects a movement in contractual dealing from the pursuit

---

[26]   Cf Joseph Raz *Practical Reason and Norms* (London, Hutchinson, 1975).

of short-term self-interest to longer-term calculations of self-interest. At minimum, we are looking for the subordination of short-term interest to longer-term interest as a matter of exclusionary reason – we are looking, in other words, for the *systematic* prioritisation of longer-term self-interest. Although it is tempting to treat such enlightened self-interest as a new contracting paradigm, it fails to make a decisive break with the classical model. To make such a break, it is suggested, we must regard co-operation as a moral phenomenon, with respect for the community of contractual interest (to which self-interest is to be subordinated) being treated not simply as exclusionary reason but as categorically binding.[27] It follows that apparently 'co-operative' conduct, guided by self-interest, not only is not to be identified with conduct which treats the contractual community of interest as a moral requirement, but that unlike the latter it is not actually a case of co-operation at all.

(iv) What kind of moral theory could support co-operation in contract?

If co-operative reason is moral reason, it remains to specify the particular substantive morality that constitutes such reason. In principle, what kind of morality might support a theory of co-operation in contract and specify the particulars of the contractual community of interest?

One obvious candidate is a utilitarian moral theory. However, utilitarianism can be formulated in many ways, so that the application of utilitarian theories of co-operation might well vary from one formulation to another. For example, if one were to work with a rigid form of rule-utilitarianism, co-operative requirements would be set in a longer time-frame than would be the case with an act-utilitarian theory of co-operation. Thus, whereas a

---

[27] Specifying the *formal* characteristics of a moral position (of moral reason) is not at all straightforward: see Deryck Beyleveld and Roger Brownsword, *Law as a Moral Judgment* (reprinted, Sheffield, Sheffield Academic Press, 1994) 23-26. For present purposes, the critical point is that moral reason must be specified in such a way that calculations of self-interest in no sense underpin the prescriptive force of morality. Moral reason must therefore be characterised as categorical – and, in no sense, instrumental – reason.

model of co-operation driven by rule-utilitarianism might prescribe against short-term opportunism and exploitation, an act-utilitarian model would weigh only the utilities and disutilities of the particular situation.[28] Another obvious candidate to support a model of co-operation is a moral theory in the Kantian tradition. Again, though, theories of individual rights and duties can vary enormously, even while claiming a common pedigree in the Kantian categorical imperative.[29]

The problem that we have here, therefore, is that there are too many moral theories competing to specify the requirements of the co-operative ideal. Moreover, it is not just that we are spoilt for choice, the problem is that these moral theories will not specify the requirements of co-operation in quite the same terms. At this stage, we need not offer any further conjectures about the moral basis for a model of co-operative contracting. An answer will be offered in due course. For the moment, it suffices to say that, if (as has been proposed) the model of co-operative contracting rests on a moral foundation, the nature of that foundation remains to be specified.

(v) Synthesis

How far do these opening questions take us in clarifying the concept of co-operation? Essentially, we have a *formal* model of co-operation in the sense that it is represented by a contractual community of interest to which self-interest must to that extent be subordinated; it has also been contended that the contractual community of interest must be viewed, not in terms of a guideline for enlightened self-interest, but as an overriding *moral* requirement. What we do not have is a specification of the scope and requirements of the co-operative model; and, clearly, we cannot make much

---

[28]   Generally, see the discussion in Richard A. Wasserstrom, *The Judicial Decision* (Stanford, Stanford University Press, 1961); and cf the controversy surrounding the so-called 'efficient breach' (see eg Donald Harris and Denis Tallon (eds), *Contract Law Today* (Oxford, Clarendon Press, 1989)).

[29]   Cf eg Ronald Dworkin, *Taking Rights Seriously* (London, Duckworth,1978); Robert Nozick, *Anarchy, State, and Utopia* (Oxford, Basil Blackwell, 1974); John Rawls, *A Theory of Justice* (London, Oxford University Press,1972).

progress with these unresolved questions until we have
sorted out the particular moral foundation on which the co-
operative model is to rest.

3. OPERATIONALISING THE CO-OPERATIVE IDEAL

The concept of co-operation, it has been suggested, sets
limits on the pursuit of self-interest by contractors; it does
this by invoking the idea of an overriding contractual community of interest; and this, in turn, presupposes that
co-operation ultimately rests on a moral foundation. Even
conceding this, there still remains the question of what precisely the contractual community of interest provides. In
this part of the discussion, two strategies will be outlined,
the first procedural, the second substantive, each offering a
way of trying to identify more precisely the particular
requirements of co-operative contracting. Because of its
relative familiarity, we can deal quite briefly with the first of
these strategies.

(i) The community standards approach

To see what would be involved in the first approach, we can
consider the analogous approach in the context of the doctrinal requirement of good faith, which as has already been
said is the most direct doctrinal device for incorporating
notions of co-operation in contract law.[30] Although the
jurisprudence of good faith is relatively under-developed in
England,[31] there is a wealth of literature elsewhere in the
common law (and, of course, in the civilian) world, particularly in the United States.

---

[30] See also Steven Fennell and Simon Ball's sketch of a 'business stan-
dards model' in the context of economic duress, in 'Welfarism and the
Renegotiation of Contracts' in Roger Brownsword, Geraint Howells and
Thomas Wilhelmsson (eds) *Welfarism in Contract Law* (Aldershot,
Dartmouth, 1994) 212, 217–22.

[31] Although see Raphael Powell, 'Good Faith in Contracts' (1956) 9
Current Legal Problems 16; J. F. O'Connor *Good Faith in English Law*
(Aldershot, Dartmouth Publishing Company, 1991); and Roy Goode
'The Concept of 'Good Faith' in English Law', Centro di Studi e
Richerche di Diritto Comparato e Straniere, Saggi, Conferenze E
Seminari 2, Rome, 1992.

Comment (a) to s 205 of the *Restatement (Second) of Contracts* states that '[good faith] excludes a variety of types of conduct characterized as involving "bad faith" because they violate community standards of decency, fairness or reasonableness'. This chimes in with Robert Summers' seminal analysis of the concept of good faith as an 'excluder'.[32] According to Summers, as we saw in Chapter 7, the concept of good faith has no independent meaning or unity; the concept of good faith is simply a reflection of so many unconnected instances of bad faith. How, then, would one decide whether a particular act was a case of bad faith? Quite simply, one would judge the matter against the standards of the relevant commercial community, for it would be the standards of this community that would determine whether there had been a violation of 'decency, fairness or reasonableness'. Initially, appeals to community standards might be somewhat unpredictable in their outcome; and this strategy could run into difficulties where contractors in a particular sector did not share precisely the same standards. However, Summers' trawl of the American case-law (as a reflection of prevailing community standards) encourages the belief that contracting communities would often have sufficiently high levels of consensus to make the approach viable.[33]

Summers' discussion indicates how the regime of good faith could serve as a model for the operationalisation of the co-operative idea of a community of contractual interest. Indeed, it might be thought that these are precisely the same ideas. However, this is not the only way of operationalising the co-operative ideal and we must now consider a second possible strategy.

(ii) A theory of a contractual community of interest

Summers' analysis of good faith has had its critics, most notably Steven Burton.[34] After a number of clarifications and revisions of position, it is not entirely clear how

---

[32] See Robert S. Summers '"Good Faith" in General Contract Law and the Sales Provisions of the Uniform Commercial Code' (1968) 54 Virginia Law Review 195.

[33] Ibid, at pp 220–52.

[34] See Steven J. Burton 'Breach of Contract and the Common Law Duty to Perform in Good Faith' (1980–81) 94 Harvard Law Review 369.

much distance there actually is between Summers and his critics.[35] However, the gist of the critics' position is that Summers undersells the concept of good faith and that it is possible to tease out a more principled and coherent view of good faith. Similarly, one might think that we do scant justice to the concept of co-operation if we refer the question of the scope and requirements of the contractual community of interest to happenstance commercial opinion. In different times and in different places, commercial standards might reflect stronger or weaker views of co-operative entitlements and responsibilities. The challenge is to articulate a strategy which offers a plausible alternative to the community standards approach.

As we have said already, there is no shortage of (independent) moral theories upon which we might try to found a theory of co-operation in contract and, with that, a more precise specification of the contractual community of interest. Most moral theories, however, suffer from a double vulnerability. First, they are often intuitively implausible – utilitarian theories, for example, are notoriously implausible in a number of respects (particularly to the extent that they fail to recognise individual human rights) but, equally, theories in the Kantian tradition are often accused of taking individual rights and duties too seriously (for example, by insisting upon hugely expensive or inconvenient acts).[36] Secondly, as we explained in Chapter 7, even if a particular moral theory convinces moralists, moral theories tend to remain vulnerable to the scepticism of amoralists. It follows that, whilst the vast corpus of moral theory offers a surplus of answers, compelling 'right answers' are in short supply. This being so, the community standards approach looks neither better nor worse, neither more nor less valid, than many independent moral theories.

Now, in Chapter 7, we suggested that, amongst modern moral theories, Alan Gewirth's theory stands out. What particularly distinguishes Gewirth's theory is not that it follows many other modern moral theories in rejecting

---

[35] See E. Allan Farnsworth 'The Concept of Good Faith in American Law', Centro di Studi e Richerche di Diritto Comparato e Straniere, Saggi, Conferenze E Seminari 3, Rome, 1993.
[36] See eg the critique in Richard Posner 'Utilitarianism, Economics, and Legal Theory' (1979) 8 Journal of Legal Studies 103.

utilitarianism, but that it purports to present a compelling demonstration (to both moralist and amoralist sceptics) of why agents[37] must regard themselves as having rights to their freedom and well-being. In the next chapter, we will consider how the law of contract would look if we were to design it with a view to ensuring that contractors' rights to freedom and well-being were respected. However, for present purposes, it is not so much the substantive outcome of Gewirth's theory that is of interest, as the so-called 'dialectical' method[38] that Gewirth employs to derive his substantive conclusion (ie that agents have rights to their freedom and well-being and, concomitantly, a duty to respect the freedom and well-being of others). For, the thought is that Gewirth's dialectical strategy, applied not to agency at large, but specifically to agents who need to exchange in order to fulfil their purposes, might be a fruitful way of developing a view of the contractual community of interest.

Before outlining the argument, it must be remembered that the strategy is dialectical. No claims are being made about moral requirements *tout court* (no claims are being made 'assertorically', as Gewirth puts it). At no stage, is it being asserted that such and such is morally required *simpliciter*. What the argument seeks to show is that a party who views itself as an agent, as one capable of free and purposive action, cannot without self-contradiction deny that its agency commits it to respecting the freedom and well-being of other agents.[39] In the argument below, the validity of Gewirth's argument is assumed and the same strategy is employed to tease out the co-operative essence (for exchanging agents) of contracting.The principal steps of the argument are as follows:

1.   Imagine some party, X, who views itself (or him- or her-

---

37   Here, it should be remembered that the term 'agent' is not being used in its technical legal sense. Rather, it is being used to denote an individual actor (but with the particular defining characteristics of voluntariness and purposivity as given by Gewirth); see further ch 10, section 4.

38   See Alan Gewirth *Reason and Morality* (Chicago, Chicago University Press, 1978).

39   Whilst it may seem a bit strange to refer throughout to an agent in terms of 'it', rather than he or she, we do this simply to signal that we are placing no restrictions on who might qualify as an agent.

self)[40] as an agent – that is, as a party capable of free and purposive action. X necessarily takes a favourable view of the particular purposes (ends) that it freely chooses to pursue.

2. X necessarily must take a favourable view, too, of having the means necessary to accomplish its freely chosen ends.

3. Viewing things strictly as an agent (as defined in (1)), X necessarily must take a favourable view of the conditions that must be possessed if *any* freely chosen ends are to be successfully pursued. In Gewirth's argument, the contention is that X must take a favourable view of having freedom and basic well-being, these being identified as the generic conditions of agency – that is, conditions necessarily implicated in the successful pursuit of *any* end.

4. Suppose that X needs to exchange in order to pursue some of its freely chosen ends, then in relation to that range of ends that cannot be achieved without making an exchange, X must take a favourable view not only of the generic conditions of agency but also of the generic conditions of exchange.

5. Assuming that X has its freedom and basic well-being (the generic conditions of agency), the generic conditions of exchange overlay these generic conditions of agency. It is suggested that the generic conditions of exchange are: (a) that X has the information to make an exchange that promotes X's desired end (the *raison d'être* for the exchange); and (b) that the exchange is performed as agreed (that promises are kept).

6. Given (4), because X needs to exchange and because X (as a prospective exchanging agent) must take a favourable view of having the generic conditions of exchange, X must take an unfavourable view of non-fulfilment of these conditions.

7. It follows from (6) that X must consider that non-fulfilment of the generic conditions of exchange by a fellow exchanging agent is impermissible, and that it (X) therefore has a right to the generic conditions of exchange.

8. Because, in X's dialectical reasoning, X's claim to having a right to the generic conditions of exchange

---

[40] But see n 39 above.

rests sufficiently on the fact that X is an agent who needs to exchange, X must consider that being an exchanging agent is sufficient reason for having a right to the generic conditions of exchange.

9.   In X's dialectical reasoning, X must now recognise that all agents who need to exchange must claim the right to the generic conditions of exchange (thus, mimicking X).

10.   More importantly, given (8), X must consider that all agents who need to exchange have a right to the claimed generic conditions of exchange. In other words, given (8), X must consider that it, X, is under a duty to respect the generic conditions of exchange to which other agents necessarily (from X's dialectical viewpoint) have a right.

This argument, just like Gewirth's principal argument, proceeds through three main stages.[41] At the first stage, a set of generic *needs* (the generic conditions of agency/exchange) is identified; at the second stage, *rights* to the generic conditions are claimed; at the third stage, a *duty* to respect the generic conditions with regard to other agents is accepted. The progression in the argument outlined above is thus: from the generic conditions of exchange (at (5)), the argument moves to rights (at (7)), and to duties (at (10)). The viability of these key moves – from needs to rights, and then from rights to duties – and, with it, the validity of Gewirth's alleged derivation of a supreme moral principle by such a dialectical method has proved highly controversial in philosophical circles.[42] Of course, this is not the place to attempt to rehearse the arguments for and against the main argument. Suffice it to say that the present argument to rights and duties in relation to the generic conditions of exchange certainly does nothing to improve on Gewirth's principal argument; and, indeed, by introducing the idea of the generic conditions of exchange (and specifying those conditions in a particular way), it adds a further dimension to an already complex debate. Accordingly, we can be confident

[41]   For elaboration of the steps in the main argument, see ch 10.

[42]   For the views of a range of critics, see Edward Regis Jr *Gewirth's Ethical Rationalism* (Chicago, Chicago University Press, 1984); and for a comprehensive defence, see Deryck Beyleveld *The Dialectical Necessity of Morality: An Analysis and Defense of Alan Gewirth's Argument to the PGC* (Chicago, Chicago University Press, 1991).

that if Gewirth's argument is invalid, the present argument will suffer from a similar defect; and, even if Gewirth's argument is valid, we cannot be entirely confident that the present argument is sound.

Suppose, though, we were to assume the validity of the above argument. What would be the implications? Would the argument assist in elaborating the scope and requirements of the contractual community of interest? On the face of it, the argument would assist in a number of respects.

First, it would seem to tie the contractual community of interest to the institution of contract itself. And, to this extent, it would invite us to adopt the institutional interpretation of co-operation – thereby giving the co-operative ideal scope to range across the entire contracting process.

Secondly, the informational aspect of the generic conditions would militate not only against fraud and misrepresentation, but also against non-disclosure of material facts (that is, facts which one's fellow-contracting agent would regard as relevant to the making of the exchange). It would, accordingly, be incompatible with the co-operative ideal for a seller to omit to mention to a purchaser some fact that would reveal the exchange to be inappropriate for the purchaser's intended purpose (cf Lord Atkin's examples of permissible non-disclosure in *Bell v Lever Brothers Ltd*).[43] Equally, it would be incompatible with the co-operative ideal for a purchaser to fail to disclose material facts to the seller (cf Cockburn CJ's examples of permissible non-disclosure in *Smith v Hughes*).[44] Contrary to the classical view, the co-operative law of contract would be very much concerned with what, as Cockburn CJ famously put it, 'a man of scrupulous morality or nice honour would do under such circumstances'.[45]

Thirdly, the generic requirement that the exchange be performed as agreed, that promises be kept, would shed light on co-operative requirements in a variety of situations where opportunism or exploitation tempts. This would cover not only blatant exploitation of the kind practised where there is an asymmetrical vulnerability between the parties (as where a contractor demands more to perform as

---

[43] [1932] AC 161, 224.
[44] (1871) LR 6 QB 597, 603-604.
[45] Ibid.

agreed,[46] or where a debtor exploits a creditor's urgent need for settlement),[47] but also cases where requirements are manipulated,[48] or termination options exercised,[49] for market advantage.

No doubt a comprehensive specification of the contractual community of interest would take some elaborating; and, it must be conceded, there is more than a little unfinished business here. However, the fundamental idea of the generic conditions of exchange should serve to keep the analysis on the right track as this substantive approach is addressed to ever more concrete questions. At any rate, enough has been said about this strategy to justify treating it as a plausible alternative to the community standards approach.

4. CONTRACT, CO-OPERATION, AND RATIONALITY

Co-operative contracting, the modern commentary holds, is rational contracting. It follows that rational contractors should aspire to co-operative behaviour; and that a rational law of contract should endeavour to promote such conduct. Given the uncertainty surrounding the concept of co-operation, however, this is easier said than done.

The key question carried forward from the previous discussion is how we might operationalise the idea of the co-operative ideal. Should we adopt a procedural strategy, such as the community standards approach, or should we try to unpack a substantive theory of the contractual community of interest? In this section, having briefly sketched the requirements of a rational law of contract and summarised some socio-legal truisms that bear on the matter of instrumental rationality, we can tackle this difficult question.

---

[46] See eg *Atlas Express Ltd v Kafco (Importers and Distributors) Ltd* [1989] QB 833.

[47] See eg *Headley v Hackley* 45 Mich 569, 8 NW 511 (1991); *D and C Builders Ltd v Rees* [1966] 2 QB 617.

[48] See eg *Orange and Rockland Utilities Inc v Amerade Hess Corpn* 59 AD 2d 110, 397 NYS 2d 814 (1977).

[49] See eg *Arcos v Ronaasen* [1933] AC 470.

(i) A rational law of contract

If legal doctrine and its administration is to be fully rational, it must satisfy three criteria. It must be formally rational, instrumentally rational (in both a generic and a specific sense), and morally rational. A detailed discussion of the concept of rationality can be postponed until Chapter 10. For present purposes, a thumb-nail sketch will suffice.

Formal rationality requires that legal doctrine must not be contradictory. For example, the law of contract would be formally irrational if, on the one hand, it provided that penalty clauses were void and yet, on the other hand, it declared that penalty clauses were enforceable. Such explicit contradictions are, of course, exceptional. Equally important for formal rationality, however, are those less obvious contradictions screened from view by traditional compartments and categories. For example, if penalty clauses are condemned on the ground that they unjustly enrich the innocent party, is it not then contradictory to enforce cognate provisions for over-compensation even though they do not fit the particular description of a penalty clause (for which a breach has to be predicated)? Again, on a broader canvas, Tony Bradney[50] has recently suggested that the concept of duress is interpreted in different ways in contract, criminal, and family law. To the extent that these different interpretations involve contradiction, the law is irrational, and formal rationality cannot be rescued by the simple expedient of setting up traditional legal divisions and categories as barriers to doctrinal comparison.

Instrumental rationality operates at two levels, *generic* and *specific*. At a *generic* level, instrumental rationality requires law to be capable of guiding action. That is to say, whatever the particular purpose of law, if there is to be any prospect of it having a purchase on conduct, it must conform to a number of generic instrumental requirements. Drawing on Lon Fuller's seminal analysis of the 'inner morality of law',[51] we can say that legal rules should be general, promulgated, prospective, clear, non-contradictory,

---

[50] Tony Bradney 'Duress, Family Law and the Coherent Legal System' (1994) 57 Modern Law Review 963.

[51] Lon L. Fuller *The Morality of Law* (New Haven, Yale University Press, 1969).

and relatively constant; they should not require the impossible; and, crucially, there should be a congruence between the law as officially declared and the law as administered.

At a *specific* level, instrumental rationality concerns the appropriateness of particular legal interventions in given situations. If we assume that particular interventions in contract (in the field of transactions) are backed by particular facilitative and protective purposes, then specific instrumental rationality focuses upon the efficacy of the steps taken to secure those purposes.There is, of course, a degree of overlap between formal rationality and instrumental rationality (because contradictory law cannot serve as a guide to action), and generic and specific instrumental rationality must work together as a set of necessary and sufficient conditions for effective law.

Finally, substantive moral rationality requires legal doctrine to be justifiable when set against rationally defensible moral criteria. But, how are we to determine whether law is morally legitimate? In the final analysis, can any moral criteria be upheld as rationally defensible (in the sense that it would be irrational to espouse any other criteria)? As indicated already, Alan Gewirth's approach to moral theory offers a strategy for identifying the contractual community of interest. More generally, however, Gewirth's theory offers a compelling response to all shades of moral scepticism.[52] Of course, the sceptical conviction that any attempt to ground an objective morality must fail will be fortified precisely by the strength of the claims made on behalf of Gewirth's argument – for, from a sceptical perspective, any argument that purports to be dialectically *necessary*, its implications inescapable by agents no matter what their initial practical predilection (amoralist or moralist, adeonticist or deonticist, and so on) must be wrong.[53] If, however,

---

[52]   See eg Deryck Beyleveld *The Dialectical Necessity of Morality: An Analysis and Defense of Alan Gewirth's Argument to the PGC* (Chicago, Chicago University Press, 1991); Deryck Beyleveld and Roger Brownsword, *Law as a Moral Judgment* (reprinted Sheffield, Sheffield Academic Press, 1994); 'The Dialectically Necessary Foundation of Natural Law', in Alan Norrie (ed) *Closure or Critique: New Directions in Legal Theory* (Edinburgh, Edinburgh University Press, 1992); and Roger Brownsword, 'Liberalism and the Law of Contract' in Richard Bellamy (ed) *Liberalism and Recent Legal and Social Philosophy*, ARSP Beiheft 36, Stuttgart, Franz Steiner, 86.

[53]   In fact, in the current context of co-operative contracting, where commentators freely presuppose that it is intelligible to talk about what

one is persuaded that the argument does work (not merely because it seems to work, but because no convincing demonstration of its invalidity has yet been made), then Gewirth's moral theory has to be the cornerstone of our thinking on legal rationality and it must set the terms for the co-operative ideal in contract.

(ii) Effective legal regulation: some truisms

Rational law-making needs to be informed by an appreciation of the conditions for specifically effective regulation. Given the many studies that have examined the impact of particular legal interventions, this is a matter about which we should have some understanding.[54] At the price of some over-simplification, we can identify two clusters of truisms that emerge from this rich seam of research.[55] One cluster concerns the phenomenon of non-compliance with law; the other cluster concerns the choice of a particular regulatory technique.

(a) The phenomenon of non-compliance

If we assume (a) that the laws in question require some act (or omission) by way of compliance, (b) that those who are required to comply know that compliance is required by law, and (c) that those who are required to comply are capable of making a conscious calculation about whether to comply with the law, then two extended law-in-action truisms can be identified. We can call these two truisms, first, the Law of Moral Rejection and, secondly, the Law of Prudential Rejection.

The Law of Moral Rejection. Where a particular legal requirement is morally rejected by those to whom the law is

---

one 'ought' to do (and possibly even what it is 'right' to do), Gewirth's argument finds itself in a relatively hospitable milieu. However, the ultimate test of the argument is not that it works in a dialectically *contingent* fashion, where the milieu happens to be favourable, but that it holds necessarily even in the most unfavourable milieu.

[54] Cf Iredell Jenkins *Social Order and the Limits of Law* (Princeton, Princeton University Press, 1980).

[55] For helpful overviews, see Bob Roshier and Harvey Teff *Law and Society in England* (London, Tavistock, 1980) chs 4 and 6; and Roger Cotterrell *The Sociology of Law: An Introduction* (London, Butterworths, 1984) ch 8.

directed (ie where a particular legal requirement is in conflict with cultural or value-commitments), non-compliance
(conscientious objection, rejection, non-recognition, or
exclusion of law) will occur unless: (a) compliance is judged
to be (morally) required all things considered; or (b) prudential considerations in the particular circumstances
dictate compliance (ie because of the particular incentives
and disincentives attached to the law) and such prudential
considerations are given priority over moral considerations.

For example, suppose that, in the state of confusion surrounding the legality of Sunday trading which prevailed
before the Sunday Trading Act 1994, some large retailers
took the view that the Shops Act 1950 was immoral because
it unfairly interfered with the freedom of traders to sell on
Sundays and of individuals to shop on Sundays if they
wished. The Law of Moral Rejection would predict that these
retailers would now break the law unless: (a) they judged
that compliance was morally required all things considered
(eg in order to set an example of respect for the law); or (b)
they judged that in the particular circumstances[56] it was in
their prudential interests to comply (thus avoiding fines,
and more importantly possible adverse publicity) and they
gave these prudential considerations priority over their
moral rejection of the statute.

The Law of Prudential Rejection. Where a particular
legal requirement is in conflict with the (non-moral)
prudential interests of those to whom the law is specifically
directed, non-compliance will occur unless: (a) overall,
prudential considerations in the particular circumstances
dictate compliance (ie because of the particular incentives
and disincentives attached to compliance or non-compliance with the law); or (b) compliance is judged to be (morally)
required, and moral considerations are given priority over
prudential considerations.

Again, consider the case of Sunday trading. Suppose that
prior to the 1994 Act some large retailers judged that the
Shops Act 1950 was in conflict with their economic (prudential) interests. Then the Law of Prudential Rejection

---

[56]   The thrust of this discussion about the effectiveness of law is that much
depends on the prudential and moral considerations of the relevant
agents. However, agents do not act in a social vacuum and the particular circumstances in which they act will constitute a set of variables
that impinge on their calculations.

would predict that non-compliance would occur unless: (a) retailers judged that, all things considered, compliance was a better prudential bet than non-compliance; or (b) retailers were guided by overriding moral considerations in favour of complying with the law in general (or this particular law).

These truisms suggest that if legal interventions are not seen as legitimate by the particular persons against whom they are directed, and if compliance cuts against the (non-moral) prudential interests of the individuals concerned, then the effectiveness of the law will depend on a particularly skilful mix of persuasion, and incentives and disincentives. Or, to put this another way, legal interventions will be viable only if they are compatible with the features of the particular field within which they are to operate; that is, if they can overcome any relevant resistances[57] within the field. Crucially, where law is not internalised, its effectiveness will depend upon the perceived balance of self-interest; and, where large economic interests are at stake, it takes powerful incentives or disincentives to shift the perceived balance of advantage – a £2,500 fine, for instance, would have been unlikely to have dissuaded, say, B & Q from trading on Sundays when Sunday sales were estimated as worth many millions of pounds to the company.[58]

(b) The choice of particular regulatory technique

A second cluster of law-in-action truisms concerns the impact of particular regulatory strategies. The use of the criminal law, for example, may have a very different impact in a particular field than if the strategy were administrative or civil in character.[59] To depart from contract for a moment, if, say, the elimination of racial discrimination were the particular desired end, it would be important to understand

---

[57] Cf Gunther Teubner 'After Legal Instrumentalism? Strategic Models of Post-Regulatory Law' in Gunther Teubner (ed) *Dilemmas of Law in the Welfare State* (Berlin, Walter de Gruyter, 1986) 299; and 'Regulatory Law: Chronicle of a Death Foretold', (1992) 1 Social and Legal Studies 451.

[58] See Catherine Barnard 'Sunday Trading: A Drama in Five Acts' (1994) 57 Modern Law Review 449.

[59] Cf Robert Bradgate, Cosmo Graham and Geraint Howells 'Regulating Fairness and Promoting Welfarism in Contract: An Institutional Perspective' in Roger Brownsword, Geraint Howells and Thomas Wilhelmsson (eds) *Welfarism in Contract Law*, (Aldershot, Dartmouth Publishing Company) 158.

which of the many legal techniques within the regulatory repertoire would be most effective.[60] We would need to consider, for example, the appropriateness of private law remedial techniques, criminalisation, agency monitoring, contract compliance measures, affirmative action, and so on (as well as various combinations of these measures).[61] Each technique would have its own debits and credits: on the one side, its limitations, costs, and resistance, on the other side, its positive prospects. Unless such calculations are made, the particular intervention may simply make no impact, or, worse, produce unintended, and undesirable, side-effects.

The conventional wisdom about regulatory techniques supports two truisms. We can call the first the Law of Private Enforcement and the second is the closely-related Trubek's Law.

The Law of Private Enforcement.   Where the effectiveness of a particular law depends upon enforcement being initiated by individuals (not acting in an official law enforcement capacity), and where the overall prudential balance dictates non-enforcement rather than enforcement of the law, the law will not be enforced (and will be ineffective) unless prudential considerations are overridden by moral considerations in favour of enforcement.

The significance of this is fairly obvious. Because private law remedial strategies rely on individual initiative, private law will fail to regulate effectively unless the prospective fruits of litigation (prudential and/or moral) outweigh the costs. Accordingly, to entrust enforcement of landlords' obligations to individual tenants,[62] to entrust enforcement of employers' obligations to individual employees, to entrust enforcement of dealers' obligations to individual consumers, and so on, is a strategy that has relatively low prospects of success. This is not to say that the alternatives are certain

[60]   See Laurence Lustgarten 'Racial Inequality and the Limits of Law' (1986) 49 Modern Law Review 68.
[61]   Consideration would also need to be given to whether reflexive or non-reflexive approaches to regulation were more suitable. Generally, see Gunther Teubner and Alberto Febbrajo (eds) *State, Law, and Economy as Autopoietic Systems* (Milan, Guiffrè, 1992).
[62]   Cf Martin Partington 'Landlord and Tenant: The British Experience' in Eugene Kamenka and Alice Erh-Soon Tay (eds) *Law and Social Control* (London, Edward Arnold, 1980) p 166. This, of course, does not apply in those many blocks of flats where the landlord is a company which actually belongs to the tenants.

to be more effective or less problematic. However, any attempt to render contract law more rational must reckon with the limitations of private law techniques.[63]

Trubek's Law. David Trubek[64] has suggested that 'economic actors will employ the litigation process to settle disputes only to the extent that (1) the present value of continuing relationships is low, and (2) the anticipated return from the litigation process is relatively high'.[65] In other words, where there are contractual disputes in the commercial sector, the likelihood of one side suing the other is a function of two variables: the amount of money at issue, and the extent to which the disputants are economically dependent upon one another (how relational the contractors are to one another). The less the money at stake and the more relational the contractors are, the less the likelihood of litigation.[66] Conversely, where a great deal of money is at stake or where contracting is more 'one-shot', the greater the likelihood of litigation – so that, following Trubek, we would assume that these variables would be material to explaining an increase in contractual litigation (for example, a litigation explosion of the kind experienced in the United States in the 1980s).[67]

(c) Synthesis

In the light of these various truisms about legal effectiveness, we might now hazard a more ambitious general

[63] Generally, see Mauro Cappalletti 'Alternative Dispute Resolution Processes Within the Framework of the World-Wide Access-to-Justice Movement' (1993) 56 Modern Law Review 282. For a succinct summary in relation to contractual claims, see Barry Reiter, 'The Control of Contract Power' (1981) 1 Oxford Journal of Legal Studies 347, at 354–5.

[64] David M. Trubek 'Notes on the Comparative Processes of Handling Disputes Between Economic Enterprises' (paper presented at the US-Hungarian Conference on Contract Law and the Problems of Large Scale Economic Enterprise, New York, 1975).

[65] See Stewart Macaulay 'Elegant Models, Empirical Patterns, and the Complexities of Contract' (1977) 11 Law and Society Review 507.

[66] It should be noted, however, that this 'law' does not hold good in the context of shipping and international trade where the same parties are constantly dealing and litigating.

[67] Cf M. Galanter and J. Rogers 'The Transformation of American Business Disputing? Some Preliminary Observations' paper presented at the 1988 Annual Meeting of the Law and Society Association, Colorado, June 1998; and Peter Vincent-Jones, 'Contract Litigation in England and Wales 1975-91: A Transformation in Business Disputing? (1993) Civil Justice Quarterly 337.

statement about all calculating conduct within the domain of law. Quite simply, it is that agents' responses to law (including making use of law) ultimately rest on prudential or moral considerations, and it is this mix of prudential and moral calculation *in the particular circumstances* that holds the key to understanding the conditions that make for the effectiveness and specific instrumental rationality of law.

(iii) Which approach, community standards or the contractual community of interest, is the more rational?

How should contract law seek to operationalise the co-operative ideal? Should it rely on the community standards approach, or should it attempt to legislate substantively for a theory of the contractual community of interest? Which approach is the more rational? The community standards approach has some obvious attractions. Apart from obviating the need to grapple with some complex moral theory,[68] it promises to have a significant regulatory effect – in other words, it promises to score well in terms of instrumental rationality. The reasons for this are twofold. First, because co-operative requirements would be judged by the standards of the commercial community of which the contractors are members, one would expect there to be a high level of knowledge about this normative background as well as an above-average degree of predictability about its application in particular cases. Secondly, because the standards of co-operation would be, in a sense, the contractors' own standards, backed by a strong mix of perceived self-interest and fairness, the legitimacy of these standards should not be an issue. The promise of regulatory effectiveness might, of course, be disappointed. For example, detailed empirical research might disclose that community standards of co-operation are shared only at a very high level of generality as a result of which disagreement soon reveals itself as the questions to be arbitrated become more specific. Or, again, there may be cases where dominant contractors can, with relative impunity, pursue self-

---

[68]   Cf Gunther Teubner 'Substantive and Reflexive Elements in Modern Law' (1983) 17 *Law and Society Review* 239.

interested advantage notwithstanding the general constraints set by co-operative standards.

The weakness of the community standards approach is
that it may not effectuate the right interpretation of the co-
operative ideal. Different commercial communities may set
different standards, some pitching co-operative requirements low, others pitching them high, some requiring
co-operation in negotiation, others requiring it only in performance and enforcement, and so on. If each of these
communities *freely* agrees to a particular set of ground rules
for contracting, some less co-operative than others, other
things being equal this could satisfy even a Gewirthian
interpretation of moral rationality. However, in so far as we
are trying to express the co-operative ideal as a default rule
for contract law, this kind of variation from one commercial
group to another simply will not do.

When we consider the credentials of the rival approach,
articulating a theory of the contractual community of interest, we find the position reversed. Unlike the procedural
approach, the substantive approach has its strong suit in
moral rationality but it looks somewhat less convincing
in relation to instrumental rationality. It is self-evident why
this approach has apparent strength in terms of moral
rationality – it draws on the particular moral theory that we
are assuming to be the key to moral rationality. Of course,
to play Devil's Advocate, it may not correctly apply Gewirth's
theory; but, at least, this is what it purports to do. However,
it is not so clear that an articulation of the contractual community of interest based on Gewirthian reasoning would
regulate very effectively.

To take the obvious difficulty: suppose that contract law
were to specify co-operative requirements which were far
more constraining of self-interest than was generally
thought reasonable by commercial contractors. With such
a disjunction between legal and commercial standards, one
would not be optimistic about the law being respected or
utilised. As we have said, the thrust of the impact studies is
that the law tends to be effective where it is seen as legitimate (and is internalised) by the relevant parties, or where,
even though it is not accepted as legitimate, the overall
balance of prudential interests dictates enforcement/com-
pliance/use and is sufficiently compelling to override any
countervailing moral considerations. Thus, if co-operative
ideals were pitched too high, one would expect that

contractors would deal, adjust, and dispute according to their own lights, leaving the formal machinery of the civil law largely unused. This would leave the law morally rational on paper, but not morally rational in practice and instrumentally ineffective. Is there any way around this?

The answer seems to be to employ the substantive approach as a way of setting the default rules for co-operative contracting. Accordingly, the contractual community of interest so specified would apply unless the parties *freely* agreed to different ground rules.[69] Such a regulatory strategy would be compatible with the Gewirthian emphasis on the primacy of agents' freedom, thus preserving moral rationality on paper, and it would promise an altogether more effective legal regime on the ground, thereby promoting both moral and instrumental rationality in practice. It certainly should not be thought that such an approach would be entirely free of difficulty. For example, some contractors might reject the regime as requiring, as it were, the parties to contract-out of the co-operative default rules (particularly if contracting-out involved significant transaction costs); there might be problems about specifying the contracting-out procedure itself; and, as ever, there would be difficulties with the condition that contracting-out be 'freely' agreed to. Nevertheless, all things considered, this pattern for a co-operative law of contract seems to be the more rational option.

5. CONCLUSION

The classical model of contract is under siege. Wherever we look, contract theorists – whether they are working in the socio-legal tradition, in law and economics, or in legal philosophy – are pressing forward with a co-operative interpretation of contract. These theorists, of course, do not necessarily have identical cognitive interests. Some are more interested in uncovering and explaining practice; others are more interested in evaluating policy and doctrine. However, there is a common conviction that contract is not

---

[69] For example, the parties might freely agree to put themselves at risk during the stage when the contract is being negotiated: see *Regalian Properties plc v London Docklands Development Corpn* [1995] 1 All ER 1005.

to be equated with competition and that the concept of co-operation needs to be built into our understanding of contractual phenomena.

In this chapter, it has been suggested that we should take the ideal-typical, or focal, case of co-operative conduct to be that which is guided by a set of moral requirements, the contractual community of interest. These requirements set the limits to permissible self-regarding conduct in contract, restraining the pursuit of self-interest and placing contractors under responsibilities to which, again, personal advantage must be subordinated. It has also been suggested that the right way of operationalising these requirements is by drawing on Alan Gewirth's dialectical method, to elaborate a substantive theory of the contractual community of interest. This, as it were, offers a blueprint for a rational legal regime, as well as for rational contractual behaviour consistent with the law.

Finally, it must be emphasised that if this kind of approach is correct, and if the moral reading of co-operation is to be treated as central, then this sets the conceptual framework for all inquiry into co-operative contracting. In other words, the moral reading does not point simply to the required features of legal doctrine or policy, it sets the bench-mark for all attempts to describe, map, and explain this transactional field.[70]

---

[70] To put this more pointedly, on this view, if conduct fails to instantiate the moral ideal, it is not then correctly characterised as co-operative conduct at all – even though the actors may regard their conduct as 'co-operative' and even though many commentators may accept the actors' own description of their conduct. Cf Deryck Beyleveld and Roger Brownsword, 'The Implications of Natural-Law Theory for the Sociology of Law', in A. Carty (ed) *Post-Modern Law* (Edinburgh, Edinburgh University Press, 1990) 126.

Chapter 10

A rational law of contract

Introduction

As we remarked in the last chapter, one aspect of the critique of the classical model emphasises that the law of contract has undergone a transformation in the hands of modern judges and legislators.[1] To some extent, this is perceived to be a transformation in the form of the law, the general rules of the classical law having given way to more particular, more discretionary, more flexible legal forms. However, there have also been some striking (substantive) doctrinal developments in the modern law. For, as we have seen in the earlier chapters of this book, the modern law has attempted to modify the classical law in two significant respects – first, by bringing doctrine more into line with the practice and expectations of commercial contractors and,

---

[1] See eg Patrick S. Atiyah *From Principles to Pragmatism* (Oxford, Clarendon Press, 1978), and *The Rise and Fall of Freedom of Contract* (Oxford, Oxford University Press, 1979); Hugh Collins, *The Law of Contract* 2nd edn (London, Butterworths, 1993); Duncan Kennedy, 'Form and Substance in Private Law Adjudication' (1976) 89 Harvard Law Review 1685; Roberto M Unger, *The Critical Legal Studies Movement* (Harvard, Harvard University Press, 1986); Thomas Wilhelmsson, *Critical Studies in Private Law* (Dordrecht, Kluwer, 1992), and 'Questions for a Critical Contract Law – and a Contradictory Answer: Contract as Social Cooperation' in Thomas Wilhelmsson (ed), *Perspectives of Critical Contract Law* (Aldershot, Dartmouth, 1993) p 9. For some reservations about the extent to which the modern law has actually departed from classical principles of market rationality, see Juha Häyhä, 'Scandinavian Techniques for Controlling Fairness in Contracts' in Roger Brownsword, Geraint Howells, and Thomas Wilhelmsson (eds) *Welfarism in Contract Law* (Aldershot, Dartmouth, 1994) p 127.

secondly, by qualifying (or re-interpreting) the principle of freedom of contract in such a way that vulnerable contractors (particularly consumer contractors) deal, as it were, under a protective umbrella.

Since much of the modern transformation has been driven by a welfarist concern that stronger parties should not be allowed to take unfair advantage of weaker parties,[2] it might be thought that the development of the modern law should be a cause for celebration rather than concern. However, for some, the modern law of contract is in crisis, formally rational law having yielded to an ad hoc interventionism which threatens a crisis of both instrumental and substantive rationality – a crisis of both effectiveness and legitimacy.[3] Moreover, whereas the classical law could at least be taken to represent the general law of contract, the modern law apparently lacks any such generality for it involves a clear bifurcation between commercial and consumer contracting. In other words, whereas there once was '*the* law of contract' (or, at any rate, so the textbook writers would tell it),[4] we now have a divided 'law of contracts'.

These cautionary remarks prompt a number of questions

---

[2]   Cf Roger Brownsword 'The Philosophy of Welfarism and its Emergence in the Modern English Law of Contract' in Roger Brownsword, Geraint Howells, and Thomas Wilhelmsson (eds) *Welfarism in Contract Law* (Aldershot, Dartmouth, 1994) p 21.

[3]   See eg James Gordley *The Philosophical Origins of Modern Contract Doctrine* (Oxford, Clarendon Press, 1991). For Gunther Teubner's seminal response to this perceived crisis, see 'Substantive and Reflexive Elements in Modern Law' (1983) 17 Law and Society Review 236. For comments on the extent to which reflexive (procedural) strategies can divorce themselves from questions of substantive rationality, see Roger Brownsword, 'Towards a Rational Law of Contract' in Thomas Wilhelmsson (ed), *Perspectives of Critical Contract Law* (Aldershot, Dartmouth, 1993) p 241, esp 242–5; and, to somewhat similar effect, see Paul Van Seters, 'Law and Purpose' in Gunther Teubner and Alberto Febbrajo (eds) *State, Law, and Economy as Autopoetic Systems* (Milan, Giuffrè, 1992), 435, 438, where it is argued that reflexive law, with purpose incorporated, can be brought close to Nonet and Selznick's model of responsive law (see Phillipe Nonet and Philip Selznick, *Law and Society in Transition: Toward Responsive Law* (New York, Harper and Row, 1978)).

[4]   For the important influence of the textbook tradition, see John N. Adams and Roger Brownsword, *Understanding Contract Law* 2nd edn (London, Fontana, 1994), esp pp 30–8.

about the modern law of contract. In particular, is the special protection of consumer contractors defensible? Is it sensible to treat commercial contracts and consumer contracts differently from one another? And, generally, are the sceptics right in suggesting that there is a crisis of rationality in the modern law?

In this final chapter of the book, we gather together the threads of our earlier discussion in three ways. First, we set out in rather more detail a (formal) framework for assessing the rationality of legal doctrine. This framework is intended to structure debate about the rationality of contract law but, in principle, it is capable of serving the same function in relation to any area of law. Secondly, we continue to explore the possibility that particular moral judgments might be rationally defensible. The question, it will be appreciated, is not whether particular criteria (or principles) are commonly employed with justificatory intent, but whether compelling reasons can be given for adopting one substantive (moral) position rather than another. If, like many, one is sceptical that a particular conception of substantive (moral) rationality can express anything more than a person's firmest moral intuitions or commitments, then it must be accepted that one's favoured critical perspective on law has no more validity than any of its rivals. The alternative is to think the relatively unthinkable, namely that moral foundationalism is not perhaps an impossible project;[5] and, as in the earlier chapters of the book, we again look to the strategy employed by Alan Gewirth as the most promising way of responding to moral scepticism.[6] Thirdly, we consider how the law of contract might be articulated if we were to attempt to express the law as fully rational. Here, taking the basic Gewirthian moral axiom (that one should respect the freedom and well-being of others) as guiding, we consider whether the modern regulatory bifurcation between

---

[5]   Cf the project in David Gauthier *Morals by Agreement* (Oxford, Clarendon Press, 1986), at p 4: 'Our claim is that in certain situations involving interaction with others, an individual chooses rationally only in so far as he constrains his pursuit of his own interest or advantage to conform to principles expressing the impartiality characteristic of morality. To choose rationally, one must choose morally. This is a strong claim. Morality, we shall argue, can be generated as a rational constraint from the non-moral premises of rational choice.'

[6]   Alan Gewirth, *Reason and Morality* (Chicago, Chicago University Press, 1978); and see our discussion in chs 7 and 9.

consumer and commercial contracting is rationally defensible. We conclude by emphasising that, although the book sets the agenda for a rational appreciation of contract law, our business is by no means complete – in particular, it must be understood that applying abstract moral principles to concrete doctrinal questions is not always a straightforward matter.[7]

1. RATIONALITY, RECONCILIATION, AND TRADITIONAL LEGAL DOGMATICS

The rationality of law is a matter of concern within both the traditional and the critical legal communities. Indeed, it would be no exaggeration to say that traditional legal dogmatics displays something of an obsession with rationality, at least with a particular form of rationality. For traditionalists, the law aspires to be (and largely is regarded as) a seamless web, each precedent, each statute, fitting into a coherent mosaic of doctrine and principle. Occasionally, mistakes are made, but they are soon addressed and rectified. It follows that, for traditionalists, the reconciliation of apparently conflicting precedents is more than a distraction. If the cases cannot be reconciled, the law is irrational. Accordingly, whereas critical legal scholars (such as Roberto Unger and Duncan Kennedy)[8] strive to expose and develop tension and contradiction, for the traditionalist every effort must be made to reconcile the apparently irreconcilable.

The English law of contract has a number of instances of cases which stubbornly resist reconciliation. The cases dealing with mistake of identity that we mentioned in our introductory chapter are one well-known example.[9] Here, however, we will use a different example, a notorious pair of the so-called 'coronation' cases – *Krell v Henry*[10] and *Herne Bay Steam Boat Co v Hutton*,[11] although nearly a century old

---

[7]   Similarly, see the caveats in Charles Fried 'Rights and the Common Law' in R.G. Frey (ed) *Utility and Rights* (Oxford, Basil Blackwell, 1985) 215. See, too, Michael J. Trebilcock, *The Limits of Freedom of Contract* (Cambridge, Mass, Harvard University Press, 1993).

[8]   See n 1 above.

[9]   See *Phillips v Brooks* [1915] 2 KB 243; *Ingram v Little* [1961] 1 KB 31, and *Lewis v Averay* [1972] QB 198.

[10]   [1903] 2 KB 740.

[11]   [1903] 2 KB 683.

and no longer important, continue to puzzle students and academics alike.[12] In *Krell v Henry*, the defendant hired a flat in Pall Mall with windows overlooking the route of the processions planned for the coronation of Edward VII. In *Herne Bay*, the defendant hired a boat 'for the purpose of viewing the naval review and for a day's cruise round the fleet', this again being linked to the coronation celebrations. When the King was taken ill, the coronation was postponed, and in both *Krell v Henry* and *Herne Bay* the question was whether the contracts (for the hire of the room and the boat respectively) were frustrated. The Court of Appeal decided that the contract in *Krell v Henry* was frustrated, but that the contract in *Herne Bay* was not. To intensify the puzzle, the same three judges sat in the court on each occasion, and the two cases were heard in the same week. Can these cases be reconciled, or was this a rare outbreak of irrationality?

For many years, the standard response has been that the cases are reconcilable. Orthodoxy has it that the contract in *Krell v Henry* was frustrated because the defendant was deprived of substantially the whole benefit of his bargain. Granted, he could have made use of the room on the days in question; but he surely would not have contemplated hiring the rooms were it not for the planned coronation processions. In *Herne Bay*, by contrast, the defendant was not wholly deprived of what he had bargained for. Not only did he have the use of the boat, the fleet actually remained anchored at Spithead notwithstanding the postponement of the coronation. The received wisdom, therefore, is that the cases are distinguishable, the difference being a matter of degree – Henry got no part of his bargain, but Hutton got at least some part of his bargain.

Whilst this is a plausible explanation of *Krell v Henry*, it surely ignores the most important point about the *Herne Bay* case. The fact of the matter was that Mr Hutton was a businessman from Southampton who hired the boat, not for his own pleasure, but for his own profit. His intention was to cram as many paying passengers as possible into the boat, to take such paying passengers as frequently as

---

[12]   See eg Roger Brownsword 'Henry's Lost Spectacle and Hutton's Lost Speculation: a Classic Riddle Solved?' (1985) 129 Solicitors' Journal 860; and Hugh Beale, W. D. Bishop, and Michael Furmston, *Contract: Cases and Materials* 2nd edn (London, Butterworths, 1990) p 362.

possible around the bay. His venture, in other words, was a purely commercial speculation – his grievance simply that of an entrepreneur who finds his anticipated profit diminished. It follows that the distinction between the two cases is not one of degree, but one of kind. Whereas Hutton hired the boat while dealing in the course of a business, Henry did not. Accordingly, the fact that the fleet remained anchored at Spithead (a fact much emphasised in the orthodox account) was entirely irrelevant: the contract in the Herne Bay case could not have been frustrated even if the fleet had sailed away. For, following *Davis Contractors Ltd v Fareham UDC*,[13] it is now settled that a plea of frustration cannot succeed on grounds of purely economic loss; and, with the benefit of hindsight, it is clear that this was the sole basis for Hutton's argument.

If this offers a more convincing reconciliation of the two cases, it does not quite lay to rest all concerns about the rationality of these decisions. Rationality has more than one dimension, and the foregoing explanation does no more than smooth over an apparent contradiction. The question now arises whether it is rational to treat those (such as Henry) who deal as consumers differently from those (such as Hutton) who deal as commercial contractors. Since this distinction underwrites much of the modern law – sometimes explicitly, as for example in the Unfair Contract Terms Act 1977, the Unfair Terms in Consumer Contracts Regulations 1994, and the Sale and Supply of Goods Act 1994 (in so far as it amends the right to reject goods); sometimes implicitly, as for example in the relative willingness to incorporate and imply terms into contracts[14] – this is no marginal matter confined to the coronation cases. Before we can tackle this question, however, we must look more carefully at the different dimensions of the idea of rationality.

---

[13]   [1956] AC 696.
[14]   Cf eg *Thornton v Shoe Lane Parking* [1971] 2 QB 163, and *British Crane Hire Corpn Ltd v Ipswich Plant Hire Ltd* [1975] QB 303. And see John N. Adams and Roger Brownsword *Understanding Contract Law* 2nd edn (London, Fontana, 1994) pp 69–70.

2. THE THREE DIMENSIONS OF RATIONALITY

As we have seen, rationality (in our employment of the concept)[15] comprises three dimensions: namely, 'formal rationality'; 'instrumental rationality', this being divisible into 'generic instrumental rationality' and 'specific instrumental rationality'; and 'substantive rationality'.

Formal rationality expresses the requirement that legal doctrine should not be contradictory. At one level, this is fairly straightforward, formal rationality simply requiring that the apparently irreconcilable should be reconciled, that the law should be rendered consistent. Moreover, as we have said, this is an axiom of traditional legal scholarship. At another level, however, the requirement of formal rationality is more complicated. For one thing, traditional legal scholars are adept at smoothing out apparent inconsistencies by relying on distinguishing categories. The law on negligent acts and the law on negligent statements, for instance, is treated as relatively discrete, existing as traditionalists put it 'in different lanes'. Thus, while liability for negligent acts can be said to be crawling along in the slow lane, liability for negligent statements can be said to be overtaking at speed in the fast lane – and no reconciliation is deemed necessary. The same is true where the more general categories of 'contract' and 'tort' are brought into play. For example, no contradiction is seen in there being different limitation periods or third-party rules in relation to a particular act of negligence (which is also a breach of contract) depending upon whether the situation is viewed contractually or tortiously – contract is contract, and tort is tort. Needless to say, formal rationality cannot be secured by such boundary-creating and category-manipulating expedients. Another problem arises from the distinction between 'contradiction' and 'tension' in the doctrinal materials. Formal rationality militates against contradiction, but it does not preclude indeterminate tensions between particular doctrinal principles.[16] Suppose, for example, that one principle (P1) provides that in construing contractual terms

---

[15]   Seminally, see Max Weber, *The Theory of Social and Economic Organization* (New York, The Free Press, 1964).
[16]   Cf Ronald Dworkin *Taking Rights Seriously* (London, Duckworth, 1978) esp ch 2.

the intention of the parties is relevant; while another principle (P2) provides that contracting parties are presumed not normally to agree to exclusions of liability for negligence. These principles may pull against one another, in one case P1 prevailing (in the sense that it is held that the parties' intention was to exclude liability for negligence) in another case P2 prevailing (in the sense that it is held that the parties did not intend to exclude liability for negligence), but this gives rise to no contradiction as such. However, if P1 provided that, for the purposes of construing the terms of a contract, the intention of the parties was paramount, while P2 provided that, for such purposes, the intention of the parties was never decisive (or that liability for negligence could not be excluded even where the parties so intended), this would involve a contradiction. More could be said about formal rationality, but this must suffice: whatever the difficulty of applying this idea, the requirement is simply that legal doctrine should not violate the principle of non-contradiction.[17]

Instrumental rationality, as has been said, can be of either a generic or a specific kind. The generic requirement is that legal doctrine should be capable of guiding action. Irrespective of whether contract law is duty-imposing or power-conferring, it purports to guide the conduct of would-be contractors. If the law is to have a purchase on conduct, it must conform to a number of instrumental requirements. Of course, this does not guarantee that the law will have a purchase on conduct, whether as a controlling or as a facilitative mechanism. However, generic instrumental rationality is a necessary, if not always a sufficient, condition of action-guidance. Specific instrumental rationality concerns the appropriateness of particular legal interventions in given situations. If we assume that particular interventions in contract (in the field of transactions) are backed by particular facilitative and protective purposes, then specific instrumental rationality focuses upon the efficacy of the steps taken to secure those purposes. If the intervention is intended to be facilitative, it should facilitate; if it is intended to be protective, it should protect. For example, if the intervention aims at eliminating certain

---

[17]   Cf Deryck Beyleveld and Roger Brownsword 'Privity, Transitivity, and Rationality' (1991) 54 Modern Law Review 48.

forms of unfair dealing by conferring upon judges a general reviewing jurisdiction (ie a discretion to strike out unfair terms), specific instrumental rationality concerns the suitability of this particular technique. There is, of course, a degree of overlap between formal rationality and instrumental rationality (because contradictory law cannot serve as a guide to action), and generic and specific instrumental rationality must work in tandem. However, we can say more about this shortly when we deal more fully with the concept of instrumental rationality.

The third dimension of rational law is substantive rationality. This requires that the substance of legal doctrine should be justified or legitimate. However, the notion of substantive rationality in relation to the law can be interpreted in at least three ways as follows:

1.   Law is substantively rational if its norms are by and large accepted as justified and legitimate;
2.   Law is substantively rational if its norms not only are by and large accepted as justified and legitimate, but also can be shown to form a consistent normative set; and,
3.   The substantive rationality of law does not depend at all on acceptance; rather, law is substantively rational if, and only if, its norms form a justified and legitimate (coherent and rationally defensible) set.

From these different notions of substantive rationality, different interpretations of a 'crisis of legitimacy' (such as we mentioned in our introductory remarks) may follow. On the first view, a crisis arises where the norms of law are no longer accepted as legitimate (which may, of course, diminish not only the standing of the law but also its effectiveness). To resolve this crisis, either legal norms must be brought into line with what is accepted as legitimate, or popular conceptions of legitimacy must be transformed. The crisis is essentially one of 'legitimation'.[18] On the second view, there may be a practical legitimation crisis (as with the first view). However, there may also be a more subtle crisis. Even if legal norms are accepted as legitimate, they may fall short of the requirement of consistency. But, so long as this crisis is confined to the world of legal theorists, the general

[18]   Cf Jurgen Habermas, *Legitimation Crisis* (trans Thomas McCarthy) (London, Heinemann, 1976).

effectiveness of the law should not be impaired. Finally, on the third view, the legitimacy crisis arises where legal norms lack any rationally defensible basis. If legal norms cannot be coherently defended and justified, it is no compensation that those norms are effectively applied and enforced as well as being generally accepted as legitimate. This really is a case of false consciousness.

Given widespread moral scepticism, many will think that the only legitimacy crisis worth troubling about is the first type – the crisis of legitimation. For, in a world of conflicting value perspectives, it cannot be assumed that substantive rationality, even in this limited sense, is viable. In the present context, however, substantive rationality is to be understood in terms of moral objectivism, of rationally defensible moral criteria, from which it follows that it is a crisis of legitimacy in the third sense which is focal. To underline this interpretation of the challenge facing contract theorists, we can recall James Gordley's view that the task is to discover general principles which explain 'the rules of positive law or the results most people regard as fair'.[19] Against this, the present interpretation of the legitimacy crisis holds that what 'most people regard as fair' is largely irrelevant to whether or not a rule actually is substantively rational (although, of course, popular conceptions of fairness may be extremely relevant to questions of instrumental rationality). This is certainly counter to the conventional wisdom which sees legal theory as a resource for mapping and capping practice rather than critically structuring and shaping that practice.[20] However, before elaborating upon this controversial thesis, a little more needs to be said about instrumental rationality.

3. INSTRUMENTAL RATIONALITY

According to Lon Fuller,[21] once it is accepted that the legal enterprise aspires to be an action-guiding enterprise, then it follows that certain minimal principles of rationality are

---

[19]   Above, ch 8 at p 257.
[20]   Cf the methodological comments in William Lucy 'Rethinking the Common Law' (1994) 14 Oxford Journal of Legal Studies 539.
[21]   Lon L. Fuller *The Morality of Law* (New Haven, Yale University Press, 1969).

presupposed, the so-called 'inner morality of law'. Legal rules should be general, promulgated, prospective, clear, non-contradictory, and relatively constant; they should not require the impossible; and, crucially, there should be a congruence between the law as officially declared and the law as administered.

The Fullerian principles can be regarded as 'procedural' matters in the sense that they generally have no substantive impingement. This is most obviously so, perhaps, with the requirement of promulgation, for this permits legal rules to have any content provided that they are published. Of course, promulgation might invoke certain resistances which would not be provoked by secret rules. Nevertheless, promulgation imposes no direct substantive constraint. The same is true for the requirements of clarity, congruence, constancy and non-contradiction (although, in these cases, reference to the content of other legal materials may be necessary in order to establish that a particular provision satisfies the requirements). The remaining Fullerian ideals (generality, prospectivity, and possibility of compliance) do have some substantive impingement, but they stop short of subjecting law to the governance of a master 'external' (as Fuller would put it) moral standard. For present purposes, it is unnecessary to consider whether the Fullerian procedural principles are correctly characterised as 'moral' principles;[22] here, their significance is that they provide some important leads in relation to the notion of generic instrumental rationality.

We have already treated the principle of non-contradiction as a matter of formal rationality. However, as we have indicated, non-contradiction is significant too in the dimension of instrumental rationality. In this context, it can be conveniently set alongside the requirements of clarity, constancy, and promulgation.

For many judges and commentators, the cardinal sin is for the law of contract to fall into a state where contracting parties and their advisers are left uncertain as to their legal position. In particular, for commercial contractors, legal calculability is of the essence. Recall, for example, Lord

---

[22]   But see Roger Brownsword 'A Synthesis of Rights and Community: In a Different Register?' in W. Watts Miller (ed) *Socialism and the Law* (ARSP Beiheft 49) (Stuttgart, Franz Steiner, 1992) p 131.

Wilberforce's observations in *Photo Production v Securicor:*[23]

> 'After this Act [viz, the Unfair Contract Terms Act 1977], in com-
> mercial matters generally, when the parties are not of unequal
> bargaining power, and when risks are normally borne by insur-
> ance, not only is the case for judicial intervention
> undemonstrated, but there is everything to be said, and this
> seems to have been Parliament's intention, for leaving the
> parties free to apportion the risks as they think fit and for
> respecting their decisions.
>
> At the stage of negotiation as to the consequences of a breach,
> there is everything to be said for allowing the parties to estimate
> their respective claims according to the contractual provisions
> they have themselves made, rather than for facing them with a
> legal complex so uncertain as the doctrine of fundamental
> breach must be . . .
>
> At the judicial stage there is still more to be said for leaving
> cases to be decided straightforwardly on what the parties have
> bargained for rather than on analysis, which becomes progres-
> sively more refined, of decisions in other cases leading to
> inevitable appeals.'

This serves to highlight an important point. Whilst the distinction between contradiction and tension is important in
the context of formal rationality, it is of no great moment
in the context of instrumental rationality. The fact of the
matter is that if the legal position is unclear, it matters little
why the problem exists. Whether the source of the difficulty
is that the law vests judges with an unpredictable discretion
(as Lord Wilberforce feared might become the case with
UCTA), or that there are contradictions or tensions in
the materials, either way, instrumental rationality is
jeopardised. And, of course, precisely the same considerations apply to the requirements of constancy and
promulgation. If legal doctrine is restless, and constantly
changing, contractors cannot be confident that they can rely
on extant principles remaining settled. If the law is not
promulgated, the position is even worse: contractors have
no doctrinal basis for reliance and they must operate more
in hope than (doctrinally grounded) expectation.

Even if the law is clear, non-contradictory, and promulgated, there must be a question mark against its generic
instrumental rationality if, nevertheless, it violates the
principle of 'ought implies can' by prescribing the impos-

---

[23]   [1980] AC 827, 843.

sible. Since much of liability in contract is strict, does this entail instrumental irrationality? After all, where strict liability applies, the defendant will be liable for breach even though all reasonable steps – maybe even all possible steps – to perform have been taken. This is not the place to have a full-scale discussion of strict liability in contract; even so, two short points can be made. First, where the law of contract sets up a permissive framework in which contractors can freely agree to accept strict liability risks, there is nothing instrumentally irrational about the law if the parties make use of that facilitative framework. Secondly, however, if strict liability applies, not because the parties have freely agreed to it, but because the law so prescribes independent of agreement, then the position is more complex. Briefly, where the law has protective concerns (eg for consumer purchasers of goods or services) a strict liability regime may be instrumentally rational. Whilst it may not be possible for the party subject to strict liability (eg the seller or supplier) to perform, it is perfectly possible for this party to compensate the other party for a strict liability breach. Granted, this may not, in the final analysis, serve the specific protective end: costs may be transferred to consumer purchasers, sellers and suppliers may avoid high-risk enterprises, and so on. Nevertheless, strict liability, even imposed strict liability, cannot be written off without a good deal more as instrumentally irrational.[24]

For Fuller, the requirement of congruence (coupled with that of generality) articulates the essential ideal represented by the rule of law. In contract, as we have emphasised in earlier chapters, a lack of congruence has characterised much of Appeal Court adjudication this century as the classical paradigm has been challenged by the new interventionism. So, for instance, until the enactment of the Unfair Contract Terms Act in 1977, the disjunction between declared doctrine and the real reasons for decisions was strikingly apparent in relation to the regulation of standard form contracts and exemption clauses. While the judges insisted that they were doing no more than effectuating the parties' intentions, they manipulated the rules on formation

---

[24]   For the question of substantive rationality, see Deryck Beyleveld and Roger Brownsword 'Impossibility, Irrationality, and Strict Product Liability' in Geraint Howells and Jerry Phillips (eds) *Product Liability* (Chichester, Barry Rose, 1991) 75.

and the canons of construction in order to protect weaker bargaining parties, especially so that a fairer deal could be struck for consumers. Officially, freedom of contract ruled, but, in practice, the judicial script was written in terms of fairness and reasonableness.[25] This phenomenon, however, was not restricted to the regulation of exemption clauses, and as we have seen it has been implicated in much adjudication concerning the privity doctrine[26] and the right to withdraw for breach of contract.[27]

Generic instrumental rationality, as it has been emphasised, must be complemented by specific instrumental rationality. To borrow Iredell Jenkins' terminology,[28] legal interventions will be viable only if they are compatible with the features of the particular field within which they are to operate, if they can overcome any relevant resistances – individual or sub-systemic[29] – within the field. As we explained in Chapter 9, rational lawmakers must consider which of the many legal techniques within the regulatory repertoire (or, which combination of techniques) is likely to prove most effective in a particular case. Each technique will have its own debits and credits: on the one side, its limitations, costs, and resistance; on the other side, its positive prospects. Unless such calculations are made, the particular intervention may simply have no impact, or, worse, produce unintended – and undesirable – side-effects.

Clearly, it is important that lawmakers are aware of the so-called problem of the 'gap' – the disjunction between the law-in-the-books and the law-in-action. One aspect of the gap concerns the lack of conformity between the intended purpose of the declared rule and the conduct or response of *non-officials*. On the one hand, if the law is meant to facilitate, it may not actually be used in practice – although such a failure of use may not always give rise to great cause for concern. On the other hand, if the law is intended to be protective, a failure to function as such may be serious. It is one

---

[25] Cf Barry Reiter, 'The Control of Contract Power' (1981) 1 Oxford Journal of Legal Studies 347, esp at 360–61.

[26] See ch 5.

[27] See ch 6.

[28] See Iredell Jenkins *Social Order and the Limits of Law* (Princeton, Princeton University Press, 1980).

[29] Cf Gunther Teubner 'After Legal Instrumentalism? Strategic Models of Post-Regulatory Law' in Gunther Teubner (ed) *Dilemmas of Law in the Welfare State* (Berlin, Walter de Gruyter, 1986) p 299.

thing for commercial contractors to make little use of the law of contract in their dealings;[30] it is quite another thing for tenants to fail to make use of fair rent provisions and rent tribunals,[31] or for poorer consumers to remain unclear about the cost of credit despite legislation designed to improve their knowledge and understanding of such matters.[32] Not only must lawmakers be aware of this problem, they must act on an understanding of why the gap exists – an understanding of why the law fails to regulate as intended.[33]

The other aspect of the gap concerns the conduct of *legal officials* rather than non-officials. In relation to judges, it is not simply that there is sometimes a lack of congruence between the law as declared and the law as administered; for the way in which the gap develops depends in no small part on the particular judicial ideologies in play. Legislative reform in the area of contract law, for example, has to reckon with the different approaches that judges display towards the interpretation of statutes, as well as with the particular ideologies that judges have with regard to consumer protection, the facilitation of commerce, and the like.[34] Of course, judges play no great part in the totality of dispute-resolution – or, at any rate, they have little *direct* involvement in everyday dispute-settlement. Nevertheless, judicial ideology has to be a factor in the calculations of any lawmaker who aspires to make a specifically instrumental rational intervention.

It should not be thought, however, that rational law-making is simply a challenge for the draftsman. We have to

---

[30]   See Stewart Macaulay, 'Non-Contractual Relations in Business' (1963) 28 American Sociological Review p 55; and Hugh Beale and Tony Dugdale, 'Contracts Between Businessmen: Planning and the Use of Contractual Remedies' (1975) 2 British Journal of Law and Society p 45.

[31]   See Martin Partington, 'Landlord and Tenant: The British Experience' in Eugene Kamenka and Alice Erh-Soon Tay (eds), *Law and Social Control* (London, Edward Arnold, 1980) p 166.

[32]   See eg Geraint Howells 'Contract Law: The Challenge for the Critical Consumer Lawyer' in Thomas Wilhelmsson (ed) *Perspectives of Critical Contract Law* (Aldershot, Dartmouth, 1993) p 327.

[33]   See our comments about the effectiveness of law in ch 9.

[34]   Generally, see John N. Adams and Roger Brownsword *Understanding Contract Law* 2nd edn (London, Fontana, 1994); see, too, 'Law Reform, Law-Jobs, and Law Commission No 160' (1988) 51 Modern Law Review 481.

come to terms with the fact that judges do not have uniform ideologies, that the impact of regulation is not always easy to predict, and that no amount of attention to drafting can be guaranteed to produce the desired response. A rational approach to the law of contract is not a panacea, simply the best that can be made of a difficult job.

4. SUBSTANTIVE RATIONALITY

In line with the position that we have taken in earlier chapters, we suggest that Alan Gewirth's moral theory offers the best guidance in relation to questions of substantive rationality. Yet, why should we take Gewirth seriously? Why should we think that substantively rational contract law must (following Gewirthian thinking) be consistent with respect for the freedom and basic well-being of agents?

In several respects, Gewirth's theory has a rather obvious appeal. For one thing, the model of agency, with which the theory starts, fits very well with the picture of rational autonomous beings (namely, beings with their own life-plans who are able to respond to various normative signals, to incentives and disincentives, and so on) that is shared by a broad spectrum of theories – in fact, by all those theories that follow Fuller in seeing law as a purposive enterprise, from utilitarian welfare-maximising theories (whether or not in the law and economics school) through to rights-based theories such as those advanced by Ronald Dworkin and John Rawls. Joseph Raz, for example, says:[35]

> 'In western industrial societies a particular conception of individual well-being has acquired considerable popularity. It is the ideal of personal autonomy. It transcends the conceptual point that personal well-being is partly determined by success in willingly endorsed pursuits and holds the free choice of goals and relations as an essential ingredient of individual well-being. The ruling idea behind the ideal of personal autonomy is that people should make their own lives. The autonomous person is a (part) author of his own life. The ideal of personal autonomy is the vision of people controlling, to some degree, their own destiny, fashioning it through successive decisions throughout their lives.'

[35] Joseph Raz, *The Morality of Freedom* (Oxford, Clarendon Press, 1986) p 369. See, too, Martin Hollis, *Models of Man* (Cambridge, Cambridge University Press, 1977).

Not only does Gewirth's account of agency fit with theories that presuppose the capacity for autonomous action, the basic moral principles derived from the concept of agency have a liberal-welfare trajectory similar to that argued for by many contemporary moral theorists.[36] In addition, unlike many theories of individual rights, Gewirth's theory establishes a coherent hierarchy of rights by focusing on the relative importance of the various needs that agents have. If these features are deemed sufficient reason to take Gewirth seriously, all well and good. However, as we have emphasised before, the reason Gewirth ultimately must be reckoned with is that he contends that agents are *logically committed* to the moral principles that he outlines. In other words, Gewirth's theory is presented as a matter of necessary truth, not as a matter of (optional) simple acceptance or reflective commitment; and it is this foundationalist claim (and its plausibility) that makes Gewirth's theory – bold though it is – the strongest candidate for a theory of substantive rationality.

As we have seen already in Chapter 9, Gewirth[37] starts with the concept of action, and with what it is to be an agent (viz, an actual, or prospective, purposive, voluntary actor). From this, Gewirth claims to derive the so-called Principle of Generic Consistency (the *PGC*). According to the *PGC* each agent is required to 'Act in accord with the generic rights of your recipients as well as of yourself'. Since, in Gewirth's contention, the 'generic rights' relate to an agent's freedom and well-being, the *PGC* effectively enjoins agents to respect one another's freedom and well-being. The derivation of the *PGC* proceeds by what Gewirth terms the 'dialectically necessary method'. Broadly, what this means is that the *PGC* is derived by an agent's own reflection on the nature, needs, and prescriptive implications of viewing oneself as an agent. This reflective process is 'dialectical' in the sense that the agent's interrogation of its[38] own agency is restricted entirely

---

[36]   For instructive applications of the concept of autonomy in relation to contract doctrine, see Hugh Collins, *The Law of Contract* 2nd edn (London, Butterworths, 1993), and 'Disclosure of Information and Welfarism' in Roger Brownsword, Geraint Howells, and Thomas Wilhelmsson (eds) *Welfarism in Contract Law* (Aldershot, Dartmouth, 1994) p 97.

[37]   Alan Gewirth, *Reason and Morality* (Chicago, Chicago University Press, 1978).

[38]   To repeat a point that we have made before, we use 'it' simply to avoid begging questions about the possible range of agents.

to its own first-person perspective. The method is 'necessary' in two senses: first, the reflective process allows only those derivations which are strictly entailed by the premises; and, secondly, the focus for the agent's self-examination is upon the necessary features of being an agent, not the contingent features associated with one's own instantiation of agency. The dialectically necessary method, therefore, generates the *PGC* as a necessary truth for agents. However, as we emphasised earlier, the argument does not make a direct 'assertoric' claim that the *PGC* corresponds to the moral furniture of the universe (nor, of course, that it is, in fact, generally accepted by agents). Instead, the claim is one about coherence: the claim is that dialectical reflection on the necessary conditions of agency entails acceptance of the *PGC*, such that it would be contradictory for one to deny the binding force of the *PGC* whilst at the same time continuing to regard oneself as an agent. If the term had not already been coined for another purpose, it might have been appropriate to have thought of the *PGC* as a 'reflexive law'[39] for agents, a law for inter-agent dealings derived by a process of rational and reflexive interrogation of one's necessary needs and attitudes as an agent.

There are three principal stages in Gewirth's derivation of the *PGC* – identifying generic *needs*, claiming generic *rights*, and accepting generic *duties*. The first stage involves an agent's dialectical appreciation that, irrespective of one's particular purposes, one's freedom and basic well-being are necessary prerequisites for the selection and achievement of one's purposes. In this sense, an agent's freedom and basic well-being must be regarded as the generic conditions of agency. Moreover, because an agent must have a positive attitude towards its particular purposes, it must have a positive attitude towards the prerequisites for the achievement of those purposes. Accordingly, an agent can only consistently have a favourable attitude towards the possession of the generic conditions of agency (ie its freedom and basic well-being). It follows that an agent must have a negative attitude towards interferences with its freedom and basic well-being (unless, of course, an agent wills such interference in order to pursue a particular purpose). The second stage of the argument – a stage which has attracted

---

[39]   Cf Teubner, n 3, above.

perhaps the lion's share of the criticism[40] – involves transforming the agent's necessarily negative attitude towards
interference with its generic conditions into the claim that
the agent has a *right* to its freedom and well-being.
Understandably, adeonticists and amoralists jib at the
introduction of the idea of a 'right'. However, it must be
remembered that the argument is constrained by both
necessity and consistency, and the only proposition which
is consistent with an (adeonticist, amoralist, deonticist, or
moralist) agent's negative attitude towards interference with
its generic conditions is that the agent must consider that
it has a right that others do not so interfere. Quite simply,
to deny this proposition is to concede that it is permissible[41]
for others to interfere with one's generic conditions and this
just cannot be squared with a negative attitude towards
such interference (the necessity of which has already been
established). Finally, at the third stage, the agent must
accept that, because the rights claim rests on the sufficient
reason that one is an agent (the Argument of the Sufficiency
of Agency, the *ASA*, as Gewirth calls it), it follows that being
an agent constitutes sufficient reason for having the generic
rights. Accordingly, the agent must consider that other
agents have the generic rights (by virtue of being agents). In
other words, the reflective agent must come to see that
agency not only grounds one's own rights claim, but also
entails a duty not to interfere with the freedom and basic
well-being of other agents.

There are four general aspects of Gewirth's argument
which invite objections. These are: (i) his specification of
what it is to be an agent (ie a voluntary and purposive actor)
and how precisely this conception of agency relates to
socially situated human beings; (ii) the internal validity of
the three-stage derivation of the *PGC*; (iii) the content of the
PGC; and (iv) the application of the *PGC* to concrete
situations.

The first of these issues is important, for Gewirth's argument is of no practical interest unless it hooks up to humans
as social beings. Clearly, though, as soon as we entertain

---

[40]   See the essays in Edward Regis Jr (ed) *Gewirth's Ethical Rationalism*
(Chicago, Chicago University Press, 1984).

[41]   Or, if 'permissible' seems to beg the question in favour of a moral viewpoint, the negative attitude certainly requires that one has reason to
resist intereference.

thoughts about what we (or others) ought or ought not to do (not necessarily in a moral sense), we assume that we are dealing with agents (as defined by Gewirth). So long as we entertain such thoughts, therefore, we are committed to viewing ourselves (and others) as agents.

The second issue (the validity of the derivation of the *PGC*) obviously is crucial and, as we pointed out in Chapter 9, it has attracted a vast critical literature, much of which insists that there is an invalid modal shift at the second stage, as a result of which the argument simply fails to carry through to the third stage. The fact of the matter is, however, that neither Gewirth nor his defenders have yet met an objection that obviously undermines the argument.[42] This does not prove that the argument is valid; but the onus is surely on its critics to show why it is invalid.

In relation to the third issue, the content of the *PGC*, some commentators read Gewirth's Chicago moral philosophy as a counterpart to Chicago economics. Whilst Gewirth's presentation tends to concentrate on negative rights (the agent's right against interference with the generic conditions), it is a serious mistake (as we pointed out in Chapter 7) to think that the argument does not entail positive rights. For, given that an agent must have a negative attitude towards interferences with its freedom and basic well-being, it must be favourably disposed towards assistance in attaining those conditions where it is otherwise unable to achieve them. It follows that an agent must consider that it has a prima facie right to support from others for its generic conditions in such circumstances; and that agents have a duty to assist one another.[43]

If the *PGC* is an amalgam of negative and positive rights, there nevertheless remains the fourth line of objection. How is a principle as abstract as the *PGC* to be applied in concrete situations? How are the inevitable conflicts of rights to be arbitrated? As we saw in Chapter 7, Gewirth offers more guidance than many rights-theorists in this respect, setting up a three-tiered hierarchy of rights, these rights

---

[42]   In addition to Gewirth's own many published replies to critics, see especially Deryck Beyleveld *The Dialectical Necessity of Morality* (Chicago, Chicago University Press, 1991).

[43]   See, too, the positive aspect of autonomy-based obligations as elicited by Joseph Raz, n 35 above, ch 15.

relating in descending order of priority to basic goods,[44] non-subtractive goods,[45] and additive goods.[46] It has to be conceded, however, that even with this structural guideline there will be plenty of cases where the correct application of the *PGC* is controversial and unclear. The resolution of this difficulty lies, in our view, in a strategy which puts the emphasis on procedure (constrained and shaped by a substantive moral theory) rather than directly and exclusively on outcome. This strategy relies on a distinction between regulation which is rational in an absolute (theoretical) sense, and regulation which, for practical purposes, must be treated as rational. Rationality in a theoretical sense exists in a transcendental strongbox of principle, to which omniscient beings would have access. Rationality in a practical sense sets a less demanding standard, a standard more in keeping with the limited cognitive abilities of human social beings. With regard to rationality in a practical sense, what matters is not that the doctrines in question are fully rational, but that those who have legislated the rules have made a 'good faith attempt' to apply the *PGC*.[47] Such an attempt involves a mixture of sincerity and competence, a

---

[44]   Basic rights concern the essential conditions of agency. Correlatively, basic harms, according to Gewirth, include 'whatever adversely affects the necessary preconditions of one's action, as by removing one's life, freedom of movement, physical integrity, or mental equilibrium . . .' (at pp 232–3).

[45]   Non-subtractive rights relate to an agent's ability to maintain present levels of purpose-fulfilment. Non-subtractive harms include 'being lied to, cheated, stolen from, defamed, insulted, suffering broken promises, and having one's privacy violated, as well as being subjected to dangerous, degrading, or excessively debilitating conditions of physical labor or housing or other strategic situations of life when resources are available for improvement' (at p 233).

[46]   Additive rights concern an agent's ability to increase present levels of purpose-fulfilment. According to the correlative duty: '[E]ach person must refrain from feeling or exhibiting contempt toward others; persons must not be insulted, belittled, or patronized, nor must they be discriminated against on grounds of race, religion, or nationality. Put positively, the duties of such respect require that persons have toward one another an attitude of mutual acceptance and toleration, including acquiescence in diversity so long as this falls within the limits set by the *PGC*'s duties regarding basic and non-subtractive goods' (at p 242).

[47]   For elaboration of this idea, see Deryck Beyleveld and Roger Brownsword *Law as a Moral Judgment* (reprinted Sheffield, Sheffield Academic Press, 1994), esp chs 7–9.

bona fide attempt to apply the PGC and an outcome which is not obviously inconsistent with the *PGC*. Without pressing the analogy too far, the test of a good faith attempt is somewhat akin to judicial review as it exists in England: the emphasis is on procedure (attention to relevant considerations, absence of bad faith and improper motive, and so on) but with marginal substantive constraint (a decision which no reasonable person could come to being declared ultra vires).[48]

5. SUBSTANTIVE RATIONALITY AND THE LAW OF CONTRACT

If the *PGC* is the yardstick of substantively rational contract law, what might this require? How can contract consistently reflect the negative rights of agents (not to have their freedom and well-being interfered with) as well as their positive rights in respect of the generic conditions? And, to recall one of our earlier questions, can the modern distinction between consumer and commercial contracts be squared with the *PGC*? We can tackle these questions in two stages, first by distinguishing between 'excluded' and 'non-excluded' transactions and, secondly, by identifying some of the substantive landmarks pertaining to non-excluded transactions.

(i) Excluded and non-excluded transactions

One of the first tasks for a regime of contract law is to draw a line between those transactions that, in principle, are to be treated as enforceable and those that are not. A line must be drawn, in other words, between those transactions that are to be amenable to civil law remedies (which we can term 'non-excluded' transactions) and those that are not (which we can term 'excluded' transactions). If contract law is to be substantively rational, and if the PGC is the criterion of substantive rationality, the line between excluded and non-excluded transactions must be drawn in a way that is

---

[48] Cf the so-called 'Wednesbury' principle in relation to judicial review: see Lord Greene MR's celebrated judgment in *Associated Provincial Picture Houses Ltd v Wednesbury Corpn* [1948] 1 KB 223.

defensible in the light of the *PGC*. This suggests that transactions should be excluded for one of two reasons: either (i)
because the transaction violates the *PGC*-protected rights of
third parties; or (ii) because the parties to the transaction
have freely agreed to deal outside the arena of the civil law.

The first of these reasons for exclusion bears some simi-
larity to the category of transactions which, traditionally, are
regarded as illegal or void on grounds of public policy. This
is not to say, however, that the present exclusions are all
substantively rational relative to the *PGC*. Consider, for
example, the well-known case of *Upfill v Wright*.[49] There, the
court refused to assist the plaintiff landlord to recover one
half-year's rent of a flat, because the plaintiff knew that the
defendant tenant, being the mistress of a certain man,
intended to receive him in the flat for the 'sinful and immoral
purpose [of fornication]'.[50] Formally, we might defend this
decision as rightly declining to enforce a transaction that
was tainted with immorality. However, if a transaction of the
kind in *Upfill v Wright* is only to be legitimately excluded
where it violates the *PGC*-protected rights of third parties, is
it so clear that the agreement for the rent of the flat fell foul
of that standard? Was there, for example, some deception
being practised by the mistress's man-friend? By contrast,
we might be rather more confident that the fraudulent
agreement in *Tinsley v Milligan*[51] (which we discussed in
Chapter 2) violated the *PGC*-protected rights of third parties
and, thus, was rightly treated as an excluded transaction.
However, this is not the end of the matter. Tinsley and
Milligan may have been jointly cheating tax-paying third
parties; and there is good reason for the law of contract to
offer no support for such an enterprise. But, when Tinsley
tries to cheat Milligan of a share in the house, should the
civil law offer any support to the victim? Until the House of
Lords decided *Tinsley v Milligan*, it looked as though English
law might be set to pose this issue in terms of a public conscience test, according to which relief would be granted
unless it would appear to assist or encourage illegality.[52]

---

[49]   [1911] 1 KB 506.
[50]   Ibid, at p 510, per Darling J.
[51]   [1993] 3 All ER 65.
[52]   See eg *Thackwell v Barclays Bank plc* [1986] 1 All ER 676; *Saunders v
        Edwards* [1987] 2 All ER 651; *Euro-Diam Ltd v Bathurst* [1990] 1 QB
        1; and *Howard v Shirlstar Container Transport Ltd* [1990] 3 All ER 366.

However, the House rejected such a test in *Tinsley v Milligan*, preferring to employ the procedurally fickle *Bowmakers* rule, which makes everything depend on whether the victim has to rely on the excluded transaction. Whilst, there is room for debate about the most defensible response to issues arising around excluded transactions, it seems unlikely that the approach taken in *Tinsley v Milligan* should be on our short-list.

The second reason for treating a transaction as excluded is the parties' preference for dealing in a context free of civil law remedies. This relates to the traditional requirement of an intention to create legal relations. In practice, we might regard this requirement as a pragmatic device used by the law to remove certain classes of transaction from the legal arena (particularly social and domestic agreements) and, occasionally, as a useful excuse for refusing to enforce agreements that otherwise would have unwelcome effects.[53] In principle, though, there is no reason why the law should not respect the freedom of the parties to choose the context in which they transact. If they choose to put the emphasis on trust rather than background civil law sanctions, they should be free to do so – and, as we have said in earlier chapters, many commercial contractors do choose to deal on the basis of trust (even though, formally speaking, the law continues to regard them as intending to create legal relations). It is important to realise, of course, that by excluding a transaction, the parties may be taking a risk. Therefore, it is imperative that exclusion by agreement is permitted only where the parties fully understand and freely accept the implications of their action. Beyond this, however, the law (like the parties) must accept that free choice and risk go together.

(ii) The features of non-excluded transactions

What would be the principal features of the law regulating non-excluded transactions in a substantively rational regime? To develop a sketch of such features, it will be helpful to outline three ideal-typical models of contract.

We can call the first ideal-type the 'classical' model of contract. According to this model, contracts are to be conceived

---

[53] See eg *Horrocks v Forray* [1976] 1 All ER 737.

of as representing the free agreement of parties. To secure the freedom of the parties, the law must protect contractors against the rather more obvious forms of coercion; and to secure the reality of their agreement, the law must regulate fraud, misrepresentation, and mistake. Within these ground rules, however, the parties must be left free to strike their own bargains (freedom of contract) and perform their obligations (sanctity of contract).

In the second-ideal type, which we can call the 'neo-classical' model,[54] contract is again conceived of as the free agreement of transactors, but the procedural safeguards must be strengthened to take account of the greater sophistication of the market. To secure the parties' freedom, the law now moves beyond transparent coercion to regulate more subtle forms of pressure. In particular, the doctrines of economic duress and undue influence are developed. To secure the reality of the parties' agreement, subtle forms of deception (in addition to the more obvious forms) must be controlled. In particular, doctrines concerning unfair surprise, due notice, and the like, are cultivated. Although the neo-classical model largely focuses upon procedural matters, it also begins to regulate outcomes by providing for the incorporation of standard implied terms. However, the parties remain in control of these implications by being permitted to exclude them by agreement.

The third ideal-type, which we can term the 'modern' model, comprises not only these various procedural restrictions, but also a significant measure of imposed substantive regulation of contracts. As Lord Wilberforce rightly observed in *National Carriers Ltd v Panalpina (Northern) Ltd*:[55]

> 'I think that the movement of the law of contract is away from a rigid theory of autonomy towards the discovery – or I do not hesitate to say imposition – by the courts of just solutions, which can be ascribed to reasonable men in the position of the parties.'

Accordingly, certain types of implied terms are no longer excludable by agreement; if the parties choose to make a certain type of contract then it is simply subject to particu-

---

54   Although this is not to be confused with Ian Macneil's terminology in 'Contracts: Adjustments of Long-Term Economic Relations under Classical, Neo-Classical and Relational Contract Law' (1978) 72 Northwestern University Law Review 854.

55   [1981] AC 675, 696.

lar stock terms. Equally, certain types of contractual terms are disallowed as unfair or unconscionable (or, at any rate, reliance on the contract is disallowed as unfair or unconscionable). Contract law in the modern model prescribes good faith and conscionable dealing, reflected by a mixture of procedural and substantive regulation confining the parties' freedom to take unfair advantage of one another.[56]

Now, whereas the classical and neo-classical models arguably show more concern for the parties' freedom than for their well-being, the modern model arguably protects the parties' well-being at the price of their freedom. How can we resolve this consistently with the *PGC*? Two approaches (one freedom-led, the other well-being-led) suggest themselves.

One approach (the freedom-led strategy) involves treating the freedom of the contracting parties as central; contract is to be understood primarily as a vehicle for the exercise of free transactional choice, for the exercise of autonomy. Autonomous contracting, however, is limited in two important respects. First, the idea of free choice itself presupposes that agreement is genuine – to this extent, a requirement of free and fair dealing is implicated. And, secondly, freedom is not tantamount to licence, for the contracting parties are constrained by the need to respect the well-being of *non-contracting parties*. Subject to these restrictions, though, the parties have freedom of contract and the way in which a transaction impinges on the parties' own well-being is simply not an issue for the law. To take the standard example, if the parties freely agree to a contract of slavery, that is their choice and the law should respect their agreement. Following this approach, therefore, contract law would have a dual focus: first, the law must ensure that only freely assumed obligations are enforced; and, secondly, it must protect the well-being of non-contracting third parties. Now, much of the modern law could be squared fairly readily with such a freedom-led approach. For example, modern attempts to modify classical doctrine in relation to, say, consideration and privity, so that the reasonable expectations of contractors are not defeated, are very much in line with respect for freely given undertakings. Again, as we indicated in Chapter 8, much of the modern intervention against unreasonable terms can be understood as an attempt to enforce only the products of free agreement; and the same

[56]   Cf John Cartwright *Unequal Bargaining* (Oxford, Clarendon, 1991).

applies to modern intervention against economic duress. However, the freedom-led approach would draw the line at paternalistic intervention (in the sense that, where there has been full and free agreement to a transaction, there is then no justification for relieving one party against the unwanted outcome of the agreement); and there is an obvious question mark about how far the freedom-led approach is compatible with those parts of the modern law which black-list particular terms.

The alternative (well-being-led) approach starts by constructing a model of contract in which the well-being of the parties is fully protected, but then it qualifies this by employing a theory of waiver. Putting this rather generally, the law of contract should be organised around a model which is compatible with the well-being dimension of the *PGC*, but the freedom dimension of the *PGC* is respected by permitting agents, who so wish, to transact on less protective terms. This general formulation of the well-being-led approach, however, glosses over a critical distinction concerning the theory of waiver. In principle, the well-being-led approach might employ a strong or a weak theory of waiver. According to the strong theory of waiver, any of the contractor's protected rights may be waived. Hence, as with the freedom-led approach, the law eschews any paternalism once it is satisfied that the contract has been freely made (in the present case, once it is satisfied that the waiver has been freely exercised). It follows that where the well-being-led approach employs a strong theory of waiver it is virtually indistinguishable from the freedom-led approach – and the question mark about the substantive rationality of the black-listing provisions of the modern law remains. The well-being-led approach might, however, employ a weak theory of waiver. On this view, it would not be open to a contractor to waive all protected rights – some rights, so to speak, would be indefeasible. For example, the law might prohibit enforcement of contracts which, although freely made, might put at risk the essential conditions of a contractor's agency (such as slavery contracts, contracts reducing one to a state of dependence on others, and so on).[57] If such a weak theory of waiver is compatible with the

---

[57]   See the discussion of 'minimal welfarism' in Roger Brownsword, n 2, above.

PGC, the black-listing elements of the modern law might be squared. However, given the distinctly anti-paternalistic script of the *PGC*, any such compromising with freedom is exceedingly controversial.

For the sake of argument, let us suppose that the well-being-led approach, with a strong theory of waiver, best fits with the *PGC*. On this assumption, we can draw on some of the ideas suggested in earlier chapters to sketch the contours of a *PGC*-inspired regime of contract law.

First, we suggested in Chapters 4 and 5 that legitimate expectation should be the basis of contractual obligation; and, as we have seen, this has important ramifications for the classical doctrines of consideration and privity. Whilst the concept of legitimate expectation needs more analysis, it fits squarely with the *PGC* (which directly enjoins that promises should be treated as binding). Accordingly, a promise seriously given must be treated as binding irrespective of whether it is supported by consideration, irrespective of whether it can be characterised as part of an exchange. In fact, as we have seen, the English doctrine of consideration is in the process of being dismantled so that the promisee is no longer required to have detrimentally relied on the promise – some practical benefit to the promisor will now suffice.[58] Whilst such dismantling of the consideration requirement is readily associated with the 'death of contract' school,[59] it would be more appropriately tagged as the 'resurrection of contract'.[60] Furthermore, where third parties have a legitimate expectation that they can rely on a promise, they should be able to do so, lack of privity notwithstanding. Again, English law seems to be in the process of relaxing the privity doctrine and this is a step towards substantive rationality.

Secondly, as we suggested in Chapters 7 and 9, a co-operative model of contract would impose a stringent duty to disclose, both pre- and post-formation[61] – and such a

---

[58] See *Williams and Roffey Bros v Nicholls (Contractors) Ltd* [1990] 1 All ER 512.

[59] Cf Grant Gilmore *The Death of Contract* (Columbus, Ohio, Ohio State University Press, 1974).

[60] See Brian Simpson *A History of the Common Law of Contract* (Oxford, Oxford University Press, 1975).

[61] Cf Hugh Collins 'Implied Duty to Give Information During Performance of Contracts' (1992) 55 Modern Law Review 556.

stringent duty would be prescribed by the default rules (as well as by the rules governing free agreement to modify the default rules). Thus, the *Smith v Hughes*[62] distinction between a mistake concerning the terms of the offer and a mistake concerning the quality or nature of the subject-matter of the contract would be broken down. If one party fails to disclose a material[63] fact to the other side, and stands by knowing that the other side is making a wasted contract, the latter would have redress against the former. In a transactional world regulated by the *PGC* passive deception is as illegitimate as active deception.

Thirdly, although there would be some room for price-variation (particularly depending upon the degree of risk assumed), the default rules would specify limitations on both the kind of risk which could be assumed and the price which could be charged. In other words, the concept of a balanced contract would be applicable (price and risk having to be balanced) but this would be within a band of fairness. If a contract specified a risk or a price which fell outside this band, it would be open to review and adjustment.[64] Possibly, one might remit the question of fair exchange to a comparable competitive market; but, in general, the question should be whether rational agents could agree to deal on the proposed terms without knowing on which side of the transaction they might stand – in a sale, for example, the test of fairness would be whether rational agents could agree on

---

[62]   (1871) LR 6 QB 597.

[63]   Of course, as we saw in ch 7, the question of what counts as a material fact is open to interpretation. Also, we need to attend to the question of whether materiality is to be judged subjectively or objectively. Clearly, a subjective failure to disclose is more culpable than a failure as judged by objective standards; but it does not follow that there should be no relief against objective non-disclosure (however innocent).

[64]   Seminally, see James Gordley, 'Equality in Exchange' (1981) 69 California Law Review 1587. Gordley points out that those modern doctrines which reflect a revival of interest in the problem of unjust exchange – for example, the doctrine of unconscionability in the common law legal systems, *Wucher* in Germany, *lésion* in France – tend to treat disparity in exchange as evidence of a procedural flaw rather than as a case of unjust enrichment. With regard to the doctrine of *lésion*, Articles 1674ff of the *Code civil* provide that, where the seller of an immovable receives less than five-twelfths of the 'just price', he may claim *rescision* of the contract: see Barry Nicholas, *The French Law of Contract* 2nd edn (Oxford, Clarendon Press, 1992) pp 137–44.

the terms proposed irrespective of whether they were the seller or the buyer.[65]

Fourthly, there would be a general requirement of good faith. This, as we have seen, would demand honest dealing and it would operate as a self-denying ordinance against opportunism. As we saw in Chapter 6, one of the implications of a good faith requirement would be that withdrawal from a contract would have to be for breach and not for collateral economic reasons.[66] But, of course, more generally, good faith would protect vulnerable parties against coerced renegotiation and shirking of obligations.

Finally, it is arguable that contractors should be protected against post-formation contingencies, which are beyond their control, and which threaten their basic well-being. This is not to say that the doctrine of frustration should be relaxed to present contractors with an easy exit from bad bargains. However, the default rules of a substantively rational law of contract should shield contractors against the effects of contracts that prove ruinous through no fault of the contracting party at risk.[67]

In the light of these remarks, what do we make of the modern split between consumer and commercial contracts? Up to a point, this division correlates to the distinction between the modern and the classical ideal-types of contract. In other words, whereas commercial contracting is largely governed (formally speaking) by the classical ground rules, consumer contracting is governed (again, formally speaking) by rules which bear some resemblance to the modern ideal-type. To regard this arrangement as substantively rational – at any rate, if we take the well-being-led approach with a

---

[65]   See Roger Brownsword's idea of a 'fair deal formula' in 'Liberalism and the Law of Contract' in Richard Bellamy (ed.) *Liberalism and Recent Legal and Social Philosophy* (ARSP Beiheft 36) (Stuttgart, Franz Steiner, 1989) p 86. And, cf Hugh Beale 'Unfair Contracts in Britain and Europe' (1989) 42 Current Legal Problems 197. Even if this test could not specify a single fair price, it might at least specify the *range* of fair prices, thereby excluding obviously unfair prices. For some illustrative examples of exploitation of price ignorance, see Melvin Eisenberg, 'The Bargain Principle and its Limits' (1981–82) 95 Harvard Law Review 741, esp at 778–85.

[66]   Generally, for the implications of a regime of good faith, see chs 6 and 7.

[67]   Thomas Wilhelmsson's elaboration of a doctrine of social force majeure indicates how this line of thinking might be developed. See Thomas Wilhelmsson *Critical Studies in Private Law* (Dordrecht, Kluwer, 1992).

strong theory of waiver as our criterion – we must be able to justify two features of this regime: namely, the imposed restriction on the freedom of consumer contractors, and the weakening of protective rights to well-being in relation to commercial contractors.

With regard to the first point, it may well be right to assume that consumer contractors generally prefer not to waive their protective transactional rights, from which it follows that freely agreed bilateral waivers of well-being-protecting rights would be exceptional. Even so, this does not justify the deprivation of freedom in the exceptional case. Here, to present itself as substantively rational, the regime of indefeasible rights for consumer contractors needs further argument – possibly along the lines that it is better to restrict the freedom of a few exceptional consumer contractors than to risk making erroneous judgments in many borderline situations where it is unclear whether a consumer contractor has freely waived his or her rights.[68]

Turning to the treatment of commercial contractors, the assumption underlying the bifurcated regime is that such contractors generally prefer to deal without well-being-protecting default rules. In two respects, however, this assumption is open to question. First, where one commercial contractor is in a dominant bargaining position, the weaker contracting party may well prefer to have the bene-

---

[68]   Cf Joel Feinberg's essay 'Legal Paternalism' in *Rights, Justice, and the Bounds of Liberty* (Princeton, Princeton University Press, 1980) at pp 124–5. Here, Feinberg is considering how one might reconcile a prohibition against slavery contracts with respect for voluntary choice. Having said that any machinery designed to determine voluntariness will be fallible, and given the general presumption of nonvoluntariness in relation to slavery contracts, Feinberg continues:

> 'the state might be justified simply in *presuming nonvoluntariness conclusively in every case as the least risky course.* Some rational bargain-makers might be unfairly restrained under this policy, but on the alternative policy, even more people, perhaps, would become unjustly (mistakenly) enslaved, so that the evil prevented by the absolute prohibition would be greater than the occasional evil permitted. The principles involved in this argument are of the following two kinds: (1) It is better (say) that one hundred people be wrongly denied permission to be enslaved than that one be wrongly permitted, and (2) If we allow the institution of "voluntary slavery" at all, then no matter how stringent our tests of voluntariness are, it is likely that a good many persons *will* be wrongly permitted.'

fit of protective default rules. Of course, in principle, it remains open to the parties to contract back into a protective regime; but, in practice, this is small comfort to a small business wholly reliant on a powerful commercial enterprise. To presuppose free waiver of rights in such circumstances is to abandon any serious concern with the concept of freedom; and, to this extent, the division of contracts into commercial and consumer agreements correlates only very crudely with the division between free and unfree waiver of rights.[69] Secondly, as we saw in Chapter 9, commercial contractors may often view their relationships flexibly, in co-operative rather than competitive terms, thereby indicating that they are presupposing the modern model rather than choosing more combative ground rules. Although the imposed waiver of the default rules does not actually infringe upon the parties' freedom to reinstate such ground rules, it is nevertheless doctrinally inappropriate.

The upshot of this is that, if one were looking for a fairly rough and ready way of instituting the *PGC* in transactions, one might do worse than to organise the law around the distinction between consumer and commercial contracts. Of course, this is a long way from suggesting that the *PGC* offers a clear rationalisation of the bifurcation between consumer and commercial contracts; nevertheless, one might see a germ of substantive rationality in this development.

---

[69]   There is also a difficult question about the rights of parties to refuse to contract. To revert to consumer contracting, what do we say about the situation where a dealer wishes to deal on classical terms but a consumer contractor is not prepared to (or is not allowed to) waive the standard protective rights? May the dealer refuse to deal? Given that the *PGC* orders rights in a three-tiered hierarchy, this must be the key to resolving this problem. In general, therefore, we can treat it as axiomatic that the dealer's freedom (unless it pertains to the dealer's own basic well-being) must yield to the requirements of the consumer's basic well-being. To coin Thomas Wilhelmsson's terminology (albeit developed in a different context) one dimension of 'need-rationality' (see Thomas Wilhelmsson, 'Need-Rationality in Private Law' (1989) Scandinavian Studies in Law 223) might be that, if a dealer is in the business of supplying 'necessaries' (items relevant to an agent's basic well-being), then the dealer's freedom to refuse to sell (or, to sell only on the basis of less protective rules) may be severely constrained.

6. CONCLUSION

The quest for rational law is a continuing and a complex challenge. It is not simply a matter of cleaning up doctrine so that it is clear, calculable, and free from contradiction; nor is it merely a matter of finding out what works, or what will serve; nor is it just about determining what is legitimate. It is all these things. Moreover, it is all these things at all levels from the micro-doctrinal to the macro-theoretical. Just as it will not do to detach our views about the concrete particulars of legal doctrine from our views about abstract theoretical matters, it will not do to detach abstract theory from concrete doctrinal questions. In a fully developed theory of rational contract law, it would be possible to move smoothly from abstract theory to concrete particulars and back again, rationality being secured and integrated at every level. No doubt, it is unduly optimistic to hope that we might achieve such a developed theory but this at least is the model to which all those who seek rational law must aspire.

In this book, we have taken no more than the first steps towards specifying a rational law of contract, setting the general framework for inquiry, identifying some of the key issues and key concepts for that inquiry, and along the way filling in a little of the detail. Sometimes, we have worked, as Ronald Dworkin has put it, 'from the inside out',[70] starting with concrete doctrinal matters and working out to more general theory; at other times (particularly in this last chapter), we have worked 'from the outside in',[71] starting with a general theory and trying to apply it back to specific doctrinal issues. Whichever way we tackle the key issues of contract, however, the canvas is a large one; a great deal remains to be done; and the work has truly only just begun.[72]

---

[70] Ronald Dworkin *Life's Dominion* (London, Harper Collins, 1993), pp 28–29.
[71] Ibid.
[72] Cf Roger Brownsword, 'The Limits of Freedom of Contract and the Limits of Contract Theory' (1995) 22 Journal of Law and Society 259.

Index

Italics indicate material in a note